ALBERTA'S
LOCAL GOVERNMENTS
AND
THEIR POLITICS

ALBERTA'S

LOCAL GOVERNMENTS

AND

THEIR POLITICS

Jack Masson

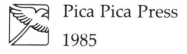 Pica Pica Press
1985

LOCAL GOVERNMENT SERIES
Adriana A. Davies, Executive Editor

First published by
The Pica Pica Press
(Textbook division of
The University of Alberta Press)
Athabasca Hall
Edmonton, Alberta, Canada

Copyright © The Pica Pica Press 1985

ISBN 0-88864-094-3

Canadian Cataloguing in Publication Data

Masson, Jack K.
   Alberta's local governments and their
politics

   Includes index.
   Bibliography: p.
   ISBN 0-88864-094-3

   1. Municipal government - Alberta.
   2. Municipal officials and employees -
   Alberta. I. Title.
   JS1721.A42M37 1985   352.07123   C85-091027-7

Typesetting by University of Alberta Printing Services, Edmonton

Printed by John Deyell Company, Lindsay, Ontario, Canada

CONTENTS

Introduction

to the

Local Government Series

The commitment to excellence made by today's leaders of public and private organizations ought to go beyond efforts to maximize organizational effectiveness and efficiency. It should also include efforts to learn more about the organization itself, its relationship with other organizations, its structure and its modus operandi. The commitment should emphasize the need to know not just how or what, but also why.

This book, which is part of what will become a unique series of publications sponsored by the University of Alberta's Local Government Studies Program, is a manifestation of that commitment to excellence, one that is shared by many practitioners and academics associated with the Program. The aim of the series is to facilitate the study of the theories and practices of public sector management, with special emphasis on the local government context. Resources from the Ministries of Advanced Education and Municipal Affairs have been made available to the Local Government Studies Program in order to achieve this aim.

Much of what will appear in these publications is produced in co-operation with provincial and municipal government agencies, professional associations of local government administrators, and numerous academic and non-academic staff from post-secondary institutions in Alberta. Even though this book can stand on its own merits, it should also be viewed as a symbol of a larger, co-operative effort among public administrators, scholars and citizens, who support excellence in public sector management.

My hope is that this volume and others planned for the series will enrich the reader's study of an important institution in contemporary society, the institution of government. Perhaps it will stimulate new ideas, fresh insights and novel approaches to public administration. I am optimistic that it will contribute to a better understanding of local government in Alberta.

Albert A. Einsiedel, Director
Local Government Studies, University of Alberta

Foreword

The long postwar boom of Alberta came to an end in 1981. The personal income per capita of the province was higher than that of any other Canadian province in that year so that adjustments to recession are being made at a relatively high level of income. There are many uncertainties about the rates of future economic growth in the province. In the long-term they are likely to be close to those of Canada and the United States.

The agricultural labour force declined from about one-half of the total labour force in Alberta before World War II to less than 8 per cent in 1981. Edmonton and Calgary grew to become the fifth and sixth ranking metropolitan areas of Canada. Many other cities and centres also experienced high rates of growth.

The provincial and local governments of the province encountered numerous problems. The movement of workers to the urban centres called for massive expenditures on schools, universities, hospitals, transportation systems, and many other public services. Accompanying the development of the Alberta economy there emerged a large number of social and political concerns.

In this book Professor Masson has provided a detailed and comprehensive account of how the provincial and local governments met the problems. It is impressive in its scope and coverage. Future trends are discussed by reference to the many uncertainties facing the residents and governments of the province. This book should be of great value and interest to all who are involved in the governments of Alberta and all the students of these governments.

Eric J. Hanson

Professor Emeritus of Economics
University of Alberta
Edmonton, Alberta
June, 1984

Acknowledgements

Many people have helped to bring this study of local government and politics in Alberta to fruition. The Faculty of Extension's Local Government Studies Program provided the encouragement and resources that made it possible for me to carry out the project. The director, Dr. Bert Einsiedel, deserves special thanks.

I wish to express my deep gratitude to Barry Clark and Gordon Tweddell of the Edmonton Metropolitan Regional Planning Commission and Professor Peter J. Smith of the University of Alberta for constructive comments on earlier drafts of "Planning and Political Process." Professor James Lightbody of the University of Alberta, Professor Stan Drabek of the University of Calgary, and Professor Paul Tennant of the University of British Columbia read the original manuscript and made innumerable welcome suggestions for its improvement. I am fortunate to have such good colleagues and am indebted to them for their constructive criticism. Other good colleagues who provided helpful suggestions and important data are Professor Edna Einsiedel of Syracuse University and Professor Edd LeSage of the University of Alberta.

I cannot express enough appreciation to John Thompson and Gilda Sanders for their many long hours of editorial assistance in making the manuscript readable. They taught me many lessons about long and rambling sentences. Charles Humphrey of the University of Alberta's Computing Services deserves thanks for his help on data analysis. Thanks also go to Stuart Munro and Jim and Ruth Rochlin for their invaluable services as research assistants. I am particularly indebted to Leah Modin who typed the original manuscript and then made a series of revisions and provided many helpful suggestions.

Finally, a very special thanks to a very special person for her encouragement and support at those times when it seemed no end was in sight for the project's completion.

1

THE NATURE

OF

LOCAL GOVERNMENT

Democracy

Although Canadians believe they live in one of the most democratic countries in the world, few give much thought to the concept of democracy. The term itself derives from the Greek words *demos*, "the people," and *kratein*, "to rule." In its broadest sense, then, democracy is found wherever the people rule. In a democracy every citizen will have the feeling of being a part of the governmental process and will implicitly consent to be governed, even though an occasional policy may strike the person as repugnant. Put another way, the citizenry gives government its legitimacy by consenting to be governed.

Few people question the theory underlying democracy, but many question the effectiveness of democracy on a practical level, for example, the claim that democracy protects minorities. Suppose, critics say, that a majority continually passes legislation oppressing a particular minority. What, in the nature of democracy itself, would protect that minority? Without necessarily questioning democratic theory, a minority in such a situation would certainly question the "tyranny of the majority"; they might even rebel against the system.

Canada has built-in safeguards to protect minorities. With its patchwork of cultural and ethnic groups and its diverse sets of economic values and life-styles, Canada has avoided a potential "tyranny of the majority" by breaking up the majority. The ten provinces and thousands of units of local government create a situation in which minorities at the national level become majorities at the provincial and local levels. People feeling oppressed in one area can move to another, where they will be members of the majority. Thus, in a country as diverse as ours, strong local governments play a leading role in maintaining a viable system of democracy.

The ancient Greeks practised a form of *direct democracy,* in which all citizens attended community meetings and made decisions by simple majority vote. As the size of the Greek population increased, direct democracy became unworkable and there was a move to *representative democracy,* where the citizenry delegated decision making to elected representatives. Direct democracy virtually disappeared after the Greek experiment and has made only a limited appearance in modern times with the village assembly, or *Landsgemeinde,* in Switzerland, and the town meeting in New England. The only other vestige is the plebiscite—a mechanism that enables the citizenry either to initiate a public proposal or to have it referred back to themselves for ratification; in both cases the citizenry votes for or against the proposal. Alberta is one of the few provinces that furthers direct democracy through provisions for holding municipal plebiscites.

Despite the advantages of direct democracy, it is extremely unwieldy except in the smallest communities. In modern democracies public policy is made by elected representatives. The perennial problem is the relationship between elected representatives and their constituents; this problem has occupied political philosophers, politicians and citizens since the beginnings of the modern legislative assembly. Should representatives simply mirror the views of their constituents, or should they exercise their own independent judgment? The former position is labelled the *mandate theory* of representation: the representative has a mandate from his or her constituents to present and represent their views in the assembly; even if these views are repugnant to the representative, he or she must represent them or resign. The latter position is called the *independence theory* of representation, since the representative is expected to remain independent of the demands of his or her constituents. Constituents, after all, cannot be expected to understand the complexities of modern government or all the facets of any given issue. Representatives are expected to be innovative in policy making instead of slavishly following the often uninformed views of their constituents. If constituents disagree with their representative's views, they can vote the person out of office at the next election. Both theories will be examined in detail in a later chapter.

Grass-roots Democracy

The New England town meeting, with the citizenry actively and directly involved in making public policy, is one of the antecedents of modern grass-roots democracy. Its other forerunner is the plebiscite introduced in the American West early in the century to bring the citizenry directly into the making of public policy. In the latter case the citizenry could bypass their elected representatives and themselves formulate and implement policy. However, only in the last 25 years has the term *grass-roots democracy* become popularized in North America. A problem with this term is that, since its definition is somewhat imprecise, it often means different things to different people.[1] For almost everyone, it implies that small governing units are better than larger ones since small units allow direct and personal contact between elected officials, administrators, and individual citizens, i.e., the citizen is an integral part of the community decision-making process. In smaller communities, elected officials are expected to make a concerted effort to determine and act upon the wishes of their constituents — to consult them on a one-to-one basis about community problems and seek advice on policies to alleviate them.

In the late 1960s and early 1970s many people, disenchanted with the impersonality of big-city government and the low rate of working-class participation, began to discuss ways of implementing grass-roots democracy at the city level. Writing in 1969, Milton Kotler advocated the decentralization of big-city government through the creation of semi-autonomous neighbourhood corporations that would have the power to tax, distribute services, etc.[2] These corporations would be governed by the neighbourhood's citizenry in an open democratic system. In essence, Kotler advocated bringing the values associated with grass-roots democracy, as practised in small rural municipalities, to the city. At about the same time others were advocating "participatory democracy" in order to involve all the citizenry in democratic governance. Carole Pateman argued that modern democratic theorists had lost sight of the values of widespread citizen participation and the ability of the citizenry to have a direct impact on governmental decisions—values found in the writings of the classical democratic theorists.[3] Although Pateman was making a case for participatory democracy in the workplace, her ideas were soon adopted by militant urban reformers wanting to bring democracy to working-class neighbourhoods. The call for participatory democracy at the neighbourhood level was taken up by community and academic activists in a collection of readings entitled *Participatory Democracy for Canada*, published in 1971.[4]

City politicians responded that these proposals were not feasible because the size of the population made direct consultation between the elected representative and the citizen impossible. Then, some politicians attempted to equate grass-roots democracy with administrative decentralization, arguing that such decentralization leads to greater accountability by civil servants who deal directly with neighbourhoods, their people, and their problems. Others have defined grass-roots democracy neither as community decision making nor as administrative decentralization, but more loosely as a particular form of electoral campaigning, that is, door-to-door electioneering. Finally, marching on city hall, packing council chambers, even stopping traffic at dangerous intersections, have all been labelled "grass-roots democracy" at one time or another.

Despite the imprecision of the term it can be said that grass-roots democracy is a process that attempts to bridge representative democracy and direct democracy. This bridging process runs the gamut from the innumerable citizen advisory groups in Alberta's larger cities to the "barbershop politics" found in the smallest communities, where councillors seek advice literally from the man on the street.

Throughout Alberta's history there has been a strong emphasis on the development of mechanisms that allow each citizen to have an effect on the community's policy-making process. An examination of municipal plebiscites in a later chapter shows that they have been an integral part of municipal policy making for well over half a century. A provision in the Municipal Government Act, Section 123(1), allows a council to hold "an annual meeting of the electors for the discussion of municipal affairs." Another provision, in Section 124(1) of the Act, gives the citizenry the ability to call a meeting of the electors by petition.[5] Although the Act is silent on the powers of the citizenry at these meetings, at the very least the exchanges between the citizenry and their representatives could hardly be ignored by the council. Admittedly, it is rare to find a council that calls an annual meeting of its electors and even rarer for a meeting to be called by the citizenry through petition; nevertheless, these mechanisms in the Act have the potential greatly to enhance grass-roots democracy.

Is Local Government Really Democratic?

More often than not when the topic of local government comes up, someone will say that the people do not make public policy; it is really made by large economic interests, the pipeline companies, the land developers, and the banks and trust companies. In some way, which is never made clear, it is said that these large economic interests are able almost completely to manipulate mayors and councils.

A similar argument has been made by a number of local government scholars throughout much of this century. During the 1920s and 1930s two sociologists examined Muncie, Indiana, and concluded

that all major public policy decisions in the community were controlled by a small economic elite.[6] Then, in the early 1950s, University
of North Carolina sociologist Floyd Hunter carried out a landmark
study of Atlanta, Georgia. He concluded that a group of the city's "influentials," composed almost entirely of business leaders, made all
decisions in the community and in some way communicated them to
the city's political leaders who rubber-stamped them and carried
them out.[7] During the 1960s in Alberta at least one study of community decision making adopted Hunter's research methods and came to
the same type of conclusion: "influentials" made the major decisions
in the community.[8] The major problem with these studies is that they
employed a research method that would almost always find a small
group of "influentials" making decisions in the community, whether
such a group existed or not.[9]

It has also been argued that local democracy is merely a myth, a
sham perpetuated by large economic interests to make the citizenry
think that they, rather than large, faceless economic interests, are
controlling the destiny of their community. Since this kind of thinking is so prevalent, it is necessary to deal with the question of whether local government is really democratic or not.

Since the substance of this question revolves around who exercises
political power in the community, it is worth defining what we mean
by power. Probably the best common language definition of power is
that formulated by a political scientist some 25 years ago. "My intui-
tive sense of power . . . is something like this: A has power over B to
the extent that he can get B to do something that B would not otherwise do."[10] It should be noted that A is able to get B to do something
against his will for one of two reasons: A can either threaten B with
physical violence, or A can exercise influence to get B to do something he would rather not do.[11] Most political power relationships are
based on influence; thus, power is a relational concept, which means
that it is exercised with respect to others—it takes at least two people.
For example, a department head who orders his subordinates to report to work at 7:00 a.m. sharp, and makes them comply even though
they dislike rising early, is exercising power.

While the relational aspect of power is important, the context in
which it is exercised always defines its scope and the resources available to its wielder. For example, in one situation a city council can
sanction a city manager for failing to perform the duties of the office;
in another situation the city council is powerless to enforce curricu-
lum changes in the local high school. Peter Pocklington, Alberta's
sports king and self-made millionaire, has the power to hire and fire
dozens of his employees, but he is unable to hire or fire teachers in

the local high school. These examples show that no individual is all-powerful: the situation and position the person occupies determines his or her ability to exercise power. In fact, one of the tenets of a liberal democracy is that elected leaders are able to exercise power only in certain prescribed contexts.

To say that power is relational and situational does not answer the question of whether members of an economic elite or elected officials wield power in the community. In order to deal with this question it is necessary to identify the resources of power available to its wielders.[12] Following is a list of resources of political power.

1. Brute force Brute force is the raw and naked use of political power. At the community level, it is used by politicians only in exceptional circumstances, such as the forcible removal of a family from a home they refused to leave even though it had been expropriated by the municipality. Another example might be the forcible ejection of an unruly council member from council chambers. Since the use of naked power usually upsets the citizenry, politicians use it with caution.

2. Wealth Wealth allows one, for example, to fund a political campaign and create a good chance that individuals favourable to one's views will be elected. The wealthy also have the ability to offer bribes to elected officials in order to sway their votes. There are, nevertheless, countless examples of well-funded candidates losing elections and of elected officials being shocked by attempts to bribe them.

3. Skill An individual with a valued skill is able to exercise power when people defer to his or her expertise. In Alberta's smaller communities, part-time councillors and mayors often defer to the clerk-treasurer's expertise in administration and knowledge about what policies should be implemented. When council and the mayor follow the advice of the clerk-treasurer, that person is exercising power based on skill. Another example of this type of power involves the city planner who presents only two alternative land-use plans to council, failing to present a third, potentially feasible plan. In effect, by narrowing council's options, the planner has exercised a form of power. An adjunct of skill as a power resource is information. The person or group that has both skills and information is a potential political force. For example, a well-educated community group with access to detailed geological and hydrodynamic information about an area a developer wishes to develop would be a formidable adversary.

4. Respect A politician who is highly respected is able to exercise political power based on this respect. An example would be an honoured and respected mayor who uses this basis of support to move a recalcitrant council in a particular direction. A very few leaders have been so highly regarded that they retain strong support even when they commit blatantly illegal acts. One such "charismatic leader" was the late William Hawrelak, former mayor of Edmonton. Although many of his activities, which were highly publicized, could be considered politically immoral, Hawrelak received overwhelming support from the citizens of Edmonton in election after election.

5. *Friendship* Many politicians play on close friendships to further their own political ends. It is common to find council members swayed by friendship to vote for or against an issue. A study of the voting behaviour of the Edmonton city council found that the major factor in council voting was the friendship patterns among council members.[13] A businessperson may be treated favourably by council because the person has many close friends on council who do not wish to jeopardize their friendship. However, an issue may be so important to a councillor that he or she is willing to jeopardize friendship; also, a friendship that is frequently used in this way is apt to become strained or to break.

6. *Legal authority* A person elected to political office is able to use the legal authority vested in the office to exercise power. For example, an elected official who is committed to regulating moral behaviour will ensure that all by-laws in the area of morality are rigidly enforced. Also, those invested with legal authority can use it to expand their basis of power. For example, a city council could pass a by-law to control new residential development, thus exercising authority that until this time was latent. Almost always, this new power is used selectively to control only certain residential development. Of course, if the citizenry does not respect its legal authority on an issue, the council will be unable to exercise power; for example, the public almost totally disregards anti-littering by-laws.

7. *Organizational ability* An individual who has the ability to motivate and organize people has a potential power resource. At the community level there are innumerable examples of individuals who have organized political parties and citizens groups that have had a major impact on public policy.

It is important to keep in mind that wielders of power usually have more than one power resource at their disposal. In one case, the successful politician may be highly respected, be a close friend of other power wielders, and make effective use of legal authority; in another, he or she may be wealthy, be an expert in a particular field of municipal operations, and occasionally make use of brute force to affect policy. Equally important is the fact that only in very rare instances do people make maximum use of the power resources at their disposal. The wealthy person does not spend all of his or her money to get elected, nor do members of a concerned citizens' group spend every waking hour lobbying council and mobilizing the citizenry.

Now we are in a position to answer the question of whether an economic elite makes all policy decisions in a community. First, wealth is an important power resource, but it is only one among many. A person whose only resource is wealth will probably be bested by someone who, while not wealthy, is able to combine a number of power resources. For this reason, one occasionally finds a well-organized community group frustrating the plans of a well-financed developer. In short, wealthy individuals and large corporations have the potential to exercise considerable political power *if* they have a number of other power resources. On the other hand, non-wealthy individuals and groups may be the power wielders in the community *if* they make effective use of power resources other than wealth. Since there is such a variation in the distribution of power resources and in their use from community to community, we cannot say that the wealthy will or will not prevail in all communities.

The Importance of Local Government

Many local government specialists distinguish between the terms "local government" and "local self government." The term local government can simply mean a mechanism or conduit used to administer higher-level government policies. Donald Higgins discusses this interpretation and writes:

> . . . there is a minimum of discretion delegated to local
> administrative officials; there need not be any locally elected
> councils, and if there are any such councils, they may have little
> more to do than to advise the centrally-appointed local officials
> and to act as a communication link between the general public
> in the area and the central government.[14]

In contrast, local self government is defined as a government with a modicum of local autonomy and citizen self-determination.

> In this model, central-local relations are not characterized by
> direction and control from above but by relative independence
> of the local organs, allowing them to establish their own

priorities according to local circumstances and local desires.[15]

Despite these polar interpretations, the two terms commonly are used interchangeably to mean local self government, as they are throughout this book.

We have been implying that there is something intrinsically worthwhile in maintaining viable local governments. Why are local governments important? After all, it would be possible for the federal or the provincial government to make all political decisions for smaller communities.

The major advantage of local government is that it brings the political leaders and civil servants in close contact with the people. For many people, grass-roots democracy has a hollow ring: in all too many areas the citizenry feels it has little control over its destiny. Even though political leaders make decisions affecting all of us, we seldom see them, except at election time. The charge has been made that at the provincial and federal levels, civil servants no longer seem to be "servants" of the people. In small communities, however, political decision makers are accessible and attempt to consult their constituents. Admittedly, few people actually attend council meetings and hearings, but there is continual informal discussion of pertinent community issues with political leaders on the streets. In a community with conscientious elected officials, people feel confident that they will be heard and taken seriously on issues that affect them: the clerk-treasurer, for example, is an accessible civil servant, not just a cog in a distant bureaucracy. Besides, a single vote can make the difference in the outcome of an election.

Some people maintain that another advantage of strong local governments is that they provide a training ground for provincial and federal politicians, teaching them how to compromise, even to the extent of working with political foes with diametrically opposed political views. Many people who would like to contribute their time and talent to government are frozen out by the ever-increasing cost of seeking political office in city, provincial and federal elections. The lack of a campaign chest is not a deterrent for the hard-working political self-starter in a smaller community.

Each justification for the maintenance of strong local governments is rooted in an aspect of the democratic process. Democracy is not a mystical concept; it is a process by which the acts of governing are carried out in accordance with the wishes of a majority of the governed. It is equally important that the minority not be hindered in its attempt to become the majority. The democratic process is difficult, time-consuming and, occasionally, frustrating to all. It is no accident that most countries have non-democratic forms of government: it is far easier to impose policies and plans upon the citizenry without consultation and compromise.[16]

Many have argued that the most fertile ground for democracy is at the local level: here the elected leader is forced to deal with constituents daily and face-to-face, not, as in large constituencies, only at election times from the distance afforded by news media. It is also argued that, unless democracy is practised at the community level, support for a democratic system at higher levels of government will be impaired.

The Responsibilities of Local Government

In Canada, local governments have dual responsibilities. First, elected officials have a responsibility to carry out the duties imposed on the municipality by the province. In Alberta, the Municipal Government Act, the Municipal Taxation Act, the Planning Act, the New Towns Act, and the Municipal Election Act delineate those functions local governments are required to perform and those that are discretionary.[17] Second, elected officials and administrators have a responsibility to maintain an open, democratic system that is accessible and responsive to the community's citizenry.

Two political scientists have argued that the responsibilities of local government can be divided into three broad classes:

> First there are the protective services of police, public safety as in fire protection, public health, and sanitation. Secondly, there are certain physical services or facilities of which roads, streets, and bridges are the best examples. The public utilities such as light, gas, water, power and transport which are increasingly owned and operated by municipalities fall in the same group. Thirdly, there are what may be broadly described as the welfare services such as education, libraries, parks and other recreation facilities, hospitals, and the care of those for whom such public provision has to be made, because of poverty, advanced age, or other defect.[18]

The difficulty with this classification system is that it is static: it does not take into account the rapid social changes that result in shifting demands on the part of the citizenry. For example, Albertans have demanded a wide range and a high level of social services, but, as costs escalated, the provincial government relieved the municipalities' financial burden by taking over more and more of these services.

Furthermore, over the last 40 years the federal government has been steadily increasing its share of welfare programs: federal programs for health care, old-age security and family allowances have relieved municipalities of a heavy financial burden.

Technological advances and changing social values have affected the scope of municipal responsibilities and priorities. For example, more effective means of birth control resulted in a rapidly declining birth rate. This decline led to an upward shift in the age distribution of the population, resulting in a slight, but decided, change in the citizenry's policy preferences. Support for educational programs seems to be declining at the same time that greater demands are being made on local governments for programs to assist the elderly and to bolster law enforcement. As technological advances make it possible to shorten the work week, people are beginning to demand that local governments provide improved leisure-time programs and facilities.

Although there are lists detailing the responsibilities of local government, demands for particular services are in a constant state of flux. In future, some services now being performed by local government will be unnecessary, or will be assumed by higher levels of government; conversely, some services now performed by the provincial government will be thought better administered at the local level.

Although legislation directs municipalities to perform limited mandatory duties and functions, local government has considerable leeway in policy making. For example, section 117 of the Alberta Municipal Government Act states:

> The council may pass such by-laws as are considered expedient and as are not contrary to this or any other Act,
>
> a. for the peace, order and good government of the municipality,
>
> b. for promoting the health, safety, morality and welfare thereof, and
>
> c. for governing the proceedings of the council, the conduct of its members and the calling of meetings.

Another example is found in section 150 which states that the "council may by by-law make provisions for the regulation of any matter or thing for the protection of life or property." It is important to note that the provincial government and the municipalities are not natural antagonists. The provincial government realizes that each community has its own unique problems that are best understood and dealt with by the local citizenry. Consequently, the Municipal Government Act allows a wide range of discretion to local decision makers. Admittedly, one can find short-sighted and shallow individuals who believe that any provincially administered program is superior to any local government program, but that attitude is the exception rather than the rule.

Centralization and Local Government

In the private sector we find a small number of large firms dominating the marketplace in industry after industry. The trend seems to be that smaller companies either merge with larger firms or are forced out of business. Larger companies justify their aggressive tactics by arguing that larger size results in economies of scale, producing savings that are passed on to consumers through lower prices. This argument is often applied to the public sector to justify the merger of units of government in order to lower the per capita cost of services. Those who make this argument tend to overlook two important factors. The first, which will be discussed in Chapter 3, is that centralization does not necessarily decrease per capita costs, in either the public or the private sector. Without becoming involved in the economic complexities of producing public or private goods and services, it can be said that a combination of circumstances, including the type of product produced, determines whether or not centralization reduces costs.

More important is that government and private businesses have different motives, different reasons for existing. The motive of business is profit; the motive of government is providing service to the people. Although elected officials must continually monitor the cost of services, cost is not the sole consideration in policy making. There are numerous examples of communities that have willingly incurred higher costs in order to preserve something worthwhile. Citizens are increasingly interested in preserving clean air, clean water, and natural forests and marsh lands in their communities at almost any cost. In fact most people are generally more concerned about the dangers of large and distant governments that are unresponsive to their needs than about arguments for slight reductions in the cost of services.

There are those in government and the universities who lament the number of local government bodies. They regard the large number of school districts, hospital districts, villages and small towns, all with overlapping governmental boundaries, as uncoordinated and untidy. Although a legitimate case can occasionally be made for amalgamating governmental units when social and economic conditions have changed dramatically, the proponents of massive governmental reorganization usually overlook the strength of diversity, which allows some people to live in communities with a larger number of amenities and accompanying higher taxes and others to live in communities with lower levels of service and taxation. Furthermore, while local governmental units may be untidy, they are not uncoordinated. Decision makers are continually working out both formal and informal bargaining arrangements; for example, several "bedroom communities" contract with Edmonton for their water supply.

If a municipality is no longer serving the purpose for which it was created, it should be abolished; if it is vital, functioning, and responsive to the citizenry, it should be retained and fostered.

The Shared Responsibilities of the Three Levels of Government

Under the provisions of the Canadian Constitution, governmental powers are allocated between the federal and provincial governments, and municipalities fall under the purview of the provinces. There are no constitutional provisions for an independent basis of power for municipalities. Professor Crawford succinctly states the constitutional position of municipalities:

> They are creatures of the provinces; their powers can be
> extended or contracted at will by the provincial legislatures or,
> in the extreme, they can quite legally be legislated out of
> existence. . . . The protection of municipalities lies, not in their
> legal or constitutional position, but rather in the needs of the
> people which must be met.[19]

Thus any provincial government could easily abolish its local units of government, but the party that attempted such a rash maneuver would be out of power at the next election.

Although local government has never been strong in Quebec or Newfoundland, it has had a long and honourable tradition in Ontario and the West. In the latter part of the nineteenth century, the population of the North-West Territories was sparse and almost totally rural. The needs of the rural population dictated the establishment of public and separate school districts, rural fire and road districts, as well as herd districts to fence out stray horses and cattle.

When Alberta became a province in 1905 it had a population of only 170,000; in nine years the population had increased to 400,000, and incorporated towns and villages blossomed across the province. Both the territorial and the provincial governments encouraged the development of local institutions. The provincial government realized that a strong network of local governments would relieve pressure on the province to provide public goods and services. Rural Albertans initially resisted the provincial government's strategy, for they had little cash and feared that the new governments would impose high property taxes and float debentures that could wreak havoc with the rates. After a small number of districts had been established and had proven responsible and conscientious, the rural population eventually supported local government. Ironically, from the beginning, the provincial government, equally concerned that municipalities might overextend themselves, imposed strict guidelines on their borrowing ability. As a consequence, local governments were limited to borrowing no more than 10 per cent of the value of their assessable property.

In 1912 legislation for the creation of the Department of Municipal Affairs was enacted along with the passage of a Town Act, Village Act, Improvement District Act, and Rural Municipality Act, which gave separate status to rural units of government.[20] The Department's activities were initially limited to auditing the books of local governments and ensuring uniformity in record-keeping. The Department was soon given much more responsibility with the passage of the Town Planning Act in 1913, which gave the Minister the power to regulate a municipality's planning scheme, or to prepare one if the municipality refused to do so. Although the Act was fairly comprehensive, it was not until 1928 that provisions were made for a comprehensive planning authority; in 1929 a new Town Planning Act provided for the establishment of regional planning commissions by the councils of two or more adjoining municipalities, with the Minister's approval.

The provincial government realized that, if local governments were to provide services successfully, they needed more powers and more fiscal resources. In 1916 the provincial government passed legislation allowing towns and villages to widen their tax base by taxing buildings and improvements. Grants were provided for road construction under the 1918 Public Highways Act, and a Board of Public Utilities Commissioners was established, one of its objectives being to help municipalities repay their debts. Alberta's oil boom, starting in the late 1940s, attracted thousands of new residents to the province's middle-sized and larger communities. Municipalities' financial capabilities were stretched to the limit in their attempts to build a service infrastructure for this new population. The province responded with programs to provide loans to municipalities at low interest rates. Monies from oil royalties permitted the province to provide grants to municipalities for a variety of local programs.

Today, the provincial government funnels monies into communities through conditional and unconditional grants.[21] In addition, the Department of Municipal Affairs provides high levels of technical expertise in many areas of local concern. Furthermore, until very recently, the province lent municipalities large sums of money at favourable interest rates for capital projects.

As has been noted, decisions relating to municipal institutions fall solely within the scope of provincial governments. The federal government, however, recognizing both the importance of maintaining viable local governments and the problems associated with urbanization, has initiated a number of programs without infringing upon the constitutional power of the provinces. When the federal government enters the municipal arena it always works closely with the pertinent provincial departments. As will be seen in a later chapter, the federal government plays an important fiscal role in municipal activities, although its contributions are but a fraction of provincial contributions.

Over the years, the federal government has formulated a number of programs to meet the housing crisis in Canadian communities, first with the passage of the Dominion Housing Act of 1935, which was as much a "pump priming" anti-depression measure as a housing act. Some $10 million were allocated for loans to private builders for construction of new housing. In 1938 came the National Housing Act that, among other things, provided low-income housing loans and funds for experimental low-income housing. In 1945, with the demand for housing for returning war veterans, the Central Mortgage and Housing Corporation was established to guide urban development through a variety of loan schemes to the public and private sectors. With changes to the National Housing Act in 1964, CMHC embarked on an urban-renewal program to eradicate blight in city cores and to restore vitality to older communities. The program provided direct grants of 50 per cent to municipalities for the preparation of an urban-renewal plan and the costs of implementing an urban-renewal scheme.

The Department of Regional and Economic Expansion (DREE) was created in 1969 to shore up the economic infrastructure of many of Canada's smaller no-growth and dying communities. With a focus on the establishment of secondary and manufacturing industries, grants were made available to the private sector for new job creation in economically depressed communities.

In 1960 the federal government embarked on a winter works program with the dual purpose of creating winter employment and helping municipalities expand their own public works programs. Under this program the federal government contributed 50 per cent, the province 25 per cent, and the municipality 25 per cent. Between 1960 and 1969 over 10,000 Albertans were employed under the program, building and improving community airports and constructing graded crossings at dangerous railway crossings.

In the late 1960s, at the prodding of the Canadian Federation of Mayors and Municipalities (since changed to the Federation of Canadian Municipalities) and with the realization by the federal government that the country had become heavily urbanized, a Federal Task Force on Housing and Urban Development was appointed to determine what the federal role should be in the urban centres. Among other recommendations, the Task Force called for the creation of a federal Department of Housing and Urban Affairs. In June of 1971 the Ministry of State for Urban Affairs was created to focus on urban policy development, to co-ordinate urban programs being carried out by a number of other federal departments, and to foster "co-operative" relationships among the federal government and the provinces, their municipalities, private organizations and the public. The new ministry was not to be a traditional agency and, for political reasons, it was prevented from absorbing CMHC. Unfortunately, it did not live up to expectations and was later dismantled. A combination of weakened federal political support and intransigence on the part of provinces fearful of a federal presence in local decision making led to its demise. It did organize two national tri-level conferences and a number of individual city tri-level conferences to promote closer co-operation between the three levels of government. An important nation-wide study of municipal public finance was carried out and the ministry developed a high level of technical expertise that was made available to local units of government.

In conclusion, it can be said that, although the Canadian Constitution quite explicitly delineates areas of responsibility for local government, the three levels of government have taken a pragmatic approach to dealing with community problems. Occasionally, disagreements occur over financial and administrative arrangements, or local governments feel their power is being eroded by the provincial governments, or a provincial government will charge that the federal government is encroaching on provincial jurisdiction; however, all of these disagreements are only manifestations of the push and pull for power under our federal system of government.

Many have argued that a country's geography and topography are influential in determining whether or not local government develops. Professor Crawford, in his exhaustive study of Canadian municipal government, argues that the physical isolation of settlements in British Columbia forced people to provide for their own needs. A number of Americans have argued that the rough justice dispensed west of the Pecos in the American Southwest was a manifestation of that area's physical isolation. One scholar argues that local government in France was retarded by the need for a highly centralized government that could mobilize armed forces in the country's hinterlands to protect the country from invaders. It is clear that, in Alberta's early history, geographical isolation was a major factor in determining how local governmental institutions developed.

Other important factors have the potential for either nurturing or retarding the development of local government institutions. In almost all developing countries, political leaders are striving to achieve industrialization and economic modernization. Local units of government are financially starved as fiscal resources are concentrated on developing a modern industrial economy. Moreover, since decision making tends to be highly centralized, local government is almost invariably sacrificed to centralized planning. The Soviet Union in the 1930s is a prime example: then, as now, few decisions were made at the local level and local government needs were totally neglected in the interests of five-year plan after five-year plan.[22]

National constitutions play an important role in the development of local self rule. In federal systems, like those in Canada, the United States and Switzerland, constitutional provisions have resulted in a diversity of municipal institutions. Although one should be extremely cautious in attributing the development of local government to any single factor, it seems that federal systems nurture local government better than do unitary systems. Great Britain is one obvious exception: it has both a unitary system of government and relatively strong local government.

It should be clear by now that no single factor determines the establishment and the vitality of local government. In Canada in general and Alberta in particular, all the factors noted have a role to play: probably the most important is the level of commitment of a community's citizenry. Where the prevailing attitude is that participation in local government is time-consuming, unrewarding and unnecessary, the demise of local self government will soon follow. If, instead, there is a commitment to grass-roots democracy and a willingness to work and to spar with the provincial government, local government will survive.

Notes

1. In 1935 the opposition of the Governor of Kansas to rural county consolidation was justified by a concern for maintaining "democracy at the grass roots." Martin, *Grass Roots*, 1. Martin then notes: "Ten years later . . . [the] Director of the United States Budget, observed that 'there are dynamics at the grass roots. These dynamics should be harnessed and used for the preservation and extension of democracy'." For discussions of democracy at the grass roots in the Tennessee Valley, see Lilienthal, *TVA: Democracy on the March;* and Selznick, *TVA and the Grass Roots.*

2. Kotler, *Neighborhood Government.*

3. Pateman, *Participation and Democratic Theory.* See also: Benello and Roussopoulos, eds., *The Case for Participatory Democracy.*

4. Hunnuis, ed., *Participatory Democracy for Canada.* A recent follow-up to this work is Roussopoulos, ed., *The City and Radical Social Change.*

5. The Act reads: "If so requested at any time by the written petition of the electors, the mayor, by public notice conspicuously posted in at least 10 widely separated places in the municipality, shall call a public meeting of the electors of the municipality to be held on the date named in the notice, for the discussion of municipal affairs . . . ." Section 124(2) specifies the number of signatures needed. In a municipality with a population of 10,000 or more, three per cent of the population is needed; for municipalities with a population between 1,000 and 10,000 the percentage is increased to five per cent; for those under 1,000 population, seven per cent is needed. An additional stipulation for summer villages is that owners of at least 10 per cent of the land parcels must sign the petition.

6. Lynd and Lynd, *Middletown in Transition.*

7. Hunter, *Community Power Structure,* 90-94.

8. The best review of these works is found in Knill, "Community Decision-Making," 17-20.

9. Hunter's method, which was adopted by countless other researchers, involved using a panel of "politically knowledgeable" people in the community to identify the "influentials." Hence it has been designated the "reputational approach" to the study of community power. The weakness of this method is that the panel of political knowledgeables often identified wealthy community members as "influentials" whether they were in any way involved in community decision making or not.

10. Dahl, "The Concept of Power," 202.

11. At times individuals are able to get others to do something against their will without realizing they are exercising power. For example, suppose B just believes that A wants him to do something and then he goes ahead and does

it. A has exercised "implicit influence" and caused B to do something without having said anything to B. A concrete example of this would be a city manager carrying out some activity because he or she feels it is something the council wants done even though council has never directly said so.

12. The best discussion of the bases of political power is found in Lasswell and Kaplan, *Power and Society,* 74-102.

13. Masson, "Decision-making patterns," 127-138.

14. Higgins, *Urban Canada,* 46.

15. *Ibid.,* 48.

16. In a few instances, governments that were initially democratic have adopted non-democratic principles in order to implement policies and programs. The classic case is Germany in 1933, when the Nazis were voted into power in free elections on an anti-democratic and totalitarian platform. Within months of the Nazi ascension to power the other political parties were dissolved, labour unions were abolished, and the free press was either Nazified or abolished.

17. *Discretionary* powers are those local government may use at its own discretion. *Mandatory* powers are those a local council is required to exercise.

18. Corry and Hodgetts, *Democratic Government and Politics,* 613-614.

19. Crawford, *Canadian Municipal Government,* 18.

20. Although the terms municipality and municipal corporation are used interchangeably, there is a subtle difference between them. Very strictly speaking, *municipality* is defined as the physical area of an incorporated community, while *municipal corporation* is used to designate the legal entity composed of all the community's inhabitants.

21. The terms conditional grants and unconditional grants are almost self-explanatory. No conditions are attached to *unconditional grants*—the recipient has the discretion to use the funds for any legal purpose. *Conditional grants* must be spent for a specified purpose.

22. The exception to this trend is Yugoslavia which, although a Communist country, has the most decentralized governmental structure of almost any country in the world. Marshall Tito was able to combine certain aspects of national economic planning with true grass-roots democracy. Workers' councils, organized at the local level, make the decisions on almost all aspects of their lives.

2

THE STRUCTURE AND MECHANICS OF COUNCIL DECISION MAKING

Four Premises of the Distribution of Powers to Municipalities

Unlike issues, such as increases in property taxes or the salaries of elected officials, the forms of local government are of little interest to most people. Only when a proposal is made to change the governmental structure do people begin to compare the merits of different forms of local government. They quickly realize that change means a shift in administrative and political power relationships. The bureaucracy may become more powerful; the mayor may become weaker; the municipality's ability to negotiate with the province may become weaker; working-class people may gain a greater share of political power while middle-class people may lose some of their power. In short, a change in the form of local government may result in major policy and power shifts in the community.

Two pairs of contrasting preferences are invariably debated in any discussion of the creation, dissolution, amalgamation or change of the political and administrative structure of local government:

1. maximizing professional management in order to achieve the most efficient use of public resources;

2. maximizing political accountability by keeping the policy makers directly responsible to the electorate;

3. maximizing local government's responsibilities and policy making and minimizing provincial control;

4. maximizing provincial control over local policy making.

In short, there are two basic preferences which are subject to debate, with two conflicting positions on each.

20

The Professional Management of Government

The professional management approach to local government in Canada has historical roots in a late-nineteenth-century, business-oriented movement to reform American city government. In an attempt to curb the power of strong local party organizations supported by large numbers of new immigrants, middle-class business groups proposed reforms that would "take politics out of local government." It was proposed that local government be run like a private business and that a strong emphasis be placed on developing a professional bureaucracy in the interests of promoting efficiency and economy. Local government administrators and elected officials in Canada were quick to espouse this approach. For example, in a paper presented to the Union of Alberta Municipalities Convention in 1909, ex-mayor of Red Deer H.H. Gaetz argued:

> It is contended by some that . . . the municipal and the business, have little or nothing in common, that the latter is conducted for the purpose of procuring a profit on the investment and operation, while the former is not conducted with this end in view. I contend however that there is no difference; that whether dividends to shareholders or the greatest material advantage to the ratepayers is the object . . . the principle is the same and that the methods which have proved successful in accomplishing the one aim will prove as effective in accomplishing the other.

Today, in many Alberta communities, the functions of government are equated with those of the private firm; a refrain frequently heard in council chambers is: "We should keep this issue out of politics and proceed in a businesslike manner."

During the 1930s an attempt was made to develop a set of scientific principles for the efficient management of government, many of which were adopted by governmental reformers in both Canada and the United States. Some of the more prominent such principles are listed below.

1. Activities should be grouped by purpose, process, clientele, place, or time and made the responsibility of small units under the direct control of supervisors.

2. Work units should be organized hierarchically, so that several are grouped under the control of a single supervising unit (or supervisor), which in turn is grouped with other supervising units under the control of a higher supervisor.

3. There should be a narrow "span of control," with a limited number of subordinates under each supervisor, so that supervisory personnel can give sufficient attention to each subordinate unit or person.

4. There should be a clear "chain of command" and "communication through channels," so that superiors will have full information about the activities of subordinates and be assured that their own directives will control their subordinates.

5. Executives should have sufficient authority to appoint and remove their subordinates.

6. Personnel appointments and promotions should be made on the basis of competence, without interference from "politicians" seeking to reward fellow partisans.

7. Executives should control the expenditures of administrative units.

8. There should be sufficient staff services to provide the executive with the information necessary to understand and control the activities of subordinates.

Underlying the professional management approach is an attempt to depoliticize local government decision making. The justification for holding non-partisan elections and electing councillors at-large is the belief that this system will ensure the election of "reasonable people" with community-wide interests rather than narrow ideological or geographical ones. This tenet is best exemplified by the expression: "There is not a New Democratic, Liberal or Progressive Conservative way to pave a street or catch a dog, there is only one right way." Those who subscribe to a professional management approach tend to view politics as being distasteful and divisive to the community; they perceive city government merely as a series of technical and management problems that can be solved by employing highly qualified engineers and administrators.

The major failing of this approach is that, when partisanship is eliminated and council members are elected at-large, council policy choices are narrowed and political accountability becomes blurred. Even in a small, relatively homogeneous community there are social and economic cleavages. Non-partisan and at-large elections blur neighbourhood and minority interests in the "public interest," which is seldom, if ever, defined.[1]

The professional management approach, with its emphasis on minimizing costs and promoting efficiency, is often used to justify local governmental consolidations and school amalgamations. Its proponents maintain that consolidating two or more units of local government will rationalize administration, broaden the tax base and lower the per capita cost of services. These arguments will be further discussed in the section dealing with governmental reorganization.

Political Accountability

A major element of grass-roots democracy is the elected official's responsiveness and accountability to the electorate. The proponents of political accountability maintain that these virtues are enhanced by a politically active citizenry. Political scientists have shown that partisan elections and ward representation lead to a higher voting turnout than do non-partisan, at-large elections. Whereas partisan politics provides the electorate with policy alternatives, non-partisan politics tends to revolve around personalities at the expense of policy issues. Furthermore, under non-partisan electoral systems, the middle class tends to vote and the working class tends to abstain from voting, resulting in a lower overall voter turnout. Finally, it has been found that, while under ward representation the interests of the working class are represented on council, they tend to be excluded with at-large elections.

Underlying the professional management approach is the view that the provision of public services should be non-political and non-controversial; underlying the political accountability approach is the idea that different segments of the citizenry will be differentially advantaged and disadvantaged by any policy. In short, the latter recognizes that local government decisions are political.

A major tenet of management in the private sector is that the lines of authority and accountability should be crystal clear. The irony is that, in the public sector, professional management often tends to obscure these lines. Under the professional management approach the bureaucrat administering a public service is often insulated from both the citizenry and the elected official. In contrast, political accountability means that the elected official is directly responsible for governmental administration.

The difference between these two approaches can also be seen in the budgeting process. Proponents of professional management maintain that the experts, the professionals, should set the budget; proponents of political accountability claim that elected representatives should set the budget in response to the demands of the citizenry, recognizing that establishing budget priorities is a highly political process.

The proponents of political accountability argue that the creation, abolition and amalgamation of local government units affects the distribution of power and resources to different segments of the community. Therefore, any evaluation of a proposed change should give as careful consideration to changes in power relationships as to matters of economy and efficiency. It is only recently that Canadian social scientists and governmental officials have recognized the importance of evaluating changes in power relationships when evaluating governmental and administrative reorganization.

Although it may seem that the premises of professional management and political accountability are diametrically opposed, in fact, in most communities the two coexist in an uneasy accommodation. Local politicians are not ideologues; rather, they make use of professional expertise in adopting programs and formulating policies that will not generate undue controversy. At the same time, professional administrators realize that they have as much responsibility to the citizenry as they have to a professional management ethic. Consequently, in any community one finds a mix of professional management and political accountability. However, if a community's citizenry has a professional management set of values it will be reflected prominently both in the governmental structure and in the policy-making process. Conversely, if the citizenry is highly politicized, this orientation too will be reflected in the government's structure and policies.

Provincial Control of Policy Making

People who believe that the provincial government should closely circumscribe the activities of local government see little value in local autonomy or grass-roots democracy. One would assume that only provincial politicians and bureaucrats would advocate greater provincial control of local policy making. Some people, however, are quite willing to let the provincial government assume greater, if not complete, control of local policy making, believing that this form of government would decrease their property taxes and protect the municipality's credit; others think that provincial administrators are more efficient than local ones.

Examples of the former attitude can be found throughout Alberta's history. In 1912 the provincial government enacted legislation that provided for the establishment of rural municipalities governed by locally elected councillors. These new units of government were empowered to levy property taxes and issue debentures to carry out their responsibilities for building and maintaining roads and bridges.

There was widespread farmer resistance, most farmers fearing the taxing and borrowing powers of the municipal councils. Even in areas where the governments were established and were acting responsibly, large numbers of farmers wanted minimal governmental activity in order to minimize their tax bills.[2] A similar phenomenon occurred in the drought-ridden southeastern part of the province during the Depression. Penniless farmers about to lose their farms requested that the provincial government disband their local unit of government, the municipal district, and administer the area directly.

Yet another example can be found in the social services area. Under the British North America Act, the predecessor of the Constitution Act, constitutional responsibility for health and welfare fell to the provincial governments which, in turn, delegated it to the municipalities. As in all the provinces, the municipality's health and welfare function during Alberta's early period focused primarily on the development of a primitive system of poor relief. With the onset of the Depression, Alberta's financially strapped municipalities were unable to provide an adequate relief program for tens of thousands of the homeless and unemployed. The citizenry then turned to the provincial and federal governments for relief. Even after the end of the Depression, the social service functions remaining with the municipalities were eroded by the two senior levels of government. Inadequate fiscal resources coupled with mounting public criticism of social services made the local units of government quite willing to have the provincial and federal governments move even farther into the social service field. By 1974 less than three per cent of health and welfare costs were being met by local governments across Canada.

It should be emphasized that it is the exception rather than the rule for the provincial government totally to absorb activities traditionally carried out by local government. Rather, as will be seen in a later chapter, the provincial government has undermined the autonomy of Alberta's local units of government by manipulating the amount and usage of their fiscal resources. Although financial influence is the primary way the provincial government exerts control over local policy making, it has the power to make basic changes in the Municipal Government Act which could narrow local autonomy greatly. However, the government is reluctant to resort to such a heavy-handed approach: the political consequences could be devastating in a province in which a large part of the population is committed to strong local government.

Local Autonomy

Even the most ardent proponent of local government autonomy

concedes that complete autonomy is an impossibility: a community with full autonomy would be a miniature nation-state. Therefore, local autonomy is always discussed in relative terms. If the provincial government exercises only minimal control and supervision over its local units of government, they are said to be autonomous. On the other hand, if local units have no independent policy-making powers and are merely administrative conduits for policies made by the provincial government, they are said to lack autonomy. In Alberta, as in the other provinces, local government autonomy falls almost in the centre of these two extremes.

In the previous chapter it was noted that, constitutionally, local governments have no independent basis of power; section 92 of the Canadian Constitution makes them creatures of the provinces. Despite this constitutional provision, many citizens and local officials feel that local governments should be given greater freedom. For a number of years the Federation of Canadian Municipalities and the Alberta Urban Municipalities Association have consistently asked both the provincial and federal governments for legislation giving municipalities greater local autonomy. During the federal-provincial constitutional debates, the Federation of Canadian Municipalities repeatedly requested that it be brought into the constitutional process to give the nation's municipalities formal recognition in the new Canadian Constitution as a distinct third level of government. Bitter and frustrated at being ignored, the delegates at the Federation's 1982 annual conference in Ottawa passed a resolution calling on the federal and provincial governments to recognize local governments in the new constitution. Red Deer's delegate, Alderman John Oldring, summed up the delegates' feelings when he said: "It is no longer good enough to be at the whim of the provinces." It is worth noting the federal government was prepared to participate in tri-level meetings, but the provinces were not.

In Alberta permissive legislation clauses in the Municipal Government Act seem to give municipalities a wide latitude of policy alternatives in certain areas. Despite this show on the part of the provincial government of granting political autonomy, local officials are acutely aware that the real key is financial autonomy and adequate fiscal resources. With revenue sources limited primarily to the property tax and user fees, municipalities depend on the provincial government for a large portion of their operating costs. The province has not been responsive to plans that would make the municipalities fiscally autonomous. Although during the last years of the Social Credit regime the province shared part of its revenue under a formula allocating a portion of oil revenue to the municipalities, the program was

terminated by the Progressive Conservatives. While the other western provincial governments all have schemes whereby they share
their resources with their municipalities, the Lougheed government
has flatly rejected such sharing, making municipalities dependent on
provincial grants.

Thus proponents of the local autonomy premise want both wide
latitude in tapping fiscal resources and an absolute minimum of provincial interference in municipal policy making. They believe the
latter condition can be met either by entrenching certain municipal
powers in the constitution or by adopting a form of local autonomy,
called the "home-rule provision," found in some American states. A
city operating under "home rule" is given a general grant of power by
the state legislature to control its own elections, annex adjoining
areas, and regulate public health, safety and morality. The Alberta
provincial government has never seriously considered implementing
home-rule legislation for municipalities.

Some General Characteristics of Alberta's Local Governments

Although there are major differences in Alberta's various forms of
local government, certain executive and council characteristics are
common to all. Paramount among these common features is that
power and control tend to be fragmented among the council, the
mayor, the administration, and a plethora of special boards and commissions.

For the most part, the mayor's powers are limited to presiding at
council meetings and sitting *ex officio* as "a member of all boards, associations, commissions, committees or other organizations to which
the council has the right to appoint members." Much more significant
are the powers mayors do not have: they do not have the power to
veto legislation passed by council, although in several other provinces mayors are given this power; more importantly, they have little
control over the municipality's administration since that power is
vested in council. It is not the mayor but the council that has the
power of hiring and firing administrative heads.[3] Although the may-
or is without powers to control the administration, under section
51(1) of the Municipal Government Act he or she is given the following charges, among others:

(b)   [to] cause the laws governing the municipality to be
executed
(c)   [to] supervise and inspect the conduct of all officials of the
municipality in the performance of their duties

(d)   [to] cause all negligence and carelessness and violation of duty to be prosecuted and punished, as far as it is within his power to do so.

The irony of the Municipal Government Act is that it clearly delineates the mayor's responsibilities but gives the mayor little power to carry them out. Perhaps section 51(1)(d) is a recognition that the mayor is relatively powerless, since it qualifies his or her responsibilities with the clause "as far as it is within his power to do so."

Municipal councils must function within the framework of the requirements and prohibitions of the Municipal Government Act, but they are given wide discretionary powers. Section 112 states that

> The council may pass such by-laws as are considered expedient and as are not contrary to this or any other Act,
>
> a. for the peace, order and good government of the municipality,
>
> b. for promoting the health, safety, morality and welfare thereof, and
>
> c. for governing the proceedings of the council, the conduct of its members and the calling of meetings.

In case a municipal council should adopt an ill-conceived by-law, the provincial government has adopted a policy of self restraint in letting local democracy prevail, as shown in section 108 of the Act, which states:

> A by-law or resolution passed by a council in the exercise of any of the powers conferred and in accordance with this Act, and in good faith, is not open to question, nor shall it be quashed, set aside or declared invalid, either wholly or partly on account of the unreasonableness or supposed unreasonableness of its provisions or any of them.[4]

Just as councils are given wide discretion in the scope of their powers, they have equally wide discretion in the mechanisms they may employ to arrive at decisions. Each council is given the power to "make rules and regulations for calling meetings, governing its proceedings and the conduct of its members, appointing committees and generally for the transaction of its business." Each council determines how many meetings are necessary and the mayor is given the power to call special meetings at his or her discretion. A majority of the council constitutes a quorum and by-laws need the vote of a majority of the members present. Finally, "Every by-law shall have three distinct separate readings before it is finally passed, but not more than two readings of a by-law shall be had at any one meeting unless the members present unanimously agree to give the by-law third reading."

In general, the real work of the municipal government takes place in the council's committees, where by-laws are drafted and special research projects are carried out, usually at the direction of the council. Of the two kinds of committees, special committees and standing committees, standing committees are by far the most important. Council will create a special committee to deal with a specific problem; when it completes its task and reports to council, it is abolished. Standing committees are appointed on an ongoing basis to deal with a specific area, such as finance, engineering or public works.

Alberta legislation gives council committees somewhat more power than is found in municipalities in many other provinces and in American states. In Alberta, a council can delegate any of its powers to its committees, with the exception of the power to borrow money, pass a by-law or enter into a contract; the final prohibition can be breached if the council passes a by-law giving a council executive committee the power to make contracts.

Council-Committee Form of Government

The council-committee form of government, the dominant form in Alberta communities, is somewhat misnamed. All municipal governments have councils and, with the exception of some villages with only three council members, they all have committees. What differentiates the council-committee system from others is that it is characterized by an extremely weak executive, who has only slightly more power than any single councillor, and by a council that oversees the municipality's administration through a small number of standing committees. As a consequence, decision-making powers are decentralized and fragmented. It is worth noting that the council-committee form of government is found primarily in Alberta's smaller communities. Of Alberta's 12 cities, only Drumheller uses this system.

One student succinctly sums up the role of standing committees in this form of government.

> The committees exercise a general supervision over the work of the staff under their jurisdiction, consult with and advise the officials responsible for such work and make reports and

recommendations to council on matters within their sphere.[5]

Since this system of standing-committee supervision of administration tends to fragment the administrative structure, the mayor, by virtue of his or her power to sit *ex officio* on all committees, often co-ordinates the activities of the municipal departments to ensure that they are not working at cross-purposes.

A prime requisite of democracy is that the citizenry be able to hold elected officials and administrators accountable. Attempting to pinpoint administrative and political responsibility under the council-committee form of government is a fruitless task. Having no formal sanctions to use on a recalcitrant council, the mayor has only slightly more power than any single councillor; this factor, combined with the independent bases of political support of mayor and council (by virtue of their both being elected), results in a complete diffusion of power. Under these circumstances it is nearly impossible for the citizenry to determine the identity of the parties responsible for a particular policy. An attempt to determine administrative responsibility is just as confusing. Since the mayor has no control over the administration, he or she justifiably refuses to assume administrative responsibility. The council will not assume responsibility, since its members maintain that the standing committees are wholly responsible for administration. The members of the standing committees maintain that, since they only make recommendations, administrative responsibility ultimately rests with the full council. In addition, the tendency for standing committees to proliferate causes a further diminution of responsibility. Clearly, the council-committee form of government has a strong potential for "buck-passing" and irresponsibility. Not only does this governmental form lack political and administrative accountability, it also runs counter to the professional management orientation toward "running government" to which most local politicians in Alberta maintain that they subscribe.

The Canadian council-committee form of government is an amalgam of features borrowed from Great Britain and the United States. The practice of placing administrators under the purview of standing committees was borrowed from Great Britain; unfortunately, the integrative mechanism, the political party, which provides political accountability, was dropped in Canada. British local government is quasi-parliamentary in form, since the mayor is either elected or appointed by a highly politicized council operating under a strong party system. The party system acts to centralize responsibility and pull together the diverse centres of power located in the standing committees. The direct election was borrowed from the United States.

However, in many American municipalities the administration is directly responsible to the mayor who has the power to hire and fire senior administrators.[6]

Council-Manager Form of Government

Like many other Canadian municipal institutions, the council-manager form of government was borrowed from the United States and modified for Canadian use. The manager form of government, which originated in Staughton, Virginia, in 1908, was rapidly adopted by community after community, first in North America and then in Europe. It is found primarily in medium-sized and smaller communities committed to bringing professionalism into government. In Alberta a number of towns and seven of the 12 cities operate under the council-manager plan. The cities are Edmonton (in conjunction with an executive committee), Camrose, Grande Prairie, Lethbridge, Lloydminster, St. Albert and Wetaskiwin.

The manager in an Alberta municipality derives his or her power from section 91(1) and (2) of the Municipal Government Act, which states:

> A council may, by by-law, provide for the delegation of any or all of its executive and administrative duties and powers to one or more municipal commissioners or to a municipal manager. The municipal commissioners or the municipal manager, as the case may be, shall exercise the powers and duties set out in this Act, and any other powers and duties vested, confirmed or delegated by by-law or by resolution of the council.

Although under the Act the council can delegate executive powers to the manager, the underlying philosophy of the manager plan is that a hired professional administers policies made by the council. The intent of the manager form of government is completely to separate policy making from administration. This purpose can be seen in the City of Grande Prairie's by-law (c-609) that established the city manager system for the municipality, and which states:

> 4. Except for the purpose of official inquiry, the City Council and its members shall deal with and control the administrative service solely through the City Manager, and neither the Council nor any members thereof shall give orders to any of the subordinates of the City Manager either publicly or privately.

The manager plan is the purest example of the professional management ethic in government, since the manager is seen as being equivalent to the private corporate manager who oversees day-to-day business operations. The city manager is responsible to the council, an arrangement which, it is argued, is equivalent to the corporate manager being responsible to the corporate board. In Alberta the manager has three primary responsibilities, to which others may be added.[7] He or she must make policy recommendations to the council, prepare the city's budget and submit it to council, and oversee and co-ordinate municipal departments.

In the United States the manager also has the power to hire and fire department heads; in Canada, however, the person can only make recommendations to council on the hiring and firing of administrators. In Alberta the council-manager form of government, like the council-committee form, is characterized by a weak executive and uncertainty over exactly who is responsible for both long- and short-range policy formulation. The manager is responsible to council, which has the power to hire and fire him or her. As with the council-committee form of government the mayor has little or no control over administration.

Two major advantages are attributed to the council-manager form of government. First, it frees the council from continually having to scrutinize the administration and enables it to devote its full attention to the formulation and evaluation of short- and long-range policy. Second, it brings into the municipality a professionally trained administrator who is given the power to co-ordinate departmental activities and evaluate staff performance. More importantly, while many council members have a relatively short-term policy perspective and evaluate and formulate proposals on the basis of their effects on the upcoming electoral campaign, the manager is not as constrained by politics and tends to take a long-term view of the policy process by planning well into the next century.

It is not unusual, however, for a manager to build an independent base of power in the community or to act as the policy formulator in smaller communities with part-time mayors and councillors unsure of their political and administrative expertise. A study of manager government in 45 American communities found that the manager assumed the role of chief policy maker as well as that of administrator in the community. The study found that the behaviour of city managers can be:

> . . . fully and exhaustively characterized by three role
> categories: managerial, policy, and political.' The first

managerial role involves his relation with the municipal bureaucracy, including supervision and control of policy administration and personnel. The policy facet of the manager's role includes his relation with city council, particularly as he is the source of policy recommendations. His political role includes efforts as a community leader and as a representative of community needs and interests before the local council, the community at large, and other units of government. . . . He bears most of the responsibility for creating the 'menu' of policy alternatives to be considered. The council will not accept everything on the menu, but the menu does set forth the policies likely to be considered seriously.[8]

Although the study was conducted in the United States, the findings are of importance in an evaluation of the council-manager plan in Canadian communities.

It is difficult to find fault with a form of government that attempts to bring professional expertise to bear on municipal problems; however, the manager form of government has two failings, one of which is relatively minor. Until quite recently a city manager tended to have a background in civil engineering, which, while an advantage in overseeing hard services, such as road, sewer, and water main maintenance, repair and construction, does not provide preparation for evaluating and administering policies in the soft service areas, such as welfare, health and recreation. The major failing of the manager concept is in its underlying assumption that the principles of the private sector can be used to administer a municipality. The clientele of a private corporation is not felt to have a legitimate interest in its policy making and administration, and is not provided with access to these areas. Thus, while in the public sector the citizenry expects to have some input into both policy making and the administrative process, the manager has little sympathy for citizens meddling with and questioning "manager technical decisions." The underlying philosophy of the council-manager form of government is that politics can be taken out of administration and minimized in policy making. What should be remembered is that local government is political: any attempt to take politics out of government invariably ends up eroding democratic principles.

Council-Chief Administrative Officer Form of Government

Since this form of government evolved from the council-manager system, the two share many characteristics. Like many other forms of local government in Canada the council-chief administrative officer system originated in the United States. In California, where the municipal reform movement was extremely strong during the first half of the century, the council-manager form of government was widely adopted. Then, during the 1940s, a number of communities became sympathetic to the concept of hiring a professional administrator, but were reluctant to relinquish direct control by making the manager "the council's agent in the administration of the municipality's affairs." The consequence was a variant of the council-manager system that had an administrator but "provided that the councillors retained and exercised all of the administrative powers." This basic power relationship is found in the council-chief administrative officer form of government found in some Alberta municipalities.

The major difference between the manager form of government and this form is that, whereas council delegates all administrative responsibilities to the city manager, it assigns specific duties to the chief administrative officer. The chief administrative officer directs and supervises other administrative officials only to the extent that the officer is specifically authorized to do so by council. Unlike a city manager, the chief administrative officer does not have a general grant of power. In addition, the administrative officer acts (as does the city manager) as an advisor to council, making recommendations and preparing technical studies.

One study of the council-chief administrative officer form of government argues that:

> In practice . . . because of the wide difference in the attitudes
> and the needs of councillors, the abilities of CAOs and the needs
> of the municipal corporations, the informal role of a CAO may
> be very similar to the formal role of a manager; and the powers
> and duties that are assigned, informally, to a CAO, may be very
> similar to the powers and duties that are assigned, formally, to a
> manager.[9]

The same study maintains that "from the council's point of view, there is no meaningful distinction between a manager . . . or a CAO"; thus, it seems to miss the essential difference between the two forms of government. When a council decides to bring a professional into its administration, it has the choice of either delegating its administrative power to a manager or holding on to the reins of administration by appointing an administrative officer. Admittedly, the chief administrative officer may be allowed to function in much the same way as does a city manager, but, at any time and on the shortest notice, the council is able to halt his or her activities. This important distinction does not escape council members, who are constantly on guard against any erosion of their powers.

Although the Municipal Government Act makes no mention of a chief administrative officer, section 60 reads:

> A council, by by-law, may provide that the duties and responsibilities of the office of the municipal secretary and the treasurer be combined into one officer to be designated as the municipal administrator and a person appointed to that office may under the title of municipal administrator do anything that by this or any other Act is to be done by the municipal secretary or the treasurer.

Under the Act every municipal council is required to appoint a secretary and a treasurer. Since the costs of hiring two administrators would be excessive for very small municipalities, section 60 is frequently invoked to combine the offices.

In conclusion, the question of whether the council-administrative officer form of government centralizes power must be addressed. The system is not as decentralized as the council-committee form but not as centralized as a manager system. With powers and responsibilities dispersed under the council-administrative officer system, the citizenry is just as confused as with the other forms of local government we have examined.

Council-Commission Board Form of Government

The council-commission form of government, like the council-manager form, attempts to bring a professional management approach to local government. It differs from the council-manager form in that the council delegates executive and administrative powers to a board composed of senior administrators and the mayor rather than to a single administrator. Hence the mayor has a much greater role in controlling the administration. This form of government, which begins to recognize the mayor as an executive with power, has been used successfully in Calgary for a number of years and has been adopted recently in Fort McMurray and Medicine Hat. The system was in use in Edmonton until 1984. A variation of the council-commission form, which will be discussed shortly, has been employed in Red Deer for some time.

Although council-commission government brings considerable professional expertise to bear on municipal problems and provides the mayor with a modicum of power, it has the disadvantage of being overly complex, with almost infinite lines of political and administrative responsibility. To unravel these complexities, Calgary's council-commission will be examined in detail. The council formulates policy, which is carried out by four professional commissioners, experts in their respective fields, appointed (and dismissed) by council. There is a chief commissioner, a commissioner of planning and transportation, a commissioner of finance and administration, and a commissioner of operations, each directly responsible for the supervision of a number of city department heads.[10]

The mayor and the four commissioners constitute the commission board, which determines how council's general policy directions are to be carried out through the administrative structure. Under the direction of the chief commissioner, the activities of the commissioners are co-ordinated to ensure that they will not be working at cross-purposes. The commission board also makes policy recommendations to council, and these recommendations are often given more consideration than policy recommendations coming directly from council's standing committees. Calgary retrogressed in 1968 when the city's by-law was amended to transfer the commission board's chair from the mayor to the chief commissioner. This action was unfortunate, for its effect has been to restrict the mayor's control of administration.[11] The mayor does sit *ex officio* on the commission board, but plays only a limited role in its activities. This restriction is unfortunate, since the mayor is the linchpin in the whole system, the bridge between the formulation of policy on council and its administration through the commission board.

The commissioners are intricately woven into the council's five standing committees. Although not formal committee members with voting privileges, the commissioners are resource personnel for the committees, and actively participate in their discussions. Normally, a standing committee meeting is not held unless at least one commissioner is present. The commissioner of finance and administration is directed to attend all meetings of the standing committees on community services, and finance and budget. Both the commissioner of planning and transportation and the commissioner of operations are directed to attend meetings of the standing committee on operations and development. The chief commissioner is given the authority to attend any standing committee meeting. In practice, he attends almost all meetings of the standing committees on legislation and intergovernmental affairs.

In addition to co-ordinating the commission board and sitting on a number of standing committees, the chief commissioner has other important responsibilities, which include keeping the lines of communication open between the administration and the mayor and council, and assisting and advising them on policy and administration. The commissioner must also consult the agenda committee to prepare the council's agenda. Potentially, this is an extremely important power, for, by acting as the "gate keeper" for policy proposals, the chief commissioner and the agenda committee can structure council's policy direction. Lightbody sums up this power, when Edmonton operated under commission government, when he writes: "Not surprisingly, most council business originates from commission board reports, which have a considerable impact in the structuring of political choice."[12]

The mayor's formal power on council is limited, as in the other forms of government: the incumbent presides at council meetings and is *ex officio* a member of all council and city committees, boards and commissions. It is worth noting that the mayor is also a member of council's agenda committee and, moreover, is the only committee member allowed to place additional items on the agenda without majority committee approval.

The administrative structures of other Alberta cities that have adopted this form of government vary slightly from those of Calgary. In Fort McMurray there are commissioners of operations, finance and community services, and the chief commissioner; the chief commissioner is the board chairperson. Medicine Hat has four commissioners (finance and administration, utilities, community services and public works) but no chief commissioner, so titled. As the board's chairman, the mayor is able to play a much more decisive role in administration than are the mayors in Fort McMurray and Calgary. Red Deer adopted council-commission government with a single commissioner who co-ordinates and has broad supervisory powers over the municipal departments. In addition, the commissioner works closely with council's standing committees. Though the mayor is also a commissioner *ex officio*, he or she does not function as an active commissioner by supervising staff, etc. In reality, the functions of Red Deer's single commissioner differ little from those of a city manager.

The major advantage of council-commission government is that, like council-manager government, it allows the council to devote its time to consulting constituents and to making policy without the distraction of having to deal with everyday administrative matters. Its major failing is its complexity: its structure and processes are confusing to the majority of citizens and even members of the administration are often baffled by poorly defined lines of authority and responsibility. Even when the mayor is chairperson of the commission board and is given more authority than under the other forms of local government in Alberta, power and responsibility remain diffused. A related problem is that council-commission government diffuses administrative responsibility among a number of commissioners. A progressive change would be to place final administrative authority with the mayor, who would be ultimately responsible for all the commission board's decisions. This improvement would require giving the mayor the power to hire and fire commissioners and making him or her a powerful chairperson of the commission board. An even more serious problem is secrecy. In an examination of Edmonton's use of council-commission government Lightbody writes: ". . . in much the same way as the environment of the newsroom rewards consistency with the general editorial orientation of a newspaper, upwardly mobile civic managers do not upset applecarts in Edmonton. Rarely do internal struggles over policy alternatives reach the public ear, even though some have been fierce."[13]

Generally, the disadvantages of council-commission government outweigh its advantages. Although it employs highly trained professionals, administrative power is diffused and quite often there is administrative infighting. The council-commission structure is extremely complex, and few citizens understand its workings. More importantly, this complex structure provides for little citizen input into either the policy making or the administrative process. With the council-commission form of government, as with other forms, if democracy is to prevail at the local level each citizen must be able to pinpoint who is responsible for political and administrative decisions. Unless power is concentrated so that deliberate long-range policies can be planned and co-ordinated, the council will wallow in a sea of indecision.

Council-Executive Committee Form of Government

The term *council-executive committee* is used in a variety of contexts and often means different things to different people. For example, the Municipality of Metropolitan Toronto has an executive committee composed of the mayors of the City of Toronto and each of the five boroughs, four City of Toronto councillors, and the committee chairperson, selected from the committee's members. [14] Its wide-ranging duties include acting as a financial policy-making and watchdog body and submitting by-laws to council. Also found in Ontario is the council-board of control form of government; the executive committee, elected at-large, is the board of control. [15] The board/committee is extremely powerful, since it is given the responsibility to: 1) submit all proposed by-laws to council; 2) call for tenders and award contracts; 3) prepare annual estimates; 4) nominate and dismiss department heads; and 5) perform any other duties assigned by council.

Despite their use of the term executive committee, neither Toronto's metro government nor the council-board of control found in cities are considered to be true council-executive committee forms of government.

The council-executive committee form of government (found in only one Alberta municipality, Edmonton) resembles most closely the executive committee-council manager form of government implemented in the cities of Quebec, Hull and Laval in the late 1960s. To enable the mayor to exercise leadership and to streamline council policy making, each city created an extremely strong executive committee. With its members chosen by the mayor, such a committee's powers closely parallel those of the Ontario board of control, with one exception: the executive committee does not nominate and dismiss department heads; this duty is left to the city manager who reports directly to the executive committee.

The executive committee-council manager system employed in the three Quebec cities is quasi-parliamentary. However, unlike the case in true parliamentary government, the executive (i.e., the mayor) is elected rather than appointed from the ranks of the majority party in the legislative body. When the council-executive committee system is combined with strong municipal party politics, as occurs in Montreal and Quebec City, the mayor has the power to carry out long-range policy making. The only criticism of this type of government is that it concentrates excessive power in the hands of the mayor and the council's executive committee. However, for people committed to decision making under a parliamentary system that pinpoints responsibility, this criticism is not a telling one.

In Alberta, section 47(1) of the Municipal Government Act allows a council to establish an executive committee with wide-reaching powers.

1. A council may by by-law provide

a. for the appointment of an executive committee which may be comprised of

1) members of the council, or

2) members of the council and officials of the municipality, and

b. for the delegation to the executive committee of the power to make decisions or orders, enter into contracts, execute agreements or documents and to affix the municipal seal thereto.

2. All decisions, orders, contracts, agreements and documents made or executed by the executive committee are as valid and enforceable as if made directly by the council that delegates the powers.

Despite this permissive legislation, only Edmonton has established an executive committee. In 1981 the city hired a private consultant to determine why policy making seemed to be directionless and how the situation could be improved. Among other recommendations, the consultant suggested that an executive committee system, with a committee composed of the mayor and three councillors, be adopted. The mayor, chairing the committee, would appoint the councillors. In June of 1982 the council supported the general concept of an executive committee and proceeded to determine how the recommendation could be implemented. However, with the 1982-83 budget crisis, the council quietly sidetracked the proposal in order to focus on the city's financial problems. Then, in the fall of 1983, Laurence Decore swept into the mayor's chair, with one of his platform promises being to dismantle the city's commission board and replace it with an executive committee and a city manager. With virtually no opposition, the council-commission board form of government that had been in use for three-quarters of a century was dismantled and an executive committee form was adopted in January, 1984.

Like its counterparts in Hull, Quebec City and Laval, Edmonton's executive committee is the nerve centre of city government. In the area of finance it is directed to: 1) prepare the annual budget, determine tax rebates and monitor the administration's financial performance; 2) call for tenders and award contracts; 3) recommend to council which civic organizations are to receive civic grants and the amounts; 4) recommend to council the rates and charges for services such as transit fares, utility rates and license fees, and; 5) settle claims on behalf of the city. In the area of policy making and administration the committee is directed to: 1) develop long-range policies; 2) act as the policy co-ordinator between the manager and the council's standing committees; 3) monitor the level of service provided to the public; 4) control and give direction to the city manager in his or her administrative capacity; and, 5) enter into collective bargaining agreements with city employees. The committee is also given the power to make recommendations and draft by-laws for presentation to council in any policy area. Finally, the committee is responsible for structuring much of council's activity. It sets the council's agenda and directs and co-ordinates the flow of information and business between council, its committees, and the administration.

It was more than two months after the executive committee was adopted before some members of council became aware of its ramifications. After the executive committee approved a controversial land swap, one council member not on the executive committee felt strongly that power to approve land sales, swaps and purchases should be returned to the full council. A member of the standing committee on utilities and finance wondered whether his committee any longer had a function now that almost all fiscal and utilities matters were being handled by the executive committee. Yet another councillor was concerned about the number of public letters being routed past the public affairs and utilities and finance committees directly to the executive committee. Concerns about the powerful executive committee were expressed by its leading council critic in a letter to the *Edmonton Journal* which states:

> We [the dissident council members] provided examples of
> where the executive committee was ignoring or interfering with
> existing standing committees and not providing adequate
> communication with other members of council. The executive
> committee has to realize it is the servant of council, not its
> master. Aldermen not on the committee shouldn't have to learn
> of major decisions from the media.[16]

Yet, in theory, the executive committee form of government, coupled with the employment of a city manager, should greatly increase accountability and administrative efficiency and should facilitate long-range planning. A close-knit executive committee, chosen by the mayor on the basis of similar values on policy and administration, co-ordinates and orchestrates both council and the administration. It works most successfully when party politics is entrenched at the local level; the mayor appoints like-minded party members and thus is able to appeal to their party loyalties in carrying out his or her policies. In short, the executive committee concept is successful when the committee is composed of like-minded individuals who are able to work together.

The flaw of Edmonton's executive committee lies in the way it is chosen. Initially, Mayor Decore proposed that the executive committee should comprise the mayor, who would be its chairperson, and the "City's six senior councillors." The city is divided into six wards, each electing two members; the member who receives most votes in the ward becomes the "senior councillor." After several councillors pointed out that a committee composed of half the council's members would be unwieldy, the mayor compromised. The committee's membership would consist of four councillors chosen in rotation from among the six senior councillors, the rotation schedule to be determined by the mayor in consultation with all senior councillors. Thus, chance determines the composition of the executive committee. Unlike Ontario's board of control-executive committee system, in which the public votes for candidates specifically running for the executive committee, in Edmonton the voter selects two candidates for council but is unable to specify which sits on the executive committee. More importantly, under Edmonton's system the mayor may be forced to work with executive committee members openly hostile to the mayor or to each other.[17] Fortunately, at the time the executive committee form of government was adopted in January, 1984, the council decided it would be reviewed "no sooner than 12 months from its adoption . . . and not later than 18 months." It is very probable that the method of selection will be given close scrutiny and changed.

Finally, although the by-law that established the executive committee provided additional remuneration for members, with council's authorization, no immediate additional remuneration was to be forthcoming. In Decore's mayoralty campaign one of the justifications for abolishing the commission board was to save money. Therefore, it would have been politically awkward for Decore to propose that executive committee members should receive a substantially higher salary, commensurate with their additional responsibilities. Undoubtedly, in the near future the executive committee will quietly recommend that its members' salaries be increased.

Fragmented Decision Making: Special-Purpose Bodies

City government in Alberta's larger municipalities is characterized by the number of boards, commissions, and committees that may formulate policy but have a tangential relationship with the mayor and the council. Each body has a a narrow focus but, when we examine them collectively, we see that a sizeable portion of city policy is made and administered by the predominently non-elected members of these bodies. The policy scope of these special-purpose bodies can be seen merely by listing the boards, commissions and committees in Edmonton in 1982 and in Calgary in 1984.

Calgary

1. Approving Authority for Campaigns for Public Contributions
2. Calgary Convention Centre Authority
3. Calgary Exhibition and Stampede Board

4. Calgary Housing Commission
5. Calgary Parking Authority
6. Calgary Regional Arts Foundation
7. Calgary Regional Planning Commission
8. Calgary Tourist and Convention Association
9. Calgary Transportation Authority
10. Advisory Committee on Animal Control
11. Boxing and Wrestling Commission
12. Calgary Auxiliary Hospital and Nursing Home District No. 7
13. Calgary General Hospital Board
14. Calgary Planning Commission
15. Calgary Police Commission
16. Calgary Regional Mental Health Council
17. Calgary Safety Council
18. Calgary Taxi Commission
19. Calgary Zoological Society
20. Calgary Research and Development Authority
21. Calgary Parks Foundation
22. Disaster Services Committee
23. Calgary Economic Authority
24. Clean Calgary Committee
25. Development Appeal Board
26. Gas and Power Committee
27. Gas Approval Board
28. Handicapped and Elderly Transportation Committee
29. Heritage Advisory Board
30. Heritage Park Society
31. Home Care Management Committee
32. Housing Commission
33. Special Needs Taxi Service Appeal Board
34. Housing Authority Recommending Committee
35. Intergovernmental Housing Committee
36. Landlord and Tenant Advisory Board
37. Library Board
38. Licence Appeal Committee
39. McMahon Stadium Board
40. Metro Calgary and Rural General Hospital District
41. Metro Calgary Foundation
42. Parks and Recreation Board
43. Planning Advisory Committee
44. Scholarship Committee
45. Mall Days Authority Committee
46. Urban Native Affairs Committee

47. Weed Control Board
48. YWCA Women's Shelter Task Force
49. Calgary Centre for Performing Arts
50. Fort Calgary Preservation Society
51. Lindsay Park Sports Society
52. Max Bell Society
53. Mobile Homes Sites Advisory Board
54. Olympic Coliseum Management Foundation
55. Ex-Sheriff King Home Committee
56. Tax Commission
57. Alberta 75 Task Force
58. Calgary Allied Arts Foundation
59. Centennial Planetarium and Pleiades Theatre Society
60. Calgary Olympic Coliseum Society
61. Calgary Economic Authority
62. Calhome Properties Ltd.
63. Centennial of Incorporation Committee
64. Community Video/Arcade Committee
65. Calgary Centre for Performing Arts—Construction Management Committee
66. Local Emergency Committee
67. Mall Days Board of Appeal
68. Municipal Building Advisory Committee
69. Calgary Municipal Heritage Properties Authority
70. Civic Traffic Management and Advisory Board

Edmonton

1. Edmonton Metropolitan Regional Planning Commission
2. Taxi Cab Commission
3. Local Board of Health
4. Royal Alexandra Hospital Board
5. Sinking Fund Trustees
6. Edmonton Public Library Board
7. Edmonton and Rural Auxiliary Hospital and Nursing Home District no.24
8. Development Appeal Board
9. Royal Glenora Club
10. Old Strathcona Foundation
11. Edmonton Area Hospital Planning Council
12. Metro Edmonton Hospital District no. 26
13. Boxing and Wrestling Commission
14. Police Commission
15. Greater Edmonton Foundation

16. Parks, Recreation and Cultural Advisory Board
17. Edmonton Historical Board
18. Convention Centre Authority
19. Edmonton Ambulance Authority
20. Landlord and Tenants Advisory Board
21. Names Advisory Committee
22. Non-profit Housing Committee
23. Edmonton Research and Development Park Authority
24. Social Services Advisory Committee
25. Charitable Appeals Committee
26. Edmonton Northlands
27. Economic Development Authority

Although, more often than not, special-purpose bodies are lumped together in any discussion of advantages and disadvantages, it is important to keep in mind that, since each is created in response to the demands of a particular group, each has a very specific clientele. For example, librarians and medical professionals have successfully insulated libraries and hospitals from the control of municipal councils by having them placed under special-purpose boards where the professionals have a major input. The professionals argue that hospitals and libraries are too important to be subject to the scrutiny of a municipal council interested in cutting departmental budgets to the bone so that it can be re-elected. As a consequence, the Libraries Act and the Alberta Hospitals Act specify that hospitals and libraries will be administered by boards. In both cases the municipal council is directed to appoint community members to the boards; almost invariably the council appoints one or two of its own members. Since it is unlikely that all board appointees will be members of the pertinent profession, professionals use other methods to ensure that board policy will reflect their views. For example, "It is not uncommon in agencies which have boards as policy making bodies for most of the policies ultimately adopted to be generated within the bureaucracy of the agency and to be 'sold' to the commission by the administrative head."[18]

The professional groups are not alone in wishing to remove some narrow interest from council's control and to become a major force in formulating policy. For example, in 1981 the Calgary Associated Dog Fanciers had a representative on the city's Advisory Committee on Animal Control, and both the Urban Development Institute (an association of property developers) and the Alberta Mortgage Loan Association had representatives on the Calgary Housing Commission. The Urban Development Institute, an especially active interest group, also had a representative on the city's Strathcona Task Force on Advance Planning.

Councils often create a special-purpose body in order to deflect a politically explosive "no win" issue from council chambers. An example of an attempt to do this can be found in Edmonton. The plan to develop the city's river valley strictly as a park or as a mix of park and residential development has had a history of controversy, with council members being "damned" whatever their stand. In the spring of 1983 a council member suggested that council resolve the issue by establishing a special-purpose body to formulate policy on river valley development. Rather than absolve itself of its responsibility, however, council rejected the suggestion.

Another important reason council creates boards, commissions and committees is to bring large numbers of potential opponents among citizens' and interest groups into the policy-making process. The hope is that, once brought into the administration, they will feel they have a stake in its success and will support a broad range of council policies in addition to their own board's policies. In short, it is a policy of attempting to co-opt one's opponents. Equally important is the fact that board appointments are often made as rewards for electoral support in a political system that has little political patronage since virtually all civil service positions are filled on the basis of merit and examination. Many people feel fully repaid by the recognition that comes with an appointment to a powerful and important board, even if there is no remuneration. Furthermore, although members of most special-purpose bodies receive no remuneration, a few such bodies do pay their board members. For example, in Edmonton the Royal Alexandra Hospital Board adopted the following pay schedule in 1981:

> that the honorarium for Board members attending regular and special Board meetings and/or standing or ad hoc committee meetings be remunerated at the sum of $75 per Board member and $100 for the Chairman of the Board.
> that Board members who attend conventions, seminars, workshops and other hospital related concerns be remunerated at the sum of $100 per day plus out of pocket expenses, per Board member.[19]

In the fiscal year ending March 31, 1982, nine board members received remuneration ranging from $525 to $2,870 for the year — not insignificant sums.

More important than the reasons why special-purpose bodies are created and why people seek positions on them is their effect on the governmental policy process. Our discussion of the forms of government employed by Alberta municipalities has emphasized the fact that, in every political system, power is fragmented and responsibility is diffused. Special-purpose bodies further fragment power and responsibility and make it virtually impossible for an administration to develop and carry out a comprehensive body of policy. Another major failing of these special-purpose bodies is that, although many formulate and implement important policy, they are one step removed from control by the citizenry because board members are appointed, not elected. Boards, commissions and committees do not take particular functions out of politics; rather they remove these functions from the control and scrutiny of the citizenry to those of special interests in the community.

An Overview of Municipal Decision-Making Structures

At the beginning of the chapter we examined four premises that shape any decisions on structural change in local government. With more and more communities adopting the council-manager and council-chief administrative officer forms of government, it is clear that Alberta's citizenry favours the professional management premise over the political accountability premise. Another indication of this preference is the provincial government's commitment to upgrading the qualifications of local government administrators: if it had a strong commitment to political accountability it would probably fund education programs for locally elected representatives, and encourage the council-executive committee form of government, ward representation, strong local citizen groups and party politics. It also is clear that the citizenry tends to favour local autonomy over the provincial control of local government. Although Alberta legislation has never provided for "home rule," it does give municipal councils wide discretion in the mix of services they can provide for the citizenry.

Two factors have stood out in an examination of the various forms of government. First, unlike the provincial government system, where the legislative function is carried out by the legislative assembly and the executive function by the cabinet, the legislative and executive functions tend to be combined in municipal councils. The bureaucracy informally and the council as a whole initiate policy proposals, formulate the proposals by passing by-laws, and oversee the municipal bureaucracy. In short, the council's legislative and executive functions are indistinct and tend to blur into one another, a feature that often leads to confusion and frustration among council members as well as the public. Furthermore, in Alberta's local governments formal power is dispersed rather than concentrated.

Table 2.1
Power Relationships in Various Forms of Local Government

	Mayor's Power	Council's Power	Administrative Power	Overall Assessment of Power
Council-Committee	very weak	strong	very fragmented	very fragmented
Council-Manager	very weak	strong	concentrated	somewhat fragmented
Council-Commission	somewhat weak	somewhat strong	concentrated	somewhat fragmented
Council-Chief Administrative-Officer	very weak	strong	somewhat concentrated	fragmented
Council-Executive Committee	strong	somewhat weak to somewhat strong	somewhat concentrated	concentrated

Neither the mayor nor anyone else is given enough formal powers to control effectively the administration or to implement major policy decisions. Table 2.1 graphically shows this weakness and fragmentation in the forms of government that have been discussed. An examination of the table should make it clear that, in Alberta, the only way leadership can be exercised and a distinct policy direction can be made is through the use of informal power, which we will examine critically in a discussion of the council policy-making process.

Notes

1. Banfield and Wilson argue that, in American communities, an "Anglo-Saxon Protestant middle class political ethos is often found." Central to this ethos is "the obligation of the individual . . . to seek the good of the [whole] community" rather than foster narrow parochial interests. *City Politics*, 40-44.

2. Crawford describes a similar phenomenon in Newfoundland's early period. "The ownership of land was essential in order to have a base of

operation for fishing, the main occupation of the settlers; their livelihood thus depended on retaining their property. Municipal government would mean property taxes and with property taxation was associated the spectre of losing property through inability to meet the taxes." *Canadian Municipal Government*, 40.

3. Under section 90(1) of the Municipal Government Act, the mayor "may suspend any official or employee, other than a municipal commissioner or municipal manager, and he shall forthwith report the suspension and the reasons . . . to the council not later than the next meeting." However, council has the last word on the suspension, for 90(2) states, "council may reinstate the official or employee suspended or may dismiss the official or employee."

4. Section 108 also serves another purpose. It prevents people who "lose" in the policy struggle from clogging the courts with continuing objections.

5. Crawford, 110.

6. This tends to be an over-simplified explanation of the American system, for there are both "strong mayor-council" and "weak mayor-council" forms of government. Under the strong mayor form the department heads are directly responsible to the mayor. In addition, the mayor has a veto over council's actions. Under the weak mayor form the department heads are responsible to a board or commission appointed by both the mayor and council; furthermore, the mayor has no veto power.

7. In Grande Prairie the manager is charged with the following duties:

> a. In addition to the powers and duties prescribed by the Act and the powers and duties as may from time to time be delegated to him by by-laws or resolution of Council, the City Manager shall:
>
> i. *provide for the enforcement of all by-laws* and resolutions of the City;
>
> ii. *attend all regular and special meetings of Council* and be entitled when required to attend or to be represented by his designee at all meetings of Boards, Committees or Commissions appointed by Council or the Mayor;
>
> iii. *keep the Council advised on all operations of the City and consider and make recommendations to Council on all matters affecting the security, welfare, and financial condition of the City* and such other measures as he may deem necessary and pertinent; keep the Council advised of the financial condition and needs of the City;
>
> iv. *cause the annual current and capital budgets to be prepared including estimates of revenue and expenditure* for the following year and in such detail as Council may prescribe;
>
> v. *provide for the supervision of all departments* of the City;. . .

vi. *provide for the supervision, care, control and maintenance of all public thoroughfares, sidewalks, public buildings and/or properties,* owned or controlled by the City, with the exception where any contract or agreement of Council provides for separate maintenance, control or construction of a City owned facility;

vii. *provide for the prosecution of all claims for damage to property owned or controlled by the City and the judgment of all claims against the City.*

8. Wright, "The City Manager as a Development Administrator, " 203-248.

9. *Ibid.,* p. 275.

10. The City Solicitor, City Clerk, Director of Corporate Resources, Director of Personnel Services, Director of Business Development, Director of Public Information and Director of Social Services all report to the Chief Commissioner. The Fire Chief, Director of the Planning Department and Director of the Transportation Department report to the Commissioner of Planning and Transportation. The City Assessor, Budget Officer, General Manager of the Electric System, Risk Manager of the Insurance Division, Director of the Finance Department, Director of Management Audit and Director of the Data Processing Services Department report to the Commissioner of Finance and Administration. The City Engineer, Director of Mechanical Services, Director of Purchasing and Stores, Director of Parks and Recreation, and the Director of the Land Department report to the Commissioner of Operations.

11. At least one student of Canadian local government disagrees with this interpretation. He writes: ". . . the idea of appointing the chief elected representative of the people to the board is questionable and may lead to difficulties . . . it is not possible for one person to carry out the duties and the responsibilities of the leader of the council and the community and, at the same time, carry out the duties and responsibilities of the chief administrative officer; either or both of these duties will suffer. . . . Since the mayor is the chief elected officer, he will dominate the discussions and the decisions of the board—even if he is not the chairman of the board. The mayor's dominance of the board is not desirable from the commissioner's point of view and many councillors are concerned with this aspect of the system." Hickey, *Decision-making Process in Ontario,* 218-219.

12. Lightbody, "Edmonton," 274.

13. *Ibid,* 274-275.

14. See the appendix to Chapter 3 for a discussion of Toronto's metro government.

15. Paul Hickey maintains the board is not a committee. He writes: ". . . it must be emphasized that the members of the board of control are not a committee of council. They are something more than a committee of the

council! They are not responsible to the council. They are responsible to the electors who elected them." *Decision Making in Ontario,* 144.

16. *Edmonton Journal,* March 9, 1984.

17. Olive Elliott, political columnist for the *Edmonton Journal,* argues that political parties would soon follow adoption of a council-executive committee form of government. She has no basis for the argument either in the executive committee experience in Quebec or the academic literature on political party development.

18. Adrian and Press, *Governing Urban America,* 353.

19. Velma Manz, Letter to C.J. McGonigle, May 4, 1982.

3

MUNICIPAL REORGANIZATION: TOWARD EFFICIENCY IN GOVERNMENT

Efficiency and Size in the Private Sector

In the last chapter it was pointed out that many people equate the activities of the municipal corporation with those of the business corporation. In addition, many knowledgeable students of government, who realize that the basic goals of government and private business are very different, believe the municipal corporation should employ businesslike methods. A great many justifications of governmental reorganization have their roots in private business theory. For these reasons, a cursory examination of the private sector must be made before the public sector can be discussed.

In the private sector, the key to profit is efficiency, which is usually equated with lower per unit costs of production. A common technique for increasing efficiency is reorganizing personnel either to maintain the same level of production with fewer employees or to increase production with existing personnel. Another method involves introducing sophisticated machinery either to displace existing employees or to increase their productivity. It is generally agreed that personnel reorganization and the use of sophisticated technology usually result in lower per unit costs and higher profits.[1] A more controversial strategy is to increase the size of the business in order to achieve "economies of scale." The "economy of scale" concept is relatively simple: the larger the business, the lower the per unit cost of production. Larger enterprises buy greater volumes, thus reducing the per unit cost of raw materials. Furthermore it is argued that, since "fixed costs" remain the same, a company that increases production will decrease the per unit cost of the product. Finally, it is thought that, because of the greater flexibility associated with a large work force in a big organization, individual workers can be employed more effectively, both by better use of their work day and by greater specialization.

The "economy of scale" argument is controversial, for there are unintended side-effects that may increase per unit costs. The most serious problem is that the larger the business the more difficult it becomes to co-ordinate its operation and its personnel. The organization may become so large and complex that no single individual or group is able to comprehend its total operation; and the consequence can be policy decisions that lead to production and managerial inefficiencies. There is an optimum size beyond which per unit costs of production increase rather than decrease. It is for this reason that many small companies successfully compete with industrial giants; for example, the per unit costs of production of the U.S. Steel Corporation, a giant in the steel industry, are higher than those of most of its smaller competitors.

Although "economies of scale" and greater profits are the reasons usually presented for increasing size, there are equally important non-economic reasons for expansion. New technology may alter the relationship of completely unrelated enterprises so that it is in their mutual interest to merge. In Japan this process is beginning in the ceramics and automobile manufacturing industries. It is also common for a company to merge with another to acquire its technological and managerial expertise. Finally, the larger the business, the greater the prestige (and salaries) of its senior employees. While little prestige accrues to the manager of a company that employs four people, a manager of a large city bank gains considerable prestige and a senior executive of a national bank acquires even more. Many expansion decisions have little or no economic justification, but reflect a desire for greater public exposure and prestige.

Efficiency and Size in the Municipality

Municipal office-holders and administrators, like their counterparts in the private sector, search for strategies to increase efficiency and decrease the per unit costs of services. Their motive is not increased profit, but better public service at the same cost or the same service at a lower cost. The centre of controversy in many municipal elections is how aggressively the administration held the line on costs, and the public has come to expect charges of administrative inefficiency as common electoral fare.

Municipal corporations and private corporations use the same strategies to increase efficiency. A new industry has developed in Canada to serve municipalities attempting to become more efficient.

Private consultants, hired to evaluate a community's administrative structure to improve efficiency, frequently recommend that professionals should manage the municipal corporation; more specifically, they advise that council-commission, council-manager or council-administrative officer forms of government be introduced. Almost invariably they recommend that a professional finance officer be hired and that standard accounting procedures be adopted. As in the private sector, this administrative reorganization sometimes results in greater efficiency, while in other cases it has little discernable effect.

The strategy with the greatest appeal for governmental reformers, academics and private consultants is to increase the size of the governmental unit to gain the advantage of "economies of scale." Proponents claim that consolidating governmental units within a region and administering the area as a single governmental unit reduces wasteful duplication of services. The strategy is controversial since advantages are often questionable.

On the one hand, as in the private sector, many office-holders and administrative personnel in large cities favour expansion for the increased prestige (and salary) accompanying larger governmental units. Not surprisingly, the "expansionists" discuss only in private the fact that their salaries and prestige would increase with the municipal boundaries. On the other hand, office holders and administrative personnel in small communities that would be absorbed by city expansion oppose consolidation for fear of losing their jobs. Many small-community bureaucrats are aware that they are not as well trained as their big-city associates and that they would be downgraded or terminated with amalgamation.

Difficulties of Service Evaluation

Before trying to evaluate governmental reorganization proposals, one should examine the difficulties involved in determining whether or not a particular service is efficient. After all, if the efficiency of a municipal service cannot be measured, or can be measured only very imprecisely, it makes little sense to attempt evaluation.

Since it is difficult to measure the benefits of many governmental services in dollars and cents, one must employ other forms of measurement. For example, there has been a long-standing controversy over whether it is more efficient in dollar terms to employ one or two officers in police cars. The advocates of one-officer cars claim tremendous savings in labour costs. The advocates of two-officer cars say that this claim is misleading; they argue that when one-officer cars patrol high crime areas, the officer's inclination is to be extremely cautious, patrolling the fringes of the area rather than the core. They

cite statistics showing a much higher officer fatality rate for one-officer patrols and argue that a price cannot be placed on human life.[2]
The question of whether it is more efficient to patrol with one-officer
or two-officer police cars remains unanswered.

Another controversial policy in the law enforcement field is
whether a single, central police station is more or less efficient than a
number of precincts located throughout the community. The advocates of a single police station argue that having several precincts
leads to unnecessary duplication of functions and substantially
higher costs. Their opponents maintain that the officers working out
of a neighbourhood precinct are better acquainted with the area and
are accepted as a part of the community; thus, they claim, precincts
help to reduce crime and its costs to the citizenry. In this example, as
in the preceding one, the proponents of each position employ different measures of efficiency. One group considers the cost of crime to
the citizenry in its index of efficiency; the other restricts the measure
to administrative costs alone.

As one might expect, the problems of service measurement are
most difficult in the area of "soft services." One reason is that various
segments of the public have different perceptions of service goals,
one segment evaluating a soft service, such as welfare, on the basis of
one factor, and another judging it by a different criterion. Evaluation
of hard services, although far easier, also presents measurement problems. For example, while it is easy to determine the per-mile cost of
asphalt paving, it is more difficult to determine the relative long-term
costs of asphalt versus gravel. Gravel is cheap but the cost to the public of broken windshields and other damage may be high. Is efficiency to be measured solely in terms of the per-mile cost of roads or
on the basis of this cost plus the cost of wear and tear on private and
public vehicles?

These examples are simple, but they show that the issues are extremely complex and the bases of evaluation are fraught with controversy. In evaluating the pros and cons of governmental reorganization proposals, it is important to ascertain whether everyone is using
the same measurement scales; more often than not, one group employs direct dollar costs while another employs non-dollar measures
or very indirect measures of dollar costs.

Intellectual Roots of Municipal Reorganization

As the next chapter will show, Alberta has been a leader in the consolidation of governmental units. During the 1930s and 1940s, hundreds of tiny school districts were consolidated to provide a higher

level of education and to effect tax savings. The Premier, William Aberhart, a former teacher, made educational reorganization a first priority when he came to power. The impetus for his program came from his own experience, rather than from the educational establishment. Today the controversy over governmental reorganization almost invariably deals with the reorganization of municipalities. Proponents of municipal reorganization argue that, in the interests of efficiency, it is best for small rural municipalities to be consolidated into a single unit and for small municipalities adjacent to a large city to be absorbed by it.

The movement toward reorganizing municipalities to increase efficiency has its intellectual roots in the American Progressive Movement, which flourished in the mid-western and western United States in the early decades of the twentieth century. [3] The Progressives initially focused on removing corruption from municipal politics; it was but a short step to proposing programs for increasing the efficiency of municipal administration.

The first systematic arguments dealing with the disadvantages of having a number of independent municipalities within a metropolitan area were made in 1922 by Chester Maxey, an American reformer and academic, who wrote:

> A very slight acquaintance with municipal conditions in the United States discloses the fact that one handicap under which practically every city of magnitude is laboring is political disintegration . . . the metropolitan district finds itself obliged to struggle for civic achievement amid conflicts, dissension and divergencies of its several component political jurisdictions. [4]

It should be emphasized that Maxey and the reformers who followed him argued from the assumption that a metropolitan region was a single social and economic entity. Urban economists and sociologists have found, however, that a metropolitan region contains a number of diverse social and economic systems.

Maxey's legacy is found in the writings of a leading authority on Canadian local government, who wrote in 1968:

> In the metropolis, where the government is politically fragmented, the problem becomes even more acute, for its inhabitants are economically and socially interdependent irrespective of the sector in which they live, and, as a result, many requirements and needs of the metropolis are area-wide in character. [5]

Maxey's assumptions were used in 1980 by the City of Edmonton in its bid, submitted to the Alberta Local Authorities Board, to bring the metropolitan area's outlying communities into the city's fold: ". . . the major components within the Edmonton boundary proposal . . . [constitute] one urban or metropolitan unit, characterized often as one socio-economic unit, within which there exists a high degree of interdependence or community of interest."[6]

Although Maxey presented a number of arguments (which were, in fact, nothing more than statements) about why municipal governments should be reorganized, he outlined the mechanics of his solution, large-scale annexation and consolidation, only sketchily. Following Maxey's seminal work, a number of articles and college textbooks were published extolling the virtues of governmental reorganization. However, it was not until 1930, with the publication of Paul Studenski's *The Government of Metropolitan Areas in the United States*, that all of Maxey's arguments and those of his followers were put together systematically. More importantly, Studenski presented in detail how the "metropolitan problem," i.e., too many governments in a metropolitan area, could be solved. He carefully examined each of the reformers' proposals in terms of its benefits and political feasibility. However, Studenski erred, just as Maxey had done, by assuming that many units of government in a metropolitan area were always inefficient and that consolidation would greatly increase administrative efficiency.

The followers of Maxey and Studenski still maintain that the ideal is a single governmental unit.[7] They consider that it makes sense to eliminate the expensive duplication of facilities, such as city halls, police and fire stations, and administrative personnel. It also seems to them that the planning process will become orderly and rational only when region-wide government is adopted; they cite case after case of fragmented planning leading to unfavourable "spillover effects" for adjoining communities.[8] Finally, the reformers believe that the adoption of a single unit of government for a metropolitan area would bring order to what seems to be the uneven, even chaotic, delivery of services by a multiplicity of local governments.

Modern Arguments for Governmental Reorganization

Although the arguments for governmental reorganization have their intellectual roots in Maxey and Studenski, changing circumstances in the modern Canadian metropolis have provided additional ammunition. The changing nature of the metropolis, it is argued, has led to tax and service inequities and a patchwork of local governments that frustrate attempts at regional planning.

The nation-wide decentralization of manufacturing, retailing and housing has had devastating consequences for many large cities. Manufacturing plants in search of cheaper land have moved their facilities from the city core to outlying industrial parks, badly eroding the industrial tax base of the core. Developers of new single-family housing for the middle class locate on cheaper land in outlying communities rather than on more expensive land nearer the city centre, with the unintended consequence that the city core is left with a disproportionate number of lower-income and welfare families. The social problems associated with large numbers of low-income people puts further pressure on the city's resources, already reeling from a declining industrial tax base.

A 1981 report commissioned to support the City of Edmonton's proposal to annex St. Albert and Sherwood Park states:

> There is a whole range of facilities and services which outlying communities cannot afford or do not wish to provide, and public housing is one example. There is none in St. Albert or Sherwood Park. . . . Edmonton currently pays for public housing not only for its own residents, but also for those from surrounding communities who for one reason or another, find it necessary to live in less expensive accommodation. In this, as in other areas, Edmonton once again carries the financial burden of a service used by all metro residents.[9]

In addition, the proponents of consolidation argue, middle-class residents of the city's outlying communities are employed in the central city and use its cultural and recreational facilities, but escape paying their fair share of the costs of services.[10] Also, they point out that there are sizeable disparities in a metropolitan region where some municipalities provide low levels of service, while ratepayers pay low taxes, and other municipalities enjoy high levels of service and many amenities, and residents pay high taxes.[11] It is argued that amalgamating all of a core city's bedroom communities would eliminate these inequities and allow the city to capture the businesses and residents who have been avoiding their fiscal responsibilities.

Finally it is argued that increased use of the automobile, coupled with changes in communication technology, has made the metropolitan region an integrated, interwoven unit; a number of autonomous communities no longer makes sense since they fragment governmental activities that are regional by nature. In the report referred to above, the city argued that annexation could co-ordinate currently fragmented services in the region. A discussion of transportation states:

> Over-lapping responsibilities occur at all levels of government operations. . . . An integrated service should offer more attractive and convenient transit routing, scheduling and service. More major destinations could be serviced between the two communities [Sherwood Park and St. Albert] in the core area, saving travel time and transfer inconvenience.[12]

The apparently reasonable argument that a number of governmental activities are regional by nature has a doubtful basis in fact. Although many students of local government attempt to distinguish local from regional services, the distinction is purely arbitrary. With the exception of planning, persuasive arguments can be made for any municipal function being either local or regional in nature. Furthermore those who attempt to make the local/regional distinction seldom base their arguments on population size or the decision-making abilities of a particular unit of government.

Another major argument for consolidating governments in a metropolitan area is the planning of land use on a regional basis. A number of autonomous municipalities each developing its own land-use plan are likely to work, unintentionally, at cross-purposes. The consequence may be that an industrial park in one municipality borders a suburban neighbourhood in another. In addition, large tracts of potential parkland and farmland are eroded in the absence of regional planning. Alberta municipalities are fortunate that regional planning can be carried out in a metropolitan area without requiring governmental consolidation. In a later chapter this planning mechanism will be discussed in detail.

All the arguments made by the proponents of metropolitan reorganization are persuasive. However, one must question whether it is necessary to embark on a drastic policy of consolidation to solve problems created by changing economic and social conditions. As has been noted, the local/regional distinction is fraught with problems, and it is possible to plan regionally without consolidating governments. Furthermore, rather than viewing a number of municipalities with disparate service levels and tax rates as disadvantageous, one could argue that this diversity gives the residents of a metropolitan area a variety of options. Then, communities experiencing a decline in their tax base while facing increasing and costly social problems

could be assisted either by government grants or by a provincially administered redistribution of revenue among the municipalities. In short all the problems can be handled without destroying municipalities in a metropolitan area.

The Economics of Governmental Reorganization

In spite of the difficulties of such evaluations, a variety of dollar and non-dollar criteria are used to measure governmental activity. As one might expect, the most common factor is dollars and cents. Therefore, an initial examination of governmental reorganization will focus on its economics.

There is no question that, under certain conditions, smaller communities would benefit by consolidating some services with other communities: many smaller communities cannot justify the expense of buying and maintaining fire-fighting and road-maintenance equipment that is used only a few times during the year; smaller communities cannot afford to employ full-time, professional municipal administrators even though they may wish to upgrade and professionalize their administrations; and many communities cannot afford to install expensive water and sewer trunks. However, certain rules of thumb should be considered before communities embark on consolidation. It is estimated that, depending on the type of services involved, maximum economies of scale are achieved for governmental units serving areas containing between 50,000 and 100,000 residents. The reasons that cost increases (diseconomies of scale) are encountered in administration units serving larger populations are succinctly stated by an urban economist who writes:

> . . . most government services require relatively close geographic proximity of service units to service recipients; this prevents the establishment of huge primary schools, fire houses, police stations, or libraries. Urban government services are also labor intensive, with wages and salaries often accounting for more than two-thirds of current costs. The resulting concentration of manpower can increase the bargaining power of labor and this, in turn, increases costs. While there are economies resulting from bulk purchases of supplies and equipment, such savings can be outweighed by inefficiencies resulting from top-heavy administration and the ills of political patronage in very large scale governments.[13]

This is not to say that all municipalities should be consolidated into governmental units with populations ranging between 50,000 and

100,000; it merely means that the per unit costs of governmental services are higher for smaller and very large communities than for medium-sized communities. Non-economic factors that should be given as much, if not more, consideration in evaluations of the merits of governmental reorganization are discussed below.

In the private sector, evidence indicates that the cost of consumer goods is lowest in openly competitive industries and highest in uncompetitive industries. For example, until recently almost all international airlines met regularly to establish fares for international travel; with the recent breakdown of the cartel, air fares plummeted. The existence of so-called natural monopolies in the private sector (e.g., telephone and power companies) often results in organizational complacency, inefficiency and high consumer prices and, in spite of heavy regulation, these monopolies turn handsome profits. Almost all economists deplore the production and bureaucratic inefficiencies of monopolies, as well as the high prices they charge.

In the public sector, one normally finds a single producer of governmental services within a municipality. Although we seldom think of a municipality as a monopoly, the organization and processes it employs to deliver public services resemble those of a classic monopoly. However, while the municipal administration has a monopoly in public services at the local level, an imperfect form of competition exists at the regional level. More knowledgeable residents become aware of the taxes and services of neighbouring municipalities and it quickly becomes known which municipal administrations seem to be most, and which least, efficient. As such information is often put to use by candidates in municipal electoral campaigns, the politicians prod the administration to be as efficient as possible. Finally, if a portion of the electorate is continually dissatisfied with taxation and services, they have the option of moving to a nearby municipality with a more efficient administration and a more desirable tax level. When governmental units are consolidated into a single regional unit, this incentive toward efficiency and cost-conciousness is lost, since the public has no measuring stick to evaluate a regional unit; the result is a decrease in efficiency.

It is important to note that this analysis makes a series of critical assumptions and claims, the validity of which will vary from one metropolitan region to another. The first assumption is that taxation levels accurately reflect the degree of municipal efficiency. In fact, however, in most metropolitan regions the level of taxation is as much a function of the presence of an industrial tax base as it is of the level of government efficiency. Second, it is assumed that the electorate has access to accurate information on levels of taxation and costs of services for all municipalities in a region. While some municipal administrations may point with pride to an efficient administration, others often attempt to distort or hide service costs, particularly if the service is inefficient. The third assumption is that the electorate is well-educated, interested in politics and economics, and motivated to seek out such information. While this may be true for a large portion of the electorate in an upper-income, well-educated community, it is probably much less so for members of a poorer community with an overall low educational level. Less well-educated members of the electorate often throw up their hands in despair over the complexity of political and economic issues. Finally, an ability to act on the conclusions drawn from a comparison is presumed to exist. However, even if the electorate has the interest and motivation to make comparisons, many people are unable to move if they become dissatisfied with their municipality. For example, a very low-income family living in an older, low-rent community cannot afford to move to a middle-class community of single-family dwellings, no matter how efficient the governmental structure. Yet, however valid or invalid these assumptions are in any given case, proponents of consolidation still have to deal with the problems of monopoly behaviour and the optimum size of a city for efficient delivery of services.

Political and Other Non-Economic Factors of Governmental Reorganization

If metropolitan reorganization policy were based solely on economic considerations, local governments in Alberta should be reorganized into units serving between 50,000 and 100,000 people. At the same time, a mechanism to promote service competition among these new governmental bodies would be required. However, non-economic factors are at least as important as economic ones, although, in their zeal to make municipalities more efficient, past reformers have given non-economic factors short shrift.

Today, the proponents of municipal autonomy seem to resort to non-economic and political arguments more than to economic ones. An exceedingly important non-economic factor is the emotional attachment people develop towards their community. Many people display a strong identification with and loyalty to their community: they identify themselves as being from Jasper, Medicine Hat or Rocky Mountain House as much as they identify themselves as being Albertans. Community "business boosters" exhort the citizenry to be loyal and shop in their own town rather than an adjoining one. "Smithville" may be far too small to be efficient at producing municipal services and its property taxes may be high, but its residents are strongly attached to their community. Their forbears founded "Smithville" and they hope their children will remain in the community and maintain its viability rather than leave for the city. When it is suggested that it would be better to have a single unit of government for the region rather than a number of "Smithvilles," many people are distressed, believing governmental reorganization would destroy their heritage and community identity. Some of the most bitter political battles in Alberta have been fought over the consolidation of school districts. Since the school is a major catalyst in maintaining community identity, townspeople are dismayed at the prospect of losing their school, seeing the loss as the beginning of the end for the community. In fact, the loss of a school often does signal the end of a community.

On the other hand, community loyalty must be kept in perspective. Alberta has experienced explosive growth in the last two decades. Since it takes time to develop community identity, it is unlikely that these newcomers have the same sense of attachment as do second and third generation Albertans. In addition, there are many extremely mobile Albertans with no emotional attachment to any community. Yet others, coolly dispassionate, regard community loyalty and identification as irrational; economic factors outweigh community identification when these people choose a location to live or evaluate governmental reorganization.

Another significant non-economic consideration involves accessibility. The political implications of governmental reorganization are of concern to advocates of grass-roots democracy. The public's perception of government is that the greater its size, the more distant and remote it becomes from the citizenry. In Edmonton and Calgary it is difficult for individuals to see their elected representatives in person to complain about services and taxation or to discuss municipal policy. Municipal policy making is exceedingly time-consuming in large cities: the elected officials put in as much as 60 hours a week. Hence, they insulate themselves from their constituents with receptionists, secretaries and administrative assistants. Many people, intimidated by the city's bureaucracy, feel it is fruitless to try to penetrate the complexities of city hall. In smaller communities, elected officials and the bureaucracy are perceived as being much more accessible. Although a number of studies of small-town politics in the United States indicate that the electorate participate in community affairs at about the same rate as do people in large cities, the studies also show that small-town residents feel that, if they wanted to participate, their elected representatives would be accessible and responsive. When a community is considering amalgamation with another, the opponents of the

move invariably argue that the larger unit of government will become removed from the citizenry. Unfortunately, so little work has
been done in this important area that it is not known precisely how
large a community can become before people feel alienated from
their government.

Governmental Reorganization in Edmonton and Calgary

Many municipal reorganizations have been carried out across Canada
and numerous proposals for governmental reorganization have been
made by academics, governmental reformers and city boosters.[14] Unlike most provinces, Alberta has not formulated an explicit policy on
urbanization, despite promises made as early as 1971 by the Progressive Conservative government that such a policy would be forthcoming in the near future. Faced with a massive influx of new residents
during the 1960s and 1970s, neither Edmonton nor Calgary has
waited for a comprehensive urban policy; they have expanded their
boundaries as fast as possible. Fortunately, Calgary has almost no outlying communities with which to contend. In 1978 it applied to annex 28,000 acres and was granted approval for the annexation of
16,000 acres with virtually no controversy. Edmonton is less fortunate, since it has autonomous communities on its doorstep.

Before examining attempts by Edmonton and Calgary to increase
their size, one must understand the annexation process, a process that
undermines local autonomy. In Alberta the Local Authorities Board
(LAB) is vested with the power to evaluate and rule on amalgamation
proposals. [15] Furthermore, the Board acts as a quasi-judicial body under powers given to it by the Local Authorities Board Act, Section 30
of which states:

> the Board has, in regard to the amendment of proceedings, the
> attendance and examination of witnesses, the production and
> inspection of documents, the enforcement of its orders, the
> payment of costs and all other matters necessary or proper for
> the due exercise of its jurisdiction or otherwise for carrying any
> of its powers into effect, all the powers, rights, privileges and
> immunities that are vested in the Court of Queen's Bench.[16]

An annexation proposal is initiated for the LAB's consideration in
one of three ways: 1) by a majority of owners of land in or adjoining a
municipality; 2) by a municipality's council with respect to land in or
adjoining the municipality; 3) by the Minister of Municipal Affairs
with respect to improvement district or special areas lands in or adjoining a municipality. After the LAB hearing, a Board Order is issued

either rejecting the petition or approving it and specifying the conditions for its enactment. In 1975 the Municipal Government Act was amended to require that decisions of the LAB be referred to the provincial cabinet for approval. In 1978 the Act was again amended to give the cabinet even more power over annexation proceedings. In addition to approving or disapproving LAB decisions, the cabinet was also allowed to "prescribe conditions that the order is subject to and approve the order subject to those conditions" and "vary the order and approve the order as varied." Thus, theoretically, the cabinet has ultimate control over municipal expansion and development, the LAB's decisions being only an interim step.

Two important factors must be considered in evaluations of the annexation and amalgamation process in Alberta. First, under the Local Authorities Board Act a favourable plebiscite on amalgamation and annexation petitions filed with the LAB is not required in the area to be annexed or amalgamated. Second, there have been a number of cases in which the Board has approved an annexation initiated by a small number of property owners in an area adjacent to a municipality that strongly objected to the proposal.

One reason Edmonton and Calgary have been frustrated in their attempts to expand is that, even though the provincial government has no stated policy on urbanization or on when and how local governments should be organized and reorganized, there has been a consistent unstated policy on community growth and economic expansion dating back to the 1930s. The Social Credit government (which ruled from 1935 through 1971) was committed to maintaining the autonomy of local municipalities.[17] Admittedly, the 1930s and 1940s saw a major reorganization of rural government in Alberta with the creation of large school and municipal districts. Then, in 1950, the County Act was passed, creating an all-purpose unit of government for Alberta. By order-in-council, the provincial government was given the power to incorporate all or any part of a municipality, school division or hospital district into a county. However, since Social Credit had a largely rural support base, it was not in its interest to promote the expansion of politically antagonistic urban centres.

The discovery of oil at Leduc in 1947 was followed by rapid economic expansion and urban growth that resulted in myriad financial problems for Edmonton and Calgary. The Social Credit government responded by providing loan assistance programs to municipalities, developing district planning commissions and, in 1954, establishing the McNally Commission to examine and make recommendations for the cities of Edmonton and Calgary on the "financing of school and municipal matters," as well as "the boundaries and the form of local government which will most adequately and equitably provide for the orderly development of school and municipal services."[18] In January, 1956, the Commission submitted its final report, which recommended "that each metropolitan area would be best governed by enlarging each of the present cities to include its whole metropolitan area."[19] The premises upon which the recommendations rested were not unlike those presented by Maxey and Studenski some quarter of a century before:

1. It is unjust and inequitable that wide variations in the tax base should exist among the local governing bodies that comprise a metropolitan area where that area is in fact one economic and social unit.

2. A metropolitan area which is in fact one economic and social unit can ordinarily be more efficiently and effectively governed by one central municipal authority than by a multiplicity of local governing bodies.[20]

The Commission then recommended that Edmonton be enlarged from 41.5 to 112.02 square miles and that Calgary be increased from 49.5 to 104.77 square miles.

These recommendations caught the government off-guard since it still had a strong commitment to maintaining local autonomy. Taking the position that "the metropolitan problem" was caused by a lack of fiscal resources, it ignored the Commission's recommendations for expansion. The government established the Municipal Financing Corporation in 1956 "to assist in municipal financing . . . by purchase and sale of municipal securities at lowest possible cost."[21] Next, direct provincial assistance grants to both Edmonton and Calgary were greatly increased: in 1954-1955, Edmonton received $6,430,000 in provincial assistance; in 1958-59, $16,190,000. [22]

Dissatisfied with the province's response to the McNally report, Edmonton managed to expand from 41.5 to 68.6 square miles through piecemeal annexation in only five years. Then in 1967, in an effort to pressure the provincial government, the city commissioned an economist to conduct "a study . . . in regard to extending the City's boundaries in all directions."[23] The economist's report recommended that the city be increased in size from 86 to 292 square miles. Since the report was commissioned by the city, the strong recommendation that a single governmental unit should govern the metropolitan area was not unexpected. Furthermore, since an economist prepared the report, it was not surprising that the arguments were based almost entirely on economic considerations.

Between 1968 and 1979, Edmonton continued its policy of piece-meal annexation while at the same time issuing reports and news releases to justify its development into a single, region-wide government. Then in March 1979, the city made a bid to the LAB to annex more than 467,000 acres (an increase in size from 123 square miles to 700 square miles), which included the City of St. Albert, the unincorporated community of Sherwood Park, the entire County of Strathcona, and significant portions of the County of Parkland and the Municipal District of Sturgeon. In a bitter political fight[24] in which Edmonton, St. Albert and the County of Strathcona spent over seven million dollars for consultants' reports to justify their respective positions, the city was eventually awarded 86,000 acres.[25] The unincorporated community of Sherwood Park and the City of St. Albert escaped annexation, but the County of Strathcona lost 54,000 acres to the city. In December, 1980, the LAB made its decision, subsequently revised by the cabinet, which made the final decision in June, 1981. Predictably, Edmonton's mayor suggested that the city would continue its attempts to increase its size. Less than a year later, the city made a bid for an additional 8,300 acres.

After the province turned down the McNally Commission's recommendation that Calgary's size be greatly increased, the city made a more modest, successful bid for 26 square miles in 1956 and then waited until 1961, when it made a major bid for slightly more than 75 square miles. Although the proposal included the amalgamation of the municipality of Forest Lawn, there was only slight opposition and the LAB gave the city everything it asked for. In 1963 the city acquired the small community of Montgomery and in 1964 the community of Bowness; in both cases there was limited opposition from citizens' groups and politicians in the communities, but the LAB ruled in favour of Calgary. The next annexation occurred in 1971, when a group of property speculators and a large real estate company filed a request for the annexation of three-quarters of a square mile of farmland on the city's northern border to develop modestly priced housing. Despite protests from the Calgary School Board, which was concerned about the area's isolation from existing schools, the LAB once again ruled favourably.

In 1974 Calgary's administrators enthusiastically floated a proposal to annex 198.5 square miles north and south of the city, a takeover which would have almost doubled Calgary's size. Concerned about the city's explosive growth, increasing capital debt and the secrecy surrounding the proposal, an anti-annexation citizens' group soon formed in the city. The controversial proposal was submitted to the city's electorate and soundly rejected by almost two-thirds of the voters. Then, less than a year after the plebiscite, six private developers submitted bids for annexation of land in the same northern and southern sectors that the citizenry had just turned down. Twenty-five square miles were annexed in 1978.

In January, 1983, the LAB approved the annexation of three parcels of land totalling 4,500 acres which, it was estimated, would give the city an additional 12-year supply of land. Shortly thereafter the city planning department made two massive annexation proposals despite the fact that the city's population growth had ground to a halt with the 1982-83 economic downturn. One proposal, based on older population and market predictions, called for the annexation of 127 square miles; the other, for 93 square miles. The latter plan soon became the centre of political controversy. A split immediately developed between city planners and Mayor Ralph Klein and other members of council who were preparing for a fall municipal election and remembered the heavy 1974 anti-annexation vote. Undoubtedly, they were also aware of an increasingly vocal anti-annexation citizens' group.

Although the city's planning department (with its unofficial motto of "bigger is better") adamantly maintained that it was necessary to annex at least 93 square miles to meet the needs of residential and industrial expansion until the year 2014, members of council and the anti-annexation group, 20th Century Calgary, suggested that the city examine other options. With increasing numbers of people settling in the outlying communities of Airdrie, Okotoks, Cochrane, Strathmore and High River, one option suggested was encouraging the growth of satellite communities in order to relieve some of the financial pressure Calgary would face in an attempt to develop a massive service infrastructure for yet another annexed area.[26] Another suggestion was that the density in the city's core be increased by encouraging people to stay in the city and by upgrading large areas of the core to accommodate a higher population density. As a result of the political controversy in the city and opposition from the Municipal District of Rocky View, which would lose its only source of industrial taxes (the Turbo refinery and gas plant near Balzac) with the proposed annexation, it is unlikely that the proposal will go to the LAB before 1986.

The Provincial Government's Unofficial Policy on Urbanization and Reorganization

Although the provincial government has no explicit policy on the future growth patterns for Alberta's two major cities, there is an unofficial policy of strengthening the vitality of smaller municipalities and of encouraging province-wide economic diversification, in order to stabilize rural-to-urban migration that accelerated in the 1950s and 1960s.[27] In a speech entitled "Alberta's Industrial Strategy," presented before the Calgary Chamber of Commerce in 1974, Premier Lougheed stated that one of the government's goals was "to spread the growth on a balanced basis across the province and capitalize upon the potential of the smaller centers--to assure a better quality of life for citizens living within the metropolitan areas and also the smaller centers as a combined result."[28] To make sure there could be no question about the nature of government's unofficial urbanization policy, the premier reiterated the provincial government's stance at a "Think West" conference in September, 1977:

> . . . part of our economic strategy is balanced growth. We want twenty Red Deers in this province. . . . We do not want to see Calgary and Edmonton grow at the expense of the smaller centers. . . . Primarily, our view as a government is to create the essential services and develop them in the smaller communities--the basic essentials of water and sewer, communication and transportation.

Then, in a 1980 legislative discussion of vocational education in Alberta, Lougheed mentioned another facet of his decentralization policy:

> In terms of regional expansion . . . we want a new thrust to expand our apprenticeship and technological courses to our college(s) . . . throughout Alberta, to follow through in our program of decentralization of government services.[29]

Although the premier has emphatically denied having a "no-growth" policy for Edmonton and Calgary, it is clear that the government's policy has been to slow the growth of its two major urban centres. In September, 1974, the then Minister of Municipal Affairs stated: "The Alberta Government does not favour continued rapid growth for Calgary and Edmonton at the expense of the smaller centers of the province."[30] In November of the same year, in an address to the Edmonton Chamber of Commerce, Premier Lougheed said, "Edmonton and Calgary . . . are large enough now."[31] In 1979 a question came up in the legislature about the decentralization of provincial government offices; in an offhand remark Lougheed said:

> . . . one has to recognize that the stated policy of the
> government in terms of decentralization of government
> operations has to do with the balanced economic growth of the
> province. Although there may be appropriate cases for
> recognizing that in terms of the City of Calgary, when last I
> checked the statistics I saw that Calgary was doing relatively
> well in terms of economic growth.[32]

The provincial government is not inherently hostile to local government amalgamation and expansion: the LAB hears 80 to 90 cases each year, most of which are successful. As a sign of the government's commitment to strengthening the vitality of government in rural areas, a special act of the legislature was passed in 1979 amalgamating a number of financially strapped municipalities in the Crowsnest Pass area and forming a much stronger unit of government with a minimal loss of responsiveness and accountability to the citizenry. The towns of Blairmore and Coleman, the villages of Bellevue and Frank, and 11 small hamlets in Improvement District No. 5, almost all of which were contiguous, were amalgamated into the Town of Crowsnest Pass.[33]

Although the Lougheed government has been in power for a number of years, it is unlikely that its informal policy on provincial urban development will be translated into official policy with a complete urban legislative program. MLAs from Edmonton and Calgary are aware of the interests of their constituents and there is little doubt there has been dissension within the government caucus and the cabinet over Lougheed's policy of diversification and slowing the growth of the province's two major cities. For example, while five Edmonton MLAs, including two cabinet ministers, went on record in 1979 as being opposed to Edmonton's annexation proposal, other Edmonton MLAs tacitly supported Edmonton's bid. It is unlikely that the government will jeopardize its urban political support by opting for a formal policy of "no growth" for its two major urban centres. One can safely predict that the government will informally allow a slow, controlled incremental expansion of Edmonton and Calgary, while attempting to foster strong local units of government in the rest of the province.

Metropolitan Reorganization in Alberta

Almost from the province's establishment, population trends and economic factors have caused some communities to annex land for expansion and others to amalgamate with their neighbours. This pattern continues today—few of the province's municipalities maintain static boundaries—although most of the changes have been and are relatively small and excite little controversy. Only in the metropolitan areas of Edmonton and Calgary has a combination of population pressure and business "boosterism" resulted in incremental expansions of thousands of acres at a time. While the sheer size of Calgary's increases have caused controversy, it has been in Edmonton that the controversy has been most intense. Efficiency and economy-of-scale arguments have been made frequently to justify expansion in both cities. Neither city has evaluated the effects of any increase on the city's administration, its fiscal capability or service delivery capacity. This apparent negligence may be caused by the realization, on the part of the cities' administrations and the provincial government, that the arguments made for expansion are ammunition in very political conflicts.

Before evaluating the costs, benefits and process of governmental reorganization and local governmental expansion in Alberta, we should briefly examine a problem that is rarely given serious consideration. One of the most detrimental effects of annexation has been the loss of huge tracts of prime farmland to residential and industrial development. Although both Edmonton and Calgary have given lip service to the preservation of farmland, the administrations in both cities have allowed expansion to erode prime farmland at an alarming rate. Edmonton and Calgary have given little thought to expanding onto non-farm lands or to "in-filling" vacant inner-city areas. A study by the Environment Council of Alberta found that, between 1977 and 1979, Calgary and Edmonton each annexed 21,000 acres of farmland for residential and industrial use. During the same period, Alberta's smaller communities were just as guilty of ignoring the importance of preserving the province's agricultural future: Red Deer annexed 1,600 acres and other central Alberta communities annexed 5,500 acres, of which 93% was prime farmland.[34]

The 86,000 acres annexed by Edmonton in 1979 is excluded from the above calculation. Eighty-five per cent of this land is number one and number two farmland. Eventually, Edmonton's council made a commitment to preserve less than 10 per cent of this prime farmland for agricultural purposes. Municipal policy on the preservation of farmland is summed up best by the area manager of one of the provinces's largest land developers, Nu-West Development. He maintained that, although municipalities pay lip service to preserving farmland, they actually give it low priority. "If the municipal officials aren't concerned about it we won't be. If all the municipal councils passed resolutions saying we won't develop class one land, we'd get the message." [35]

Edmonton has not been atypical in failing to calculate carefully the costs and benefits of annexation. In 1979, in an attempt to convince metro Edmonton residents of the virtues of annexation, the city distributed a fact sheet titled "About the Edmonton Boundaries." In this publication, Edmonton's Mayor Purves promised: "Regional service levels would remain at current standards or higher in present Edmonton, and will improve in the outlying urban areas. This is particularly so for the protection services such as fire and police." [36] The exuberance felt by Edmonton's administration after the award of 86,000 acres began to wane in the early 1980s, with the downturn in Alberta's economy. The province experienced a net increase of only 9,235 in 1982, and Edmonton's residential, business and industrial growth ground to a halt. Taxes in the annexed areas skyrocketed and the city was unable even to maintain the level of services the areas had enjoyed before they became part of the city.

Although businesses located in rural areas annexed to Edmonton were to receive far lower levels of service than their counterparts in the "core city," a decision was made to have their tax structure conform to taxes paid in the "core city." The tax increase was 100 per cent. The 175 farmers residing in the newly annexed areas fared even worse since the city's taxation policy, different from rural policy, includes taxation on buildings as well as land. A report prepared by the city's assessor demonstrated how rural land-holders would substantially increase the city's coffers. For example, the taxes levied on one Strathcona County farm would increase from $439, under the county's tax structure, to $1,498, under the city's structure; a Parkland County farm would experience an increase of 366 per cent from $279 to $1,300. [37]

As taxes went up in the annexed areas, the minimal pre-annexation levels of service began to decline. Outlying residents were particularly concerned about fire protection, feeling they were not nearly as well protected as they had been before annexation. [38] The city was experiencing continuing fiscal crisis and, in 1983, had no funds budgeted to service industrial and commercial lands in the newly annexed areas. In the spring of 1984, a former Edmonton councillor and a number of other disgruntled property owners living in the annexed area attempted to organize the residents into a ratepayers association to fight city hall. The unhappy group, who saw their property taxes increase substantially with annexation but who still had to truck in their water and truck out their garbage, wanted the city to lower tax rates for those receiving minimal city services or none at all.

With services cut below minimal standards and taxes substantially increased, some 5,000 of the newly annexed residents presented a petition to Edmonton's council requesting that taxes be rolled back to pre-annexation levels. The petition was dismissed by council. Council experienced unique problems in phasing the servicing of the new areas into the city; however, they made no special provisions for the new residents to have input into city departments or to exercise political power. Hence, these residents have been submerged into a political system composed of 6 wards with 12 councillors who perceive their constituents as being "core city" residents.[39]

Some Edmonton councillors have become as disenchanted with annexation as have the new residents. In January, 1983, Councillor Jan Reimer complained: "Annexation hasn't benefitted Edmonton at all, we'll be paying years down the road for road maintenance and snow clearance in the new areas."[40] Another councillor came up with a unique idea to solve the city's annexation problem: he proposed that the city "de-annex" a sizeable portion of the land it took over in 1981 by turning it over to the province or back to its original owners.[41] The proposal came to nothing since other members of council were unwilling to decrease the geographical area of the city.

Edmonton is not unique in having a sizeable segment of the citizenry disenchanted with a successful boundary expansion. Many residents in the Crowsnest Pass area were "sold" on amalgamation when they were told that it would bring higher levels of service with little added cost. Once amalgamation was carried out, the province provided "one-time" grants to help offset servicing imbalances among the amalgamated communities. However, these funds were quickly spent and the new administration embarked on an ambitious program of road paving and curbing and gutter installation. In 1982 the cost of this program, added to the $200,000 needed for facilities for the 1984 Alberta Winter Games (held in the Crowsnest Pass area), resulted in a property tax increase of 17 per cent for homeowners and 10 per cent for businesses.[42] The Crowsnest Pass Ratepayer's Association came into being in response to the probability of another substantial tax increase in 1983. The new organization, almost 600 strong, first sought a referendum on abolishing the amalgamated municipality but, finding that that could not be done, focused on downgrading service levels and freezing spending.

Crowsnest Pass is a classic case showing the result of bringing together a number of communities whose residents have different expectations of services and taxes, and imposing a single tax and service standard. Moreover, having become a much larger municipality, it has seen the emergence of a professional municipal bureaucracy that favours higher levels of professional administration. For example, in addition to being criticized for upgrading roads and installing curbing and gutters, the administration was admonished for spending funds on professional meetings, conventions and travel. There is little likelihood that the disagreement between those favouring higher service levels and a more expensive, professionalized administration and those favouring lower levels and a more accountable, grass-roots administration will be resolved in the near future.

An evaluation of governmental reorganization in Alberta should emphasize that many more annexations and amalgamation proposals have been successfully implemented with minimal controversy than have resulted in failures and continuing conflict. Two factors determine whether or not a governmental reorganization proposal will be ridden with conflict: first, whether the proposal involves substantial numbers of people and/or communities, or only vacant land; and second, whether the strategy involves an attempt to reach an accommodation with the governmental unit losing territory or depends upon uncompromising "power politics."

In the case of Edmonton, the city has been reluctant to restrict its growth to the relatively unpopulated southern sector of the region and, until quite recently, has been less than willing to negotiate with the municipalities and counties involved.[43]

Examples of minimal conflict and animosity are found in recent annexation bids by Medicine Hat, Fort Saskatchewan, Lloydminster and Lethbridge. All four communities have adopted a policy of annexing land rather than people, and this policy has reduced conflict substantially. Fort Saskatchewan and the County of Strathcona recently established a "joint planning process" to reach accommodations over land needed for the city's expansion. In 1981 Medicine Hat entered into protracted negotiations with Improvement District No. 1 over a proposed 9,000 acre annexation. The city was convinced by the improvement district to annex a road allowance that would require substantial improvement with the expansion of the city boundaries. As a result of the improvement district's concern about the annexation of prime farmland, the size of the area to be annexed was reduced by 640 acres.[44] In a 24,000 acre annexation bid made in 1981, the City of Lethbridge established a joint planning committee with the County of Lethbridge. A series of compromises was hammered out that included a reduction of the annexed area to 13,760 acres; an agreement on the part of the city to pay $60,000 per year for five years for lost tax revenue; and a property tax reduction of almost $400 a year for the 36 county residents in the annexation area.[45] In late 1982 Lloydminster was partially successful in working out an accommodation with affected governmental jurisdictions in its bid to annex 3,500 acres. The city negotiated a compromise with the County of Vermilion River and the rural municipality of Wilton; however, although it agreed to freeze taxes of farmers living in the proposed annexed area for five years, the city was unable to work out an agreement with the rural municipality of Britannia.

Although many communities are able to adjust their boundaries through a series of mutual accommodations and compromises before approaching the LAB, irreconcilable differences between the proponents and opponents of annexation may occur. Such conflict is exacerbated by the nature of the LAB hearings. An essay by two political scientists directly involved in Edmonton's annexation proposal makes the point that the LAB hearings are adversarial in nature.[46] "What is important to recognize is that both the applicant and the principal intervenors perceived the hearings of this tribunal as a judicial type process and structured their cases accordingly. . . ." The authors note that in "run of the mill" annexation proposals where requests are made for the annexation of outlying unincorporated areas ". . . the issues raised . . . are confined to a consideration of property assessment implications for the jurisdiction losing territory and the matter of urban service availability for the territory in question." They note:

> . . .the LAB process works reasonably well in dealing with the
> conventional or typical annexation requests. But the Edmonton
> application did not fit into this category for it raised other
> substantial issues not generally dealt with in the conventional
> annexation hearing, for example, the amalgamation of two
> existing and viable municipalities. . . . Because the City was, by
> the nature of the process, the initiator of the annexation
> application it also became quickly designated as the aggressor
> by the intervenors who emerged as the defenders of the status
> quo. It was in the interests of the latter, by virtue of the
> adversarial process which quickly emerged, to smother any
> attempt to maintain a focus on the wider issues involved. . . .

They further point out that the quasi-judicial nature of the LAB hearings "inhibited the intervention of individual citizens and groups." In conclusion, they suggest that if the province had employed

> an investigatory task force comprised of the municipalities in
> the metropolitan area. . . this approach would have eliminated

the adversarial process, might have initiated research independent of municipal bias and could have provided a means of hearing all parties concerned without resort to tedious cross-examination. . . .

Implicit in the authors' conclusions is the belief that such an approach would facilitate co-operation among municipalities rather than the conflict built into the current procedures.

Appendix: Local Government Reorganization in Canada

In Alberta's government reorganization controversies, both proponents and opponents often cite the successes and failures of governmental reorganization in other parts of Canada. For this reason, a very brief summary is presented of these reorganized governments.

In the early 1950s both the government of Ontario and the municipalities in the greater Toronto region examined the feasibility of governmental reorganization and, in 1953, the Ontario government imposed a two-tier form of metropolitan government on the region's 13 municipalities. Services deemed to be local in nature (such as fire protection) were to remain the responsibility of the municipalities while area-wide services (such as health and planning) were to be the responsibility of the new, first-tier metropolitan government. Representation on the metropolitan council, the decision-making body, was indirect, with each of the 12 smaller municipalities having one representative, chosen from its council, and Toronto's city council having 12 representatives. The 25th member of the council, its chairperson, was appointed by the Ontario government.

From the earliest discussions of metropolitan government, the City of Toronto's position has been that it is desirable to amalgamate all the suburban communities into a single governing body, i.e., the City of Toronto. In 1963 the province established the Royal Commission on Metropolitan Toronto to examine the experiment and recommend improvements. In June, 1965, the Commission presented a report that recommended amalgamating the 13 municipalities into four and greatly increasing the powers of the first-tier metropolitan government. The provincial government responded by increasing the powers of Metropolitan Toronto and amalgamating the 13 governments into six large units; this structure still exists in Toronto.

Another major metropolitan reorganization took place in the greater Winnipeg area where, in 1960, a two-tier metropolitan government was introduced. Service functions were divided, some being given to the new metropolitan government and others being retained by the municipalities. Unlike Toronto, Winnipeg instituted a system of direct representation: 10 metropolitan councillors were directly elected to the metropolitan council although the 11th, the chairman, was appointed by the provincial government. Beginning shortly after metropolitan government was introduced in Winnipeg, various commissions were established to evaluate its accomplishments and recommend changes. In 1969 metropolitan organizations became a provincial campaign issue and, with the election of the New Democratic Party, the Winnipeg metropolitan government was drastically restructured. Twelve municipalities were replaced by one governmental unit. To keep government close to the people, the city was divided into 50 single-member wards; in 1977 the number was reduced to 29. In addition, several "resident advisory groups" with very limited powers were created to foster close relationships between the citizenry and their elected representatives. The "resident advisory groups" have not been as successful as envisioned, since participation in the groups has been minimal.

Another major reorganization of government took place in the greater Montreal region where, in 1970, 29 municipalities were organized into a two-tier metropolitan government. The Montreal Urban Community somewhat resembles the Toronto metropolitan structure in that the 29 communities are proportionally represented by population on the Montreal Urban Community Council and the service functions are divided between the municipalities and the metropolitan government.

In almost all provinces, reports and royal commissions have recommended the abolition and consolidation of smaller rural municipalities in the interests of efficiency. In the Atlantic Provinces, Newfoundland's Whalen Report recommended the creation of several two-tier regional governments, while Nova Scotia's Graham Commission recommended the elimination of smaller, inefficient municipalities, and the gradual reduction of others with the transfer of their powers to the province. A similar recommendation was made in New Brunswick. In Ontario and Quebec, recommendations have been made for regional governments to blanket each province.

One of the more innovative approaches to regional government is found in British Columbia where virtually the whole province has been divided into 28 regional districts, the purpose of which is not to absorb local municipalities but to complement them. The regional districts provide services, such as mechanisms to regulate pollution, that smaller units of local government are unable to afford.

Notes

1. Needless to say, an unsuccessful reorganization of personnel often has unintended effects. It may result in decreased employee morale, increased absenteeism and greater worker turnover, all of which may result in lower productivity with a consequent higher per unit cost of production. If the business uses inexpensive unskilled workers, their replacement by expensive machinery may not be justified: the per unit cost of using machinery may be higher than that of using cheap labour.

2. This argument is fallacious since municipalities do "cost out" human life by the size of the insurance premium they pay: the premium for personnel in one-officer cars is much higher than that for patrolmen in two-officer cars.

3. Governmental reorganization took place in the United States from the early nineteenth century: Boston, 1821; Baltimore, 1851; San Francisco, 1856; New Orleans, 1874; St. Louis, 1875; New York, 1898; and Denver, 1903. Almost without exception, the reorganizations were based primarily on political considerations rather than those of efficiency. It should also be noted that, in England, attempts were made to rationalize services and gain efficiency through reorganization as early as 1829, with the passage of the London Police Act. In 1899 the passage of the London Government Act resulted in a major reorganization of governmental units. However, the London experience had little impact on the thinking of governmental reformers in Canada.

4. Maxey, "Political Integration," 229.

5. Plunkett, *Urban Canada and Its Government*, 80.

6. *Submission to the Local Authorities Board*, iii.

7. Donald Rowat, one of Canada's leading academic authorities on governmental reorganization and a consultant to numerous municipalities, has said that Victor Jones, who wrote *Metropolitan Government* in 1942, shaped many of his ideas for metropolitan government in Canada. Jones' ideas are directly descended from those of Paul Studenski.

8. *Spillover effects* are defined as effects on a municipality caused by the actions of an adjoining municipality. As an example, if one municipality permits heavy industry on its perimeter there may very well be unfavourable spillover effects of noise, smoke, dirt and odour for the residents of the adjoining municipality. Conversely, if a municipality builds an attractive park on its perimeter, residents of the adjoining community would enjoy the favourable spillover effects of increased recreational facilities and aesthetic enhancement.

9. *Edmonton: The Annexation Issue.*

10. On the other hand, it can be argued that satellite bedroom communities provide basic, costly services to employees working in Edmonton, thus in effect subsidizing the core city.

11. The proponents of governmental reorganization also point to communities that have no industrial tax base, yet have high fire and policing needs. These communities can afford no amenities and are able to provide only minimal services, although residential taxes are high.

12. *Edmonton: The Annexation Issue.*

13. Hirsch, "Supply of Urban Government Services," 509. Hirsch also found that there are some services in which there are no economies of scale, the most notable being education.

14. The Appendix to this chapter gives a very brief discussion on some of the major reorganizations and proposals. Much of the material on Edmonton in this section is excerpted from Masson, "Edmonton: The Unsettled Issues."

15. Forerunners of the Local Authorities Board were the Board of Public Utilities Commissioners (1915 through 1960) and the Public Utilities Board (1960-1961), LAB's immediate predecessor.

16. *Revised Statutes of Alberta, 1980.*

17. Bettison, Kenward and Taylor, *Urban Affairs in Alberta*, 69-117.

18. Province of Alberta, *Royal Commission on Metropolitan Development*, iv-v.

19. *Ibid.*, Chapter 14.

20. *Ibid.*, Chapter 14.

21. *Statutes of Alberta*, 1956, chap. 3, sec. 3 (3).

22. Bettison, Kenward and Taylor, *Urban Affairs in Alberta*, 151.

23. Hanson, *Potential Unification*, xii.

24. A recent discussion on metropolitan reorganization in Canadian cities argues that "Although Canadian suburbanites have generally tried to resist either annexation to the central city or metropolitan government, they have done so without the passion or commitment of their American counterparts." Sancton, "Conclusion: Canadian City Politics," 301. Although the argument may be true for Canadian cities generally, it certainly does not hold up in the case of Edmonton's attempt to amalgamate all of its neighbours. Residents of St. Albert and unincorporated Sherwood Park held a number of open air rallies and marches, displayed bumper stickers, gathered petitions with thousands of names, and wrote innumerable letters to their community newspapers as well as to the *Edmonton Journal*, all adamantly opposing amalgamation. It should be noted that, while the Edmonton citizenry was uninterested in the campaign being carried out on its behalf, the *Edmonton Journal* and a group of downtown businesspeople, all of whom were interested in slowing the decentralization of the region's population and business activity, were quite active.

25. In March, 1981, one of Edmonton's consultants stated that, estimating conservatively, the city had spent three million dollars on consultants. As of

March 1, St. Albert had spent $660,000 on attorneys and consultants; the Municipal District of Sturgeon and the County of Parkland, $450,000; the County of Strathcona, $2,982,549 (since 1977). *Edmonton Journal,* March 6, 1981, and March 12, 1981. These extremely large sums suggest that it would be much cheaper to let the citizenry decide the fate of an annexation proposal by plebiscite.

26. A study by the Calgary Regional Planning Commission found in June, 1982, that Airdrie had a population of 9,981, an increase of 21 per cent since June, 1981. Sixty-seven per cent of the employed adults in the community commuted to work in Calgary. Okotoks had a population of 4,521, an increase of 19.5 per cent over the previous year. Fifty-eight per cent of Okotoks' employed adults worked in Calgary. Cochrane, Strathmore and High River had smaller population increases during this period and a smaller proportion of employed adults working in Calgary. *Calgary Herald,* December 1, 1982.

27. Surprisingly, some politicians were unaware of the province's unofficial urban policy. As an example, Edmonton councillor Olivia Butti responded to the annexation decision as follows: "I'm dismayed after all the work and study that's been done for the LAB hearings, that the province still turns around and makes a political decision." *Edmonton Journal,* June 13, 1981.

28. It perhaps should be noted that the premier was aware that his decentralization policy was "moving against trends that exist in North America." Alberta Legislative Assembly, 18th Legislature, 2d Session, 782.

29. Alberta Legislative Assembly Debates, 19th Legislature, 2d Session, 1140.

30. *The Leader Post* (Regina), September, 1974.

31. *Edmonton Journal,* November 10, 1974.

32. Alberta Legislative Assembly Debates, 19th Legislature, 1st Session, 652.

33. No single unit of government attempted to "swallow up" its neighbours but, rather, a plebiscite was held in the area: 67.2 per cent of the residents supported amalgamation. The provincial government provided "transitional capital assistance" to smooth the amalgamation process.

34. *Red Deer Advocate,* July 21, 1982, *Calgary Herald,* July 20, 1982.

35. *Edmonton Journal,* March 29, 1982.

36. *Mainstream,* April 18, 1979.

37. *Edmonton Journal,* November 24, 1981.

38. The president of the firefighters' union pointed out that the fire department had added only 20 men to the city's 960 member force, although annexation had doubled the area the department had to serve. The city's fire chief admitted that the department would be unable to provide the same level of service in the newly annexed areas as that provided in the rest of the

city. He explained: "It would take 30 new stations to do that." *Edmonton Journal,* June 30, 1982.

39. Edmonton's Councillor Bettie Hewes advocated expanding the number of wards to eight, each served by two councillors, since the annexed areas were not being adequately represented by the existing ward system. *Edmonton Journal,* April 14, 1982. The council has been unwilling to act on her suggestion.

40. *Edmonton Journal,* January 30, 1983.

41. *Edmonton Journal,* March 8, 1983.

42. Municipal administration and general staffing decreased from 69 before amalgamation in 1979 to 44 by 1983.

43. It should be noted that, during his last term of office (October, 1974, through November, 1975), Mayor Hawrelak was very close to putting the finishing touches on an expansion agreement with the County of Parkland and the Municipal District of Sturgeon. Subsequently, the region has been in a constant state of political turmoil with much bitterness among local governmental officials. Since Calgary's proposals have involved primarily unpopulated land, conflict from this source is minimized; also, the city's attempts to negotiate with land-losing municipal districts and counties have further reduced potential conflict.

44. This annexation has not been without controversy. Since over 400 people lived on the 8,300 acres to be annexed, the improvement district's chairperson was concerned about the loss of provincial grants awarded on a per capita basis: "We lose all that tax base and all that grant base and that's going to make a difference to the ID." *Medicine Hat News,* March 17, 1982.

45. The annexation area included $2.06 million of taxable property; however, while the area contributed $227,600 in revenue to the county in 1980, service to its residents cost $212,800.

46. Plunkett and Lightbody, "Tribunals, Politics, and the Public Interest," 207-221.

4

SPECIALIZED FORMS

OF

LOCAL GOVERNMENT

Misunderstood Specialized Forms of Local Government

As most of Alberta's population lives in urban areas, some people may think of local government only in terms of large municipal governments. Local government in rural areas, governmental structures for education, and special purpose districts are often misunderstood, and even regarded as anachronisms in an age of big-city living and increasing governmental consolidation. Even people living in rural areas do not always fully understand the importance of specialized forms of local government.

The Recent Politicization of Rural Government

Until the mid-1960s, rural residents and their elected representatives perceived rural governmental units primarily as vehicles of administration, rarely as sources of political controversy. Then, the burgeoning population of Alberta's cities produced friction between traditional rural dwellers and suburbanites commuting to the city from country acreages. Although attracted by the "country life-style," the new suburbanites were dissatisfied by the low level of services in the country and almost immediately began demanding improvements in roads, recreational facilities and other amenities. They also placed pressure on the school systems; for example, a 1974 educational survey of Parkland County found that the average new suburbanite family was larger and had more pre-school and school-age children than did families of traditional rural dwellers. This new trend introduced escalating costs for school busing and facilities that were not covered by existing educational funding programs.

Another contentious issue for traditional rural dwellers has been the establishment of residential subdivisions that take valuable farmland out of production and allow speculators to drive up the price of adjoining farmland. In fact, a 1981 survey of Alberta farmland prices revealed that farmers selling land near urban centres for high prices and re-investing in outlying areas were causing a ripple effect throughout the province: number one farmland was selling for as much as $1,900 an acre in Olds and $1,100 an acre in the Peace country near Dawson Creek.

Other factors associated with Alberta's growing population directly affect traditional rural dwellers and their governments. Urban dwellers continually place pressure on the provincial government to develop more recreational land. Although land set aside for recreational use constitutes less than one-half of one per cent of the province's total land area and is primarily unsuitable for agriculture, a sizeable proportion is agricultural land located near urban centres. An even greater threat to agricultural land has been the growth of the province's primary highways. It is estimated that in Alberta almost 800,000 acres of land is devoted to highways, and the figure increases substantially each year. With more urbanites living on outlying acreages and others making greater use of rural areas for recreation and transportation, it has been necessary to establish controls on rural land use. Many traditional rural dwellers feel that their freedom and "rural way of life" are threatened by these controls.

Rural areas and their governments, at one time thought of as the backwaters of politics, now are often embroiled in fierce political battles. The battle lines are frequently drawn between the new suburbanites and the traditional rural dwellers. However, other factors also work to politicize rural governments. For example, some traditional rural dwellers have rising expectations about the services local governments should provide, while others believe that services and taxes should be held to an absolute minimum. In addition, although citizen activism is not as prevalent in rural areas as in urban ones, citizens' groups in some rural communities are beginning to question what were once thought to be purely administrative decisions.

Historical Development of Rural Government

During Alberta's early period of settlement, crops were destroyed by stray livestock and prairie fires. The territorial council responded by providing mechanisms for establishing herd and fire districts.[1] Later, in 1887, the Statute Labour Ordinance was passed to provide for the development of local units of government to build and maintain roads. The Statute Labour Ordinance recognized both the need for roads in rural areas and the cash-poor position of many settlers. Poorer residents of road districts could work on road crews to fulfill their obligation; more affluent settlers could pay cash. The amount of land a person held determined the amount of the obligation. Road labour was valued at $1.50 a day. In 1890 the functions of labour and fire districts were combined with the passage of the Statute Labour and Fire Ordinance. The 1890 ordinance was amended in 1893 so that any township with a population of eight residents could be designated a labour and fire district. Upon passage of the amended ordinance, Lieutenant-Governor MacIntosh said:

> It is pleasing to know that under the Ordinance authorizing the erection of statute labour districts, sixteen new districts have been created with eminently successful results. Thus, without unduly creating machinery for excessive taxation, an element likely to encourage organized local improvement has been introduced, and will no doubt result in educating these communities in methods so necessary for the promotion of self-reliance.[2]

The 36 fire and labour districts in existence by 1896 were indicative of the success of this unique form of local government.

Although Alberta had a population of only 170,000 in 1905, news of its rich agricultural land brought waves of immigrants and the population grew to over 400,000 by 1914. Since the province could not afford to provide services in rural areas, it encouraged new and innovative local units of government, financed by their residents, to provide a multiplicity of services.

In 1897 the statute labour and fire districts were enlarged and renamed local improvement districts. Controversy over the fact that farmers ill-equipped with engineering skills were building roads resulted in the abolition of most of the local improvement districts in 1903 and the creation of much larger districts, governed by three to six elected councillors who made policies within the guidelines established by the territorial government.

The next major impetus for rural self-government came with the Rural Municipality Act, passed in 1912. Eric Hanson, in his seminal work on local government in Alberta, describes the Act's provisions:

> . . . the province was divided into nine-township squares.
> . . . The numbers grew as units were located farther westward and northward. . . . Once these new nine-township units were laid out their residents could apply for incorporation of the unit

as a rural municipality provided there was at least one person per square mile in the area. If the areas concerned had been organized as small local improvement districts before 1912 and if their residents did not petition for municipal organization, the minister of municipal affairs could *direct* reorganization of the areas as nine-township local improvement districts operating under The Local Improvement Act of 1907. Finally, units which did not request incorporation of organized local improvement district status became unorganized local improvement districts *at the discretion* of the minister of municipal affairs.[3] [Emphasis added]

The Act created two new forms of local government for rural areas: the rural municipality and the organized local improvement district. In 1912 there were 55 rural municipalities and 90 local improvement districts, the main difference being that the rural municipality had a much stronger financial base than the organized local improvement district. The rural municipality was given the power to issue debentures and levy taxes on land while the organized improvement district could assess taxes only on an acreage basis at a rate not to exceed seven and one-half cents an acre.[4] There were slight differences in the political structure in these two forms of government. Improvement districts had ward representation while the electorate in rural municipalities chose between a council elected at-large or from wards. In almost all rural municipalities, the electorate opted for ward representation.

By the winter of 1917 there were 80 local improvement districts and 88 rural municipalities, most of which had been organized in newly settled areas. In these areas a few rural municipalities were created and then dissolved as people became fearful of their taxing powers. Perhaps not surprisingly, people were reluctant to form rural municipalities for fear that their financial muscle would result in excessive taxes and municipal debt. In 1918 the province stepped in and changed the name "rural municipality" to "municipal district" and made it compulsory for all existing organized improvement districts to organize as municipal districts. By the end of the year there were 167 municipal districts. In very sparsely settled areas with limited financial resources, the provincial government established improvement districts that it made policies for and administered.

In Alberta, agriculture was in trouble throughout the 1920s and finally, with the onset of the Great Depression, farm income completely dried up. As a consequence, a number of municipal districts collapsed because of their inability to collect taxes. Three reverted to improvement district status in the late 1920s, and a number in south-eastern Alberta were dismantled, designated special areas and wholly administered by the provincial government.

Despite these reverses 143 municipal districts were operating in 1940. After the demonstrated success of school consolidation in 1936 it was thought that, in the interests of economy and efficiency, the 143 municipal districts should be consolidated and enlarged. Despite opposition, the provincial government managed to reduce their number to 60 by 1944. The principles upon which the Department of Municipal Affairs effected consolidation were that the new units were to reflect common social and economic interests; their boundaries were to follow township and range lines; and their administrative centres were to be accessible to people from all their parts. On balance, the consolidations seem to have been successful since, although the elected policy makers became slightly more remote from their constituents, consolidation resulted in a greater equalization of the tax burden and increased uniformity of service standards.

Historical Development of Educational Government

In Canada's early period the educational system was administered, operated and financed by various churches, with limited government support. The Loyalists who fled to Canada during the American revolution brought, as a part of their philosophical baggage, the belief that the state had a moral responsibility to provide education for the masses. Although the Common School Act enacted in Upper Canada in 1816 provided for the establishment of a school by the residents of any town, village or township by local option, almost half a century passed before universal education financed by the public purse was fully accepted. Egerton Ryerson became Superintendent of Schools for Canada West in 1846 and his ideas indelibly shaped all aspects of Canadian education during the rest of the nineteenth century and left their stamp on educational practices well into the twentieth. Ryerson was committed to free, universal, compulsory education that would be uniform and would further Canadian values. His fascination with the highly centralized French and Prussian educational systems had a profound influence on his thinking. He advocated a school system tightly controlled by a central authority with limited administrative duties to be carried out by locally elected school trustees. The system was to be financed at the local level. "The Ryerson tradition," as it came to be called, soon spread westward and, by the turn of the century, was firmly established in the west.[5] At about the same time, the importance of public education was recognized in the

British North America Act and, after Confederation, the federal government set aside one-eighteenth of all Dominion Lands as an educational endowment.

A series of bitter educational struggles led to the establishment of separate and "common" schools, both of which received provincial funds and were given the power to tax. As a consequence of Ryerson's educational philosophy and the early political battles over education, it was thought that a specialized form of government was required for educational policy making and administration.

In 1884 the Northwest Territorial Council passed a school ordinance providing for the establishment of public and separate schools; in the same year, public school districts were established in Edmonton and Calgary. The 58 public schools and one separate school operating in the territories in 1885 had increased to 243 public and 11 separate schools by 1891. Hanson, describing the financial status of the early school districts, writes:

> At first the school districts levied and collected their own taxes, but the territorial government often had to help in collecting arrears. A directive from the territorial government to recalcitrant ratepayers usually had more effect than notices sent out by local trustees who did not like to dun their neighbors or seize their property. Gradually the districts arranged to have their taxes collected by the municipalities concerned. . . . Some school districts . . . especially the village districts, continued to levy and collect their own taxes until recent years [1956] when the Provincial Government abolished the practice entirely. Dominion and territorial grants to schools were paid to the treasurers of the districts or directly to teachers as part salary.[6]

One of the first acts of the new Alberta provincial government was the passage of a school act and the establishment of a department of education. In an area designated as a school district, the new act provided that the majority religious group would form the public school district, while the minority religious group could form a separate school district. There was little change in educational financing under the new school act. Nevertheless, as waves of new immigrants flowed into the province, new school districts were organized and schools were built. The number of districts jumped to 1,784 by 1911 and to 3,231 by 1921. Most districts requisitioned their funds from municipal and local improvement districts, while the rest levied and collected their own taxes. Whatever the method, if the district was poor it often had difficulty obtaining sufficient funds to make payments on its debentures and pay its teachers.

During the 1920s a few districts were consolidated voluntarily to provide high-school facilities and were called consolidated school districts. Even these new districts had financial trouble, for they were still too small. When school divisions were created, almost all consolidated school districts were brought under their umbrella.

Despite consolidations, the number of school districts proliferated and, by 1936, there were 3,771 districts. Ironically, at the same time new districts were being created, they were being destroyed by the Depression. In some of the smaller, poor districts, tax collections had dried up and teachers were left unpaid. When the new Social Credit government came to power in 1936, conditions were ripe for a massive school consolidation. The new government, with Premier Aberhart managing the education portfolio, "passed legislation enabling the department of education to proceed with a policy of merging school districts to form large units . . . the minister of education established divisions by ministerial orders; votes of the electors were not taken."[7] As one might expect, many parents did not take kindly to what they perceived as a loss of community control over education and a dictatorial stance by the provincial government. Despite strong opposition, however, the government proceeded with its comprehensive reorganization plan.

The new administrative unit was the school division, which included up to 60 rural school districts. Educational policy making and administration shifted from the school district to the new school division and, although the districts were left intact, they became primarily attendance units with limited advisory powers. In describing the policy-making and administrative structure of the school division, Hanson wrote in 1956:

> A school division is administered by a board of trustees, three to five in number, each trustee representing a subdivision. A full-time secretary-treasurer is hired by the board to carry on the day-to-day administrative matters of the division. He is usually provided with stenographic assistance. A supervisor of schools, appointed by the department of education, is stationed in nearly every school division. His duties are to supervise school operations and to serve as an adviser of the board of trustees. Finally, the local school districts elect three trustees each; their duty is to advise the divisional board on local matters.[8]

From the perspective of school consolidation, the government's policy was a success: by 1941 there were 50 school divisions where there had been 3,450. By 1954 the number of divisions had increased to 59 but it dropped to 30 by 1971 as a result of the creation, in 1950, of counties with educational functions, and the alignment of school division boundaries, in 1953-54, by the Co-terminous Boundaries Commission.

Despite the continuing consolidation of school districts, approximately 140 school districts remain independent of school divisions and counties. One hundred are in cities, towns and villages; most of the rest are either in extremely remote areas or are connected with defence bases. There is little doubt that the future will see further consolidations.

There is no question that many school districts were much too small to support an adequate educational system. Consolidation produced greater equalization of the tax burden and a higher degree of administrative specialization, but there have been drawbacks, such as a lessening of community control over educational policy. The consolidation of physical facilities meant that children had to be bused some distance to adjoining communities. In addition, some people argue that the loss of a school through consolidation leads to a decline in community identity. On balance, however, few people would advocate a return to the conditions extant in 1936, with almost 4,000 school districts duplicating facilities and making and administering educational policy.

Education: Turbulent Local Politics in the Eighties

During the 1950s and early 1960s, education at the local level was rarely beset by political controversy. A recent report characterized this period as one in which "the authority or wisdom of the school was rarely questioned" and "education was held in high esteem by all."[9] For the most part, students were well-behaved and the local educational system was strongly supported by the community. Teachers thought of themselves as professionals above "haggling" over wages, and the education profession and the community agreed that teachers were expected to make economic sacrifices in the interests of the community. But the 1970s changed all that. A more permissive society made teaching much more arduous, with teachers facing classrooms of unruly and rebellious students. Teachers became militant, demanding higher salaries and better working conditions. At the same time the public was becoming disenchanted with the educational system: many people saw an inverse relationship between the amount of money spent on education and "Johnny's ability to read." Property taxes increased dramatically and education became the scapegoat. For example, while the average personal income in Alberta increased 293

per cent between 1972 and 1982, the average property tax soared 415
per cent in Calgary and 433 per cent in Edmonton. Similar increases
took place in other Alberta communities.

Table 4.1
Educational Funding in Alberta, 1970-1980

	1970	1971	1972	1973	1974	1975
Total Revenue from Province for Education (000)	287,540	310,943	331,650	359,839	398,334	483,802
Per Cent of Total Revenue	83.8	82.8	81.5	81.5	79.7	77.9
Total Revenue from Supplemental Requisitions (000)	38,847	42,776	50,348	56,299	74,041	106,963
Per Cent of Total Revenue	11.3	11.4	12.4	12.8	14.9	17.3

	1976	1977	1978	1979	1980
Total Revenue from Province for Education (000)	526,693	579,791	624,331	679,317	740,719
Per Cent of Total Revenue	75.6	74.1	72.4	70.2	68.1
Total Revenue from Supplemental Requisitions (000)	130,325	161,194	192,076	232,623	281,341
Per Cent of Total Revenue	18.8	20.7	22.3	24.1	25.9

One of the major reasons people have become acutely aware of
educational costs is that, during the 1970s, the provincial
government's grants did not increase as fast as communities' spending. School boards were forced to resort to "supplementary requisitions" (i.e., requisitions from municipalities that raised additional
funds through additional property taxes). Table 4.1 shows that, although provincial grants for education have increased in absolute
terms each year, in relative terms, the provincial share of total educational revenue consistently decreased. In 1970 the province picked

up 83.8 per cent of total educational costs; by 1980 this proportiom had dropped to 68.1 per cent. During the same period supplementary requisitions increased from 11.3 per cent to 25.9 per cent. In community after community, taxpayers became acutely aware of the costs of educational programs as they watched their property taxes increase.

To understand the politics of education it is necessary to understand its funding. Each year the provincial government examines projected enrolments, transportation costs, debt retirement and other related factors, as well as overall projections in the inflation rate, in order to determine the amount to be budgeted for the coming fiscal year. Another important consideration is the size of the education budget in relation to other budgets. The Provincial School Foundation Program provides the lion's share of monies for school jurisdictions.

Although the School Foundation Program's regulations and formulas governing the distribution of monies are relatively complex, basically, funds are distributed for four functions. The largest amount is expended for per-student grants. In 1981 a school jurisdiction received $1,399 per student in grades one through six, $1,466 per student in grades seven through nine, and $1,679 per student in grades 10 through 12. Second, grant monies are provided for the transportation of students. Third, the province provides each jurisdiction with funds for administrative costs (three per cent of the transportation and per-student grants). Finally, funds are given for debt retirement and capital expenditures.

It is important to note that an equalization formula is not built into the grants given to the province's school jurisdictions.[10] However, the province has devised a form of equalization on the revenue side, a provincial levy on commercial and industrial property that goes to the School Foundation Fund. For the 1980-81 budget year, the levy generated revenues of $103,296,000.

School jurisdictions have been forced to resort increasingly to supplementary requisitions. Table 4.2 shows the total funds requisitioned by school jurisdictions in Alberta in 1981 and 1982.

In 1981 Edmonton requisitioned $67,475,000 for public schools and $23,137,000 for separate schools; the comparable sums in Calgary were $80,208,012 and $16,957,379, respectively.

Educational costs doubled between 1974 and 1982, while other service costs rose at a lower rate; hence, education has become more and more politicized as it has been forced to compete with other local governmental services for funding. In counties, education must compete directly with other services. In other units of municipal government, the competition is equally intense but much less direct, since school districts requisition their funds from the municipalities. At election time, school board candidates advocating increased spend-

Table 4.2
Amount of Supplemental Requisitions
by School Jurisdiction, 1981 and 1982

Jurisdiction	Requisition 1981	Requisition 1982
Divisions	50,836,608	63,194,806
Counties	65,454,509	83,208,427
City School Districts	236,208,178	300,869,520
Town School Districts	9,822,299	12,227,037
Village School Districts	318,090	365,815
Consolidated School Districts	301,832	365,815
Rural School Districts	5,644,572	6,705,369
TOTALS	$368,586,008	$478,837,608

ing attempt to counter candidates favouring ongoing and reduced spending levels. This election rhetoric often evolves into a comparison of educational and municipal needs.

Evolution of the County Form of Government and County Government Politics

The economic prosperity generated by a wartime economy in the early 1940s was followed by a full-fledged oil boom, beginning in 1947, and local units of government revived and again became financially sound. However, many such units were beset with problems of policy co-ordination and, perhaps more importantly, many of their citizens were confused by the overlap of school divisions and municipal and hospital districts. As Hanson reports:

> Tax rates differed within municipal districts because those districts embraced parts of several school divisions and hospital districts, and each of the latter units requisitioned amounts that necessitated the levying of different rates in different parts of a municipal district.[11]

In short, a farmer living in a school district and a hospital district on one side of the road often would pay substantially higher taxes than his neighbour across the road in a different district. This disparity caused confusion and charges of inequities.

Many municipal districts were frustrated by school and hospital requisitions in their attempts to hold down taxes. After being denied a portion of municipal reserves, many school officials criticized municipal councillors for being unconcerned about the importance of education. Other school officials felt that municipal councils' only interest was to keep mill rates and taxes at an absolute minimum, a practice that, school officials believed, undermined educational goals. On the other hand, many municipal councils argued that school boards were irresponsible. They built up huge cash reserves at a time when municipalities were not merely short of cash but facing a taxpayers' rebellion. However, the major criticism made by municipal councils was that the system of requisitioning by the school boards meant, in effect, that the school boards exercised an unofficial veto over municipal financial policies. More often than not, school officials, hospital officials and municipal district councillors planned and made policy without consulting each other.

The provincial government became increasingly concerned about what it perceived as uncoordinated policy making, which confused and alienated people residing in municipal districts. The government made several attempts to remedy the problem, first, in 1946, by providing that the school board and municipal council would each send a member to the other's meetings to facilitate communication and then, in 1948, by providing an appeal procedure for a municipal district whose school board(s) requisitioned an amount exceeding the previous year's requisition by more than 20 per cent. Unfortunately, these remedies did little to alleviate the conflict between the school districts and municipal districts. Then, in 1950, the government passed the County Act providing for the creation of an omnibus authority with a single body to make policy and plan and administer all local governmental services within its geographical boundaries.

At about the same time, the provincial government established the Co-terminous Boundaries Commission to straighten out the tangled and overlapping boundaries of municipal districts and school divisions. After devising seven criteria (physical features, nature of production, ability to pay, size in relation to administration, inclusion of non-divisional schools, existing pattern of school centralization, railroads and highways and market centres), the commission negotiated with municipal councils, school boards, teachers associations and other interested groups until "boundaries common to both types of administrative units were determined wherever possible to the general satisfaction of all concerned." There is little doubt that the Co-terminous Boundaries Commission played an important role in Alberta's county movement by resolving political and administrative conflict and, thus, allowing county government to become acceptable to the area's residents.

The province was more circumspect in its policy on the establishment of counties than it had been in its earlier policies on school reorganization and municipal district consolidation. Under the County Act the provincial government could not form a county unless it first received a resolution to do so from a municipal council or a school division. Furthermore, four years after the implementation of county government, a plebiscite had to be held on its continuance.

Very shortly after the County Act was passed three counties were formed. Grande Prairie and Vulcan commenced operations on January 1, 1951; Ponoka, a year later. Only in the case of Sturgeon County, which was incorporated in 1960 and dissolved in 1965, did the electorate reject the county form of government after the four-year trial period and revert to separate municipal district and school division status.

Despite the provincial government's attempt to bring all local government policy making and administration under the aegis of a single authority, hospital districts have remained independent of the county. The County Act originally provided for the amalgamation of municipal, school and hospital districts under a single unit. However, many rural dwellers strongly opposed the abolition of hospital districts, and the provincial government, deciding not to jeopardize its policy on counties, left the hospital districts intact. As one might expect, county councils are unhappy when they are forced to produce funds under requisition for hospital districts over which they have almost no control.

Governmental reformers and proponents of county government see independent hospital districts as forestalling completely rational and efficient policy making and administration at the county level.[12] Nevertheless, it is unlikely that the provincial government will be willing to face, in the near future, a political showdown by abolishing hospital districts and transferring their functions to the county.

In 1967 the County Act was amended so that an improvement district and its towns, villages and school divisions would be able to merge into a single "Metroplex County." Such a drastic reorganization would need the support of a majority of the residents, expressed in a plebiscite, and not a single "Metroplex County" has been created since the Act was amended. Since such a political and administrative unit would take in both rural dwellers and residents of small towns, groups with divergent interests, it is unlikely that Metroplex Counties will be created in the future.

The provincial government deliberately kept the county's political structure simple and straightforward. Its policy-making body was to be composed of no more than 11 councillors who would select the county's chief executive officer, the reeve, from their own ranks. At its first meeting of the year, the county council was to appoint three members to a school committee and three to a hospital committee. The school committee was to be augmented by school representatives appointed from towns and villages within the county.

In 1977 the County Act was amended to clarify educational representation on the county council. The council's education committee, which is the county's board of education, was to consist of at least three county council members and additional school representatives appointed from the county's educational units (i.e., the towns and villages within the county). An educational unit with a population of 2,000 or less was allowed one representative; one with a population of 2,000 to 4,000, two; and one with a population greater than 4,000, three. Since the county's board of education formulates the education budget and is responsible for its administration, the amendment ensured that it would be impossible for the number of the council's educational representatives to exceed the number of councillors on the committee. The Act reads: "The number of school representatives appointed to the board of education shall not exceed the number of electoral divisions that exist within the county." This provision caused a problem since, in most cases, the number of authorized representatives exceeded the number allocated to form the school board. For example, in 1981 the County of Lacombe had seven councillors (seven electoral divisions), yet six towns and villages were authorized to have one educational representative each, and the Town of Lacombe, with a population of 5,000 was authorized to have three representatives, for a total of nine. When this situation occurs, the newly amended Act states: "the county council shall meet with those school representatives . . . and determine a system of rotation which will permit those positions on the board of education to be filled." In the case of the County of Lacombe, the towns of Lacombe and Blackfalds, with a total of four educational representatives, were exempt from the rotation, and the five other representatives rotated monthly to fill three positions.

Most county school boards have dealt with the problem of educational representation and the rotation system by allowing all authorized educational representatives to sit on the school board, but permitting only some of them to vote. Since the rotation system is often based on a population formula, representatives of some smaller communities are almost always relegated to non-voting status. This system has been an extremely contentious issue in almost all counties since 1977, as the smaller towns and villages feel that they are being squeezed out of the educational policy-making process.[13]

Local self-determination and local control over educational policy became major issues in 1981 when the government introduced Bill 25 to amend the County Act. Bill 25 would have abolished the power of the county council's education committee/school board to formulate and administer the county's education budget; the effect would have been to reduce the committee/school board to little more than an advisory body, leaving the county council to formulate and administer the education budget alone. Small towns and villages fought the proposal, feeling that it would spell the end of local control over educational policy. Their opposition, in concert with strong lobbying against the bill by the Alberta School Trustees Association and the Alberta Teachers Association, resulted in its being quietly dropped after second reading.

An interesting quirk in the County Act is that a municipality with city status is prevented from being represented in the county school system; the effect is to allow a city located in a county to have its own school system. In 1983 this provision became an issue when the Town of Leduc wanted to expand its high-school facilities. After the county turned down a request by the town for $11 million to match previously approved provincial funds for the expansion of the town's high school, Leduc's administration decided to apply for city status to enable it to establish and run its own school district.[14]

Although educational policy making and "school politics" is an extremely important component of county government, it must be kept in perspective, for the county council exercises the same powers as any municipal council. The County Act states: "Except as otherwise provided by the Act, the county council has and shall exercise all the rights, powers, privileges, duties and functions conferred on a council by The Municipal Government Act and The Municipal Election Act." (The Municipal Election Act has been superseded by the Local Authorities Election Act.) The administrative structure is equally straightforward; the council is given the power to appoint a secretary-treasurer who has the same powers and duties as in a municipal district.

In 1982 there were 30 counties throughout the province, with annual revenues ranging from Thorhild's over $6 million to Strathcona's nearly $80 million. Table 4.3 shows that the counties range in population from less than 25,000 to nearly 50,000. Economic and social diversity are equally wide and, hence, there are wide variations in levels of service. Diverse spending patterns are found with roadways, protective services, education and recreation taking different proportions of the budget.

Table 4.3
Counties in Alberta and their Populations, 1982

Grande Prairie No. 1	12,078	Mountain View No. 17	8,832
Vulcan No. 2	3,715	Paintearth No. 18	2,495
Ponoka No. 3	7,536	St. Paul No. 19	6,101
Newell No. 4	6,199	Strathcona No. 20	48,024
Warner No. 5	3,460	Two Hills No. 21	3,380
Stettler No. 6	5,092	Camrose No. 22	7,564
Thorhild No. 7	3,323	Red Deer No. 23	13,664
Forty Mile No. 8	3,451	Vermilion River No. 24	7,533
Beaver No. 9	5,347	Leduc No. 25	13,258
Wetaskiwin No. 10	9,026	Lethbridge No. 26	8,779
Barrhead No. 11	5,517	Minburn No. 27	4,041
Athabasca No. 12	5,974	Lac Ste. Anne No. 28	7,614
Smoky Lake No. 13	2,910	Flagstaff No. 29	4,507
Lacombe No. 14	8,783	Lamont No. 30	4,687
Wheatland No. 16	5,513	Parkland No. 31	23,626
TOTAL POPULATION			252,029

For the most part, county government in Alberta has been a success, with the county councillors developing policies, overseeing county administration and providing services their constituents desire at reasonable costs. Self-serving elected representatives have been the exception rather than the rule, although there have been occasional abuses of power. In the spring of 1980, an investigation by the Department of Municipal Affairs revealed a scandal in the County of Vermilion River. Councillors' relatives had been hired without authorization, county-owned culverts and gravel had been sold at cost to a private developer, and it was common practice for councillors to allocate funds for each electoral division, rather than for the county as a whole, a practice prohibited under the Municipal Government Act. The adverse publicity generated by the report alerted the electorate and changes in administration and a new council rectified the situation.

Most of the major controversies faced by county councils are products of urbanization, industrialization, inflation and demands for higher levels of service. In 1982 violent political controversy erupted in Beaver County over the province's plans to locate a hazardous waste plant there. Residents who favoured the plant pointed to the $750,000 in annual tax revenue that would accrue to the county, and to the 80 jobs that would be created. Opponents, led by environmental and farm groups, feared the plant's potential adverse effects. The county council was caught in the crossfire of these deeply divided opinions. The counties of Parkland and Strathcona, faced with demands that service levels be raised without increases in the residential mill rate, are in competition with Edmonton for high-tax industrial development. In 1980 some acreage owners in the County of Lethbridge were faced with 500 per cent property tax increases. Since acreage owners and farmers are pitted against one another over land use classification and tax assessments, Lethbridge County Council meetings are often contentious affairs. The same phenomenon is found in the County of Grande Prairie. Farmers, industrial land owners and acreage owners are all pitted against one another over taxes and the levels of service.

The Municipal District Today

By 1982 the number of municipal districts had been reduced to 18, the smallest being the M.D. of Acadia, with a population of 604 and total revenue of $1,241,700 (1982); the largest, the M.D. of Rocky View, with a population of 17,362 and revenue of $15,435,892. Table 4.4 presents the municipal district population figures for 1982. A municipal district gains its authority from the Municipal Government Act. Briefly, municipal districts enjoy almost the same powers as any town or city; they have full taxing and spending powers and are able to borrow money. In addition, the Act gives a municipal district powers applicable for the governance of a rural area; for example, a municipal district can make a grant to encourage a veterinarian to practise in the district, or can make cash advances to district farmers for "spring feeding" to sustain livestock and "for any other good and sufficient reason."

The governing structure of a municipal district is straightforward as the Act specifies that the council "shall consist of the same number of councillors as there are electoral divisions." These divisions range in number from four to nine. Once elected, the councillors choose a chief executive, a reeve, from their own ranks.

The municipal district's administrative structure is equally straightforward. The secretary-treasurer is selected by and is responsible to the council, as are other administrative personnel. To bring a higher level of expertise into their administration, some municipal districts have hired professional managers. The manager, too, is hired by the council and is responsible to it.

Table 4.4
Municipal Districts in Alberta and their Populations, 1982

Cardston No. 6	4,292	Provost No. 52	2,611
Pincher Creek No. 9	2,970	Wainwright No. 61	3,837
Taber No. 14	5,637	Bonnyville No. 87	9,407
Willow Creek No. 26	4,534	Sturgeon No. 90	13,682
Foothills No. 31	8,725	Westlock No. 92	7,059
Acadia No. 34	604	Smoky River No. 130	2,858
Rocky View No. 44	17,362	Spirit River No. 133	891
Starland No. 47	2,068	Peace No. 135	1,520
Kneehill No. 48	5,761	Fairview No. 136	1,889
TOTAL POPULATION			95,707

Municipal districts, which are exactly like counties without their educational component, are faced with many of the same problems as confront the counties in the 1980s. Those adjacent to large cities, such as Taber (east of Lethbridge), Rocky View (adjoining Calgary), and Sturgeon (north of Edmonton) must reconcile the demands of commuting "hobby farmers" for suburban amenities with the demands of farmers for fewer services and lower taxes. Another difference between "hobby farmers" and those who farm for a living is the tax structure; since acreage owners are taxed on both buildings and land, while farmers are taxed only on land, acreage owners feel they are carrying an undue tax burden.[15] For example, acreage owners revolted when the Municipal District of Foothill's school board requisition increased 93 per cent between 1981 and 1982 and the council was forced to make a 50 per cent increase in its tax assessments. The acreage owners, with almost no support from district farmers, formed the Foothills Ratepayers Association, which encouraged ratepayers to withhold the increase when they paid their 1982 taxes. A manifestation of this cleavage in Rocky View was a battle, in 1983, between the two groups over political representation. The municipal district was badly apportioned: its seven electoral divisions ranged in population between 1,200 and 4,600. The Minister of Municipal Affairs stepped in and increased the electoral divisions to 11 by splitting the populous non-farming divisions, thus giving them more representation. This division, in conjunction with minor adjustments to the other electoral division boundaries, reduced the variation in electoral division population to no more than 600 people. As the examples illustrate, the population of many municipal districts is becoming more heterogeneous, with the consequence that conflicting demands are made on the districts' councils. The councils find themselves dealing more with controversial political issues and less with purely administrative ones.

Lloydminster

Almost as if its founders wanted to play a cruel joke on the community, when Lloydminster was founded in 1903 the main street was located on the fourth meridian that was to become the boundary between Saskatchewan and Alberta. As a result of the vagaries of urban settlement, the Saskatchewan side grew much faster than the Alberta side; by the time amalgamation was being considered, the Saskatchewan portion was twice as large. Being substantially larger, the Saskatchewan side had town status, while the Alberta side was still designated a village. Although the two communities were a single economic and social unit, sharing a common main street, churches and social institutions, there was an occasional outbreak of bitter political rivalry between them. More importantly, however, neither community was large enough to develop badly needed water and sewer systems. Finally, in the early spring of 1930, elections were held in the town and village to ascertain whether or not the respective electorates favoured giving their representatives the authority to approach the provincial governments for the necessary legislation to amalgamate. The electorate in both communities voted overwhelmingly for amalgamation. On March 21, 1930, An Act Respecting the Amalgamation of Lloydminster was passed in Alberta and on March 27 an almost identical act (the Lloydminster Municipal Amalgamation Act) gained assent in Saskatchewan. The two provincial acts were relatively simple. They amalgamated the two municipalities and their school systems; the new governmental units were to be governed by a council/board "under the provisions of an approved Act." Assets and liabilities of the two municipalities and school districts were transferred to the new amalgamated units. Perhaps the only extraordinary provision was the inclusion of a supremacy clause. Section six of the Act read: "In the event of there being any conflict between the provisions of this Act or any Order in Council . . . and those of any other Act . . . the provisions of this Act and any such Order in Council shall prevail."

Today, Lloydminster is completely politically integrated, with the electorate ignoring whether council candidates reside in the Alberta or Saskatchewan portion of the community. The city's (it became a city in 1957) financial affairs and powers are somewhat more complicated than those of other Alberta municipalities since it operates under separate Saskatchewan and Alberta acts and must receive approval from both provinces when borrowing money. The charter specifies which of the provincial acts apply to the whole city and which apply only to one or other portion. For example, while Alberta's Agricultural Pest Act (chapter 2) and Saskatchewan's Gas Inspection and Licensing Act (chapter 368) and Special-care Home Act (chapter 275) apply to the whole city, there are several Alberta acts that apply only to the Alberta part. [16] Despite these complexities there are advantages in being located in two provinces. The city borrows money from the province that gives it the best terms, an arrangement other Alberta municipalities must surely envy.

New Towns: Interim Economic and Democratic Development

Following the discovery of oil at Leduc, oil companies embarked on a massive exploration effort across the province. When an oil field was discovered, hundreds of men would move into the area. Hanson writes of this phenomenon:

> . . . new towns sprung up almost overnight in new oil fields. These contain a transient population of oil drillers, 'roughnecks', technicians, and even camp followers who instead of pitching the proverbial tent move in with trailers. Some of these new towns consist mainly of a main street with hastily constructed business buildings and hundreds of trailers . . . during the usual hectic period of initial growth of a new town . . . most 'residents' are transients and take little interest in affairs pertaining to the town. [17]

Over a period of time a permanent, family-oriented population would settle in the new town, but their demands for services and taxation would be blocked by the transients, who had no interest in taxing themselves for educational facilities, parks, and adequate water and sewer systems. Recognizing this problem and the difficulty of financing a town service infrastructure from scratch, the provincial legislature enacted the New Town Act in 1956 to provide provincial assistance for the development and planning of new, almost instant, communities.

The basic intent of new town legislation was two-pronged: to establish democratic institutions and to provide financial support. The province initially administers and makes decisions for the community through a town board of administration with a chairperson appointed by the province and other members provincially appointed and elected from the community. Grand Cache is a typical example of the democratic evolution of a board of administration. When it was designated a new town in 1966, it had a board composed of three provincial public servants from Edmonton. Then, in 1970, the board grew from three to five members, the two additional members being Grand Cache residents chosen in a community-wide election. The following year, the board again grew, to seven members. Two appointed members were removed and the residents elected a total of six to the board. The only provincial board member was the chairperson, who had to be a provincial appointee under the provisions of the New Town Act. Concurrent with a town's democratic development is its fiscal development. The province provides the initial money for large capital projects and the community is expected to repay these investments once it is financially stable. A new town is expected to meet its own operating expenses.

Shortly after the Act was implemented, a number of new towns were incorporated and the process continued until 1967: Cynthia, Drayton Valley, Hinton and Lodgepole in 1956; St. Albert in 1957; Swan Hills in 1959; Whitecourt in 1961; Fort McMurray in 1964; High Level in 1965; Grand Cache and Rainbow Lake in 1966; and Fox Creek in 1967. All of them now have hamlet, town or city status, with the exception of Rainbow Lake.

Other communities applying for new town status were turned down after the provincial government decided that they were unlikely to become well enough off to pay back the province's loans. For example, the hamlet of Smith applied to the Alberta Provincial Planning Board for new town status in 1968. After an economic feasibility study the board concluded that, as there was little prospect that Smith would attract new industry or expand existing ones, the request should be denied. The most curious instance of a community being denied new town status occurred in the town of Slave Lake, the population of which increased from 500 to 3,500 in a 10-year period. The provincial government, as much as the town's administration, was responsible for putting the community in a precarious financial position. In 1970 the Alberta government and the federal Department of Regional Expansion signed a federal-provincial agreement to promote long-term economic expansion in this area. Incentive grants of slightly over $5 million encouraged $14 million of investment in wood and wood product plants just outside the town's boundaries. A Department of Municipal Affairs publication describes the financial chaos that resulted:

> While the 1970 regional development plan was for the provincial and federal governments to provide the administrative, planning and financial support for the development in Slave Lake over a five year period, no new funding was available after 1972 when the impact of growth was the greatest. . . . During the 1970-1972 period the town . . . received a total of $440 per capita ($978,400) from the federal government and $250 per capita ($557,600) from the provincial government for services and facilities. The town also benefitted from a grant of $443,000 for the construction of two schools. During the same period the municipal government . . . was required to spend approximately $3 million ($1300 per capita) from its general budget to upgrade roads, the water system and the sewer system. The rapid growth of the town and Mitsue Lake Industrial Park [where the new wood and wood product plants were located], which is outside the town's taxation area, committed the town's tax base and borrowing power to providing only the most basic public works infrastructure. The development of recreational and community facilities suffered as a consequence.[18]

Faced with an ever-increasing financial burden and encouraged by the Planning Division of the Department of Municipal Affairs, the town's council applied for new town status in order to obtain provincial funds, even though it knew that, with a change in status, the community would no longer be self-governing. The application went to the cabinet, which turned it down.

In 1969 the New Town Act was completely rewritten, although the basic philosophy of the 1956 Act remained unchanged. As under the 1956 Act, the board of administration requires the approval of the proprietary electors (property owners) "on any by-law for the expenditure of money, the issuance of debentures or for any other matter or thing that shall take place or be required except in the case of an election of members of the board of administration." The Alberta Planning Board must approve all matters relating to the planning and development of the town and the Local Authorities Board all matters relating to the town's development and operation. The provincial government provides a new town with grants and loans, and purchases of its debentures.

Since 1967 the province has not designated a single fast-growing hamlet or municipality a new town. Moreover, the new towns created in the 1956-1967 period have had their status changed as soon as they seemed fiscally viable. In 1982, with Grand Cache, Fox Creek, High Level and Rainbow Lake still retaining new town status, the Department of Municipal Affairs both scolded them for denying their citizens their democratic rights and encouraged them to change their status. All made the change in 1983, except Rainbow Lake where the citizenry rejected any change in status.

A concern with democratic institutions has not been the province's only motive in its refusal to designate more communities as new towns and in its encouragement of new towns to change their status. A new town is a costly enterprise for the provincial government. As in improvement districts, if it can shift the support of a number of costly services to the local citizenry, the provincial government can effect considerable savings.

Improvement Districts: Toward Self-Government?

Improvement districts, which are administered by the provincial government, have been located primarily in sparsely populated rural areas which lacked the ability to finance their own local government services. With 216 improvement districts organized across the province by 1942, the provincial government embarked on a policy of reducing their number. While some were amalgamated, economically viable ones with adequate population were turned into municipal districts. This policy sharply decreased the number of districts until, in 1969, only 24 were left. Since 1969 there has been a further reduction; today there are only 20 improvement districts, five of them coterminous with national park boundaries. The 20 improvement districts in Alberta account for 75 per cent of the province's land area (177,430 square miles) and yet have a population of only about 84,500 people. Table 4.5 shows that there are striking disparities in population among improvement districts. This imbalance results in an equally striking disparity in their fiscal resources. Improvement District No. 17 had a population of 11,699 and total revenues of $9,838,498 in 1982, while Improvement District No. 13 contained only 36 people and had total revenues of $55 in the same year. Five Improvement Districts are national parks, and federal lands comprise a sizeable portion of two districts, the Experimental Range being located in No. 1 and the Primrose Lake Air Weapons Range in No. 18.[19] Most improvement districts have such small populations and limited tax bases that the formation of a self-governing municipal district has not been feasible. As a consequence, Alberta's Department of Municipal Affairs is responsibile for providing services to the residents. Alberta Transportation provides substantial assistance for the construction and maintenance of roadways, and the Forestry branch provides fire protection in forested areas. The school districts and divisions make requisitions to the Department of Municipal Affairs for their funds.

Table 4.5
Improvement Districts in Alberta and their Populations, 1982

No. 1	5,029	No. 14	9,238
No. 4 (Waterton		No. 15	2,670
National Park)	176	No. 16	5,350
No. 6	119	No. 17	11,699
No. 7	1,258	No. 18	9,605
No. 8	1,268	No. 19	1,757
No. 9 (Banff		No. 20	3,000
National Park)	6,949	No. 21	2,936
No. 10	9,201	No. 22	4,250
No. 12 (Jasper		No. 23	5,837
National Park	3,970	No. 24 (Wood Buffalo	
No. 13 (Elk Island		National Park)	188
National Park)	36		
TOTAL POPULATION			84,536

Despite the pervasive influence of the provincial government in the affairs of improvement districts, they are so much like municipal districts that they are often referred to as "rural municipalities" in legislation. They have municipal planning commissions, development appeal boards and courts of revision that function in the same way as they do in incorporated municipalities. They also receive municipal assistance grants like those received by other municipalities. However, they differ from municipalities in two important areas, policy making and administration.

As can be seen by the administrative organizational chart in Table 4.6, the Department of Municipal Affairs controls the upper levels of administration. Only recently has Municipal Affairs decentralized administration at the grass-roots level.

In the area of policy making, until the mid-1970s the Department of Municipal Affairs was extremely paternalistic toward improvement districts. The only mechanism the residents had for expressing their policy preferences were "resident advisory committees" whose members were appointed by the government and whose advice was not taken very seriously.[20] In 1974 Marvin Moore, who was later to become Minister of Municipal Affairs, said: "at least their views [resident advisory committees] are taken into consideration much more than they were during the early years when they were first established with regard to levying mill rates . . . road construction and a variety of other services."[21] Surprisingly, however, few residents were dissatisfied with this arrangement, as they felt that autonomy would mean a substantial loss of provincial government revenue and a corresponding increase in property taxes, a belief the provincial legislature did nothing to dispel.[22]

In the mid-1970s the government began to change its policy toward the districts. The passage of the Improvement Districts Amendment Act allowed the districts to have the same services as municipal districts. In the course of the legislative debate it was brought out that the Minister of Municipal Affairs intended to give the advisory committee much more responsibility in the determination of district policy. More important was the implication that the government intended to encourage financially viable improvement districts to become municipal districts by plebiscite. However, the government's new policy languished until 1979 when the Minister of Municipal Affairs announced that improvement districts would be undergoing major changes during the 1980s. He then announced three goals for the districts: 1) to increase the number of advisory councils and councillors, particularly in the northern and remote areas of the province; 2) to encourage self-government; and 3) to decentralize decision making and administration to the local level in order to provide a higher level of service.

In a parallel development, the administration of the eight Alberta Métis settlements, which had been the responsibility of the Department of Social Services and Community Health, was transferred to the Department of Municipal Affairs and placed under the jurisdiction of the Assistant Deputy Minister of Improvement Districts. Municipal Affairs was directed to encourage Métis settlements to become self-governing communities. Each settlement has a five-member elective advisory council that makes recommendations to the Metis Development Branch. It would seem that the program was placed in

Table 4.6
Improvement District Organization Chart

	Minister of Municipal Affairs	Executive Assistant
	Deputy Minister	
Director Personnel Branch	Assistant Deputy Minister I.D. Operations	Director of Finance and Administration
Special Projects Manager		
Research Assistant	Secretary	
	Director Support Services	
	Director Land Tenure	Director Métis Development
Support Staff		
Regional Director North	Regional Director Central	Regional Director South
Manager ID 23	Manager ID 18	Manager ID 1
Manager ID 21-22	Manager ID 17c	Manager ID 7
Manager ID 19-20	Manager ID 15	Manager ID 6, 8
Manager ID 17w	Manager ID 14	Manager ID 10
Manager ID 17c		
Manager ID 16		

the Improvement District section of the department because that section had been directed to develop programs that would lead to self-government for some of the improvement districts. Municipal Affairs, in conjunction with the Department of Advanced Education, is developing training programs for the Métis settlements to develop the residents' political and administrative skills.[23]

The underlying policy of the Department of Municipal Affairs is to provide support and incentives to some of the more populous improvement districts to induce them to assume full responsibility for their affairs by becoming municipal districts. The newly created elective "advisory councils" (the successors of "advisory committees") have much greater powers, and the department expects that a taste of real democracy will encourage the residents to opt for the self-governing status of a municipal district. In 1980 the Minister of Municipal Affairs, in a speech to advisory council members, stated that the advisory councils would have to become much more knowledgeable about the revenue-raising function of local government and should begin to consider "a lot of new things that we can best call services to people."

In order to decentralize policy making and administration, the department's office in Edmonton has begun to function as a co-ordinator and advisor to district offices. More importantly, beginning in 1981 the district offices were given the responsibility to tender, purchase and make payments for local goods and services. As a consequence of Municipal Affairs' new policy, a 150 per cent increase in services and a 42 per cent increase in taxes occurred in Alberta's improvement districts between 1980 and 1982.

The first test of Municipal Affairs' policy of encouraging improvement districts to become self-governing came in July, 1979. The advisory council for Improvement District No. 1, located in the southeastern corner of the province, asked the Minister of Municipal Affairs to undertake a study to assess the feasibility of the improvement district becoming a municipal district.[24] Municipal Affairs' Special Projects Branch prepared a comprehensive study examining the financial and administrative implications of the proposed change in status. Not surprisingly, the study's report concluded: "Improvement District No. 1 appears to be capable of operating as a viable rural municipality. The assessment and population base [5,400] are more than adequate to meet the responsibilities of incorporated status." Minister of Municipal Affairs Marvin Moore almost immediately began to mount a campaign to convince the area's residents of the virtues of self-government. Funds were budgeted for pamphlets, newspaper ads and radio announcements.

In the fall of 1980 and early spring of 1981, Municipal Affairs held a series of meetings throughout the improvement district to discuss the department's report and put forward arguments demonstrating why the district would be better off as a municipal district. The meetings were well attended and the discussion periods made it clear that the residents were opposed to the change in status. They felt that they would lose their large provincial transportation grant and other subsidies, with the result that their taxes would rise by at least six mills. The Minister attempted to counter this concern by pointing out that taxes would increase whether incorporation proceeded or not. He then said, "No one is going to be able to remain in an improvement district situation merely to be able to take advantage of lower taxes." One cause of the change in attitude was that elections had changed the composition of the advisory council. The new council was evenly split over incorporation, which the previous council had favoured. The opponents actively spoke out against incorporation in community meetings and newspaper interviews.

On April 8 the residents went to the polls and answered the question: "Are you in favour of self government for Improvement District No. 1 providing the Local Advisory Council is able to negotiate the terms?" With an estimated 40 per cent of the eligible voters turning out, 295 voted "Yes" and 518 voted "No."

After Municipal Affairs lost this first skirmish, and with the appointment of a new minister, Julian Koziak, the department changed its tactics. Discussions were held on the feasibility of calculating transportation grants to improvement districts as though they were municipal districts. In addition, other provincial subsidies were cut to put the improvement districts on a more equal financial footing with municipal districts. However, rather than working to convince residents of the value of local autonomy, self-government and grass-roots democracy, Koziak decided to change several improvement districts into self-governing municipal districts unilaterally. On February 16, 1984, Koziak announced that I.D. No. 1 would become an M.D. on January 1, 1985. A similar announcement was made to a group of citizens in I.D. No. 10 on March 4. Shortly thereafter, the Minister announced that the agricultural and rural areas of I.D. No. 7 would be absorbed by the County of Wheatland and the Municipal Districts of Starland and Kneehill. The remaining portion of the I.D. either will be absorbed by its neighbours or will be given M.D. status.

Despite the minister's persuasive argument that both I.D. No. 1 and I.D. No. 10 had a far more secure financial base than most M.D.s, a number of residents in both I.D.s were opposed to the change, fearing that it would involve a substantial increase in taxes.[25] When

Municipal Affairs Assistant Deputy Minister Robin Ford told an I.D. No. 1 meeting "I don't believe the improvement district system is a democracy, it actually gives the minister of municipal affairs the powers of a kind of dictator," a member of the audience retorted, "so we have democracy imposed by dictatorship."[26]

Whether Municipal Affairs' actions are motivated by a desire to transfer some of its costs to I.D. residents or whether the government has a commitment to local autonomy and grass-roots democracy, in the long term one can hypothesize the residents will be much more satisfied running their own affairs and making their own decisions than having them imposed from offices in Edmonton. If self-government is imposed, the citizenry will probably be suspicious and less receptive. If local democracy is to take hold, Municipal Affairs should first educate I.D. residents about the advantages of local autonomy and grass-roots democracy and then let them put it into practice by voting either to change their status and become self-governing or to remain as they are. If the educational process is successful the residents will opt for self-government.[27]

Special Areas: Problems in Democratic Development

In the 1920s the federal government and the railroads placed thousands of farmers in the semi-arid parts of southeastern Alberta on small land holdings that could not support them. With little knowledge of the region's climate and no understanding of dry-land farming practices, these farmers overgrazed the land and broke sod in areas where wheat should never have been planted. During the 1930s the region was ravaged by drought and Depression commodity prices. Many farmers had no crops; others could not sell what they produced, even at the Depression's low prices. The combination of drought, Depression and inability to pay property taxes led to massive failures that saw a majority of southeastern Alberta's farmers walking away from their farms. Tax sales were held, but there were no buyers. Farm families remaining had virtually no income and, by 1932, the 37 improvement and municipal districts in the area had tax arrears of $1.25 million. Conditions continued to worsen as district after district went bankrupt until, in 1938, the province abolished all municipal and improvement districts in the region and established six special areas, comprising 7 million acres, to be administered by the Department of Municipal Affairs. Since then, 2 million acres have been amalgamated into adjoining municipal districts and the remaining 5 million acres have reorganized into three special areas. The government tidied up the fiscal loose ends in 1939 by writing-off all tax arrears up to 1935.

Eric Hanson, discussing the government's initial policies for the special areas, writes:

> One of the first objectives in setting up Special Areas was to assist people to move out so that the remaining farmers could get enough land to make their operations economical. The province provided grants to farmers who wished to move to other farming districts. Land surveys were undertaken during the 1930s and land was classified into three categories—that suitable for grazing only, for both wheat-growing and grazing, and for wheat-growing. Water surveys were also undertaken to devise the best ways of utilizing river, lake and creek waters, and run-offs.[28]

In order to exert direct control over farming practices and to return the land to grass, the province froze sale on the 1.5 million acres of Crown lease land in the area and the 2 million acres the province had seized under the Tax Recovery Act. Then the province leased the land to individual farmers under strict land-use regulations. When the province seized the land for non-payment of taxes it was generally understood that titles would remain in trust until back taxes had been paid and the land rehabilitated. However, long after these conditions were met, the province still held the land.

All of the special areas are governed by a three-member board responsible to the Deputy Minister of Municipal Affairs. Until January 1, 1982, appointments to the board were made by the Deputy Minister, who appointed long-term residents well acquainted with the problems peculiar to the special areas. The only disquieting note to this process is contained in a 1977 legislative interim report that stated: "They have tended to sit for very lengthy periods. . . . The negative aspect of such lengthy tenure has been a certain lack of innovation in approaching continuing problems—for example, water development." The board is responsible for all public land administration, including the issuance of cultivation and grazing permits and leases; it is also responsible for tax assessment and road construction and maintenance. In short, in addition to its public land control duties, it performs many of the functions of any municipal council. To maintain contact with area residents, the board has decentralized its administrative structure: the main office is located in Hanna and field offices in Consort, Youngstown and Oyen. Since a number of government departments are involved in service delivery to special areas, the Department of Municipal Affairs has created a special areas branch to co-ordinate administration and policy making by the special areas board, the Deputy Minister and other concerned government departments.

The Special Areas Act provides for resident participation in the policy-making process through a 13-member elective advisory council. The council was originally composed of 18 members but, as the geographic area of the special areas shrank, its size was reduced. The special areas are divided into 13 subdivisions which constitute the geographic areas from which taxpayers elect their representatives to the advisory council. The residents of each subdivision also meet annually to assist in the preparation of the road program. Curiously, representation on the advisory council is based on land area rather than population, since electoral areas roughly correspond to former municipal boundaries. The elections are staggered and the tenure of office is two years.

When the advisory council makes a recommendation to the board it is always given serious consideration; nevertheless, the council has no binding powers. As its name implies, it acts only in an advisory capacity. A small step to democratize the policy-making process was made on January 1, 1982, when the government appointed two advisory council members to the board. The third member, its chairperson, is still appointed to the board by the Deputy Minister of Municipal Affairs. Despite this change, the residents of special areas are left with only a modicum of power, and one can speculate whether or not potential community leaders have been discouraged from taking an active role in the governance and administration of the special areas by their knowledge that they would be unable to exercise any real political power. Surprisingly, the opposition parties in the province have never made an issue of the government's paternalistic stance on policy making for special areas.

Perhaps this lack of criticism is a sign that the provincial policy for special areas has been successful for, although the population is sparse, almost all of the farms are prospering and the residents are relatively satisfied with the services they are receiving. A land area about two and one-half times that of Prince Edward Island is held by some 3,500 farmers. Individual holdings range in size from 160 to 25,000 acres, the average being 3,000 acres. In 1982 Special Area No. 2 had a population of 2,565; Special Area No. 3, 1,701; and Special Area No. 4, 1,776. Proper soil management practices, a buoyant farm economy, over 2,000 gas and oil wells in production, and a vast network of pipelines, gas plants and compressor sites, have resulted in an economic revival in the region. Nevertheless, the population is much too sparse to assume the burden of financing and administering the programs that are normally the responsibility of local residents. The Alberta government provides municipal assistance grants, road grants, and culture, youth and recreation grants, while the board strikes mill rates, and collects royalties, taxes, crop shares, fees and a variety of other revenues—all retained and applied in the interests of the region. With an enlarged revenue base and efficient administration, the special areas had a $7 million surplus in 1981. Despite minimal road, police and fire services, the residents are satisfied, for their taxes are relatively low. Many older residents haven't forgotten that they lost their land holdings because they were unable to pay their taxes and, as a consequence, there is a real fear of property taxation.

Residents, while satisfied with the provincial government's benevolent administration of special areas, became increasingly dissatisfied with the government's land-lease policy. During the years when no one was interested in acquiring land in special areas, the farmers felt secure with their provincial land-lease agreements. Then, during the 1970s, entrepreneurs became aware of the farming potential of the lands, and lease assignment values doubled and redoubled. At the same time, oil and gas activity was increasing and a decision was made to build a $700 million generating station in the area. As a consequence, farmers became fearful that the province might change its policy on the 1.5 million acres of Crown lease land and the 2 million acres of tax recovery land, and sell it to the highest bidder. Farmers who had been leasing land wanted the opportunity to buy it from the government, although a few farmers felt the government should give them the land since they had spent a number of years bringing it back to productivity. All the farmers on leased land maintained they had fulfilled the government's ownership conditions; back taxes had been paid and the land was rehabilitated. To resolve the problem, special area residents authorized their advisory council to negotiate with the Minister of Municipal Affairs for the return of the 2 million acres of tax recovery land. Immediately, a split developed on the council between farmers who held leases and those who did not, the latter opposing lease sales that could make their lease-holding neighbours millionaires. The faction on the advisory council favouring sale of lease lands to residents prevailed and negotiations commenced with the Minister of Municipal Affairs. In February, 1982, the Minister announced that 800,000 acres of lease land would be offered to residents at bargain prices averaging $28.50 an acre for grazing land and $67.50 an acre for cultivated land. Approximately 1,400 resident farmers were eligible, the minimal requirement being that they had leased their land for three years or longer. It remains to be seen whether the advisory council's success in convincing Municipal Affairs to sell residents a substantial portion of the government's lease land will encourage the council to exert greater pressure on the government in other policy areas.

By virtue of their isolation and sparse population the three special areas face a unique problem in the 1980s. As Alberta's oil and gas industry has developed, an unwanted byproduct has been an ever-increasing supply of hazardous waste material. Hazardous waste plants are generally undesirable but must be located somewhere. Rather than risk a recurrence of the intense political battle that occurred in Beaver County, the provincial government has been examining the possibility of locating hazardous waste treatment plants in some of the least populated portions of the special areas. After the government hired drilling crews to test for the presence of water and water movement (a waste treatment plant cannot be located on land that has underground water or drainage problems), the special areas advisory council requested that a plebiscite be held on the issue. The Minister of Municipal Affairs agreed and, on March 7, 1983, voters in each special area overwhelmingly opposed locating a hazardous waste plant in their area. The residents have won the first battle; it now remains to be seen whether they will win what will undoubtedly be a long war.[29]

The Park Towns of Jasper and Banff

Because Jasper and Banff are located in national parks where the federal government has exclusive jurisdiction, their residents have been denied the rights of self-government enjoyed in other Alberta municipalities. The Rocky Mountain Park Act of 1887 established the communities as train and park service towns entirely under federal jurisdiction. From their beginning the communities were operated as fiefdoms, with the citizenry passive observers of town policy made by the federal government. Furthermore, the policy that land in the townsites could only be leased, not sold, gave the federal government an iron grip on long-range municipal planning and development.

The Natural Resources Transfer Agreement of 1930 does give Alberta limited and carefully circumscribed jurisdiction; it allows "Alberta laws to operate . . . to the extent they are not 'repugnant' to Federal laws and . . . taxing Acts to apply . . . unless expressly excluded by Federal laws."[30] As a consequence, the aspects of municipal functions now under provincial jurisdiction are: education, police protection, hospital and health services, recreation and culture (library services, etc.), building and fire inspection, and social services. But although the federal government has relinquished jurisdiction in these areas, two federal employees make and administer townsite policy: in each townsite the Park Superintendent formulates policy that is carried out by the Townsite Manager.

Citizen dissatisfaction with the federal government's autocratic municipal policy making led to the establishment of citizen advisory committees in Banff, in 1921, and in Jasper, in 1927. Members of these locally elected committees sat on various park committees administering the two communities. Over time, with the federal government pushed and cajoled to loosen its grip, the two administrations were given a modicum of power. In each town the advisory committee is especially important in providing representation on the school board, which has become an embryonic municipal administration. In recognition of the two municipalities' special status, provincial acts have been amended to allow the school board to levy taxes and provide library, recreation and social services, as well as educational ones. Furthermore, "the Banff and Jasper School Boards are considered as incorporated municipalities and thus eligible to receive certain local government grants and transfers."[31] The residents receive water, sewer and garbage collection services on a user pay basis.

After the federal government began to change its policies on leasing townsite lands in 1958, a number of studies looked at changing the status of the two communities to permit self-government.[32] The studies provoked an examination of the residents' plight but have not led to substantive policy changes. The federal government would like the residents to assume more of the communities' costs but is reluctant to allow self-government for fear that policies conflicting with general Parks Canada policy would be implemented. It seems that the federal government does not trust the judgment of the residents of Banff and Jasper.

Hospital Districts and the Changing Role of Health Responsibilities

The government's medical and public health responsibilities have changed dramatically in the past hundred years. At the turn of the century the only health responsibilities the government assumed were those involved in controlling epidemics and maintaining minimal health standards. Medical care and hospital service were regarded as purely private matters. For the most part, hospitals were administered and supported by churches and charitable societies. When the public finally accepted a governmental role in the provision of health facilities, the responsibility was felt to be a local one. Initially, hospitals were publicly supported in the large cities but were woefully lacking in rural areas, which did not have an adequate financial base.

In Alberta, a Public Health Act was enacted in 1906, but it was not until 1919 that health was considered important enough to justify establishment of a cabinet-level department of health. To stimulate the building and operation of hospitals by local governments, the provincial government provided a grant of 70 cents a day for each hospital patient. For financially strapped rural units of government the grant was far too small, and they could not afford to operate hospitals. The government enacted legislation to allow rural areas to assume health responsibilities. The Municipal Hospitals Act allowed a municipality to establish an independent hospital district and develop a hospitalization scheme to serve the district's residents.

The districts were designed to be strictly local institutions with strong policy-making and financial powers. To ensure continued political support, a district's creation was dependent on a favourable plebiscite. An elective board was the district's policy-making body and had wide-reaching power to purchase land, construct hospital facilities, operate an ambulance service and generally oversee hospital operations. The district obtained its revenue from three sources: patient fees, the 70-cents-per-day provincial grant, and requisitions from local units of government within its boundaries.

The first three districts were formed in 1918 and, by 1929, 19 were operational. Constrained by the scarcity of local fiscal resources during the Depression, few new districts were established during the 1930s, but when more local funds became available after the Second World War, their numbers grew rapidly, reaching 80 by 1960.

A new hospital policy was enacted in 1959 when plans were made to divide the province into 32 auxiliary hospital districts that would provide long-term treatment and care for patients with chronic illnesses. Then a curious policy twist was made in 1964. It is described in a recent Municipal Affairs bulletin:

> Upon the establishment of the Nursing Home Plan in 1964, it was decided to utilize the auxiliary district geographical divisions for the purposes of setting up nursing home districts in order to avoid a proliferation of district boards. By 1964, eighteen of the thirty-two auxiliary districts had been formally incorporated. The boards of these districts were empowered to construct and operate auxiliary hospitals. With the passing of the *Nursing Homes Act* that year, these eighteen boards exercised their option to apply for nursing home facilities in their districts

and became known as auxiliary hospital and nursing home districts.[33]

In areas not served by auxiliary hospital districts, nursing home districts have been established.

Another major change occurred in 1961 with the enactment of a new Hospitals Act that, among other provisions, provided for the establishment of general hospital districts. [34] In order to straighten out the tangle of the differing kinds of districts, the Hospitals Act was again changed in 1970, allowing establishment of multi-purpose health care districts. Municipal and general hospital districts were allowed to amalgamate with auxiliary hospital and/or nursing home districts and to operate under a single district board.[35]

Table 4.7
Alberta Hospital and Nursing Home Districts, 1982

Municipal and General Hospital Districts	49
General Hospital/Nursing Home Districts	15
General/Auxiliary Hospital/Nursing Home Districts	29
Auxiliary Hospital/Nursing Home Districts	13
Nursing Home Districts	4
Inactive Districts (those without established boards)	8

An examination of Table 4.7 shows well over 100 medical districts in Alberta. Despite the growth of publicly supported hospitals, many are still financed and administered by churches and charitable organizations. They are an important part of the province's overall health policy program since many contract with municipalities for the provision of health services.

With the provincial government increasingly accepting responsibility for health care, there have been major changes in the financing and policy making of hospital districts. The 1970 Alberta Hospitals Act eroded some of the grass-roots principles governing the establishment of earlier hospital districts. The Act empowered the Minister to establish a new hospital district through the Alberta Hospital Services Commission. The Commission would formulate the new district's program and submit it to the municipalities within the district's boundaries for their approval. Popular control over the district's policy-making body, the district board, were also eroded.

The district was divided into wards with some board members being appointed and others elected: ". . . the municipality with the largest population in each ward determines whether the representative (or in some cases representatives) from the ward shall be appointed or elected by all electors in the ward."[36] As a consequence of this arrangement, which potentially could have allowed the municipalities to control district policy making, only about half the hospital districts now have directly elected members and only a quarter are controlled by elected members.

In 1959 the province assumed full responsibility for hospital capital costs and previously incurred debt charges for capital projects. Since 1961 the province has assumed full responsibility for hospital operating costs. When a hospital district is formed it requisitions funds from municipalities within the district for the purchase of the hospital site; once the hospital is built, the district requisitions funds for external landscaping, paving and upkeep. Following are some 1981-1982 examples of site and paving costs to municipalities:

Metro Calgary Rocky View site development	$277,800
Medicine Hat General Hospital parking facilities	$71,578
Drumheller General Hospital parking lot	$25,000

The only other way a hospital district incurs capital liability is by purchasing equipment and making renovations the province feels are not necessary. The same rule applies for operating costs. The province will fund the hospital's operating costs at a specified level; if the hospital district wishes to provide additional service, it must either charge its users or requisition funds from the municipalities. It is much more common for a hospital district to requisition funds from its municipalities than to bill its users.

A particularly interesting aspect of the requisition process, which recognizes the importance of provincial support for hospital districts located in sparsely settled areas, is found in section 30 of the Alberta Hospitals Act: "When the funds available to an improvement district or special area included within a hospital district are insufficient to meet any requisition of the district board upon it, the Minister of Municipal Affairs may pay the sum . . . or in the absence of an appropriation therefore from the General Revenue Fund of the Province."

In addition to hospital districts, the provincial government has provided for the creation of auxiliary hospital districts (normally much larger in area than hospital districts) to serve the chronically ill and infirm. Auxiliary hospital districts use the same elective-appointive mechanism to fill their board positions as do hospital districts.

Irrigation Districts

Southern Alberta, with its sparse vegetation, long winters and hot, dry summers, was not attractive to settlers during the province's early period. It became apparent that, without irrigation, agriculture was much too risky. As a consequence, several large irrigation projects were developed with private financing, but they never became economically feasible. A legacy of this early entrepreneurship is the Alberta Railway and Irrigation Company and Canadian Pacific Railway irrigation works in southern Alberta that form part of the works of the present irrigation districts. Recognizing that private ventures would be inadequate, in 1915 Alberta enacted the Irrigation District Act allowing farmers in a given area to organize for the purpose of floating bond issues for construction of an irrigation project. From 1919 through 1968, six additional irrigation district acts were enacted for the benefit of the region's farmers. Then, in 1968, the government enacted a single uniform act to replace all previous irrigation legislation.

Today, almost one million acres in southern Alberta are serviced by 13 irrigation districts ranging in size from the Ross Creek District, with 1,319 acres, to the St. Mary River District, with 274,301 acres. The farmers holding land in an irrigation district elect a board of directors charged with policy making and administration. [37] The board has wide-ranging powers that may have a major effect on every farmer in its jurisdiction. Each year the board establishes an annual water rate to cover the cost of operating and maintaining the district. This is an extremely important function, since:

> Irrigation district rates are a charge against the land, and unpaid rates are a first lien against crops and other produce grown on that land. Such rates may also be the subject of 'rate-enforcement', a legal process described under the Act in which the title to the land in question may be transferred to the district and sold to recover the rates owing.

In addition, the Irrigation Act allows the board to arrange for government guaranteed loans for operating costs or capital replacement. Section 44(1)(F) of the Act also makes provisions for the board "to enter into agreements with the Government of Canada, the Government of Alberta, or with one or more local authorities for the cost sharing of constructing, extending, or rehabilitating the works of the district."

The size of a district's board of directors is determined by the size of the district. Under the Irrigation Act, the board consists of three directors where the assessment roll of the district shows 90,000 acres or less classified as irrigation land, five directors for 90,000 to 200,000 acres of irrigation land, and seven directors for districts containing more than 200,000 acres of irrigation land. The directors have a three-year term of office and the district has the discretion of having all members elected every three years or staggering the elections and holding them annually. Although board members are often elected by acclamation, the electoral turnout is relatively high: in the United Irrigation District and Western Irrigation District elections in 1980, the turnout rate was approximately 33 per cent, in the Eastern Irrigation District election in 1982, 37 per cent.

A district's administration is carried out by a manager appointed by and responsible to the board of directors. The manager is responsible for hiring and overseeing an administrative and operating staff and for keeping the district's records.

The irrigation district would seem to exemplify local self-government and grass-roots democracy. Its formation depends on a petition of landowners within the proposed district boundaries and the elected board of directors is given wide-ranging policy making and administrative powers. In addition, the Irrigation Act outlines in detail the procedure whereby a board is able to poll the district's electorate on questions of policy.[38] However, from the first Irrigation Act passed in 1915 to the present, the provincial government has been apprehensive about the amount of power it has given farmers to manage their own affairs: the irrigation council, a provincial agency members of which are appointed by the government, has the power to check and curb district boards.

The Irrigation Council consists of six water users and persons who are not members of the civil service appointed by the Minister of Agriculture, the Assistant Deputy Minister of Environmental Engineering Support Services, and the Director of the Irrigation Division of the Department of Agriculture. The chairperson of the council is selected by the Minister of Agriculture from the appointees.

Although the ostensible purpose of the council is to develop and co-ordinate a province-wide irrigation policy, in fact, at every turn it has the power to shape or overturn policy made by the locally elected boards. The all-important policy of setting an annual water rate by the district board must be approved by the Irrigation Council. The district board needs permission from the council before it is allowed to borrow money for capital projects. If the council finds that a board of directors has defaulted on its payments or decides that the board has not abided by the Irrigation Act, it has the power to dismiss any or all board members and appoint new ones. In short, irrigation district boards throughout the province are always operating in the shadow of the Irrigation Council.

The irrigation district boards work amazingly well. Most misunderstandings over rates, water flows and delinquent accounts are settled informally by the district manager and the board members. In the event that a question over assessment rates cannot be settled informally, the complainant has recourse to a Court of Revisions made up of all the board's members; dissatisfied complainants can appeal to the Alberta Assessment Appeal Board.

Irrigation districts have recently faced issues that are either insoluble or beyond their powers. A problem of the former type would be an expansion of the storage facilities of an irrigation reservoir, the likely effect of which would be to flood adjoining farmland. Although the district could expropriate the land, the result might well be an angry farmer bearing a life-long grudge against the district; also, taking a large acreage out of production means a loss of tax revenue. Such a divisive issue taxes a district's board to develop equitable policies.

Although irrigation districts have seldom been newsworthy in the past, they may become major political participants in the future as the provincial government considers a massive water diversification scheme. For several years the government has been studying the feasibility of transporting water from the Mackenzie Valley to drought-prone areas of southern Alberta. If the project is approved, new irrigation districts will be created and existing districts will be given greatly increased responsibilities. Hundreds of miles of new canals will be constructed and decisions will have to be made about who is to receive the water and at what price.

Drainage Districts

Irrigation policies and proposals for water diversion projects receive much publicity, but little is heard of drainage districts. In fact, few Albertans are aware of the existence of this grass-roots form of government in the central and western parts of the province. Nine drainage districts, ranging in size from 2,600 to 74,720 acres, have been established for flood control, lake-level stabilization, and improvement of soil drainage. The first, the Holden Drainage District, established in 1918, was followed by the Dickson and Daysland Districts in 1919, and the Hay Lakes District in 1922. The other five districts were not formed until the late 1940s and 1950s.

The policy-making and administrative structure of drainage districts is similar to that of irrigation districts. A board composed of three elected trustees is the policy-making body for the district and has the power to set drainage rates and to borrow money for drainage capital projects within the guidelines of the Drainage Districts Act.

Since the number of eligible voters in each district is very small (the largest has 166 ratepayers), an annual meeting is held where the eligible voters express their concerns and policy preferences to the district's board of trustees. Usually, members of the board of trustees are at the annual meeting and, in most cases, candidates are unopposed. An interesting twist in the election procedure is required under the Act. The district's secretary places the names of the trustees on a list "in order of the number of votes given for them, the trustee obtaining the lowest number of votes being placed first."[39] The trustee whose name appears first on the list retires to make room for the trustee elected. At their first meeting after the election the trustees elect a board chairperson from their own ranks. The board of trustees appoints the district's secretary-treasurer and other administrative and engineering personnel, although the secretary-treasurer often comprises the entire administrative structure.

Despite these trappings of a democratic form of government, the powers of the board of trustees have been neutralized by the provincial government. Overseeing all drainage districts is a drainage council composed of three members appointed by the Lieutenant-Governor in Council. Under the Act the drainage council has almost unlimited powers to curb district boards; it can require a board to furnish information on anything the board has done or is proposing to do; it must approve the rates set by the boards each year; and it has the power to "forbid an act or course of conduct proposed to be done or entered upon by a board." In short, drainage districts only appear to be autonomous institutions practising grass-roots democracy.

Those Confusing Hamlets

Since 1905 various provincial acts have made reference to hamlets, even though they have never been precisely defined. This imprecision has caused confusion about the number of hamlets in Alberta: several years ago the Peace River Planning Commission estimated approximately 900; more recently, a member of the Department of Municipal Affairs placed their number at around 300.

The 1981 federal census contains a belated reference to hamlets in the following definition of an unincorporated place: "A cluster of 5 or more permanently occupied dwellings, known by a locally recognized name and located within a rural municipality or unorganized territory. Unincorporated places do not have a local government; most of them do not have legal boundaries."[40] A footnote to the definition states: "Sometimes referred to as a VILLAGE, SETTLEMENT or HAMLET." In contrast, The Municipal Government Act defines a hamlet in terms of land rather than numbers of dwellings. Section 1(f) states that a hamlet "means":

  i. an area of land subdivided into lots and blocks as a townsite, a plan of which is registered in a land titles office,

  ii. an area of land as defined by clause(s) (i) and (iii) on which are erected improvements used for purposes other than farming purposes, or

  iii. an area declared by an order of the minister to be a hamlet.

But section 277 of the Act also refers to numbers of dwelling units. Upon petition by a majority of a hamlet's property owners, a municipal district is required to spend at least 50 per cent of the taxes collected in the hamlet on "public works within the hamlet." However, this provision "applies only to a hamlet in which there are at least 10 dwellings." The County Act has yet another definition of a hamlet: section 1(a)(v) states that, for the purpose of the Act, a hamlet is a unit "(as defined in the Municipal Government Act) that has a population of 5000 or more persons." This definition was made to bring a single hamlet under the aegis of the Act, since only the County of Strathcona's Sherwood Park met the definition and so became a hamlet.[41] Although hamlets are imprecisely defined and are not recognized as governmental units, they are recognized in several municipal financial assistance programs and for very limited electoral and taxing purposes. The Alberta Hamlets Street Assistance Program provides grants for street improvements, and there are other assistance programs for the construction of hamlet water and sewer systems. In addition, for some time the provincial government has treated the hamlet of Sherwood Park as if it were a city for policing grants. Section 177 of the Municipal Government Act gives legitimacy to an election held in a hamlet for the remission of tax revenue to it. Section 261 of the Act allows a municipal district to levy a special tax on all property in a hamlet to pay for "the drilling of a well, the provision of a reservoir, and the provision of equipment therefore in any hamlet to provide a supply of water for the residents."

With municipal administrators and elected officials confused by the different, imprecise definitions of hamlets, the delegates at the

1983 convention of the Alberta Association of Municipal Districts and Counties passed a resolution requesting the provincial government to define a hamlet precisely. Shortly thereafter, the County of Strathcona proposed a boundary for the hamlet of Sherwood Park, which was to be renamed an Urban Service Area. The county's reasoning was twofold: to enable Sherwood Park to "be recognized by all Provincial Departments as an urban area for the purpose of calculating provincial grant eligibility"[42] and to define boundaries for the purpose of representation on the county's education committee. With the confusion over what is and what is not a hamlet, there is little doubt that the government will either have to define the term precisely (along with its legal status) or delete it entirely from legislation.

The Northeast Alberta Regional Commission: Unique, Controversial and Undemocratic

With the development of the Syncrude oil sands plant at Fort McMurray in 1973 and 1974, men and materials were being brought into the area so quickly that a public service catastrophe seemed imminent. The provincial government responded by creating the Northeast Alberta Regional Commission on June 6, 1974. Its mandate was to ensure that the public services, facilities and accommodations needed for the development of the oil sands were "provided in an orderly and efficient manner." More specifically, the commission was to co-ordinate provincial government policy and interests with those of municipalities and the private sector in the provision of housing, educational facilities and urban planning in the Fort McMurray area. The commission's secondary function was to ensure that, if the area's unprecedented growth continued, there would be minimum friction between government and the private sector. From the time it was created the commission was controversial, for it gave almost unlimited powers to its single commissioner appointed by the Lieutenant-Governor in Council.

The commissioner's powers allowed him to override certain provincial legislation and to formulate policy and carry it out at will. Under Section 7(2) of the Act the commissioner could:

    i. in the name of the local authority, exercise the power, duty or right so as to bind the local authority,

    ii. by his order, do anything that a local authority is required to do by by-law or resolution, and

iii. by his signature alone, execute any agreement or other document to be signed on behalf of the local authority.

Under the same section it goes on to say that a local authority *may not exercise*:

i. the power, duty or right assigned, or

ii. any other power, duty or right so as to effectively interfere with the exercise by the Commissioner of any power, duty or right assigned to him.

Finally, Section 8(1) states:

In order to enable the Commissioner to carry out his functions with the diligence and dispatch that the circumstances may require, the Lieutenant Governor in Council may make regulations, with respect to the Region, varying, substituting, adding to or making inapplicable any of the provisions of the following Acts and the regulations thereunder: (a) The Improvement Districts Act; (b) The New Towns Act; (c) The Municipal Government Act; (d) The Municipal Election Act; (e) The Municipal Taxation Act; (f) The Planning Act; (g) The Local Authorities Act; (h) The School Act; (i) The School Election Act; (j) The Northland School Division Act; (k) The Alberta Hospitals Act; (l) The Health Unit Act.

The only power denied the commissioner was the authority to levy a tax or impose a license fee in the region.

Fortunately, the commission's first and only commissioner, R. V. Henning, was "low key" and had no interest in exercising all of his powers. As the Fort McMurray boom gained momentum, Henning ensured that the necessary public service infrastructure was put in place. In 1975 he took one of his first major actions when he over-ruled provincial legislation preventing new school construction until the existing schools were 80 per cent filled. Without additional space, the expected influx of new families would be unable to place their children in the school system. Henning knew that the situation had to be rectified.

In September of 1982, the commission discontinued its operation and, in the spring of 1983, the Alberta government phased it out, the Minister of Municipal Affairs explaining that circumstances had changed. However, the commission's demise began in 1980 when Fort McMurray was granted city status and the power to manage its own affairs. With the collapse of the Alsands Project and a delay in the Cold Lake Project, the boom had clearly ended, and with it the need for the commission. It is only an oversight by the government that the Northeast Alberta Regional Commission Act has never been rescinded.

Regional Service Commissions: New Form of Local Government For the Future?

On December 2, 1981, the provincial legislature passed the Regional Municipal Services Act which created a new and innovative form of local government, the multi-purpose regional service commission. Section 3 of the Act states that the objectives of the commissions are "to provide water, sanitary and storm sewerage and waste management services, or any of them, with respect to more than one municipality." The Act gave a newly created commission substantial powers, including expropriation of a municipal utility within the district's boundaries and the ability to float bonds and debentures to finance the building and operation of water and sewer plants and lines, and sanitary disposal sites.

Since the boundaries of a service commission would encompass several municipalities, representation on a commission board is by individual municipality, each of which designates members from its council. This mechanism provides indirect representation for the district's public. The size of the commission board and the number of representatives from each member municipality is determined by the Minister of Municipal Affairs.[43] Since no commissions have been established it is unclear whether each municipality will have a single vote or whether there will be proportional representation.

It is not coincidental that the functions and political structure of regional service commissions closely resemble those of the regional service districts in existence in British Columbia for a number of years. In 1975 the Alberta Department of Environment decided to carry out a study to determine "the most appropriate way to develop the water supply and sewage disposal facilities . . . to the year 2001" for the Edmonton metropolitan region.[44] With a number of provincial departments, the Edmonton Regional Planning Commission, and a number of private consultants involved, a comprehensive study was carried out and a seven-volume report released in July, 1978, just before Edmonton's expansion bid. When the report recommended that several regional authorities be established to develop and provide water and sewer facilities on a regional basis, the City of Edmonton criticized the study proposals since they undercut the arguments the city was making for its massive expansion. However, the region's outlying municipalities gave guarded approval to the proposals, for they could see regional authorities as a feasible alternative to amalgamation with the City of Edmonton.[45]

The provincial government's decision allowed the city some expansion but the government also maintained the autonomy of outlying governmental units. Still, it was thought that there was a need for some services to be carried out on a region-wide basis. The Department of Municipal Affairs then employed a consultant to determine a commission's boundaries and the functions and membership of a planned Edmonton Regional Municipal Services Commission. Surprisingly, the report recommended that Edmonton should not be given a vote on the commission, although the city would be central in any commission to be established since it owned the major facilities. Undoubtedly, the key factor was Edmonton's resistance to being a member.

There is little doubt that regional service commissions will eventually be established throughout the province. This new form of government somewhat dilutes local autonomy though it does serve regional needs.

An Overview of Alberta's Specialized Forms of Government

At first glance it may seem the province is covered with a patchwork quilt of specialized units of government, the boundaries or, for that matter, the very existence of which show little logic; but closer examination shows clearly that each unit provides its residents with useful services. The multiplicity of governments is a testimonial to local self-determination and grass-roots democracy. However, unless local units of government are responsive to socio-economic changes, viable local government will not survive. The demographic profile of the province is changing. In some rural areas the population is aging, while in others resource development has brought in many new families. Needless to say, areas with aging populations have far different needs than do those with surging young populations. The people living in a particular area are best able to identify problems and to formulate the most appropriate policies to deal with them. However, if the locally elected officials abrogate their responsibilities and fail to respond to new and diverse demands, the provincial government cannot be faulted if it takes over badly managed functions of government.

If there has been a weakness in the activities of Alberta's specialized units of government, it has been the tendency of their elected representatives to see themselves primarily as administrators. Even an efficient administrator using the most modern budgetary procedures cannot identify a community's needs; only adequate communication between the citizenry and its elected representatives will allow those representatives to ascertain the citizenry's needs and respond to them.

Although much has been written about political accountability, its importance has been neglected in the study of specialized forms of local government. For whatever reason, it seems that political accountability in Alberta has never been an important issue outside the province's two largest cities.

Finally, unless the provincial government has a firm commitment to community self-rule and grass-roots democracy, all the time and effort dedicated to democratizing local government and making it responsive to the citizenry will be lost. The Department of Municipal Affairs is to be commended for its new policy of encouraging self-government for financially viable improvement districts; but this is only a small step in the province's progress toward local self-government. A commitment to having educational policy made at the community level is needed. Some mechanism must be devised to democratize the policy-making process in special areas. Hospital districts are no longer popularly controlled by elective boards, as the boards have come to be dominated by appointed members. The province should reverse this trend if it is committed to local democracy. Self-rule for irrigation and drainage districts is only a veneer, since provincially appointed boards can circumvent the district's locally elected governing bodies. This situation must be rectified.

No one will deny that the provincial government should have the power to implement province-wide policies dealing with local government issues. Nevertheless, the provincial government also should have a commitment to local autonomy and grass-roots democracy. The two are not incompatible. If the provincial government would meet, confide in, and negotiate and exchange information with the local governments, it would find the citizenry at the local level at least as concerned as itself about solving vexing local government problems. Rather than taking a paternalistic stance toward local government, the province should treat local governments as equal partners. Only by establishing this kind of relationship can the provincial government implement province-wide policy while simultaneously maintaining a commitment to local autonomy and grass-roots democracy.

In summary, one can say that the province's local units of government are a bit untidy and must engage in constant negotiation and compromise among themselves and with the provincial government. In short, each unit of government acts politically to further the needs of its own citizens; collectively, this activity promotes the general interest of all the citizens. The patchwork quilt of special units of government is a recognition that, for democracy to flourish, government must be small enough to be responsive to the citizenry. Moreover, it is an acknowledgement that government in rural areas is more than administration; it requires a political unit that is responsive to its constituents.

As the province moves toward the 1990s, some outmoded special units of government will be replaced by governmental structures better able to respond to social and technological changes. Undoubtedly, units of government will be amalgamated to meet unforeseen challenges. The extent of the province's commitment to grass-roots democracy will determine the shape, structure and viability of Alberta's specialized units of government for the coming decades.

Notes

1. A herd district could be formed when two-thirds of the voters in not less than four townships made application to the Lieutenant-Governor. To form a fire district, a majority of persons with three months residence in the proposed district (minimum area 36 square miles, maximum area 144 square miles) made application to the Lieutenant-Governor. Each resident was taxed four dollars a year, payable by labouring at the rate of one dollar a day, or two dollars a day for a person with a team of horses.

2. MacIntosh, 'Opening speech."

3. Hanson, *Local Government in Alberta*, 24-25.

4. The rural municipalities were also empowered to co-operate in the formation of hospital districts and hail insurance districts. In addition, the collection of tax arrears was transferred from the Department of Municipal Affairs to the rural municipalities.

5. For a discussion of "the Ryerson tradition" see Child, "The Ryerson Tradition in Western Canada."

6. Hanson,*Local Government in Alberta*, 11.

7. *Ibid.*, 47.

8. *Ibid.*, 48.

9. Kratzmann, Byrne and Worth, *A System in Conflict*, 6-7.

10. When an equalization formula is applied in the funding of any government program, provisions are made so that poor jurisdictions receive

more funds than wealthy ones. For example, if an equalization formula were used in computing the per-student education grant, a poor district might receive $1,600 per student for those in grades one through six, while a wealthy district might receive only $1,400.

11. Hanson, *Local Government in Alberta*, 62.

12. For example, Eric Hanson wistfully writes, "It is to be hoped that the number of counties will increase in the future, and that, somehow, hospital districts can be tucked in under the county quilt." *Ibid.*, 69.

13. In recent years another serious problem in educational representation has arisen: if a county councillor or the reeve is a sworn elector of a separate school district he or she is ineligible to sit on the council's education committee, since it is the county's public board of education. If only one or two councillors are separate school supporters it is possible, although difficult, for the council to carry out its educational responsibilities. However, if most of council's members are separate school supporters, the council is prevented from carrying out its responsibilities. If a reeve is a separate school supporter he or she is placed in an impossible position: the reeve sits *ex officio* on all county boards, commissions and committees and, therefore, automatically is a member of the education committee; however, being a separate school supporter the encumbent is ineligible to be on the committee. The problem will remain irresolvable until changes are made in County Act.

14. Leduc had been considering applying for city status for some time. A study had found an independent school district feasible. In addition, with city status the municipality would be eligible for larger transportation grants from the province. Fort Saskatchewan and Spruce Grove have also considered applying for city status in order to control their own school systems.

15. A manifestation of the tax controversy occurred at the 1983 annual convention of the Alberta Association of Municipal Districts and Counties. Rural councillors voted down their association's recommendation "that all residences be assessed at 65 per cent of depreciated replacement value, with no exemptions, and the base rate of farmland, with residences on them, be lowered." *Red Deer Advocate*, March 31, 1983.

16. Alberta acts applying only to the Alberta portion of the city are the Municipalities Assessment and Equalization Act (chapter 252), the Electric Power and Pipeline Assessment Act (chapter 119), the Crown Property Municipal Grants Act (chapter 82), the Municipal and Provincial Properties Valuation Act (chapter 248), section 41 of the Alberta Government Telephones Act (chapter 12) and section 129 of the School Act (chapter 329).

17. Hanson, *Local Government in Alberta*, 87-88.

18. *Municipal Counsellor*, 20, 2.

19. The improvement districts are numbered one through 24. However, district No. 1 is an amalgamation of districts No. 1, No. 2 and No. 3, and district No. 10 is an amalgamation of districts No. 10 and No. 11.

20. Section 14(1) of the Improvement District Act states, "The Minister may in any district appoint an advisory committee of one or more persons."

21. *Alberta Legislative Assembly Debates*, 17th Legislature, 3rd Session, 1975.

22. In the first session of the 1972 legislature, when the issue was whether "resident advisory committees" should have more power, both the government members and the opposition suggested that some improvement districts should be upgraded so that they might contribute a much larger share of funds for their operation. *Alberta Legislative Debates*, 17th Legislature, First Session, 76-77.

23. The Department of Municipal Affairs is also encouraging economic development in the Métis settlements. The three goals of the economic development program are: "to support employment and ownership opportunities for settlement residents, to promote steady economic growth on a local level, and establish an independent system to assess capital resources." In the spring of 1982, five Métis settlements received a $610,000 provincial grant to be used as seed money for economic ventures.

24. At an annual ratepayers meeting in 1978, a motion was passed requesting the Local Advisory Council to initiate a study on the feasibility of greater local autonomy for the district.

25. I.D. No. 1 residents were told that the average equalized assessment for municipal districts and counties is $82 million whereas, in their I.D., it is $185 million. Residents in I.D. No. 10 were told that, "the average assessment per capita in the area is $19,821, nearly double the per-capita figure of $11,423 in other M.D.s in Alberta." I.D. No. 10's manager also pointed out that the I.D. could easily bear the cost of the change in status, for it had a $5 million reserve for capital expenditures and a $4 million operating reserve.

26. *Medicine Hat News*, March 22, 1984.

27. Alternatively, the government could employ the same strategy it used to introduce the county system.

28. Hanson, *Local Government in Alberta*, 87.

29. *Calgary Herald*, March 9, 1983.

30. *The Park Town of Banff*, 5.

31. *Ibid.*, 37.

32. Crawford, *Report of the Institute of Local Government*, 24-28; Canada, *Report of the Royal Commission on Government Organization*, vol. 2, 38-40; Plunkett, *et al.*, *Municipal Government for Banff Townsite*, 36-44; Canada, *Sixth Report on*

Northern Affairs and National Resources, 131-182; Parks Canada, *Resident Involvement in Park Townsite Administration; The Banff-Jasper Autonomy Report; The Park Town of Banff.*

33. *Municipal and Local Administrative Bodies in Alberta,* 44.

34. General hospitals were defined as those providing "acute" or "active" care.

35. If an amalgamation involves a municipal hospital district, the newly amalgamated unit is called a general hospital district.

36. *Task Force on Urbanization and the Future,* 29.

37. Technically, two types of district are designated by the Act. In one, the district has an outer boundary with all of the parcels encompassed by the boundary considered to be in the district. However, only those parcels receiving water are on the assessment roll. The second type is described as a "parcel system" in which only those parcels on the assessment roll are considered to be in the district.

38. However, the provincial government does not completely trust the judgment of the Irrigation District's voters, for section 105(7) of the Act states: "The Board is not bound by the results of a vote on a question . . . to do or to abstain from doing any act or thing."

39. Under section 32(2) of the Act "if there has been no voting or the number of votes cast for one or more trustees is equal, the trustees shall be placed on the order unanimously agreed on by the trustees, and in default of unanimous agreement then in the alphabetical order of their surnames."

40. *1981 Census Dictionary,* 55.

41. Sherwood Park is also singled out in the Election Act. Section 26 states: "On or before September 30 the enumerator shall prepare for his subdivisions a complete list of names of those persons indicated by the enumeration to be qualified electors, organized . . . (b) for a rural electoral division . . . in the case of . . . (c) a hamlet that has a population in excess of 10,000 persons . . . ." This provision was inserted specifically for Sherwood Park since no other hamlet in the province meets the population provision.

42. "A Proposed Boundary for Sherwood Park," 3.

43. It should be noted that the Act allows representation on the commission board of pertinent improvement districts, special areas, Indian reserves and military bases, all at the discretion of the Minister of Municipal Affairs.

44. *Edmonton Regional Utilities Study,* i.

45. In April, 21 councillors and government officials primarily from Edmonton's outlying municipalities spent three days in Vancouver examining the regional district concept employed in British Columbia and the advantages and disadvantages accruing to municipalities that were

members of the Greater Vancouver Regional District. They learned that the district had begun some 10 years before as a water and sewer board and had grown to include hospitals, pollution control, regional planning, regional parks, and even labour relations (today it also includes regional transportation). Although Edmonton's chief corporate planner did not believe a regional district was appropriate for the Edmonton region, most representatives from the outlying areas were enthusiastic about the concept.

5

ELECTED OFFICIALS
IN THE
POLICY-MAKING PROCESS

Introduction: Policy Theories and Explanations

A lot of inkwells have been drained by armies of academics, government reformers and practitioners, newspaper reporters and citizen's groups on how and why politicians and administrators make and carry out public policy. Some argue that the community's wealthy, in some way controlling the politicians and administrators, indirectly control public policy.[1] There are, however, so many examples of municipal policies discriminating against wealth and position that this model must be regarded as failing to explain all facets of municipal policy making.[2]

Not too long ago it was assumed that decision makers arrive at decisions through a rational, step-by-step process. Two students of policy making sum up the central theme of the "rational model":

> The ideal way to make policy is to choose among alternatives after careful and complete study of all possible courses of action, all their possible consequences and after an evaluation of those consequences in the light of one's values. That is to say, ideally one treats the policy question as an intellectual problem; one does not look upon a policy question as calling for the exercise of something called "political forces."[3]

The steps employed in this model are:

1. identify the problem;

2. identify and clarify which goals would solve the problem and then rank them according to their relative importance;

134

3. identify all alternative policies that would achieve each identified goal;

4. assess the costs and benefits of each alternative policy;

5. select the goal and the policy to achieve it that would provide the maximum benefits at the least cost with the least number of unwanted side effects.

In short, the rational theory of policy making maintains that policy makers who employ this strategy are above bureaucratic politics, internal council dissension, personality politics and the influence of neighbourhood and other interest groups. The rational model makes a number of other questionable assumptions, the first being that a problem can be clearly identified and that policy goals can be delineated and then ranked. In the real world, the definition of problems and policy goals often turns out to be subjective, and all too often policy is formulated, although "the problem" has never been clearly defined. Moreover, identifying problems and ranking policies constitute a substantial part of the politics on city councils, since this process reflects the members' different definitions of problems and of the weights to be assigned to policy goals. The second assumption is that governments have a large number of administrative personnel assigned to gathering and processing information. This is not even the case in large cities and, in smaller communities, the secretary-treasurer has little or no time to gather and process information on policy issues; hence, most decision making tends to be a "seat of the pants" exercise. Third, the assumption that decision makers have unlimited time to identify problems and rank goals is implicit in the model. In the real world, some issues require an immediate decision; seldom can a problem be put aside for six months or a year while the council explores all the goals it affects and all the policies that could be used to deal with it. Finally, the rational approach assumes that, once the particular goal and policy is found, council will adopt it in spite of politics. But politics is integral to the policy process. In short, while the rational model of decision making has some appeal for practitioners and students of local government, it neither recognizes the complexity of issues facing municipal councils nor accounts for political issues, which are most often the primary factors in municipal decision making.

It should now be clear that there is no single method of policy making but that community and political circumstances generally determine the way policies are made. A general principle underlying almost all policy making is that decision makers tend to eliminate policies that are unpredictable. A council feels more comfortable making policy by relying on past policy precedents; hence, while innovative policies may be discussed, they are usually discarded in favour of more predictable and familiar policies. The fact that council members tend to be no more disposed to gamble with the municipality's resources than they are with their own is an almost equally important consideration. For these reasons, community policy making tends to perpetuate the status quo.

Incremental Policy Making

If there is another general principle of municipal policy making, it is that councils attempt to avoid controversy by relying on routine methods in making decisions. Incremental budgeting is an example. At budget time, rather than evaluate the merits of each policy area, the council increases all departmental budgets by a fixed percentage, which usually approximates the inflation rate. The "spend-service" routine is also common: rather than evaluate an inadequate service and its administration, councils tend to pour in more money, hoping to rectify the inadequacy.

This policy-making process takes place in the context of general municipal goals. Almost all municipalities have general goals, such as making the community a good place to raise a family and preventing population decline. Such goals are often couched in terms so general that two diametrically opposing policies can be interpreted as leading to the same goal.[4]

Moreover, although policies are often rationalized in terms of furthering a general community goal, the impetus for a specific council policy decision is normally a response to a problem at hand. Over time, the council makes a series of adjustments to keep community conflict, tensions and criticism within bounds. One year the major problem may be a deteriorating road network; the next year it may be property destruction by gangs of juveniles. Each time the council tackles the problem at hand. This "real-world" process of decision making (designated *incrementalism*) was first outlined by Charles Lindblom and further refined by Amitai Etzioni.[5] Lindblom coined the term *muddling through* to describe the activities of decision makers who are continually making incremental changes in policy rather than employing a comprehensive, rational approach. He further postulated that issues and problems were political and demanded political responses. Thomas Dye added another dimension to incrementalism when he wrote:

The characteristics of policy-makers themselves also recommend the incremental model. Rarely do human beings act to maximize all of their values; more often they act to satisfy particular demands. Men are pragmatic: they seldom search for the "one best way" but instead end their search when they find "a way that will work." This search usually begins with the familiar—that is, with policy alternatives close to current policies. Only if these alternatives appear to be unsatisfactory will the policy maker venture out toward more radical innovation. In most cases modification of existing programs will satisfy particular needs, and the major policy shifts required to maximize values are overlooked.[6]

Lindblom was unduly criticized for advocating conservatism in policy making, despite the fact that he was only attempting to explain how the process actually operates. A more telling criticism was that the theory failed to explain policy makers' concern with long-range goals, since incrementalism, by its nature, prevents decision makers from working towards general goals.[7] Amitai Etzioni developed a hybrid model of incrementalism, dubbed *mixed scanning*, that met the criticism. He suggested that policy makers pursue very general long-range goals by occasional "scanning," while making a series of incremental policies. If they are moving too far from their general goals, policy makers will change the direction of their line of incremental decisions. Thus, in dovetailing general goals with incrementalism, Etzioni seems to explain the real world of policy making.

How the Fundamental Direction of Policy Making is Changed

A dramatic change in the socio-economic composition of a community invariably results in a fundamental change in its policy direction. An example is found in an examination of a community on the outskirts of Edmonton. Spruce Grove had a population of 465 in 1961, 598 in 1966, 1,110 in 1970, and 10,784 in 1982. In two decades Spruce Grove had become a large bedroom community for Edmonton as many young families were attracted by its cheaper housing. In 1966 the community spent $2.47 per capita for recreation and community services; by 1970 this amount had increased to $13.34. The younger population increased the demand for recreation, resulting in a substantial policy shift in only four years.[8]

For very different reasons, the fundamental direction of municipal policy making is often changed by the provincial government, either directly through legislation or indirectly through manipulation of the grant structure. Legislation is often enacted to force municipalities to make major policy shifts, from taking new directions in planning to giving greater consideration to environmental factors. Other provincial policies may have unanticipated and unintended but dramatic spin-off effects on municipalities. As a hypothetical example, a new provincial agricultural policy supporting a particular segment of agriculture may encourage young farmers to move into certain municipalities or farmers' children to remain on the farm. In either case, affected municipalities would face new problems and would be forced to re-evaluate their spending priorities.

The grant structure, which will be examined in a following chapter, is often used to induce municipalities to make major policy shifts without making the province seem dictatorial. *Conditional matching grants* (i.e., grants, designated for a specific project, that require the recipient to allocate funds for the project equivalent to a percentage of the provincial grant) often require a municipality to make major shifts in its spending priorities.

Finally, a well-organized community group is often able to bring about fundamental changes in policy direction. More often than not, if a group has politically astute leadership and committed members, the council will heed its demands, even if it means a radical departure from existing policy.

Although campaigning councillors and mayors often pledge to shift municipal policy to an entirely different direction, they seldom carry out their promises. The principal reason for this failure is that a member of council simply does not have the political power to mobilize other council members to change policy direction. As was emphasized in Chapter 2, the various structures of local government in Alberta act to fragment political power at the local level. Moreover, when this fragmentation is combined with the absence of an informal mechanism to consolidate and concentrate political power (i.e., a well developed local party system), the council member with "deviant ideas and program proposals" gives up attempting to bring about major policy changes. Furthermore, the newly elected "firebrand" is soon socialized into the "norms and ways of doing things" on council; the new member either conforms or is ignored or even ostracized.

Since the bureaucracy generally resists change, it plays an exceedingly important role in any attempt to change the fundamental direction of policy making. There are several reasons for this resistance. First, the nature of any bureaucracy is to settle into a routine that has been established with much effort, time and money; any major change will force its members to learn a new routine. Second, the greater the change in policy, the less predictable are its effects on the organization. Thus, a major policy change may threaten job security, personal power, bureaucratic status and income. Another reason for bureaucratic resistance is presented by a leading authority on administrative behaviour, who presents the following propositions:

The more officials affected, the greater will be the resistance to significant change. Hence:

1. The larger the organization, the more reluctant it will be to adopt any given change.

2. Small bureaus tend to be more flexible and innovation minded than larger ones.

3. One way to speed the adoption of a given change is to design it so that it affects the smallest possible numbers of persons.[9]

The irony is that the highly professionalized bureaucracy has the expertise to develop well-conceived, innovative policy alternatives for the elected decision makers, yet the bureaucracy is one of the most conservative forces in government.

The Mayor as Chief Policy Maker?

The second chapter pointed out that, in Alberta, the mayor does not have the powers normally given to a chief executive in government; the mayor has neither the power to hire and fire members of the administration nor the very limited veto power over council's activities found in several other provinces. Therefore, to build a power base for the exercise of leadership in policy making, the politically astute mayor attempts to gain widespread public support. Council members tend to defer to a mayor with strong public support, realizing that they may not be re-elected if the public sees them as engaged in an attempt to sabotage the mayor's program.

Building Public Support

Being elected at-large, the mayor is seen as having a much broader mandate than do councillors elected from wards. In addition, the fact that he or she is perceived as the community's leader gives the mayor a distinct advantage over other council members. It is the mayor who is invited to perform ceremonial functions, from commemorating new municipal projects to entertaining visiting dignitaries. The mayor attends endless business, ceremonial and testimonial breakfasts, lunches, dinners and after-dinner events, along with an occasional wedding reception and christening. Such functions give the mayor the opportunity not only to build political support but also subtly to reward supporters and punish detractors by attending some events and politely refusing to attend others. Depending upon the occasion, the astute mayor may make a subtle (and often not so subtle) plea for community unity and policies.

In larger communities, where personalized politics is less feasible, the mayor often relies on the news media. Reporters are given "inside stories" on city hall in a tacit exchange for favourable publicity. In both Calgary and Edmonton, radio stations have donated public service time to the mayor for the presentation of non-political reports to the people. These "non-political reports" occasionally include mild recriminations of a balky council. When the council is discussing an important issue, it is the mayor's opinion reporters seek. The mayor, by virtue of the office, has an overwhelming advantage in reaching the public. Other elected officials and administrators are rarely invited to make their views known on radio and television and are given much less coverage in community newspapers. Perhaps their only advantage is that their activities are scrutinized much less closely by the news media than are those of the mayor.

Both Calgary and Edmonton have had mayors who were masters at marshalling public support. In Edmonton, William Hawrelak, who served as mayor from 1951 through 1959, had such strong public support that even when found guilty of "gross misconduct" in a land transaction and forced to resign, he was re-elected in 1963. He assiduously cultivated his own Ukrainian community and other ethnic communities. Bolstered by the overwhelming support of the electorate and by the sheer force of his personality, his policies were supported by council after council. In the same city, in the fall of 1983, Laurence Decore wove together a coalition of ethnics, young professionals and youth to capture the mayor's chair.[10] A disarming and shrewd politician, Decore won with an overwhelming vote and continued to maintain his popularity by immediately embarking on a number of innovative policies. His high level of public support, coupled with regular pre-council "tea parties" with council members has gained the support of almost all of the councillors for his new programs. This support is particularly unusual since the council has a 15-year tradition of divisiveness, in-fighting and opposing its executive. Rod Sykes, mayor of Calgary from 1968 to 1977, used a different strategy: he found that he could maintain a high level of public support by being abrasive with councillors who threatened his programs. This tactic, combined with his "boosting" of business in a city with a strong business ethic (Sykes had been vice president of Marathon Realty, the real estate arm of Canadian Pacific), intimidated council members, who grudgingly supported his policies. Like Hawrelak and Decore, he had a strong personality, but he used it in a very different way.

A mayor's power base depends in part on a set of community traditions elevating the status of the mayor. Donald Higgins briefly discusses the implications of these traditions:

> It is . . . not unusual for certain traditions to develop around the office of mayor, traditions that in effect endow it with extra power. For example, the decisions on which members of council or which non-elected citizens should sit on which committees, boards, commissions, and authorities is sometimes delegated to the mayor. Similarly, it is common for mayors to initiate much of the action in council, and to represent the city in negotiations with other governments and other outside interests . . . .[11]

The Mayor's Power Base on Council

A mayor relying only on his or her position as community leader is in a tenuous position: an astute council member attuned to the electorate and unwilling to defer to the mayor's leadership may undermine his or her authority. An example is found in Blake's 1967 study of the Edmonton council. Five of the councillors he interviewed stated that they were the equal of the mayor in policy making. One told him: "As I see it, in Edmonton there was a tendency on the part of councils to accept that their mayor and commissioners run the city. Council has equal responsibility with the mayor in the development of policy."[12]

The most effective way to build and maintain power on council is to control a strong and cohesive local party organization.[13] For some time there have been sporadic attempts in Edmonton and Calgary to build strong party organizations but, as we shall see in Chapter 10, they have encountered a number of obstacles, not least of which is the public's reluctance to having full-blown party politics at the local level. Consequently, the mayor is forced to rely on other methods.

Although the mayor has little more formal power on council than any single councillor, it is the mayor who is looked to for direction in policy making at the first meeting of a newly elected council. Unless the mayor loses momentum in his or her role as council's leader, members of council and the administration will bring forward suggestions, expecting them to be synthesized into concrete legislative proposals that the mayor can present to council. Normally, it is the mayor, working in conjunction with the clerk, who sets the council's agenda; a shrewd mayor can manipulate council's behaviour by placing a contentious issue at the end of the agenda, where it is likely to be dispensed with quickly by tired council members. Under the Municipal Government Act, the mayor presides at all council meetings. The astute mayor can give the appearance of being fair and even-handed and still steer the council subtly in a particular direction.

But exercising leadership is far more than having the aura of authority by virtue of setting the council agenda and presiding at its meetings. If the mayor falters in setting the direction of policy making, the vacuum may be filled by an ambitious councillor, although this rarely happens. It hardly needs to be said that the wielder of the gavel has power only if council members heed his or her dictates; there are innumerable instances of mayors pounding their gavels to no avail while the council is in a state of bedlam.

To exercise leadership while one has access to few formal powers is truly an art. Politics is compromise and a mayor can exercise leadership only by knowing when to compromise and how much can be conceded without emasculating the legislative program. The politically discerning mayor knows which council members are serving from a sense of duty, which are there to further business connections and which are politically ambitious; the mayor's appeals, promises and compromises are different for each group.

Nothing can be more destructive to legislative programs than a council fraught with politics revolving around personalities. The astute mayor focuses on issues and avoids personality discussions so as not to compromise his or her ability to gain support. However, this strategy does not require that the mayor avoid close personal friendships. Fragmentary evidence indicates that a mayor's friendships with key council members are extremely important in gaining support for his or her policy proposals. An examination of council voting behaviour in Edmonton found that friendship patterns among council members and the mayor was the best predictor of how members would vote.[14] It would be logical to assume that friendship patterns would be equally important in other Alberta communities.

In Alberta's smaller communities some of the most acrimonious politics have arisen because a mayor failed to exercise leadership: the consequence is often a power vacuum on council. For example, in the Town of Hanna in 1981, the mayor, elected to office on a platform of tax reduction, failed to gain council's support. Frustrated at having no formal powers to enforce policy or to sanction council, he resigned. A similar situation developed in the Town of Irvine in 1982. The mayor seemed to be politically inept, for he was charged by one dissident council member with "dictatorial tactics" and with not allowing councillors "the opportunity to participate in decisions." Another councillor charged that "the decisions are all reached beforehand by the mayor."[15] The mayor resigned. Two months later, in the Town of Granum, four of the town's six councillors resigned after accusing the mayor of being an autocrat. The councillors maintained that he made many important decisions without advising council and often arbitrarily reversed council decisions without its knowledge. In some instances council members have made conscious effort to undermine the mayor's image as the community leader. For example, in the Village of Cayley in 1981, a councillor refused to accord the mayor the respect to which he felt he was entitled as a community leader. The councillor, an avid proponent of "open government," consistently tried to undermine the credibility of the mayor in council meetings. In Hinton, a two-year resident and political novice won the mayoralty contest in 1983 on a reform platform. Charging that the previous council was a tool of private land developers and that many of its members were in conflict of interest, she alienated those members of council who had been re-elected. After a stormy four months in office, she in turn was charged with conflict of interest and she resigned. In a parting shot at council she said, "Enough is enough. They never allowed me to do my job because of who I worked for."[16]

The Council's Policy-Making Function

In Alberta, with the mayor having few formal powers, the administration being responsible to the council and local party organizations lacking, one might assume that council members would play a major role in formulating policy. In fact, most council members merely go through the motions of attending meetings and performing their duties. In effect, council members tend to practise old-fashioned incrementalism in policy making. There are a number of reasons for this pattern.

There are no Alberta councils of which the members are considered to be full time. In smaller municipalities, where only a few hours a week are devoted to council business, policy issues are left to the mayor and the administrator by default.

Even in the province's large cities, individual councillors have little if any staff assistance, other than, perhaps, a shared secretary. Councillors are expected to do their own research and deal with constituent problems themselves. Consequently, in Edmonton and Calgary, where as many as two hundred motions will be made during a council session, individual councillors, understandably, are often unprepared on some issues. Important policy motions are often made and passed in a perfunctory fashion. At budget time the volume and complexity of information makes it impossible for council to consider more than a small number of budget items in detail. For this reason, a council member often focuses on the merits, or lack of them, of a very minor budget item in order to show that he or she is on "top of the budget."

As we have seen, the whole or a portion of the council will occasionally revolt against an inept mayor. However, even when there is a complete leadership vacuum, most councillors hesitate to fill it, feeling that the time and energy required would be wasted. An individual councillor attempting to exercise leadership is in a much less opportune position than is the mayor. The councillor cannot, as the mayor can, claim to speak for the whole community and, inevitably, there are fellow councillors who, out of jealousy or other motives, are unwilling to support a councillor's attempt to exercise leadership.

Occasionally, a council is so rent with dissension that its energy is dissipated in internal fighting, rather than being directed to policy making. Civic workers' morale is impaired and the municipality's government functions only in fits and starts. In 1979 in Morinville, there was a deep split between councillors who were long-time residents and newly arrived councillors who commuted to work in Edmonton. The newcomers wanted to preserve the charm of the community with a no-growth policy, while the old guard wanted policies that would attract industry in order to reduce the town's dependence on the residential property tax. With neither group willing to compromise, council business ground to a halt and some councillors resigned in frustration. The same kind of old-guard new-commuter split developed in the Carstairs council in the early 1980s. Lower housing costs and a location only 37 miles north of Calgary caused the community to be inundated with Calgary commuters who were perceived by the residents as a threat. The two groups were unable to work together and four councillors resigned over a 21-month period.

Sometimes, a personal feud between two councillors will impair the council's performance. During the 1978 session of Calgary's council, Donald Hartman called Brian Lee a "liar" a number of times. When Hartman was away on vacation, Lee wrote to the city clerk, asking: "Can you confirm from your notes and minutes that the only occasion . . . that council managed to complete its deliberations on a single day was . . . when we experienced the absence of the bark, heckling, innuendoes and interruptions from Alderman Hartman, who was resting his tongue in Hawaii?"[17] In the spring of 1982 an exchange between two hostile councillors in Cochrane's council chambers became so heated that one councillor told the other, "I'll punch you in the mouth."[18] In Edmonton a long and bitter feud between two veteran councillors, Ed Leger and Ron Hayter, has affected the morale and performance of all council members. The combatants have had to be separated in the committee structure and council debate often has degenerated into a discussion of personalities.

Despite the publicity generated by conflict-ridden councils, they are the exception rather than the rule. Since councils in most Alberta communities subscribe to the professional management premise, which blurs the ideological positions of the members, and since council members working together over time tend to develop close personal ties, councils tend to be close knit. Moreover, as we will see shortly, council members tend to share the same socio-economic characteristics, a factor that diminishes conflict. In fact, in most Alberta communities council members work together amicably and outbursts of animosity are rare.

Council Committee Policy Making

Although council members do not normally initiate comprehensive policy proposals, they play an important role in the policy process through standing committees. Policy is legitimized in the council meeting through the passage of by-laws, but most of the work and political bargaining takes place in the council's committees. To understand council politics one must understand the dynamics of the committee system. With the exception of small villages with three councillors, where committee work is normally carried out by a committee of the whole, committees structure council discussion and determine policy direction. They are able to do this because, normally, council accepts its committee recommendations and enacts them into policy with little discussion or dissent. It is understood that committee members have developed special expertise in the particular policy area and that many hours have been spent in discussions of the pros and cons of the committee's proposal. Only when there is a deep-seated council cleavage, or when other council members have lost confidence in the abilities of committee members, are committee recommendations subject to close scrutiny and vigorous debate.

One potential disadvantage of council policy making revolves around the fact that, since most councils have several standing committees, policy proposals from any single committee tend to be narrowly focused. In the absence of a strong mayor to exercise leadership and given the narrow focus of standing committees, policy proposals often work at cross-purposes and overall municipal policy tends to be directionless. It is not unusual for a leaderless council to drift until the election of a strong mayor.

Members of standing committees develop expertise respected by other members of council. When these "committees of experts" recommend one type of by-law rather than another, they have structured the council's policy alternatives. Conversely, if a committee wants no action taken on a particular issue, it makes no report to council and the status quo is maintained. Both private and public interests in a community are well aware of the importance of committees: they do their best to influence committee members, realizing that the work of committees is a crucial step in the policy process.

Over time, most committee chairpersons gain the loyalty and support of committee members. In the full council it is not unusual for committee members to vote on the basis of loyalty to committee chairpersons, even for a by-law they do not support wholeheartedly. Astute chairpeople, aware of this "loyalty support," often use it to build a power base on council. On the other hand, a committee chairperson can quickly lose this support by speaking for the committee before council without having consulted the other committee members.

Council Members Socio-economic Composition and Policy Making

A newly elected council member brings council predispositions and values that are partially shaped by his or her social class. Many studies have shown that working-class and middle-class people have different perceptions of the role of business and labour in the community. They also differ in their views on the importance of thrift, mortgaging the future to pay for the present, community amenities, education, etc. Therefore, the socio-economic background of the council's members is an important factor in community policy making.

It is, perhaps, obvious that council members do not mirror the socio-economic composition of their communities. Some years ago, a study of municipal councils in the United States found that most councillors were of the middle and upper-middle class, whereas both working-class and upper-class members of the community were under-represented on council.[19] Although limited, research in Canada indicates that Canadian municipal councils have similar socio-economic compositions.[20] A 1971 study of political recruitment in Edmonton, Calgary, Red Deer, Lethbridge and Medicine Hat found that:

> Whereas 49 per cent of the councillors have incomes over
> $20,000 just slightly more than 1 per cent of the populace from
> which they were selected have comparable incomes. Similarly,
> while less than 10 per cent of their constituents have gone
> beyond high school, over two-thirds of the councillors received

some university or post-secondary education . . . 80 per-cent of the aldermen . . . fell into the traditional middle class white collar occupations of the managerial, professional and clerical nature.[21]

A recent study of Edmonton politics corroborates these findings. "For the decade commencing in 1974, 87 per cent of successful candidacies have come from professional (including teachers) or business ranks."[22] Only one working-class person has been elected to the Edmonton council since 1974. In smaller Alberta communities the only divergence from this trend is that farmers are often found on municipal councils.

A number of factors contribute to the predominance of the middle-class managerial and professional elite on councils. First, many studies have found a direct relationship between level of education and political participation. Many people with minimal education find it difficult to cope with complex political issues and tend to avoid active political participation. On the other hand, a disproportionate number of better educated, middle-class citizens are interested in politics and seek public office. In addition, it is the better educated who tend to be involved in community organizations and such involvement acts as a catalyst to running for political office. Another important factor is that people in occupations with flexible hours are better able to dovetail their work with public service than are people in occupations with rigid work schedules. This flexibility permits large numbers of school teachers, business owners and managers, lawyers and farmers to become involved in politics. Finally, there are people whose occupations are such that the high visibility of public office is an economic advantage: insurance and real estate brokers often seek public office, feeling that they will gain a competitive business advantage. These factors produce municipal councils dominated by professional and business people.

With this domination it is not surprising that the professional management ethic dominates the policy-making process. Even in municipalities with ward representation, professionals and businesspeople are over-represented on council. It is not uncommon to find a businessperson "representing" a working-class ward yet consistently voting with a business coalition on council. However, in the last decade the public has begun to recognize the political nature of city hall: in communities with ward representation it is becoming more common to find working-class wards represented by working-class individuals.

Unlike federal and provincial legislative bodies, where women have only token representation, municipal councils have a sizeable number of women representatives. Although Alberta's large city councils are still dominated by men, women dominate the councils of a few smaller communities. Social scientist Susannah Wilson explains why municipal politics provides a more fertile political environment for aspiring women politicians.[23] She points out that at the provincial and federal levels the cost of waging a successful political campaign disadvantages women, who have far less earning power than men and who are not as well "plugged in" to the network of campaign funding sources. The lower cost of municipal campaigning allows more women candidates to participate. She also points out that at the provincial and federal levels "the support structures necessary for a woman politician simply do not exist." Women legislators with children must cope with finding adequate child care facilities and deal with the problems and costs of maintaining two residences suitable for children. These barriers are much less formidable at the local level.

In the coming decade it is likely that the entry of increasing numbers of women into professions that have been traditional stepping-stones into politics, combined with the lower financial and social costs of contesting local elections, will lead to sex parity on most of Alberta's municipal councils.

Council Size and its Representative Function, Factors in Policy Making

Generally, municipal legislative bodies are much smaller than are those at the provincial and federal levels. Although Montreal's council has 54 members and Winnipeg's has 29 (reduced from 50 in 1977), Alberta's municipalities have had small councils, largely because provincial legislation limits their size. Section 27(1) of the Municipal Government Act states:

c.the council of a village

i. shall consist of three councillors, or

ii. if the council of a village having a population of at least 250 persons so authorizes, by by-law, shall consist of five councillors, one of whom shall be mayor;

d.the council of a town shall consist of a mayor and six councillors;

e.the council of a city shall consist of a mayor and

i. six councillors, or

ii. a greater even number of councillors, not exceeding 20, that the council, after the first election in the city, authorizes by by-law.

Among Alberta's cities Calgary has the largest council, with 15 members, followed by Edmonton, with 13. The Camrose, Grande Prairie, Lethbridge, Medicine Hat and Red Deer councils each have nine members. The cities with the smallest councils are Drumheller, Lloydminster, St. Albert and Wetaskiwin, all of which have seven-member councils. As prescribed by the legislation, all Alberta towns have seven-member councils, with the exception of Crowsnest Pass, which has a 10-member council. The Crowsnest Pass Municipal Unification Act (c-38), which amalgamated the area's municipalities, specified that the council was to consist of a mayor and nine council-lors.[24] Fifty-three of the province's villages have five-member councils; 110 have three-member councils.

In order to ensure that the city's diverse social and economic interests are represented, each of Canada's large cities, with the exception of Vancouver, have ward representation (i.e., representation based on a defined geographic area) and larger councils. The proponents of large councils with ward representation maintain that such a system furthers grass-roots democracy. Conversely, smaller communities with smaller councils generally have at-large representation: it is felt that councillors should represent the whole community, which is thought to be socio-economically homogeneous. The proponents of at-large electoral systems maintain that the "community interest" should be served rather than the "narrow parochial interests served by ward representation."

There are advantages and disadvantages associated with both small councils elected at-large, and large councils with ward elections. The main advantage of the ward system is that major interests in the community are usually represented; the main disadvantage is that a councillor will occasionally lose sight of his or her representational role and engage in petty, demeaning politics. For example, in a Michigan city with a ward system, one councillor shouted at another during a council meeting, "You bastard, you had three more blocks of black-topping in your ward last year than I had, you'll not get another vote from me until I get three extra blocks."[25] The main advantage of the small council elected at-large in a smaller, homogeneous community is that (theoretically) all councillors are "like minded," and, hence council conflict is reduced to a minimum. One disadvantage is that a small socio-economic minority located in a relatively small geographical area may never get represented. Another disadvantage is that small councils elected at-large tend to have a professional management ethic that refuses to recognize minority interests and defines the "community interest" solely in terms of efficiency and fiscal responsibility.

For almost 300 years, the proper relationship between representatives and their constituents has been the subject of debate. There are two diametrically opposing theories of representation: the mandate theory and the trustee (or independence) theory. Mandate theorists start from the premise that the ideal is to have all members of a community assemble in a hall to be directly involved in governmental decisions. However, since this policy-making mechanism tends to be impractical in all but the smallest communities, the best alternative is to elect a representative who has a mandate from his or her constituents to do their bidding. The representative may exercise some discretion but must consult all constituents before voting on any controversial proposal. If the representative cannot in good conscience give unqualified support to the views of the constituency, he or she must resign.

The counter-argument made by the trustee theorists is based on the premise that the business of government is too complex for the ordinary person. Therefore, constituents elect a representative to exercise good judgment in making legislative decisions whether they conform to the views of the constituency or not. It is further argued that if representatives are bound to rigid positions by their constituents, it would be impossible to effect the political compromise central to any legislative body.[26]

In fact, no representative completely subscribes to one theory or the other. When first elected, most representatives are determined to represent the positions and demands of their constituents. They soon find that it is extremely difficult to ascertain their constituents' positions: some issues evolve so quickly that it is impossible to poll constituents, and other issues are too complex for constituents to understand fully. Thus, at the municipal level, the norm appears to be that representatives lean towards the trustee position and vote according to their conscience rather than following the dictates of their constituents. Yet, when large numbers of constituents petition their representatives to vote for a particular position, the representative takes their views seriously and usually votes accordingly. In short, although representatives may lean towards either the mandate or the trustee theory of representation, they adopt a position incorporating both.

Limited research has been carried out in Canada on councillors' perceptions of their representational role. A study carried out in Port Arthur and Fort William, Ontario, in 1970, indicated that the councillors in the two communities perceived themselves more as trustees than as delegates representing the views of their constituents.[27] Journalistic accounts of council proceedings in Alberta seem to corroborate these findings. It must be emphasized, however, that, although many councillors may lean towards the trustee theory, they usually adopt their constituents' positions when pressed to do so.

If the usual mechanism for translating the views of the citizenry to their representatives (i.e., the political party) is absent, how do councillors learn what their constituents want? In the very small town or village, council members consult their constituents on a one-to-one basis; however, such a process is impossible in larger communities. A 1967 study of the Edmonton city council found that councillors felt that business and welfare groups were the ones providing council with the information required for formulating policy.[28] A study of council behaviour in five Alberta communities came to a similar conclusion: the councillors belonged to, and were recruited into politics by, community organizations, service clubs, churches, and civic and business groups. The study concluded, "the high degree of involvement of secondary groups in the recruitment process . . . helps to define the structure of effective political opportunity, in the sense of who can compete for local office with a fair chance of electoral success."[29] In short, these organizations were both consulted and listened to by members of council. In Edmonton, Calgary and Red Deer, neighbourhood groups have become increasingly important in providing councils with information useful in policy formulation.

Other major sources of information are the professional meetings, such as the annual meeting of the Alberta Urban Municipalities Association, where council members from different communities meet. Studies of state politics in the United States have found that fiscal and administrative innovations have come about primarily as a result of information sharing at meetings of state officials. Although no one has examined the introduction of innovative concepts in Canadian communities, at various times council members have stated that they were introduced to new ideas at professional meetings.

Council's Public Responsibilities and Conflict with Private Economic Interests

In the last 25 years a number of factors have led to one conflict of interest affair after another in Alberta municipalities. First, the legislation (in the Municipal Government Act) governing conflict of interest is confusing and ambiguous. Moreover, the penalty for conflict of interest violations is minimal, merely requiring that the guilty party resign his or her seat on council or failing that, "the council may, by resolution, apply to the Court of Queen's Bench for an order declaring him to be disqualified to be a member of the council." The ambiguous section of the act under which most conflict of interest charges are made is section 30(2)(d), which reads: "A member of council shall not vote in the council on any question in which he has a direct or indirect pecuniary interest."

Until some amendments were adopted in 1975 there were no guidelines in the Act defining "a direct or indirect pecuniary interest." As a result, councils were often left without a quorum as councillors abstained from voting on issues that even remotely touched them for fear of being in conflict of interest. For several days in 1975 the Edmonton council, dealing with a rent control bill, was without a quorum since councillors abstained because they were either landlords or tenants. Shortly thereafter, one of the key amendments to the Act, section 30(5)(f) was made:

> This section does not apply to a member of a council by reason
> only that the question affects any thing in respect of which the
> member has a direct or indirect pecuniary interest if the
> member's interest in it is one which is in common with all other,
> or a substantial number of other, persons in the municipality.

But even the amendments do not make the Act clear. For example, in a complex conflict of interest case in the Town of Cochrane in the early 1980s, the affected councillor "thought pecuniary interest meant receiving some gain, like money under the table."[30] Although the Alberta Urban Municipalities Association has repeatedly requested that the government delineate clearly what constitutes conflict of interest and the Minister of Municipal Affairs has promised to do so, no such definition has yet been made.

A second reason for the increase in conflict of interest cases is that many of Alberta's growth communities are one-industry towns in which it is difficult to recruit councillors who are not connected with the dominant industry in one way or another. For example, after the 1980 election, all five members of the Wabamun village council were employees of Calgary Power, an industry which dominates the community. Since the council is continually dealing with questions involving Calgary Power, the councillors were constantly faced with a potential conflict of interest. A similar situation exists in the Town of Grande Cache, in which most of the community's workers are employed by McIntyre Mines Ltd. Fort McMurray is yet another one-industry town troubled by conflict of interest cases, because the community is dominated by two major oil companies that employ many of the councillors.

Despite the vagueness of the legislation and the problems of governance in one-industry towns, the major reason for the growth of conflict of interest cases is simply that some elected officials are unwilling to forego business activities that place them at risk of abrogating public trust. And, of course, in local government as elsewhere, a few people are greedy. Several years ago in the Village of Hairy Hill, the mayor voted to extend a sewer line to service one additional residence, his own.[31] In 1980 the mayor of Coutts voted to have water and sewer taxes imposed on properties in the village's northern sector. The by-law was drafted so as to exclude the mayor's own property in that sector.

Two of Edmonton's mayors have been involved in business dealings resulting in conflict of interest charges. The late mayor William Hawrelak was ousted from office by the court in 1959 for "gross misconduct" in a land deal with a relative. Re-elected, he was again ousted in 1965 when he sold some land to the city.[32] Mayor Cecil Purves was in the public spotlight shortly after he was elected to office in 1977 over some of his controversial business dealings. In 1980 the city administration released a report showing that, from the time he had taken office, some $88,000 in contracts had been awarded to companies the mayor had an interest in. The following month another report showed that one of his companies received over $10,000 from the city for leased dump trucks. Then, in September, 1979, the mayor acquired a quarter interest in 40 acres just outside the city's boundaries. Three months later he apprised the city clerk of his interest but failed to make it known to the public. In December, 1980, the mayor voted in favour of a resolution approving a pre-annexation agreement for a large area of land, which contained his own holdings. When the case was brought to court, the judge in a controversial decision ruled that having "found that no direct or indirect pecuniary interest existed on the part of the respondent in the question before council . . . the applicant is accordingly dismissed."[33] Although the mayor was exonerated by the court, his business dealings with the city became a major issue in the October, 1983, municipal election, when he was defeated by a margin of more than two to one.

The importance of conflict of interest goes much further than whether or not a council member is found guilty of extending a sewer line for his own benefit or doing business with the municipality. For democracy to work it is necessary that the public trust its local officials and believe that they are more committed to the public's interest than to their own. Hence it is essential that, rather than skirting the edge of the province's legislation on conflict of interest, public officials be beyond reproach in their private dealings. This is not to suggest that only the propertyless and the impoverished stand for local elections, but that, if there is the slightest doubt whether a councillor's action is in conflict of interest, the councillor should always err in the public's favour. [34]

Professionalization in Politics?

If there is a single issue that will stir up an apathetic public and generate countless news stories it is an attempt by council to raise its salaries. The Alberta public is committed to efficient administration and professional management in local government. High-powered and high-salaried commissioners and managers oversee municipal departments in a number of cities, and professionally trained city managers and municipal administrators are employed by a number of towns. In smaller towns and villages, clerks and treasurers are encouraged to upgrade their skills. However, there is no equivalent public support for professional politicians. Despite the fact that mayors and councillors make policy on multi-million dollar projects there are no training programs, nor for that matter any professional qualifications, for these jobs.[35] Various beliefs contribute to this lack: first, that making public policy is not so complex that it cannot be carried out by the ordinary educated citizen; second, that municipal politicians should view their stint on council as public service rather than as an opportunity to make a career in politics.

In smaller communities where council meets less frequently, few if any local politicians maintain they should be paid as full-time political professionals. With frequent rotation of council positions, members of the community are exhorted to "do their civic duty" and stand for election. Members of these councils sacrifice a fair amount of time and receive little remuneration for their public service.

Despite the feeling that municipal politics should not be a full-time vocation, astute mayors in larger Alberta municipalities often hold office for a number of terms, are expected to devote all their time to running the city, and are paid accordingly. Table 5.2 shows that the mayors of Calgary, Edmonton, Fort McMurray, and Red Deer all make annual salaries of over $40,000, i.e., salaries comparable with those of other professionals. There are obvious disparities in the salaries received by the mayors of Alberta cities. When the mayor of Fort McMurray (population, 33,000) and the mayor of Red Deer (population, 48,000) were asked in 1981 whether their salaries were not out of line with those in comparable communities across Canada and Alberta, they vehemently denied it. Both defended their salaries by arguing that they were governing boom towns with problems of almost unprecedented growth. Red Deer's mayor also justified his salary on the basis that he was chief commissioner as well as mayor.[36]

Table 5.1
Salaries of Mayors and Councillors in Alberta's
Smaller Communities, 1982
(approximate salaries per month)

	Mayor	Councillor		Mayor	Councillor
Towns (population 1500-3499)			Villages		
High	$150	$100	High	$275	$225
Median	60	55	Median	40	35
Low	35	35	Low	18	18
Towns (population 1000-1499)			Summer Villages		
High	$130	$100	High	$ 40	$ 40
Median	60	55	Median	30	30
Low	35	35	Low	20	20
Towns (population below 1000)					
High	$ 80	$ 60			
Median	40	30			
Low	30	18			

With few exceptions, the salaries of Alberta mayors have caused little public outcry; rather, the public has directed its wrath against councillors who press for substantially higher salaries. Perhaps the explanation for this attitude is the public's awareness that the mayor normally makes a substantial financial sacrifice to hold public office. In 1978 the Edmonton council voted itself a 60 per cent salary increase, which was rescinded after an angry group of citizens circulated a petition calling for a plebiscite on the issue. The same year, Calgary's council angered the citizenry by voting a salary increase of 48 per cent for councillors and 24 per cent for the mayor. As in Edmonton, the threat of a plebiscite forced the council to revoke its position. In 1981 the Calgary council adopted a pension plan for its members, providing a pension of 20 per cent of a councillor's base salary (or a minimum of $3900 a year) for life, beginning at the age of 55, provided the person had served on council for five years. The public was enraged and the council reversed its position.[37] Then, in 1982, Mayor Klein of Calgary proposed that the October, 1983, municipal ballot ask the electorate whether four of the council's councillors should be made full time, with salaries of $40,000 a year. Klein argued that the full-time councillors would chair the council's four

Table 5.2
Salaries of Mayors and Councillors in Alberta's Cities, 1982
(approximate salaries per year)

City	Mayor	Councillor
Edmonton	$ 53,000	$ 23,500
Red Deer	43,900	10,900
Calgary	41,000	14,650
Fort McMurray	27,300	9,000
	13,500 expenses	
St. Albert	22,500	4,700
	11,250 (not taxable)	2,350 (not taxable)
	1,800 expenses	
Camrose	16,150	5,500
Medicine Hat	20,000	4,550
	10,000 expenses	2,300 expenses
Grande Prairie	21,000	7,800
Lethbridge	20,000	6,350
Lloydminster	14,100	3,600
Wetaskiwin	12,000	6,000
Drumheller	8,250	5,200

standing committees and be made members of the commission board. The press almost immediately dubbed the proposed full-time councillors "Super Aldermen" and reported unfavourably on the proposition. [38]

An examination of Table 5.2 is somewhat misleading since, in the very large cities, councillors supplement their salaries substantially by sitting on independent boards and commissions that pay their members from $75 to $100 for each meeting.[39] Since salaries are such a sensitive issue with the public, council members are reluctant to divulge how much additional income they derive from sitting on the plethora of independent boards and commissions.

Whether councillors in particular cities are underpaid or overpaid is of little importance in itself. Rather, the controversy over salaries is a manifestation of two much larger issues: whether recognition should be given to the work of professional politicians at the local level and whether paying council members a substantial salary would enable people to sit on council who would otherwise be unable to do so. There is no doubt that council members in large cities put in 30 to 60 hours a week on council business: sitting on council and its committees, sitting on independent boards and commissions, consulting with managers or commissioners, and meeting with constituents. Over time, councillors learn how the city operates and who are the key participants in the administration. In addition, those who advocate the professionalizing of local politicians argue that they are making decisions for a multi-million or even billion dollar enterprise and should, like their counterparts in the private sector, be well paid for doing so. Finally, it is argued that paying councillors a living wage ensures that no one is barred from council solely for financial reasons.

The counter-arguments are nearly as persuasive. There is the fear that if council members are well paid, people will be attracted primarily by financial rewards rather than by a commitment to public service. In a related argument it is noted that the financial barrier to public service is limited primarily to campaigning: it is becoming increasingly expensive to win a seat on a large city council. It is argued that if councillors are paid high salaries, people would spend even more on campaigning in order to win a well-paying job. Finally, many people feel that grass-roots democracy is now found only at the local level and that professionalized local government could become as distant from the public as is government at the provincial and federal levels.

Notes

1. In addition to the examples presented in Chapter 1, there are a number of studies examining public policy from the perspective of elite theory or class analysis that maintain that as the elite comes primarily from the upper socio-economic strata of society and shapes the public opinion of the masses, therefore, public policy is really the preferences of the economic elite. One of the best explanations of elite theory is found in Dye and Ziegler, *The Irony of Democracy*. Two well-regarded class analysis studies are Clement, *The Canadian Corporate Elite*, and Panitch (ed.), *The Canadian State*.

2. A number of policy studies have employed a "systems theory" developed by Easton in "An Approach to the Analysis of Political Systems," and *A*

Framework for Political Analysis. Thomas Dye succinctly describes "systems theory" when he writes: "Systems theory portrays public policy as an output of the political system. The concept of 'system' implies an identifiable set of institutions and activities in society that function to transform demands into authoritative decisions requiring the support of society. . . . Inputs are received in the political system in the form of both demands and support. Demands occur when the individuals or groups, in response to real or perceived environmental conditions, act to affect public policy. Support is rendered when individuals or groups accept the outcome of elections, obey the laws, pay their taxes and generally conform to policy decisions." Dye, *Understanding Public Policy*, 18-19. The advantage of the systems approach is that it provides an encompassing framework for analysing policy. The disadvantage is that it is at such a high level of abstraction that "the political system" (often called the "black box" in the model), where policy is made, is never clearly defined. Another social science theory, currently out of fashion, that has been used to analyse public policy is "group theory," best explained in Truman, *The Governmental Process*. Group theory posits that interest groups, not individuals, are central to the political process in the sense that elected decision makers and bureaucrats respond to the strongest group(s) pressuring them. Consequently, at any given time, public policy is the group equilibrium reached on a given policy issue. The theory tends to be overly mechanistic, somewhat simplistic and often misleading to the policy analyst.

3. Braybrooke and Lindblom, *A Strategy of Decision*, 40.

4. This is especially true in the human policy field since the complexities of human behaviour are just beginning to be understood. As an example, in order to curb the crime problem some people maintain the policy should be the strict punishment of offenders, while others maintain that the policy should be rehabilitation. It is still unclear which program leads to the greatest reduction in crime.

5. Lindblom, "The Science of Muddling Through"; Etzioni, *The Active Society*.

6. Dye, *Understanding Public Policy*, 31-32.

7. Yet another criticism of incrementalism is made by a Canadian policy analyst who writes: "Perhaps the most serious shortcoming of the incrementalist model is that it does not account for qualitatively different innovations, that is, changes based on value assumptions alternative to prevailing ones. Unless the investigator can uncover no fundamental alterations in policy occurring (or having occurred), then the incrementalist model suggests only partial explanations for the process." Aucoin, "Theory in the Study of Policy Making," 14.

8. Another example in which a change in the socio-economic composition of a community leads to a major change in policy direction is found in the United States where some communities have become "retirement havens." School districts, which formerly were well supported, are in a continual state

of crisis, as the retired will not support school expenditures. In fact, in isolated instances in Oregon, public schools have been closed when the citizenry would not support school expenditures at any level.

9. Downs, *Inside Bureaucracy*, 196.

10. Lightbody, a participant-observer, describes Decore's electoral strategy in detail in "The First Hurrah."

11. Higgins, *Urban Canada: Government and Politics*, 96.

12. Blake, "Role Perceptions and Local Decision-Makers," 95.

13. In many cities in Great Britain and the United States the council is organized by one of the political parties and the mayor exercises leadership through his role as party leader. In addition to controlling council through the party machinery, the mayor has party linkages to higher levels of government which are important in obtaining grants and influencing policies favourable to municipalities. In the past, American mayors had almost unlimited political resources through control of widespread political patronage; the mayor's office had the authority to make hundreds and even thousands of municipal appointments. For the proponents of patronage the rallying cry was, "to the victor belong the spoils." However, civil service reform virtually killed patronage at the municipal level in the United States. In Canada only Mayor Jean Drapeau in Montreal has built an exceptionally strong party machine through which he exercises political leadership and controls council. Higgins describes how powerful Drapeau has become: "The relationship between Drapeau and the party is not unlike that between a strong individual prime minister and the governing party in the House of Commons, except that Drapeau's control over his party's members of council is, if anything, more complete than that of a prime minister." Higgins, *Urban Canada: Government and Politics*, 231.

14. Masson, "Decision-Making Patterns and Floating Coalitions." The friendship strategy is touched upon in a study of Toronto's past mayor Crombie. Jon Caulfield notes how Crombie would nurture friendships, "with special care given those who may be most useful in years ahead." Jon Caulfield, *The Tiny Perfect Mayor*, 144.

15. *Alberta Report*, April 12, 1982.

16. *Edmonton Journal*, February 16, 1984; *Alberta Report*, March 5, 1984.

17. *Alberta Report*, October 17, 1980.

18. *Alberta Report*, March 22, 1982.

19. Prewitt, *The Recruitment of Political Leaders*, 23-51.

20. Canadian studies have found that councillors are predominantly professionals and businesspersons. See: Easton and Tennant, "Vancouver Civic Party Leadership," 19-29; Clarkson, "Barriers to Entry of Parties in Toronto's Civic Politics," 206-223; Alexander, "The Institutional and Role

Perceptions of Local Aldermen," 124-140; Bourassa, "Les Elites politiques de Montreal," 87-109.

21. Long and Slemko, "The Recruitment of Local Decision-Makers," 553.

22. Lightbody, "Edmonton: Gateway to the North," 271-272.

23. Wilson, *Women the Family and the Economy*, 120-125. A study that compared all of the women candidates who contested federal and provincial elections between 1945 and 1976 and women who contested municipal offices in 24 selected communities during the same period found that "women are significantly more likely to achieve election at the municipal level." Of women who successfully won office in their first attempt, 58.9 per cent did so in municipal elections, 18.26 per cent in provincial elections, and 6.85 per cent in federal elections. Vickers, "Where are the Women in Canadian Politics?" 45-46.

24. Section 3(2) of the Crowsnest Pass Municipal Unification Act states: "The council of the Municipality may, by by-law, change the number of councillors to a number of not less than 6 and not more than 20 . . . ."

25. Williams and Adrian, *Four Cities*, 264.

26. The best exposition of the trustee theory of representation is that made by Edmund Burke, who, in 1774, was elected to the British House of Commons. "[The constituents'] wishes ought to have great weight with [the representative]; their opinions high respect; their business unremitted attention. . . . But his unbiased opinion, his mature judgment, his enlightened conscience, he ought not to sacrifice to you, to any man, or to any set of men living. . . . If government were a matter of will upon any side, yours, without question, ought to be superior. But government and legislation are matters of reason and judgment, and not of inclination; and what sort of reason is that in which the determination precedes the discussion, in which one set of men deliberate and another decide, and where those who form the conclusions are perhaps three hundred miles distant from those who hear the arguments? . . . Parliament is not a congress of ambassadors from different and hostile interests, which interests each must maintain, as an agent and advocate, against other agents and advocates; but parliament is a deliberative assembly of one nation, with one interest, that of the whole—where, not local purposes, not local prejudices, ought to guide, but the general good, resulting from the general reason of the whole." Burke, "Address to the Electors of Bristol," 95-96.

27. Alexander, "The Institutional and Role Perceptions of Local Alderman."

28. Blake, "Role Perceptions of Local Decision-Makers," 83-93.

29. Long and Slemko, "The Recruitment of Local Decision-Makers," 559.

30. *Calgary Herald*, February 26, 1983.

31. Surprisingly, when a case of conflict of interest was brought before the

court the judge ruled that the mayor's vote on the three-person council was an error in judgment and that he was not guilty.

32. It should be noted that, some years later, the Supreme Court of Canada cleared Hawrelak of the later charges made against him.

33. During the same period another member of Edmonton's council admitted that her husband was the director of a company with large land holdings in an area the city wished to annex. During the controversy over Purves' "misconduct," she voted against a motion calling for a judicial inquiry into the land dealings of the mayor and council members.

34. In a discussion of conflict of interest, Grant MacEwan, long-time respected politician and former Lieutenant-Governor of Alberta, has written: "Under no circumstances should the public official be party to transactions between government in which he has a voice and any company or agency in which he holds an interest. People confining themselves to the business world may hold interlocking directorships and interests but the man in public office, if acting wisely, will remove all possibility of serving himself through his position. In other words, there must be no grounds for suspicion that he could be serving two masters." MacEwan, *Poking Into Politics*, 176.

35. The Municipal Government Act specifies certain conditions an individual must meet in order to remain a councillor, but the conditions are not of a professional nature. For example, under section 29(1) a person is disqualified to remain on council if convicted of "an indictable offence punishable by death or imprisonment for 5 or more years." Other reasons for disqualification include being an undischarged bankrupt, being indebted to the municipality (there are many qualifications to this condition) and being absent three consecutive council meetings without authorization.

36. *Alberta Report*, June 19, 1981.

37. *Alberta Report*, December 4, 1981.

38. *Calgary Herald*, March 2, 1982.

39. For example, in Edmonton one councillor received a total of $10,105 between 1977 and 1982 for sitting on the board of the Edmonton and Rural Auxiliary Hospital District no. 24; during the same period another councillor received $18,802.50 for sitting on the City Planning Department's Development Appeal Board.

6

MUNICIPAL CIVIL SERVANTS

AS

POLICY MAKERS

Bureaucratic Policy Making at the Local Level

Democratic governments elect decision makers to formulate policies, but since few policies administer themselves, the decision makers rely on a professionalized bureaucracy to carry them out. In short, the theory is that elected representatives make policy and the bureaucracy carries it out. However, part-time elected officials, even in a small municipality, can hardly be expected to be familiar with all aspects of government operations, let alone well informed about their current status. Hence once council decides on a general policy, the senior bureaucrats (municipal managers, department heads, section chiefs and their assistants) are delegated responsibility for its implementation and draft the detailed rules and regulations necessary to apply it. If a by-law is ambiguous, the senior bureaucrats interpret and "fine tune" it to make it workable. Over time, administrative rulings establish precedents about the parameters of the policy: if the policy is a regulatory one, they work out who it applies to; if a service or fiscal one, they determine who is eligible for its benefits. Of necessity, elected officials seek advice from their career civil servants and delegate lower level decision-making powers to them in the interest of rational policy formulation and efficient implementation. Democratic values can be preserved in spite of this dependence if:

1) Decisions made by administrators . . . fall within the limits of overall policy set by elected officials.

2) Discretion is exercised so as to further or at least not conflict with the objectives that the appointed decision-makers know or can find out are held by their relevant elective superiors.

3) The information, advice, and recommendations . . . are designed to facilitate the elective decision-makers' choices and are not seriously slanted toward some particular point of view in order to close their options.[1]

Unfortunately, administrators do occasionally attempt to usurp the elected officials' policy-making functions. And a few bureaucrats maintain that they should participate in policy formulation, arguing that they should have a major input in the development of police, fire, planning and other service policies.[2]

The career administrator who has long been involved in managing the municipality's affairs is viewed as the resident expert by elected officials. The council relies on this expert to identify issues of concern to the public and to provide council with an array of alternative solutions to particular problems. However, career bureaucrats are seldom more neutral than are elected decision makers: often their advice and recommendations are biased. Two social scientists describe the process by which administrators are subtly able to change policy recommendations:

> . . . the amount and kind of information, the method of presentation, the manner in which alternatives are identified and appraised, and the making of, or abstention from, recommendations—all provide opportunities for the bureaucracies to impress their own discretion and preferences. . . . The . . . techniques are many. The information may be incomplete, omitting data which point away from the preferred decision. It may be overdetailed, confusing the [elected] official until he is led to clear ground by the recommendation preferred by the reporter. The report may omit alternative solutions . . . or it may subject an alternative proposal to devastating criticism while leaving the preferred solution unexamined. . . . The object is constant: to guide the official's decision into the channels which the bureaucrats regard as wise and prudent.[3]

Elected officials are not oblivious to this potential problem, but seldom do they have the time or expertise to evaluate administration proposals. Moreover, administrators rarely make their proposals to increase their own power, prestige and salary so blatant that council would see them as motivated by bias.

Astute politicians and students of administration have long been aware that senior administrators can "make or break" a policy by the way they administer it. In essence, senior bureaucrats shape and give meaning to the policies enacted by council. Policy makers normally formulate new programs in general terms in order to give the bureaucracy a certain amount of flexibility. Most administrators resolve program ambiguities in their favour, i.e., to minimize their own workload while, at the same time, increasing their power and prestige. Policy directives are necessarily broad since it is impossible to anticipate all the day-to-day decisions required for making a policy work. Administrative flexibility, more commonly called *administrative discretion*, permeates the bureaucracy, but it is greatest at the top. For example, a municipal manager directed by council to formulate a proposal to provide for greater citizen participation in municipal affairs might believe that council has been sold a bill of goods by a few citizen "do-gooders," and might stall in the hope that council will forget the issue. A manager might refer council's proposal to a citizen study group or private consultant "for further study," calculating that it either would be forgotten or buried in political controversy. Similarly, a manager hoping to stall or reorient council's policy direction might caution council that its proposal did not follow precedent or that it was unclear whether or not council had the proper legislative authority.

With a few important exceptions, lower-level civil servants, such as mail clerks and stenographers, do not have the individual authority to influence policy, but they can have a significant collective effect. If they under-perform, the policy may become so expensive or so ineffective that it must be terminated. For example, if employees balk at a policy of office automation, the costs of implementation can balloon and become higher than those of the older "tried and true methods."

A category of lower level civil servants, called *street level bureaucrats*, who have a fair amount of discretion in the performance of their duties, can change policy direction within their sphere of influence.[4] Street level bureaucrats are civil servants directly involved with a segment of the public. Examples include building, fire and public health by-law enforcement officers, who have the discretion to enforce a regulation strictly or merely to issue a mild warning. Another example is the police officer who decides whether a minor traffic offense deserves a warning or a ticket. Even school teachers can be thought of as street level bureaucrats because they have the ability to undermine or change existing educational policy. An example was found in the small community of Eckville, Alberta, where, unknown to the school board (so it maintained), a high-school teacher had been preaching anti-semitism for a number of years.

Policy makers face a dilemma if they attempt to reduce bureaucratic discretion. While detailed policy directives curtail bureaucratic discretion, the result is extreme rigidity in policy implementation. Moreover, it is difficult to develop detailed long-range policies. Another consideration is the time required for a council to formulate detailed policy directives. On the other hand, a bureaucracy with wide discretionary powers is able to subvert the council and shape policies to its own ends.

Normally, the bureaucracy balks only when a council adopts a particularly innovative policy or radically changes an existing one. In the discussion on council policy making, the point was made that most policies are merely a continuation of the status quo. Municipal administrators, probably even more than council members, oppose change because it makes for an unpredictable future; hence, while they seek to expand their budgets and activities, they are reluctant to support innovative programs. Several writers and theorists, noting this fact, have argued that the bureaucracy is a conservative force that tends to temper many new government programs.

In fact, although they could potentially undermine policy making, most bureaucrats are conscientious public servants with a deep-seated belief that it is the council that must ultimately formulate policy. Sensitive to the criticism that they often subvert the will of the public, bureaucrats make a conscious effort to be impartial. Often when it seems that administrators are expressing a policy preference, they are merely anticipating the preferences of the council. And often their objections to council policy are objections to technical aspects that would make it difficult to implement. Thus, while most bureaucrats shape policy, they do so within parameters allowed by council.

The Municipality and its Civil Servants

Section 57(1) of the Municipal Government Act prescribes that, as soon as possible after a municipality is formed, the council shall "by by-law appoint a municipal secretary and prescribe his duties"; section 59(1) requires a similar by-law for the appointment of a treasurer. However, recognizing that very small municipalities may not be able to afford both a secretary and a treasurer, the Act allows the two positions to be combined. The incumbent of the combined position is designated a municipal administrator. The Act also dictates that every municipality must appoint at least one senior civil servant as an assessor and one as an auditor, and gives it wide discretion in making other senior and junior appointments. For example, the Act specifically allows the council to appoint a comptroller, to maintain books and records, and a municipal engineer. The council is also given the option to employ a municipal solicitor, either on a full-time or a fee basis. However, in fact, all the sections allowing specific appointments are redundant, as section 82 of the Act allows a council to appoint any civil servant it considers necessary in order to meet its responsibilities as specified in the Act. This section allows a council to appoint the almost endless kinds of employees needed to make local government work, from sanitary and building inspectors to playground attendants and community nurses. More importantly, this section allows a council to appoint one or more commissioners or a municipal manager, who may be given wide-ranging powers defined under section 91 of the Act which states that, "council may, by by-law, provide for the delegation of any or all of its executive and administrative duties and powers" to commissioners or a manager.

Recognition is given to the powers of commissioners and of the manager in the procedures a council is required to follow in order to dismiss them. While other civil servants serve at the pleasure of council or under the terms of the by-law governing their appointment, commissioners and managers can be dismissed only by a two-thirds majority vote of all council members. While the mayor has the power to suspend any other municipal servant, a commissioner or manager can be suspended only by a council resolution, which has to give a written statement of the reasons for suspension. The Act clearly attempts to insulate commissioners and municipal managers from council.

Senior municipal administrators, be they clerks, treasurers, municipal administrators, or commissioners and municipal managers, have joint responsibilities, i.e., responsibilities assigned to them by their council and statutory responsibilities laid down in the Municipal Government Act. Although the two sets of responsibilities are almost always complementary, a senior administrator will occasionally be given a council directive that conflicts with the Municipal Government Act's statutory requirements. Needless to say, the Act takes precedence. However, since a council's actions are equally governed by the statutory provisions of the Act, an administrator is rarely put in the uncomfortable position of having to choose between serving council or following the dictates of the Act. In fact, the Municipal Government Act's statutory provisions on the duties of administrators are not overly restrictive: they are meant to further, not hinder, the interests of municipalities. These provisions relieve a council from having continually to specify the duties and responsibilities of their administrators.

The Duties of Senior Administrators

In smaller Alberta municipalities the secretaries, treasurers and municipal administrators are at the apex of the administrative structure. With statutory responsibilities under the Municipal Government Act, the Local Authorities Act, the Municipal Taxation Act and the Tax Recovery Act, they are obviously expected to be administrative jacks-of-all-trades.

Section 58 of the Municipal Government Act delineates the responsibilities of the secretary. In addition to a number of minor responsibilities, the secretary is directed to 1) attend all regular and special meetings of council and record the minutes and the names of council members present; 2) ensure that council's by-laws in their original form are safe; 3) keep a record of all other materials committed to his or her charge by council; 4) prepare and deliver to the Department of Municipal Affairs all reports and other data the municipality is required to prepare; and 5) call a special meeting of council when required to do so by a majority of its members, by the mayor or, in a municipal district, by the reeve.[5] In addition, the council may direct the secretary to consolidate one or more by-laws and remove expired or repealed sections.

Provisions in the Local Authorities Election Act assign a number of additional responsibilities to the secretary. During election time, the secretary is particularly harried. While large municipalities will appoint a returning officer to carry out election procedures, in smaller municipalities often "the secretary is deemed to have been appointed as the returning officer." Even in a municipality with a returning officer, the Local Authorities Election Act gives the secretary many election procedure responsibilities. He or she is directed to 1) provide the returning officer with information and assistance and a sufficient number of ballot boxes; 2) safeguard the nomination papers and safely keep the ballot boxes for six weeks after the election; 3) destroy relevant electoral materials after the returning officer examines the voting results; 4) be present with the sealed ballot boxes if a recount is necessary; 5) record the name of any person guilty of election bribery; 6) have all election materials available for examination by a judge in the event of an election irregularity; and 7) order a new election if a judge decrees the election invalid or the elected members disqualify themselves. In addition, if a council by-law requires a voters' list, the secretary may be directed to prepare it and to appoint enumerators.

The responsibilities assigned to the secretary in the Municipal Taxation Act are equally onerous. The Act directs the secretary to 1) prepare an assessment roll for the municipality and the relevant school districts with a description of each assessable and non-assessable parcel, with its assessed value and owner's name and address; 2) prepare and maintain a supplementary assessment roll if directed to do so by council; 3) prepare a tax roll, send out the tax notices, issue receipts for payment and issue a statement as to whether taxes have been paid or not; 4) mail assessment notices and keep a record of the date of mailing; 5) keep a record of property owners with tax arrears; 6) notify the complainants and the assessor of the annual assessment Court of Revisions and keep a record of its proceedings; 7) amend the assessment roll immediately after the court's decision; 8) notify a property owner if an assessor appeals the court's decision to the Alberta Assessment Appeal Board; 9) notify the Alberta Assessment Appeal Board of Court of Revisions' appeals along with the particulars of assessments under appeal, and prominently post a list of the appellants and the time and place of the board's sitting; 10) appear at the appeal board hearing with the assessment roll and other materials pertinent to the appeal and, after the board's decision, amend the assessment roll accordingly; 11) notify the affected parties whenever a change is made in the assessment roll; and 12) post public notices of tax seizures. In addition, myriad other, minor, duties are prescribed by the Act.

Section 59 of the Municipal Government Act directs the treasurer to 1) collect all the municipality's monies and pay its bills; 2) maintain its fiscal records; 3) ensure that the books, records and accounts are up to date and ready for the auditor; and 4) ensure that either a complete or an abbreviated financial statement and the auditor's report are published "in such manner as the council considers advisable in order to give such information to the ratepayers concerning the financial affairs of the municipality as the council considers reasonable and proper."

Further duties are assigned to the treasurer under the Tax Recovery Act, which directs the treasurer to 1) notify authorities collecting taxes if they have attempted to collect taxes on property that is not taxable; 2) prepare a list of properties in tax arrears for more than a year and send it to the officers of the concerned municipalities; 3) post a list in the treasurer's office of properties in tax arrears; 4) send to every relevant authority a list of the parcels offered for sale because of tax arrears two months prior to the sale; and 5) send a registered letter to the property owners in tax arrears four weeks before the tax sale.

As was noted earlier, the Municipal Government Act does not delineate explicitly the responsibilities of a municipal manager, but rather gives council the authority to assign the person wide-ranging "executive and administrative duties and powers." Section 91(2) of the Act reads:

> The municipal commissioners or the municipal manager . . . shall exercise the powers and duties set out in the Act, and any other powers and duties vested, confirmed or delegated by by-law or by resolution of council.

Whether the senior administrator is a secretary, treasurer, municipal administrator, municipal manager or commissioner, the statutory duties and responsibilities constitute only a part of the job. Especially in smaller municipalities the secretary, treasurer and municipal administrator are expected to be generalists well versed on any activity that remotely touches the council and the administration. The senior administrator is the key link between the municipality and the public. Whether it is a question about the interpretation of a significant new by-law or about whether one needs a building permit to build a patio, it is the senior administrator who is contacted. Often a village or small town administrator will be given a general mandate by the council to encourage business expansion and tourism through a promotional campaign. This program often entails collecting data and preparing brochures on the community's amenities, labour force, markets and transportation. The administrator is expected to be well versed in personnel management and contract negotiations. Besides being a competent office manager, he or she is expected to interpret and prepare simple contracts and to understand basic legal documents. It is the administrator who deals with neighbouring municipalities and the Department of Municipal Affairs on a day-to-day basis. Unless the administrator is current with provincial and federal grant programs and regulations, a municipality may miss substantial grant monies. All rural administrators are expected to be familiar with such matters as weed control and forest fire prevention and control. In addition, county administrators are expected to be knowledgeable about the School Act and school administration.

Finally, the administrator is obliged to advise council on its statutory responsibilities. For example, the Municipal Government Act requires that council appoint one or more auditors each year to examine the administration's financial statement. If this appointment is neglected, the administrator has the duty of reminding council of its responsibility. In short, the administrator is expected to be as conversant with council's statutory duties as with his or her own.

Profile of Senior Municipal Administrators

In the past decade the profile of the senior municipal administrator in Alberta has changed substantially. Province-wide surveys carried out in 1976 and 1983 show that senior administrators are much better educated and better paid than they once were. However, there have been only minor changes in age distribution, and no change in distribution by sex. [6]

The most dramatic change has been a substantial educational upgrading of local administrators. The 1976 survey showed that 25 per cent of administrators had neither obtained a high-school diploma nor taken other academic courses. In the 1983 survey, very few administrators fell into this category. While in the 1976 survey 23 per cent of respondents had "some college," in 1983 the percentage had doubled to 46 per cent. In 1976 only one administrator reported having a college degree; in 1983, 22 administrators (14 per cent) did so. As might be expected, the educational level of senior administrators is highest in larger municipalities and lowest in villages and summer villages. Yet the 1983 survey found that among village and summer village administrators 30 per cent had "some college" and seven per cent held college degrees. The impetus for increasing educational qualifications has come from the Department of Municipal Affairs, the Local Government Administrator's Association of Alberta, and the University of Alberta's Faculty of Extension, which offers a comprehensive set of courses leading to a professional certificate in local government. In addition, although there are no statutory requirements for municipalities to follow when hiring municipal administrators, municipal councils are increasingly recognizing the importance of having well-educated employees.

The inflationary pressures of the 1970s pushed up senior municipal administrators' salaries, as it did those of all other occupational groups. But, in addition, many councils had to increase the salary scale for senior administrators substantially to attract better-educated candidates. The effect of this upgrading is particularly apparent for very small municipalities, which have traditionally paid their administrators relatively low salaries. Following are the salaries of senior administrators in smaller municipalities in 1983. [7]

under 500 population	$8,400 to $14,200
500 to 2,499 population	$12,800 to $31,000
2,500 to 4,999 population	$24,000 to $60,000
5,000 to 12,000 population	$40,000 to $60,000

Salaries of managers and commissioners in the province's larger municipalities are comparable to those of senior administrators in the private sector, ranging from $60,000 to slightly over $100,000.

The 1983 survey found the highest salaries reported were for county and city administrators. Surprisingly, a higher percentage of county administrators than city administrators reported salaries of over $45,000: 43 per cent for county people, 25 per cent for city people. The widest variation in salaries was reported by town administrators: four per cent reported salaries of less than $10,000; and nine per cent, of more than $45,000. The smallest variation was found among special area and improvement district administrators. Sixty-two per cent reported salaries between $25,000 and $35,000; 38 per cent, between $35,000 and $45,000. As one would expect, village and summer village administrators had the lowest salaries, with 26 per cent reporting salaries of less than $10,000; however, 11 per cent reported salaries of between $25,000 and $35,000.

The age category capturing the largest percentage of local administrators in both surveys was the 36 to 45 year old group: 29 per cent in 1976 and 40 per cent in 1983. The most striking difference between the two surveys is the percentage of senior administrators over the age of 55: in 1976 almost 18 per cent, in 1983 only eight per cent. With older members retiring and younger ones being recruited, one would expect a similar difference between the percentage of administrators in the younger age categories. There is, however, only a slight difference: in the 1976 survey 27 per cent reported being 35 years or younger, while in the 1983 survey 32 per cent did so.

The two surveys show that the ratio of women to men among senior administrators has remained the same: approximately one-third are women and two-thirds men. More importantly, few women hold senior administrative positions in larger municipalities; most women are village and summer village administrators. Administration is a part-time job in half of these municipalities. In the 1983 survey, 78 per cent of village and summer village administrators were women, 25 per cent of senior administrators in cities and towns, and 15 per cent of those in municipal districts. Not a single woman in the sample was a senior administrator in a county, special area or improvement district. Without entering the debate on covert sexual discrimination in the workplace, we must conclude that men enjoy a clear advantage as senior municipal administrators in Alberta.

The 1983 survey shows that, while almost all administrators have a strong commitment to their career and their community, there is a wide disparity between the ideal and the actual job. Although most municipal councils give their senior administrators financial recognition, a number fail to give them professional recognition: they are often treated as little more than glorified clerical help.

A key question asked of the administrators related to the importance of personal fulfillment and growth. Ninety-nine per cent said it was very important but, when asked how much opportunity for growth and fulfillment they had on the job, only 30 per cent replied that there was a lot and 15 per cent responded that there was none. Municipal district administrators were the most satisfied, with 42 per cent saying that their job gave them ample opportunity for personal growth; the special area and improvement district administrators were the least satisfied, with not a single person giving his or her job high marks for personal growth. Associated with personal growth is the opportunity to learn new job skills. Almost all respondents replied that it was very important to learn and develop new skills, but only 28 per cent said their job gave them the chance to do so, while 21 per cent replied their job gave them no such opportunity. This disparity can be partially accounted for by the stance municipal councils have taken on educational upgrading. A 1983 survey asked 108 Alberta reeves, mayors and a small number of councillors whether their municipality had established policies for training and development of senior administrators.[8] The responses were evenly divided: 50 per cent did and 50 per cent did not have policies on personnel development. A follow-up question asked whether their municipality had an annual budget item for educational upgrading of their senior administrators; only one-third indicated that they had.

A related question dealt with the importance administrators placed on having highly marketable skills: 91 per cent said that this was very important, but only 18 per cent replied that their job provided them with such skills, while 25 per cent replied that their job provided no marketable skills.

Another question concerned the importance of personal autonomy on the job. Well over 90 per cent of respondents said that it was very important, but only 47 per cent said they had "a lot" of personal autonomy. Once again, municipal district administrators were most satisfied, with 73 per cent having "a lot of autonomy"; special area and improvement district administrators were least satisfied, with only 25 per cent replying that they had substantial autonomy.

Job security is important to municipal administrators, as it is to most salaried employees. However, while 88 per cent of those surveyed replied that job security was very important to them, only 41 per cent felt their job to be completely secure and 15 per cent replied they had absolutely no security.

Not only were many administrators dissatisfied with their job, 38 per cent felt their job responsibilities were unclear, a factor which also must contribute to job dissatisfaction. But the most surprising finding was that, although a substantial number of administrators were dissatisfied with their job, and often lacked professional recognition by council, almost all had a strong commitment to their profession, to their employer, and to doing a good job.

Political Relationships of Alberta's Senior Municipal Administrators

In the 1983 survey of 108 Alberta elected officials, none said that they had an unsatisfactory relationship with their senior administrator.[9] Rather, 66 per cent stated the relationship was excellent, 30 per cent that it was good, and only four per cent that it was fair. When asked, "in your relationship with the chief administrator, what do you see as the most difficult problem?" 48 per cent replied they did not have a problem.[10] Results from the 1983 administrators' survey indicate that administrators have a slightly different perception: while 59 per cent replied they had an excellent relationship, at the other end of the spectrum four per cent (six individuals) indicated a poor relationship.

Perhaps even more important is the relationship between the senior administrator and the council, for, although the mayor is directed to exercise control over the administration, it is the council and its committees that the administrator is responsible to and it is the council that has the power of hiring and firing. In the 1983 survey of administrators the question was asked, "how much pressure (e.g., unreasonable demands) do you get from the council?" The response, by type of municipality (shown in Table 6.1) indicates that two-thirds of the administrators are working under some duress. The percentage with some or a lot of pressure from council varies little by type of municipality, except for county administrators. For reasons not easily explained, a much higher percentage of municipal district councils placed little or no pressure on their administrators. On the other hand, their rural counterparts, i.e., county councils, pressure a higher proportion of their administrators than do councils in any other rural type of municipality.

Although almost 60 per cent of senior administrators replied they were subject to unreasonable demands by council, 98 per cent stated their relationship with council was good to excellent. Only one county and two village/summer village administrators replied they had a poor relationship with their council. Perhaps the reason for these seemingly contradictory findings is that, while councils attempt to maintain good relations with their senior administrator, they rely so heavily on him or her that many administrators interpret this dependence as pressure.

Table 6.1
Administrators Feeling Pressured by their Council
(in per cent)

| | Pressure on Administrator by Council | | |
Governmental Unit	Hardly any Pressure	Some Pressure	A Lot of Pressure
County	23	32	46
City	25	13	63
Municipal District	62	0	39
Town	36	25	39
Village/Summer Village	28	39	33
Special Area/ Improvement District	25	50	25
AVERAGE	32%	29%	39%

To ascertain how much a council relies on its senior administrator for policy and administrative direction, the 1983 survey asked administrators, "When making policy recommendations to council, how often would you say your recommendations are adopted?" Table 6.2, which presents the responses by type of governmental unit, shows that 72 per cent had 75 per cent or more of their recommendations adopted by council. Even the governmental units adopting the lowest percentage of their administrators' recommendations, the municipal districts, had an adoption rate of 54 per cent. In villages and summer villages, which have part-time councils that meet infrequently, the administrator provides continuity from one administration to another. Thus, while one would expect an extremely high percentage of administrator recommendations to be adopted, 28 per cent had 50 per cent or less of their recommendations adopted. An intriguing finding is the 10 per cent of senior administrators who said they did not make recommendations; even more intriguing is the question of why this figure balloons to 25 per cent in cities and 23 per cent in municipal districts. Either the administrators have abrogated some of their responsibilities or their recommendations have been rejected so many times that they have stopped making them.

Serious discord between a council and its senior administrator is seldom publicized before the administrator quietly resigns. Public charges of administrative mismanagement hang like an albatross around an administrator's neck, making it impossible for him or her to find another municipal position. In the few instances where dissension has been publicized, the administrator was almost invariably forced out. In Coronation and Carstairs the competence of the senior administrators became a highly publicized issue in the 1980 election; in each case, the administrator was ultimately dismissed.[11] In 1981 the Brooks council appointed one of its members as town manager, al-

Table 6.2
How often Council Adopts the Policy Recommendations
of Senior Administrators

Governmental Unit	Percent of Recommendations Adopted					Don't Make Recommend-ations
	0%	25%	50%	75%	100%	
County	0	10	10	33	43	5
City	0	0	0	38	38	25
Municipal District	0	0	23	46	8	23
Town	0	0	11	45	38	7
Village/ Summer Village	4	4	20	24	38	9
Special Area/ Improvement District	0	0	13	63	13	13
AVERAGE	1%	3%	14%	38%	34%	10%

though he had no relevant experience. For the next two years controversy about his appointment and competence divided the council, becoming a major issue in the 1983 election. With a change in council, he was immediately dismissed. In 1981, Drayton Valley's two senior administrators resigned after the council brought in an economic consultant to evaluate the town's finances. When asked about his resignation, one replied: "Let's just say we've [the administrator and the council] come to an agreement on an early retirement."[12]

The 1983 survey asked how much pressure (unreasonable demands) administrators received from the general public, developers and community businesspeople. Eighty-eight per cent of respondents from cities, special areas and improvement districts reported some or a lot of pressure. The lowest sense of pressure was felt in municipal districts, and even there 54 per cent reported some or a lot of public pressure. Although an administrator can usually defuse a citizen's complaint or unreasonable demand with little fanfare, there are instances in which a member of the public has led a public campaign against an administrator. For an example, in Bon Accord, the town's only plumber was told by the administrator that, because his work was unsatisfactory and his prices too high, the town would no longer employ him. In 1982 the plumber circulated a petition demanding the administrator's dismissal. Almost half the town's electors signed the petition, although the administrator had the unqualified support of the mayor and all six councillors.[13]

From the administrators' responses it is clear that many businesspeople attempt to work through municipal administrators to further their own ends. Land developers seem to give administrators the most trouble: overall, 54 per cent replied that developers attempted to exert some or a lot of pressure on them; in special areas and improvement districts, the percentage shoots up to 88; in cities, it reaches 100. Most village and summer village administrators are spared developers' incessant demands: 64 four per cent replied that developers seldom if ever made unreasonable demands. On the other hand, almost 50 per cent of the village and summer village administrators replied that businesspeople often placed unreasonable demands on them; for city and town administrators the percentages were 63 and 58, respectively. However, a sizeable percentage of county and municipal district administrators escaped unreasonable demands from the business community; 69 per cent of municipal district administrators and 64 per cent of county administrators replied that they were hardly ever plagued with pressure from the business community.

Asked to name others who attempted to pressure them, only a few administrators replied. Five town and two village and summer village administrators named local organizations that attempted to exert substantial pressure. Only one respondent, a town administrator, reported that a labour union attempted to influence him unduly. Considering the number and activity of local organizations, it is surprising to find so few attempting to influence senior municipal administrators.

Professionalism and Public Policy

The surveys show that most Alberta municipal administrators are pressured and buffeted by council and assorted business interests.

Resisting this pressure requires that an administrator have a strong commitment to the service of the public and to professionalism. Particularly in the last decade, Alberta's municipal administrators have risen to the challenge and have become better educated, actively involved in their professional association, and increasingly aware of the role they play in policy making. Many, though not all, municipal councils have given their senior administrators recognition by awarding them salaries commensurate with those of other professionals. Still, there is a wide gap between the professional recognition administrators feel they deserve and the recognition they receive.

The survey of administrators asked how much commitment they had to professional values. Fifty-six per cent replied that they had a strong commitment; 37 per cent, some commitment; and only seven per cent, no commitment at all. Thus most administrators are committed professionals, yet many do not have professional status. When asked how much status their job gave them in the community, only 19 per cent replied "a lot," while 22 per cent replied "none."

Only well-qualified and highly professional senior administrators ensure that council policies will be competently implemented and administered, yet many councils have been tardy or unwilling to implement policies to professionalize their administration. It has already been shown that many municipalities have no policy on educational upgrading. This lack is reflected in the fact that, when asked whether they had an opportunity to learn new job skills, 21 per cent of the administrators replied they had none at all. Another indication of professionalization is the opportunity for job advancement within an organization. In the administrators' survey 69 per cent stated that they had no opportunity for job advancement.

One would expect councils' attitude to be reflected in the public's perception of senior municipal administrators, and both in turn to shape senior administrators' commitment to their work and perception of themselves as professionals. Commissioners and managers in larger cities and towns are, for the most part, recognized by the public as highly trained professional administrators, and the astute council realizes that success or failure of most council policies rests squarely on the shoulders of those people. It is in smaller communities and in those with less percipient councils that opportunities for educational upgrading are limited and administrators have little status in the community. Ironically, it is these same communities, often with part-time councils, that need highly trained and professional senior administrators.

The Department of Municipal Affairs is aware of the difficulties faced by councillors and administrators in smaller rural and urban municipalities and helps to keep them abreast of reporting deadlines, new regulations, and pertinent planning and legal decisions through its publication, the *Municipal Counsellor*, and through departmental directives. In addition, the department strongly encourages part-time administrators to upgrade their skills and councillors to become more knowledgeable about their responsibilities.

Notes

1. Caraley, *City Government and Urban Problems*, 268.

2. The public administration profession makes a distinction between administrative generalists and specialists; both groups claim to have special expertise. Specialists have expertise in particular service areas; for example, a knowledge of fighting fires and of administering a fire department or a knowledge of educational practices and administration. Generalists have a general knowledge of the administrative process that they are able to apply to any organization, no matter how specialized its goals.

3. Sayre and Kaufman, *Governing New York City*, 420-421.

4. Lipsky, "Street Level Bureaucrats and Urban Reform"; Lipsky, "Toward a Theory of Street-Level Bureaucracy"; Gardiner, "Police Enforcement of Traffic Laws"; Derthick, "Intercity Differences in Administration."

5. This provision applies only to villages, summer villages and municipal districts.

6. In 1976 Edward LeSage and Charles Humphrey, using a proportional stratified sample, selected 192 administrators (from larger municipalities, villages, counties and municipal districts) who were sent questionnaires relating to the skill requirements and training needs of municipal administrators. They had a 70 per cent return rate—158 questionnaires were returned, of which two were not usable. LeSage and Humphrey, "Alberta Municipal Administrator's Survey." In 1983 a follow-up study of municipal administrators was conducted by E. Einsiedel. She too used a proportional stratified sample, with 153 respondents replying to a questionnaire, a response rate of 67 per cent. Einsiedel, *Survey of Alberta Chief Municipal Administrators*.

7. Dean, Letter to Jack Masson, February 10, 1984.

8. Einsiedel, *Survey of Planning Needs and Training Preferences*.

9. *Ibid*.

10. The problems that were cited did not fall into any single category but rather covered a spectrum. The two problem areas mentioned most

frequently were "no management skills" and "poor communication skills." However, only seven per cent of the mayors cited each of those areas as a problem.

11. In Carstairs the replacement administrator, who had previously served in Spirit River for seven years as manager, lasted only two months before he resigned. Despite speculation that he too was caught up in dissension with the council, he refused to discuss the reason for his resignation. *Edmonton Report*, July 3, 1981. Perhaps, being circumspect, he realized that the publicity could only impede his appointment as a municipal administrator in another community.

12. *Ibid.*

13. *Alberta Report*, October 18, 1982.

7

GROUPS AND ASSOCIATIONS
IN THE
POLICY PROCESS

Interest Groups in Municipal Policy Making

A substantial segment of the citizenry has a major, if indirect, impact on local government through membership in interest groups. A straightforward, general definition of an *interest group* is presented by Frederick Engelmann and Mildred Schwartz, who write: "Interest groups . . . are organizations designed to put forward group demands, to infuse them into the political system and thereby take the first step toward obtaining political outputs in response to these demands."[1] Thus, the interest group links the ordinary member of a group with elected decision makers and the bureaucracy. Very few interest groups have lobbying as their sole purpose; for most, politics is a secondary activity and only occasionally necessary for furthering primary goals. For example, a religious organization, whose primary goal is providing religious sustenance, could lobby city hall for a zoning variance to enlarge the church parking lot. Finally, a small number of prestigious interest groups have much more potential influence than do most.

The following sections will concentrate on overtly political groups, one of whose primary goals is lobbying governmental officials in order to further their other primary goals. A characteristic differentiating their members from members of other groups is that a larger segment belong to the organization specifically to make their views known to city hall. These interest groups can be categorized by the *narrowness* or *broadness* of their membership base. A downtown merchants' association organized to make downtown more attractive for shoppers may have 20 or 25 members; an action group organized to prevent a freeway from bisecting a neighbourhood may have an active membership of several hundred and the passive support of several thousand. The following discussion begins by examining narrow-based membership organizations and concludes with broadly based ones.

Business Associations

We wouldn't be surprised to find business associations lobbying council continually for policies promoting business. An indicator is the time and energy council devotes to business-related matters, from rezoning applications to requests for variances permitting erection of advertising signs larger than those currently allowed. From the 1960s to the present, a number of social scientists have emphasized the pervasive influence of business on municipal policy making. They have focused on the activities of real estate developers, builders and land speculators. Arguments have often been made that these three groups act in concert, furthering their goals to the detriment of the public interest.[2]

Although businesses, independently and through their associations, lobby city council extensively, their inherent competitiveness prevents their acting in concert except on a few issues that affect them equally, such as a business tax increase and the promotion and growth of the community. A case in point is the Chamber of Commerce, found in almost every medium-sized and large municipality in the province. A chamber will lobby council, present briefs and often develop a close relationship with councillors, yet will rarely take a strong stance on issues.[3] A chamber's membership encompasses large and small businesses throughout the community. Since almost any business issue before council benefits some businesspeople and disadvantages others, a chamber's stance on most issues is either extremely moderate or non-existent. For example, on such issues as the redevelopment of the downtown core and Sunday shopping, a chamber's membership will be deeply divided. Redevelopment arouses strong support among core businesspeople and strong opposition among those in suburban shopping centres. Sunday shopping will be supported by newer businesses and opposed, as an expensive marketing gimmick, by established ones. A zoning variance allowing the entry of a new business into a neighbourhood will be opposed by existing local businesses. Then there are the "parriahs," such as escort services, massage parlours, "love shops" and video arcades, opposed by the "respectable business owners" in the community.

The irony of the reluctance of a chamber to take strong policy stands is that many citizens and elected officials believe the chamber is a unified organization that is potentially the most powerful local political force. A perceptive political scientist offers a plausible explanation of this belief when he writes:

> Public and reporters alike are relieved to believe both that there is a 'they' to make civic life explicable and also to be held responsible for what occurs. . . . The community needs to believe that there are spiritual fathers, bad or good, who can deal with the dark: in the Middle Ages the peasants combated a plague of locusts by a High Mass and a procession of the clergy who damned the grasshoppers with bell, book and candle. The Hopi Indians do a rain dance to overcome a drought. The harassed citizens of the . . . city mobilize their influenials at a civic luncheon to perform the equivalent and exorcise slums, smog, or unemployment. We smile at the medievals and the Hopi, but our own practices may be equally magical.[4]

The Urban Development Institute (UDI) and the Canadian Home Builders' Association (CHBA), formerly the Housing and Urban Development Association of Canada (HUDAC), represent the real estate industry at the national level. Both have well organized Alberta affiliates with professional staff versed in the techniques of lobbying municipal councillors and bureaucrats.

The UDI, Alberta division, has well over 400 members and associate members organized regionally into the Calgary, Red Deer and Edmonton chapters. Full membership is restricted to land developers; associate members include architects, engineers, bankers, and even municipal and provincial government bureaucrats. The UDI has an elected Board of Directors whose political activities are carried out by its Provincial Liaison Committee.[5] Both board members and professional staff maintain working relationships with bureaucrats and elected officials in provincial and municipal governments. In addition, the organization is prepared to bring legal action against policies that adversely affect developers. The ultimate end of this activity is to ease the difficulties of developers, making their business less costly and more profitable. The UDI is continually attempting to thwart policies requiring developers to build costly community facilities free of charge or to donate valuable land for transportation corridors as a trade-off for obtaining approval for subdivision developments. An example of the organization's legal activities occurred in Cochrane in the early 1980s. The town council passed a by-law prohibiting a development that would block the view of an existing development. The UDI successfully challenged the by-law in court.

In addition to its political activities, the UDI carries out a public relations program, for it is well aware of the public image of land developers. The programs, intended to brighten developers' tarnished image, include a speaker's bureau which provides experts to community groups at no cost, and various attempts to develop ties with colleges and universities.

CHBA is the parent organization of an integrated, two-tier Alberta group with municipal chapters. The CHBA Alberta Council, with approximately 1,000 members, constitutes the upper tier; the seven CHBA chapters, in Medicine Hat, Lethbridge, Calgary, Red Deer, Edmonton, Edson and Grande Prairie, its lower tier. Membership in a municipal chapter automatically confers membership in the Alberta and national organizations, and the last two are funded by a portion of the municipal chapter members' annual dues.

CHBA's political activities are simply divided: CHBA Canada lobbies the federal government; CHBA Alberta Council lobbies the provincial government; and the local chapters lobby their respective municipal councils. Since many housing programs and policies involve more than one level of government, CHBA's three levels often co-ordinate their activities.

In Alberta CHBA subscribes to an ethic of a free market in housing. Yet, realizing that a free market ethic is unrealistic and that government involvement in housing is increasing, the organization has followed a strategy of developing close relationships with the provincial and municipal governments. This tactic has been so successful that CHBA will be consulted at every stage in the formulation of government policy on housing. Not only do the Alberta Council and the local chapters attempt to develop relationships with elected officials, they also try to develop ties with bureaucrats in departments concerned with housing. Individual members are encouraged to use political and bureaucratic contacts to serve as a "low profile intelligence network . . . for early identification of legislation or regulatory issues."[6]

A few very powerful business people prefer to lobby council at the local level on an individual basis rather than to have their views expressed through an umbrella organization. In Edmonton, the Ghermezian brothers, major city property developers, provide an example. They have had a history of involvement in the city's political campaigns, making presentations before council, and threatening the city administration with dire consequences unless their demands are met. Unlike most property developers, they maintain a high level of public visibility.

Associations of Municipal Employees

The associations of municipal employees are important actors in the policy-making process of many Alberta municipalities, counties and municipal districts. A major problem faced by all municipal associations is the erratic policy stance councils take on issues concerning the well-being of their employees. A council's decisions on such policies fluctuate with the community's economic viability: during periods of prosperity municipal councils give generous wage and benefit settlements rather than face the possibility of a bitter strike, an irate, inconvenienced public and unforeseen political consequences; in hard times, however, councils often claim that their duty is to lay off municipal employees and keep wage increases to a minimum. Although the latter policy stance usually divides councils and embitters municipal employees, it generally has substantial public support.

The first association of municipal employees founded in Alberta was a local of the militant Industrial Workers of the World, made up of Edmonton outside-city labourers who organized in 1912. Almost immediately, 250 of their members struck for higher wages. The city broke the strike, with the men returning to work on the city's terms.[7] More importantly, the abortive strike broke the union. Less than a month later the Lethbridge police force went out on strike and, as in Edmonton, the city administration broke the strike.[8] Four years later, Edmonton's outside workers again organized and were issued a charter by the Trades and Labour Congress. A labour historian chronicles labour's rapid expansion from that point:

> Their lead was soon followed by city inside workers in Calgary and municipal employees in Lethbridge and Medicine Hat. By 1919 a municipal federation had been formed in Calgary to negotiate with city council. It included, in addition to city hall staff and labourers, police and fire fighters, teamsters, electricians and street-railway workers. In 1919, the first local of hospital workers in the province, Local 8, City Hospital Employees, was organized to represent workers at the Calgary municipal hospital.[9]

For the next three decades municipal unions used the strike threat as their principal strategy. In more recent times, they have become much more politically sophisticated, recruiting widespread public support in order to influence councils. This new sophistication seems to have come about with the formation of the national Canadian Union of Public Employees (CUPE) in 1963. CUPE, with a 1983

Alberta membership of over 22,000, has organized aggressively at the municipal level since its founding in Alberta. Not only are there strong CUPE locals in Edmonton (2,700 municipal employees in one local) and Calgary (5,119 in three locals), but the union has also organized municipal employees in almost all Alberta cities and in many smaller communities. In total, there are 42 locals in 37 municipalities, counties and municipal districts. Fire and police department employees have also been organized in some communities, although not into CUPE locals. Fire department employees are unionized in eight cities and in the County of Strathcona. Nine municipalities have a unionized police force.[10]

The Alberta Teacher's Association, with 26,000 members and 79 locals, is the most powerful political force at the local level today. With teachers' attempts to gain professional recognition in salary and status, the organization has had a stormy history. Its predecessor, the Alberta Teacher's Alliance, splintered from the Alberta Educational Association in 1918 because the parent organization seemed to be unconcerned with the issues of teachers' salaries and tenure, and with teachers' broader concerns about the inadequacies of the educational system. Both the Department of Education and the Alberta School Trustees' Association were alarmed over the militancy of the new organization, which, among other things, had employed a paid organizer; the two fought the Alliance throughout the 1920s and 1930s. When militant Edmonton high school teachers went out on a two-week strike in 1921, the ATA won. But, in 1926, the organization suffered a severe setback when the teachers in Blairmore were locked out and the trustees hired an entire new staff. The teachers sued the district for unlawful termination, and lost.

When the United Farmers of Alberta (UFA) came to power in 1921, one of their first pieces of legislation lowered the entrance requirements for Normal Schools (the teacher colleges of the time) in order to flood the province with new teachers who could be hired at a very low wage. Both the UFA's Department of Education and the school trustees bitterly fought the Alliance's proposals for a pension scheme, tenure and procedures for dismissal. In 1935 the Teaching Profession Act changed the name of the Alliance to the Alberta Teacher's Association (ATA), the only gain teachers received from the legislation.

It was not until Premier Aberhart swept into power under the Social Credit banner in 1935 that the ATA received support from the government. Small and financially weak districts were consolidated into stronger units that were unable to argue that they could not afford to pay adequate salaries. Teachers were given job protection and, in 1939, the Teachers' Superannuation Act was approved, a first step towards the creation of an adequate pension scheme.

Today, the ATA is a powerful association that is the collective bargaining agent for every Alberta teacher. It also has the power to discipline its members for unprofessional and unethical conduct. Acutely aware that the economic well-being of its members is directly related to the provincial basic education grant and to districts' supplemental requisitions, the ATA is continually lobbying both sources. Teachers are encouraged to run for political office and to become involved in local educational politics. As the ATA has become more and more powerful, the Alberta School Trustees' Association (ASTA), feeling increasingly threatened, has attempted to counter its influence, with only limited success.

The tactics of municipal administrations and associations of public employees are exemplified by a series of events in Edmonton and Calgary in 1982-83. In the winter of 1982, the administrations of both cities decided to minimize tax increases by laying off a large number of civic employees, including many policemen and firemen. To garner public support, the administrations leaked information on the generous salaries and benefits received by police and firefighters, benefits bestowed on the two groups with little hesitation during the prosperous 1970s. In addition, the public was led to believe that civic employees were primarily responsible for the cities' financial crises. The unions responded by initiating legal action to prevent the layoffs and by mounting a public relations campaign either to win-over the citizenry or to frighten it into supporting their position.[11] The disputes were eventually settled with only a small number of people losing their jobs and with a decrease in municipal employees to take place by attrition. The legacy of the battle is a demoralized public service and a public confused by the charges and counter-charges made by the administrations and public employees' associations.

A province-wide survey conducted in 1971 found that Alberta's union members were relatively complacent.[12] However, in the 1980s, if municipalities follow Edmonton and Calgary's example of using municipal employees as scapegoats for their financial woes, one can safely predict that municipal employees will become far more militant than they have been.

Citizen Groups, Associations and Committees

For many years committees of citizens have been part of the political scene in Alberta's municipalities. It has been common practice for council to strike a "blue ribbon citizens' committee" to handle an issue the council was unwilling or unable to deal with. However, these committees were seldom representative but, rather, were composed of businesspeople, professionals and politicians.[13]

It was not until the 1960s and 1970s that citizen groups, especially neighbourhood groups, came to be accepted as a legitimate part of the municipal political process in Alberta. The neighbourhood organizations have their roots in the student activism of the late 1960s and early 1970s. Activists learned organizational techniques and the tactics of using direct confrontation to gain a say in administration. Once graduated, they changed their life-style but they didn't forget the effectiveness of well-organized group action or the desire to have a direct input into the democratic process. In his analysis of the changing atmosphere of Edmonton's politics, James Lightbody describes another facet of the growth and legitimization of citizen participation in Alberta. He writes:

> The source of this challenge was an unintended consequence of the rapid expansion of the University of Alberta's faculty (which tripled in size) and the research staff at other agencies such as the Research Council of Alberta. By far the greatest number of recruits for these institutions were either American by birth or Canadians who had received their post-graduate education in the United States. They were not only highly qualified but had also been subject to . . . the rhetoric of direct citizen participation then associated with the American war on poverty programs.[14]

Providing dedicated members and leadership skills, these academics and a multitude of recently graduated students were instrumental in forming neighbourhood citizen groups committed to political action.

City halls in Edmonton and Calgary, quick to recognize this new political force in the community, haltingly made provisions to plug it into the political system. In 1971 Edmonton embarked on an ambitious three-year experimental pilot project combining the decentralization of social services with citizen participation for 10 communities with a population of 40,000. The West Edmonton Social Task Force, or West 10 as it was popularly known, brought together into a central community office people from the provincial Department of Health and Social Development, city social services, city parks and recreation, the public school board, Canada Manpower, the federal Local Initiative Program and a number of volunteer agencies. Two community-development officers were employed to activate the communities' residents, who were to "oversee" the project through a 15-member citizens' area council. In reality, the council was merely advisory, as the various federal, provincial and city employees were responsible only to their respective departments.

This anomaly eventually led to a drastic restructuring of the citizen participation component of the project. When the politically naive West 10 council took its mandate seriously and attempted to integrate all the departments and bring them directly under its own control, the departments resisted and, eventually, caused the provincial government to pull out of the program. Although the first West 10 area council chairman, Joe Jansen, said he was committed to "participatory democracy" with "most decision-making lying with the people and higher levels of government serving in a co-ordinating capacity,"[15] he later admitted that the citizens' area council had been a "sham."[16] To keep the "radicals" from taking control, the organization was restructured, with a board composed of representatives from established community groups, such as the Westmount Christian Council and the Westmount Ministerial Association. The low level of citizen involvement was related to the council's lack of power. Initially, approximately 900 residents were minimally involved, with a much smaller number of activists. However, the activists soon saw that the council was powerless and that "citizen participation" was merely "window dressing." At its first annual meeting in 1972 approximately 100 people turned out to elect council members; at its third, fewer than 45 people showed up, only eight of whom agreed to stand for election to the 15-member council.

Although the West 10 project was renewed at the end of its three-year trial, its funding kept shrinking and its citizen participation component was eventually discarded. Today it serves primarily as a referral body for social services.

An equally ambitious and unsuccessful effort to promote citizen participation was made in Calgary. Mayor Sykes attempted to mobilize community leaders as a nucleus for a broadly based citizen organization intended to have major input into city hall decision making. The "Citizens' Open Government Study" (COGS) was composed of middle-class professionals from civic organizations and prominent individuals representing the citizenry. These people were expected to recruit additional participants.

> The tacit, working assumption was that these people and the organizations behind them in the search for improvement would bring about a dual cure for dissatisfaction with local government. First of all, participants would increase their own awareness of civic politics, their confidence to pursue it, and their commitment to its success. Secondly, the committee's

recommendations would open the door to greater opportunities for participation in government by Calgarians.[17]

Either the organizational structure was faulty or the COGS members were unable to generate greater citizen interest, for the study failed to develop a broadly based citizens' organization. After 15 months it did submit a number of recommendations for greater citizen input to council but, by that time, the bloom was off citizen participation and little action was taken on the recommendations.

Although municipally sponsored citizen participation has been more or less a failure in the province's two largest cities, there have been successes when citizens have spontaneously organized around an issue. For example, when in April, 1981, the Brooks town council appointed a town manager many people thought unqualified, the Brooks Concerned Citizens Committee sprang into existence almost immediately. It circulated a petition protesting the appointment and held several well-attended meetings, eventually forcing the council to hire a management consulting firm to evaluate the town's administration. When the town manager was finally dismissed, the citizens' committee disbanded. After a severe 1981 storm in Edmonton caused extensive basement flooding and sewer backups in the southeastern part of the city, a Southeast Edmonton Flood Action Committee formed to pressure city council to upgrade the area's sewer system. Over nine months, the group held a number of well-attended meetings, distributed 7,000 flyers throughout the community, and had several interviews with city councillors. As a result of this incessant pressure, in April, 1982, council decided to start sewer improvement work in the area approximately 15 years ahead of schedule. Its work completed, the committee disbanded. At about the same time and in the same area, the Mill Woods Cultural and Recreational Facility Association came into being and convinced city council and the parks department to build a $4.8 million leisure and recreational centre. In the summer of 1983 an ad hoc group of 30 middle-class residents on Medicine Hat's Fourth Street organized to halt a developer's plan to build a five-story apartment building in the neighbourhood. A petition accompanied by individual appeals to council members was successful: council quashed the development.

Ethnic communities in Calgary and Edmonton have developed broadly based citizen groups that have functioned as their political arm. When, in 1982, Calgary's administration was considering scaling down the size of its Chinatown by one-third, the Chinese community quickly organized and convinced the administration that the proposal was faulty. Both the United Calgary Chinese Association and the Chinatown Ratepayer Association, long active on the Calgary political scene, have been moderately successful in maintaining the viability of the Chinese community. Edmonton's small Italian community spent six years in a tenacious attempt to convince city council to rename a small park in their neighbourhood to commemorate John Cabot. The Giovanni Caboto Society was formed, held a number of meetings, fed information to the press, and met with various councillors and senior city administrators. Its efforts came to fruition in 1981 when the park was renamed Giovanni Caboto Park.

The organization of ratepayer associations is a recent rural phenomenon. Although Donald Higgins found that ratepayer associations had "developed at least as far back as the early part of this century in many municipalities, both large and small, in Canada,"[18] there is little mention of them in Alberta newspapers before the 1930s. In Calgary and Edmonton a ratepayer association would form spontaneously to vent the wrath of property owners over an aspect of council mismanagement. It would capture newspaper headlines and then disappear. Having no staying power, such organizations were not a major political force in either city.

With the explosive suburbanization in Calgary and Edmonton in the 1960s and 1970s, hobby farm suburbanites on the cities' outer fringes found themselves locked in political battles with traditional farmers. Perceiving that property was inequitably taxed, that there was some evidence of fiscal mismanagement and that they were being denied services, hobby farmers formed ratepayer associations. There are at least eight of these associations, most on the outskirts of Edmonton and Calgary.[19] Almost all have a substantial membership cutting across social class, though most of their members are middle to upper-middle class. In a letter from the President of the Bearspaw, Glendale Ratepayer Association, the membership is described as "upper-middle to upper levels . . . the acreage owners and large farmers are in the $70,000 plus per year level; some small farmers and older residents, $40,000 plus. Most acreage owners tend to be professional management or own their own companies".[20] The President of the Leduc Residents Association describes his members as "farmers and acreage owners of middle to upper middle level incomes."[21]

When the associations were founded, most dealt with a variety of issues. Over time, they have come to focus almost entirely on property tax inequities. However, their levels of political activity vary widely. While all are involved in lobbying, there is wide divergence in their electoral activities. The Strathcona Acreage Owner's Association, which, in 1983, had existed for over 10 years, has never endorsed a county council candidate. On the other hand, the 800-member

Foothills Ratepayers Association endorsed a full slate of candidates in the 1983 Municipal District elections and convinced the Minister of Municipal Affairs to change the district's electoral boundaries to guarantee equal representation. In a candid moment, the President of the Bearspaw, Glendale Ratepayer Association wrote:

> We supported a candidate in the last councillor election to try and get acreage owners to vote for a non farmer; unfortunately the man was a hobby farmer and lost badly. This election we will try again but it might be the kiss of death to any serious contender to be supported by a ratepayers association with the large farmer vote.[22]

While the ratepayer associations have had moderate success influencing councils' policies, they have been less successful in encouraging their members to attend their meetings, despite the fact they are the only broadly based grass-roots organization in rural areas. The Brooks Renters' and Ratepayers' Association (80 per cent of whose members are ratepayers), with a membership fluctuating between 50 and 60, has been the most successful, as 15 to 25 members regularly attend meetings. On the other hand, the Bearspaw, Glendale Ratepayer Association with several hundred members averages 10 members at each meeting. Several association presidents have said that only a fiscal crisis will activate a sizeable percentage of their members to attend meetings; as it is, only a very few "hard-core" members actively participate.

Edmonton's extensive network of community leagues and Calgary's community associations with broadly based neighbourhood membership have the potential to become powerful neighbourhood political groups; with a few exceptions, however, their main focus has been recreation. Ironically, Edmonton's first community league, established in 1912, was a ratepayer association active in making demands on city hall. Other leagues soon formed and, in 1921, the Edmonton Federation of Community Leagues was established. By that time the leagues' activities had shifted from politics to recreation. Community associations formed later in Calgary, the first being the Mount Royal Community Association, founded in January, 1934. The organizations proliferated in both cities: by 1983 there were 134 leagues in Edmonton and 110 community associations in Calgary.

In both cities most organizations have been minimally involved in politics, though, during the controversy over licensing video games arcades, several took positions and sent letters to council. James Lightbody writes of the leagues' political involvement in Edmonton:

Although the Edmonton Federation of Community Leagues hovered on the fringe of issues such as the ward system, or the proposed downtown coliseum, it was not able to command the allegiance of its constituents who, in any case, were more concerned with the expansion of recreational services to their rapidly growing clientele.[23]

There are exceptions, however. In Calgary the Hillhurst-Sunnyside Community Association convinced council to change a proposed LRT route. In Edmonton the River Valley Community League played a major role in council's decision to reverse a long-standing policy of acquiring river valley land for parks and open space.

It remains to be seen whether the community groups in the two cities will change their recreational orientation. Middle-class areas in the two cities are only beginning to awake from a long political sleep. The few middle-class neighbourhood groups have had little encouragement from the municipal administration. Frustrated by unanswered letters and unreturned phone calls, given too little time to respond to proposals affecting their neighbourhood, and refused requests for information they need to respond intelligently to council proposals, many of these fledgling political groups have reverted to non-political status. Working-class neighbourhood groups bear additional burdens. With less education, they have fewer members who are able to comprehend complex policy issues and fewer members with the negotiating skills so crucial in dealing with council. They are less socially "connected" with the community's socio-economic elite, who often tend to dominate the local political scene. In short, these groups have less political influence than do middle-class ones. Yet, despite these roadblocks, a potential grass-roots apparatus is in place. Astute leadership, organizational skills and a basic change in citizen attitudes towards local government will be key factors in determining whether the community organizations will further grass-roots democracy at the neighbourhood level.

The News Media as a Political Interest Group?

Associations of broadcasters and newspapers lobby for legislation ranging from reduced newspaper mailing rates to zoning changes for proposed newspaper plants and radio and TV towers. However, most students of politics are far more interested in the effects the media have on public opinion; unfortunately, this is one of the murkier areas in social science. One problem is that "empirical studies . . . which have actually demonstrated influence relationships or tested formulations, seem to have lagged far behind the conceptual part of the enterprise."[24] Another difficulty is that newspapers, radio and television serve diverse segments of the public in varying formats — there is not a single media influence but rather different media, each with wide-ranging influences. Moreover, since virtually all forms of media compete with one another for advertising dollars (which are directly related to the size of their reading, viewing and listening audiences) they tend to *follow* public tastes and interests rather than *lead* them. As a consequence, the media provide a mix of entertainment and news to a fickle public that often complains about the inadequacies of both.

Despite their own commercial focus and the vagaries of the public, the media do play a vital role in determining whether democracy is to be a success or failure. In community after community, it is the media upon which the public relies for open political discourse. In theory, the media can bring politicians' views to their constituents and those of the citizenry to their representatives; both activities further grass-roots democracy.

In shaping public opinion at the community level, newspapers are much more important than radio and television. In an American survey of city managers in cities with populations over 100,000, newspapers were seen "as much more interested in, associated with, and influential in municipal affairs than either television or radio."[25] Sketchy evidence indicates a similar pattern in Canadian communities.[26] Radio and television stations carefully tailor their programming to the public's demand for entertainment. Radio focuses on providing music with occasional capsulized accounts of national and international news as it happens. It is the unusual station that devotes any time to council events or local political issues, let alone to in-depth analyses of them. Local television stations are reluctant to commit resources to cover council meetings and local political issues. When they do, coverage tends to be superficial 15-second to one-minute segments.

Large city dailies have a somewhat different news focus than do smaller community weeklies and urban "throw-away" advertising newspapers. A substantial amount of the political news in a large daily is national and international and is supplied by the wire services. Even more prominent is provincial political news; full-time reporters are assigned to cover the legislature and provincial departments in Edmonton. City hall and local political issues are covered, but must compete with international, national and provincial events. By contrast, weekly and community "throw-aways," whose *raison d'être* is the community, focus on community events, politics and personalities.

Whether the newspaper is a daily, weekly or "throw-away," there are constraints on the news that is reported and on the tone of writing. Since newspapers depend on the good-will of advertisers (who are generally among the community's social and economic elite), the astute editor is careful not to offend them. Edwin Black, in a study of the news media in Canada, defines four factors that result in "the tendency for small newspapers to support community notables." They are:

1. The publisher's vulnerability to local social and business pressure.

2. Vocational training of traditional gatekeepers (city and news editors, etc.) which leads them to omit or bury news items that might call into question the socio-cultural structure and people's faith in it.

3. Reporter's reliance on authority figures for news sources.

4. The journalistic concept of professionalism which emphasizes rationality, decisions rather than discussion, depersonalisation of local legislative proceedings, legal language, and respectful treatment of local notables.[27]

By deferring to the established norms of the community's socio-economic elite and by selecting which news is published and which is not, the newspaper is extremely important in establishing the community's political agenda. However, newspapers differ in their effect on different segments of the community. An American study found that members of lower-income groups were more prone to obtain their news from radio and television than from newspapers. While 41 per cent of the general population relied on newspapers for local news, only 22 per cent of the study's low-income respondents did so.[28] Yet a study of the media in the 1968 Edmonton election found that respondents with a low interest in the election and low levels of political competence "showed the closest association between voting and both editorial reading and information."[29] The same study found that the endorsement by the *Edmonton Journal* of the major civic party running candidates for office "had virtually no effect at all on the way its readers voted in the election."[30]

Although editorial endorsements are largely ignored by the citizenry, letters to the editor are followed closely by the council members. Every community has a small number of educated, informed people who follow the issues and express their opinions in the local letters-to-the-editor column. Collectively, all of these letters are taken into consideration by council, although council is seldom sure whether the self-proclaimed political knowledgeables represent the community's general interests or individual opinions.

Little is known about the extent to which newspaper "agenda setting" influences council policy making. In a recent study of this phenomenon, Edwin Black looked at three smaller Ontario communities, Belleville, Kingston and Peterborough. With mixed findings, he concluded:

> The ability to influence local decision schedules appears—on the basis of the interview data—to be a function of the prevailing structures of debate and decision making. The ability may not be generally inherent in local newspaper reporting as such.[31]

One might anticipate finding a similar pattern of influence in Alberta; that is, in many communities there will be a close relationship between issues raised by newspapers and those dealt with on council, while in others the newspaper will be looked upon as an outsider attempting to "stir up" issues the council does not consider relevant. One would expect to find many more council—newspaper relationships in the former category, since a crusading paper would normally put its advertising revenue in jeopardy by alienating either the business community or the council, both normally committed to the status quo. For example, in Edmonton in the late 1970s, the *Edmonton Journal* took persistent political potshots at a council it considered inept. The council responded by encouraging a second daily, the *Edmonton Sun*, to begin publishing in the city. Shortly after the *Sun* started up, councillor Ed Leger, the butt of numerous *Journal* editorials and editorial cartoons, proposed that all city advertising be given to the *Sun*. An examination found the *Sun's* circulation to be only one-sixth that of the *Journal* and Leger's proposal was quietly shelved. With no letup in the *Journal's* criticism of council, in October, 1979, the city published its own eight-page tabloid and distributed it free to 190,000 Edmontonians. The tabloid's in-house, city hall editor admitted the paper was "relatively bland" but explained, "elected and administrative officials obviously do have a vested interest in what goes out."[32] The public evidently agreed, for the tabloid was little read and the costly venture was terminated.

Small-town weeklies are particularly sensitive to their financial balance sheets and may rely on the publication of municipal legal notices and council minutes for their continued existence. In return for publishing its minutes and notices the council contracts with a weekly newspaper for free distribution to all of its ratepayers.[33] In 1974 it was estimated that half of the municipal districts and counties in the province had such an agreement.[34] Occasionally, it is charged that a council attempts to muzzle the press by withdrawing its advertising revenue from an offending newspaper. In 1981 the editor of the *North Peace Pictorial* charged that the Grimshaw council was trying to drive him out of business because he criticized the financial arrangements of a proposed curling complex and called for the mayor's resignation. He complained that the council gave all of its business, payment for 1800 subscriptions, to his competitor without asking the electorate their preference in newspapers.[35] In 1982 the publisher of the *Sturgeon Gazette* charged the Bon Accord council with terminating a $36,000 contract to supply the community's 600 residents with a newspaper at half cost because the paper published a letter to the editor criticizing the municipal administrator.[36] One can only speculate how many weeklies with municipal contracts "tread carefully" when reporting on council and administration activities.

Electioneering provides another important source of revenue for small-community weeklies. It is common for a candidate to drop off a political biography or news release when making arrangements to place paid political advertising. It is to be expected that the weekly will be more interested in candidates who buy political advertising than in those who do not.

Both the public and students of local politics are intuitively aware that the media have as much influence over the citizenry and council decision makers as does any other interest group. However, the full potential of this influence is constrained by the fact that media are commercial enterprises that cannot afford to run too far ahead of prevailing political norms. The long-range effect of this factor is that the media tend to be relatively conservative, supporting the status quo except on rare occasions. Investigative reporting and political exposés of local political events are found, if at all, in the larger cities, not in the smaller towns and villages.

Private Consultants

Private consultants form a hybrid group in that they are not strictly an interest group as defined by Engelmann and Schwartz. Except among elected officials and the bureaucracy, private consultants tend to be invisible. Yet, in the last two decades, municipal governments have made increasing use of private consultants, who are now nearly as important in the policy-making process as are elected officials.[37] As municipal services have become more technical and complex, small as well as large municipalities require skills unavailable in their administrations. And some service areas have become so technical or the circumstances so unique that the elected representatives do not even know what policy options are open to them. Municipalities find they need expert advice in areas that used to be serviced adequately by municipal employees, for example, swimming pool and ice arena design and construction. Municipal councils have been persuaded to hire consultants in non-technical areas as well, for example, public participation specialists.

There are other equally important reasons for the recent, almost exponential growth in the numbers of consultants employed by municipal governments. Some provincial legislation requires that a municipality hire a private consultant to protect the public, whether it is felt to be necessary or not. Under section 20 of the Architects Act, a municipality requires the approval of a licensed architect before the council can approve funds to erect, enlarge or alter:

> e. a building of more than one storey to be used for public assembly where the gross area exceeds 2500 feet,

> f. a building with a capacity of over 12 beds, to be used as a hospital, sanatorium or home for the aged, other than a veterinary hospital,

> g. a school building containing more than 3 rooms for . . . teaching . . . or containing a gymnasium or auditorium, or,

> h. any other building of which the aggregate area of all floors exceeds 5000 square feet. . . .

Under Part I, Section 1.5, of the Alberta Building Code, a municipality needs the approval of a licensed engineer before certain types of public buildings can be erected. While such provisions are intended to prevent the erection of faulty buildings, the unintended effect is to provide engineering and architectural firms with a certain amount of public business and the ability to influence the policy-making process through their recommendations and reports.

Large segments of the public in municipality after municipality have become increasingly critical of the size and cost of local bureaucratic structures. By employing private consultants rather than hiring additional personnel, a council is able to claim that it has put a cap on bureaucratic expansion and costs, even though using consultants is often as costly as employing additional municipal personnel.[38]

However, the cost of hiring consultants shows up in a different budget category; thus, the use of consultants quiets critics of big government and administration.

In recent years a strategy of many municipal councils has been to depoliticize a contentious issue by shifting its disposition to a private consultant. One student of politics explains this strategy when he writes:

> The shifting of issues to private consultants by public officials has a great deal of middle class, business oriented responsibility. Further, since the private consultant is an unknown to the general public, and often from a distant city, the potential political retaliation or economic retaliation is removed.[39]

Both Edmonton and Calgary have employed private consultants to evaluate Light Rail Transit (LRT) as a means of shifting responsibility to consultants.[40] The hope is that the public will fail to realize that policy (whether it promotes public transit, private transit or a mix of the two, or decides which neighbourhoods are to be divided by thoroughfares and public transit routes) is a political problem, not an engineering problem that can be "solved" by private consultants.

Another strategy of many councils is hiring private consultants to legitimize a policy decision they have already made.[41] The private consultant gives a stamp of "scientific approval" to a decision that is wholly political. An example of this practice occurred in the Edmonton region in the late 1970s. A horde of private consultants gave approval to diametrically opposing policies when Edmonton attempted to expand its boundaries. Each governmental unit hired one or more consultants to legitimize its position, paying the following approximate amounts:

Edmonton	$2,355,000
County of Strathcona	$2,800,000
St. Albert	$700,000
Municipal District of Sturgeon and County of Parkland [42]	$450,000

Not surprisingly, none of the consultants made recommendations out of accord with the views of their employers.

Local Government Associations

A government association's primary role is to act as a single voice for its members in expressing their concerns to the provincial and federal governments and to press for legislation of benefit to its members. Secondary roles are to mediate differences among its members and, in limited cases, to act as a co-operative providing them with goods and services.

The four most powerful such associations in Alberta are the Federation of Canadian Municipalities (FCM), the Alberta Urban Municipalities Association (AUMA), the Alberta Association of Municipal Districts and Counties (AAMD & C), and the Alberta School Trustees' Association (ASTA). The Department of Municipal Affairs works closely with the Alberta members of the FCM, the AUMA and the AAMD & C, while the Department of Education has close ties with ASTA. On issues that affect the members of the various associations equally, they form alliances to present a common front to the government.

The four organizations closely follow proposed changes in legislation in their respective areas and often present position papers to the government. It is not uncommon for the Departments of Municipal Affairs and Education to approach one of the associations informally for comments on administrative and legislative proposals. In short, there is a close working relationship between particular provincial departments and the associations that benefits both sides since it reduces acrimony and conflict.

Perhaps the most powerful local government association in the province is ASTA, which has power legitimized in the Alberta School Trustee's Association Act. From its founding in 1907, the organization has received strong support and funding from the provincial government. It was the Premier and Minister of Education A.C. Rutherford who thought it would be a "good idea" to call together all the school trustees in the province to a convention at which ASTA was founded.[43] The first provincial support came when the province "paid for the notices and the publishing of proceedings of the first convention and also assisted in this matter with subsequent conventions."[44] ASTA's close relationship with the Department of Education came about in 1909 when the Acting Deputy Minister of Education told its president that the Department intended "to incorporate the suggestions of the trustees, as far as possible, into the Amendments of the School Ordinance and Regulations." This relationship has continued to the present; for example, when in 1970 the Department of Education requested that ASTA help rewrite the School Act, more than half of ASTA's suggestions were incorporated into the new Act.[45]

During the 1930s the organization foundered as trustees of cash-starved school districts withdrew. The provincial government brought the organization back to life with its passage of the Alberta

School Trustees' Association Act, which directed that "the board of trustees of each non-divisional school district and of each school division in the Province shall be members of the association." This legislation solved the membership problem but not the financial one, which was finally resolved in March, 1941, by an order in council (no. 285) that gave the Department of Education the power to deduct unpaid fees from the provincial education grant.[46]

Perhaps the reason the provincial government has favoured ASTA is that ASTA's goals are largely the same as its own. First, ASTA has had a long battle with the Alberta Teachers' Association (ATA), opposing teacher collective bargaining, minimum salaries and continuous contracts. Undoubtedly, both Social Credit and the Progressive Conservatives were acutely aware of the potential power of the ATA and sympathized with the efforts of ASTA to check it. Second, most school trustees have the attitude that it is their duty to protect ratepayers from "inordinate tax increases and irresponsible educational empire building." This concern with local "irresponsibility" has been shared by both Social Credit and Progressive Conservatives parties.

The FCM underwent a name change in 1976: before that time it had been the Canadian Federation of Mayors and Municipalities (CFMM). It is a national organization whose purpose is to further the goals of municipalities and assist them in dealing with the federal government as well as facilitating co-operation between municipalities and the two senior levels of government. Its organizational and membership structure is complex since it includes both individual municipalities and associations of municipalities across Canada. In 1983, 22 individual Alberta municipalities (of which a small number were founding members of the CFMM in 1937), as well as the AUMA and the AAMD & C, were members of the FCM.[47]

The FCM aggressively lobbies the federal government for greater financial resources and legislative changes to ease the task of municipal government. An example of the former purpose has been its efforts to obtain a direct portion of income tax revenue for municipalities; an example of the latter one has been its attempt to convince the federal government to amend the criminal code to enable local police to clear the streets of prostitutes. Under an agreement worked out with provincial associations of municipalities, the FCM does not involve itself with strictly municipal-provincial issues. However, working with the provincial associations, the FCM recently expressed its concerns to the Alberta government about the province's declining investment in municipal capital projects and the need for a new intergovernmental structure to facilitate provincial-municipal cooperation.

Although the FCM is a major actor in the formulation of federal policies that affect municipalities, the association has some inherent weaknesses. Feldman and Graham point out that many municipalities don't see any advantage in belonging to the FCM, since, with municipal matters falling under the purview of the provinces, the federal government is not perceived as a major player in municipal policymaking. As FCM's membership represents only a minority of the nation's larger cities the organization is not seen as being very representative. The two social scientists also note that "Canadian urban municipalities have also exhibited a tendency to act alone when dealing with the federal government".[48]

Almost all municipalities in the province are represented by the AUMA. In 1980 its membership consisted of 100 per cent of the province's cities and towns, 94 per cent of the villages and 71 per cent of the summer villages. Originally organized as the Union of Alberta Municipalities in 1905, its objectives were 1) to co-ordinate assessment in the various municipalities in order to achieve uniformity; 2) to protect municipalities from unscrupulous corporations and promoters; 3) to lobby for legislation benefiting municipalities; and 4) to make "better arrangements in reference to indigent persons chargeable to municipalities".[49]

For years, functioning as an informal association, the union kept increasing its membership and, in 1966, was formally incorporated as the AUMA. In 1969, at the request of its members, the AUMA established a Labour Relations Service to assist individual municipalities in their labour negotiations. In the 1970s and early 1980s it became increasingly powerful as the provincial government began to rely more and more on its recommendations on policies for municipal governments.[50]

The main reason the AUMA has not wielded even more power in shaping municipal legislation is its own inherent tensions. Although all municipalities want to increase "no-strings" provincial assistance, in some policy areas small towns and villages have much different policy concerns than do large cities. This difference makes it difficult for the Association to take a firm position on some issues. On others, in the interest of small municipality-large city compromise, proposals can be made only in the most general terms. For these reasons, despite strength in numbers, the organization may splinter in the future.

A smaller municipal organization, some of whose members also belong to the AUMA, is the Alberta Association of Summer Villages. Founded in 1958 to promote the specialized interests of summer villages, the organization has continued to grow, and its 1983 membership consisted of 35 of the 40 summer villages in the province. Some of its members belong to the AUMA in order to obtain attractive municipal insurance, but they rely on their specialized organization to lobby and present briefs to the government for their primary concern: adequate roads and bridges.

The Alberta Association of Local Improvement Districts (the forerunner of the AAMD & C) was incorporated in 1910 to: 1) forward the interests of all local improvement districts in the province; 2) endeavour to secure legislation relating to local improvement work; 3) guard the interests of Local Improvement Districts in any proposed legislation; and 4) work closely with the Department of Public Works. Since its inception it has strongly resisted provincial encroachment on local autonomy and has cautioned the provincial government against excessive centralization. Despite the province's urbanization, the AAMD & C has successfully lobbied to ensure that the government maintains a rural point of view. Ray Speaker, the independent MLA from Little Bow, speaking before the Association's 1983 annual convention, said, "you are one of the strongest lobby groups in the province and closest to the people's needs."[51] In addition to its lobbying activities, the Association provides its members with comprehensive insurance through its Jubilee Insurance Agency and acts as a co-operative for heavy equipment and supplies used by its members' engineering departments.

Two relatively new organizations are the Alberta Federation of Métis Settlements Association, founded in 1975, and the Alberta Association of Improvement Districts, founded in 1976. The Federation of Métis Settlements represents the province's eight Métis settlements through a board consisting of the chairperson of each settlement council and four other members, elected at-large. The Association of Improvement Districts represents the 24 improvement district advisory councils through a seven-person board representing the various areas of the province. Both organizations formulate briefs and pass resolutions that are presented to the appropriate provincial departments. Since the Association of Improvement Districts and the AAMD & C are both rurally based and share many common concerns, they work very closely together in making presentations to the government. One can only speculate whether improvement districts and Métis settlements will become politicized through representation by forceful associations.

Despite the important role municipal government associations play in intergovernmental relations, questions and concerns have been raised about their legitimacy, representativeness and independence. Feldman and Graham have summarized these issues in their study of Canadian intergovernmental relations.[52] They suggest that since associations are not accountable to the public and are "somewhat immune to public opinion ... the use of municipal associations ... for the conduct of important intergovernmental affairs ... may well have stifled the emergence of much public concern about important [municipal] intergovernmental concerns." They also question whether or not an association can adequately represent an individual municipality's unique concerns. It is argued that associations "generally represent the lowest common denominator of opinion among the membership" with the consequence that the interests of individual municipalities become blurred. Feldman and Graham argue that "the important locus of initiation and response on intergovernmental matters involving municipalities in Canada should be the individual municipality. This is particularly true for Canada's larger municipalities." They also question whether or not municipal associations partially financed by provincial funds become captives of their financial benefactors. Equally important is the fact that a provincial government may be able subtly to change the fundamental direction of a municipal association so that it becomes a vehicle for dissemination of information about provincial government policy rather than an articulator of a municipal position. It is said "in this situation municipal representatives tend to be thought of at best as glorified office boys and at worst as whipping boys."

Alberta's associations need to ponder the issues raised by Feldman and Graham in order to avoid making the same mistakes municipal associations have made in other provinces. There should be no question regarding Alberta municipal associations' legitimacy, representativeness and independence.

An Overview of Interest Group Activity

A political scientist writing on interest group activity in the United States maintains that they have become so powerful they have completely undermined the democratic process.[53] He argues that the contract between government, which guarantees each person protection, and the individual citizen, who gives the government obedience and loyalty, originated in the Americans' call for freedom in their Declaration of Independence.[54] But over time, it is argued, the contract has been subtly twisted by interest groups and they, rather than the people, have become the cornerstone giving the government its legitimacy. Admittedly, many interest groups have become politically powerful and play key roles in the formulation of policy in both Canada and the United States. Occasionally an interest group will engage in political activities outside the sphere of legitimate politics. But, for the most part, rather than undermining the democratic process, interest groups enhance it by providing a voice for individuals unheard among the many in a mass society. Without interest groups only the rich and the powerful would be heard by government.

Alberta's municipalities, with their relatively small populations and direct democracy provisions, are not exceptions to the argument that interest groups represent and voice the demands of ordinary citizens. Without the interest group, few demands could be voiced and it would be difficult for a council to differentiate among those that were, since each would represent the voice and demands of but one narrow segment of society.

Notes

1. Engelmann and Schwartz, *Canadian Political Parties*, 142.

2. See: Lorimer, *The Real World of City Politics*; Fraser, *Fighting Back*; Sewell, *Up Against City Hall*; Lorimer and Ross, eds., *The City Book*; Lorimer and Ross, eds., *The Second City Book*; Aubin, *City for Sale*; Lorimer and MacGregor, eds., *After the Developers*; Roussopoulos, ed., *The City and Social Change*. Issues of the on and off *City Magazine* also contain interesting examples. For more systematic treatments of the role of the real estate development industry in city policy making, see Spurr, *Land and Urban Development*; Markusen and Scheffman, *Speculation and Monopoly in Urban Development*.

3. A recent letter from the Red Deer Chamber states: " We meet frequently with the mayor and chief commissioner and when necessary with the aldermen. It has resulted in a friendly, productive arrangement which we believe will continue in the forseeable future." Henry, letter to Ruth Rochlin, October 26, 1983.

4. Long, "The Local Community as an Ecology of Games."

5. The Provincial Liaison Committee's subcommittee structure is as follows. The Municipal Affairs Committee is active in the areas of annexation policies, the Provincial Planning Act, assessment and the Municipal Government Act.
The Housing and Public Works Committee is engaged in the various provincial housing and development subsidy programs, housing and serviced lot supply, innovative design and studies related to development of resource towns.
The Environment Committee is involved in Restricted Development Areas (R.D.A.s), lake shore development guidelines, energy line rights of way and environment reserves.
The Transportation Committee concentrates its efforts on establishing a special Transportation Revolving Fund.

Urban Development Institute, "Information sheet, 1983."

6. CHBA," Statement of Strategic Plan," 1983.

7. Caragata, *Alberta Labour*, 48-49.

8. *Ibid.*, 51.

9. *Ibid.*, 82-83.

10. The Edmonton and Calgary police forces are each organized into two unions: in Calgary, the Calgary Police Association and the Calgary Police Officers Association; and in Edmonton, the Edmonton Police Association and the Edmonton Police Officers Association.

11. An advertisement run in the *Edmonton Journal* by the Edmonton Firefighters Association warned "a child's life may be lost" if firefighters were laid off.

12. Masson and Blaikie, "Labor Politics in Alberta."

13. An example of the blue ribbon citizen committee was the five-person ad hoc committee struck by the Medicine Hat council, in February 1983, to review the role of city council members. Appointed to the committee were Frank Riddle, former public school board superintendent; Gordon Sissons, president of I-XL Industries Ltd. and former councillor; Roy Hoffman, field consultant with the apprenticeship branch of Alberta Manpower; Eugene Eaton, owner of Freddie's Paint and past Chamber of Commerce President; Lucy Milne, president of the Canadian Federation of Business and Professional Women's Clubs and retired school teacher. Town councillor Ken Sauer "and Riddle both say the committee's composition is a fair 'cross-section' of the community." *Medicine Hat News*, February 26, 1983.

14. Lightbody, "Edmonton," 269.

15. *Poundmaker*, May, 1973.

16. *Edmonton Journal*, December 19, 1973.

17. Dickerson, Drabek, and Woods, "A Performance Approach to Urban Political Analysis," 68.

18. Higgins, *Urban Canada*, 206.

19. The associations are: the Bearspaw, Glendale Ratepayer Association (Calgary); the Strathcona Acreage Owner's Association (Sherwood Park); the Leduc Residents Association (South Cooking Lake); Ratepayers Association, County of Ponoka (Ponoka); Parkland Rural Residents Association (Winterburn); Whitecourt Rural Residents Association (Whitecourt); Residents Association County of Vermilion River (Lloydminster); Foothills Ratepayers Association (Okotoks). The President of the Bearspaw, Glendale Ratepayer Association has written that there are nearby associations in Foothills, Springbank and Bragg Creek and expects an association to be formed soon in Rockyview.

20. Pilkington, Letter to Jim Rochlin, August 19, 1983.

21. Price, Letter to Jim Rochlin, undated, 1983.

22. Pilkington, Letter to Jim Rochlin, August 19, 1983.

23. Lightbody, "Edmonton," 268.

24. Gilsdorf, "Voter Susceptibility to Influence," 624.

25. Wright and Boynton, "The Media, the Masses, and Urban Management," 15.

26. Gilsdorf, "Voter Susceptibility to Influence," 633.

27. Black, *Politics and the News*, 202.

28. Greenberg and Dervin, "Mass Communication Among the Urban Poor," 236.

29. Gilsdorf, "Voter Susceptibility to Influence," 637.

30. *Ibid.*, 633.

31. Black, *Politics and the News*, 201.

32. *Alberta Report*, November 2, 1979.

33. The Municipal Government Act's section 150 reads: "(1) A council by by-law may provide for publication of the minutes of its meetings and of information concerning other municipal subjects and for that purpose may cause circulars to be prepared and distributed to all proprietary electors or to all proprietary electors and all other adult residents of the municipality. (2) If one or more weekly newspapers are in circulation in a municipality the council by by-law may provide for the publication of the matters referred to in subsection (1) in those newspapers, and for the distribution of a copy thereof to each proprietary elector or to all proprietary electors and all other adult residents of the municipality."

34. *Edmonton Journal*, December 20, 1974.

35. *Ibid.*, March 20, 1981.

36. *Ibid.*, October 2, 1982.

37. One study of private consultants and their relationship to municipal governments identifies six types who operate in the public sector.

1. *Legal*: (a) a person appointed as permanent legal counsel, (b) firms hired as continuing legal counsel, (c) ad hoc arrangements in specific situations either litigated or precluding possible litigation.

2. *Financial*: (a) bonding brokerage firms for placement and issue, (b) banks as trustees for public agency funds, (c) financial consulting firms, (d) independent auditing firms.

3. *Management*: (a) reorganization, (b) personnel systems analysis and control, (c) efficiency or effectiveness analysis . . . (d) data processing equipment adaptation and/or innovation, (e) curricula redevelopment and/ or evaluation, (f) charter revision.

4. *Engineering*: (a) feasibility studies, (b) cost studies, (c) highway and capital construction planning, (d) review of filed studies and plans by other engineering firms.

5. *Urban Development Planning*: (b) land-use maps, (c) conservation, (d) zoning laws and constraints, (e) economic base and feasibility studies by nongovernment firms, (f) transportation studies.

6. *Ad hoc and Other*: (a) university or government research bureaus, (b) individual university professor contracts, (c) insurance review, (d) architectural review etc.

Kagi, "The Role of Private Consultants," 48-49.

38. Seldom is a careful cost-benefit analysis done to determine whether it is cheaper to employ a private consultant or to employ additional municipal employees. In most cases the very small municipality is financially better off contracting with private consultants. As the size of the municipal administration increases, the administrative overhead cost per municipal employee decreases and, for the very large municipality, it is usually less expensive to hire additional specialized employees. Yet the City of Edmonton spent $13,800,000 in 1980, $18,950,000 in 1981 and $18,495,000 in 1982 for the services of private consultants. Although the city had a highly trained and professional planning department, $523,371, or 7.1 per cent of the departmental budget, was paid to consultants in 1981; $281,132 or 3.12 per cent, in 1982; and $323,500, in 1983.

39. Kagi, "The Role of Private Consultants," 54-55.

40. In both cities the transportation department carried out several studies for the council.

41. Of course a council can use experts within its own administration to prepare technical reports. However, most councils are aware that a sizeable segment of the public does not trust a council's own departments to prepare objective and unbiased reports.

42. *Edmonton Journal*, June 6, 1981; *St. Albert and Sturgeon Gazette*, December 19, 1981.

43. Weidenhamer, *A History of the Alberta School Trustees Association*, 26.

44. *Ibid.*, 33.

45. *Ibid.*, 43.

46. *Ibid.*, 427-428.

47. The Association's Alberta member municipalities are Airdrie, Brooks,

Calgary, Camrose, Edmonton, Fort McMurray, Fort Saskatchewan, Grande Prairie, High River, Lethbridge, Medicine Hat, Okotoks, Peace River, Red Deer, Redcliff, St. Albert, Slave Lake, Spruce Grove, Swan Hills, Sylvan Lake, Vegreville and Westlock. Although the cost of the services the FCM provides to its smaller member municipalities are subsidized by the fees of larger municipalities, perhaps one reason smaller municipalities have not joined the FCM is the membership fee: six cents per capita with a minimum yearly fee of $350 for municipalities and $1,000 for a municipal association.

48. Feldman and Graham, *Bargaining for Cities*, 20-21.

49. *Commemorative Brochure of the Alberta Urban Municipalities Association*, 5.

50. The association has taken credit for: "1) Police Grants—now unconditional; 2) Library Grants—were increased; 3) Municipal Assistance Grants—change in formula resulting in increased benefits; 4) Debt Reduction Program—while it is recognized that this was a political move prior to the 1978 Provincial Election, nevertheless the Premier indicated in his press release that this decision was reached partially due to the pressure brought to bear by the AUMA and similar organizations."*Ibid.*, 7.

51. *Edmonton Journal*, November 16, 1983.

52. Feldman and Graham, *Bargaining for Cities*, 21-27.

53. Lowi, *The End of Liberalism*.

54. The pertinent section of the Declaration reads: ". . . all men are created equal, that they are endowed by their Creator with certain unalienable Rights, that among these are Life, Liberty and the pursuit of Happiness— That to secure these rights, Governments are instituted among Men, deriving their just powers from the consent of the governed."

8

THE ACTIVITIES
OF
LOCAL GOVERNMENT

Introduction

For many people working in the Department of Municipal Affairs and for most mayors, council members and clerk-treasurers in Alberta, the functions and activities of local government are simply whatever is stated in the Municipal Government Act. But a close reading of the Act shows that it focuses on the *powers* of local government rather than on its functions. In fact, every municipality is required to perform only a limited number of functions, such as preparing an annual financial statement and, with the exception of cities, holding an annual meeting where "the latest municipal inspector's report" is read. The Act gives municipalities wide-ranging powers, from prohibiting horses from walking on sidewalks and streets to controlling the placement of billboards. More importantly, these powers are permissive (i.e., discretionary) rather than mandatory.

Thus, examination of the Municipal Government Act is not a reliable means of determining what local government does. A more useful strategy involves examining the activities of local government and their effects on the citizenry. Such an examination of policy outcomes includes determining unintended as well as intended effects of governmental actions.[1] Expenditure decisions are just as difficult to deal with as are revenue decisions, for, as one student of the budgetary process has written, budgeting "is the translation of financial resources into human purposes."[2]

Government activities usually take place in conventional areas familiar to the public and the government practitioner: taxing, planning and service areas, such as transportation, public safety, fire protection and prevention, garbage removal and disposal, and sewage removal and treatment. The public and its representatives may lose sight of the reason an activity is deemed public and is therefore carried out by municipal personnel and paid for by the municipality. In theory, certain activities can be carried out only by the public sector either because they are uneconomical for the private sector or because a service is so vital that no one should be denied its benefits through inability to pay. Over time, communities have opted to carry out an increasingly wide range of service activities; the consequence is a long-standing controversy over whether municipalities should extend their services or whether some services now provided by municipalities should be delivered by the private sector.

Budget Making, Taxing and Spending Policy

Every council is concerned with making "right" and rational decisions on setting the rate and distribution of taxation, the amount and mix of public services, and the financing of capital projects. But few councils give much thought to the budgeting process that provides the framework for these decisions. A council typically grapples with four interrelated budget problems. Is the budget balanced? Is it, at least, adequate to maintain existing service levels? Does it provide for an increase in the wages of municipal employees? Does it avoid excessive tax increases? If the answer to any of these questions is negative, either the budget will have to be reworked or the council will have to be prepared for sustained criticism and controversy. In their attempts to minimize conflict and to satisfy the citizenry and municipal employees, budget makers perform a simple but delicate balancing act. Although much has been written on "rational budgeting" almost all municipal councils employ the same simple rules. First, taking into consideration an increase in property taxation equivalent to the rate of inflation, they calculate revenue statistics for the coming year. Then they make expenditure decisions, with each department receiving an increase approximately equivalent to the rate of inflation. Department heads play a key role in this incremental process. Their budget requests are almost always only incrementally larger than the current year's budget; an estimate that is substantially larger would probably be subject to close scrutiny. Thus, the budgeting process rests upon the fundamental proposition that past experience is the best guide to future policy; this is incrementalist, conservative approach to policy making.

In Alberta another important factor, economic growth, operated during the halcyon years of the 1970s: property values and property taxes were increasing substantially each year; the provincial government was much freer with local government funding; and there was less concern with budgetary snafus than there is today. The prospects of larger revenues year after year provided a safety net that would prevent the administration from being embarrassed by a fiscal miscalculation. During this time, the size of many local bureaucracies increased substantially and wage increases well above the rate of inflation were routinely negotiated with civic employees. With the economic downturn of the 1980s the safety net collapsed, and allegations of fiscal mismanagement as well as outcries against the size of the municipal bureaucracy and civic wage demands divided many communities and became front page news in almost all. Consulting firms were hired by municipality after municipality to recommend more efficient and/or less costly procedures. Some communities, including Edmonton and Calgary, began moving towards Zero Based Budgeting (a procedure requiring each department to justify its total operations and total budget every year). As early as 1978, an independent auditor-general appointed in Edmonton had not hesitated to criticize some of the decisions made by the powerful commission board and to recommend improvements to the city's administration. In the hard-pressed 1980s, all Alberta municipalities are acutely aware that their ability to govern is directly related to their ability to raise sufficient revenue and to spend it efficiently.

Local governments have four major sources of revenue: locally collected taxes, charges for public services (i.e., user fees), borrowing and aid from higher levels of government (i.e., grants). Within each category, choices must be made. What kinds of taxes should be collected? What services should the municipality charge for? How much should the charge be? Should the municipality apply for every cost-shared grant offered by the provincial government? How far should the municipality go into debt? Municipal councils are faced with enormous difficulties in making expenditure decisions: invariably there are many worthwhile projects, each with its own advocate, and not enough money to fund them all.

Local governments in Alberta receive the largest percentage of their revenue from the property tax: in 1980 the figure was approximately 42 per cent for cities; 41 per cent for towns, counties and municipal districts; and 33 per cent for villages.[3] Even though the property tax is the single largest generator of revenue for municipalities, the principle of property taxation is controversial since it is generally regarded as a regressive tax. That is, since a person's income is not taken into consideration in the levying of the tax, the percentage of tax paid in relation to total income declines as income rises. As a consequence, wealthy people pay a smaller percentage of their income for property taxes (as well as other service charges) than do working-class and middle-class people.[4]

Although the provincial government specifies both methods and standards for property assessment, the responsibility for conducting the assessment is delegated to the municipalities. When this power is coupled with the municipality's ability to exempt certain properties from taxation, split the mill rate between residential and non-residential properties, and base assessment on valuations made as long as seven years earlier, the council has considerable discretion in property taxation policy making. On the other hand, provincial legislation requires the municipality to collect a certain number of mills for schools even though it has no control over how the funds are spent. Two other programs for which municipal governments are responsible for collecting revenue are the Alberta Planning Fund, which funds regional planning commissions, and the local hospital authorities. The combined revenue submitted to the province for these three programs (especially schools and hospitals) severely limits the flexibility of councils: when they try to generate significant revenue from the property tax to fund local programs, they face the spectre of a taxpayer's revolt. As a consequence, the municipalities repeatedly have requested that the province require school and hospital authorities to levy their own taxes.[5]

Two contentious taxation issues that arise from time to time are the number of non-profit facilities exempt from property taxes and the split mill rate that allows taxation of residential and non-residential properties at different rates. The most controversial of these issues seems to be exempt properties that receive full servicing paid for by taxpaying property owners. Under section 24 of the Municipal Taxation Act, most church, school and hospital lands and buildings, as well as cemeteries, irrigation works, equipment owned by a gas co-operative, and land and buildings for senior citizen housing are exempt from property taxation. Then, under section 25 of the Act, lands and buildings used for a number of other purposes are exempt "unless a municipality, by by-law authorized an assessment to be made with respect to any or all of the undermentioned properties." The "undermentioned properties" are: 1) land used by an agricultural society; 2) land used for community purposes; 3) land used by Ducks Unlimited (Canada); 4) land on which there is a government contracted nursing home; 5) land used by a non-profit organization for a summer camp; and 6) land used by "a branch or local unit of the Royal Canadian Legion . . . and any other organizations of ex-servicemen and college buildings used for residential purposes." Together these exemptions mean a substantial loss of revenue to the municipality.[6]

But the proponents of exempting churches and a potpourri of non-profit organizations point out that, if the organizations were forced to curtail their activities, the municipality would have to pick many of them up at great expense; in short, non-profit organizations are saving the municipality large sums of public funds. The split mill rate that advantages residential property owners, who comprise by far the largest segment of ratepayers in the municipality, is also contentious, but only among the small minority of business and rental property owners. The Municipal Taxation Act's section 96(2)(a) states that a council may "establish a rate applicable to residential property that is less than the rate applicable to non-residential property and less than the rate applicable to farm land." In almost every Alberta community the mill rate has been split to cater to the vast numbers of homeowners. For example, in 1983 in Edmonton, for every $1,000 of assessment, homeowners paid $11.16 in property taxes, owners of multi-unit rental housing paid $15.71, and owners of business and industrial property paid $19.44. Although owners of rental, business and commercial property seem to be disadvantaged under the split mill rate, they seldom mention it, since they can deduct business and property taxes from their income tax; in fact, they ultimately pay only about half of their tax assessment.

The sale of electricity, water, natural gas, telephone services, etc., and user fees and fines are second after property tax as an "internal" source of revenue for Alberta municipalities. In 1980, cities and towns received seven per cent and villages six per cent of their revenue from these sources.

Although it might seem that municipally owned utilities are lucrative and uncontroversial, in fact, municipalities owning public utilities are constantly embroiled in turmoil over whether these utilities should maximize profits or operate at a break-even level. Some people maintain that utilities should make substantial profits to reduce property taxes, while others maintain that consumers of public services should get the benefit of "break-even" utility rates. An example of how utility rates can be manipulated for political purposes occurred in Edmonton in 1983. The city administration was committed to holding property tax increases to eight per cent; hence, water, sewage and telephone rates were increased substantially. The effect was that all consumers of public utilities subsidized property owners. Medicine Hat has had a much different policy. The city, which owns a natural gas field and which produces its own electricity, has worked out a compromise price on utility rates that results in one of the lowest property tax and utility rates in western Canada.[7]

User fees also generate political controversy. For example, it is common practice to charge a fee for the use of municipally owned recreational facilities. Critics argue that this practice deprives poor people of the use of publicly owned facilities and subsidizes recreation for middle- and upper-class people. A seminal article by an urban economist puts the problem into perspective and suggests some ways of using user fees equitably to pay for services.

> . . . we must recall that it is the middle- and upper-income classes who typically visit museums, so that free admission becomes, in effect, redistribution toward greater inequality, to the extent that the lower-income nonusers pay local taxes (e.g., property taxes directly or indirectly through rent, local sales taxes). The low prices contemplated are not, moreover, likely to discourage attendance significantly and the resolution of special cases (e.g., student passes) seems well within our competence. . . . 'No, I would not put turnstiles in the playgrounds in poor neighborhoods, rather it is only because we do put turnstiles at the entrances to the playgrounds for the middle- and upper-income-groups that we will be able to afford playgrounds for the poor.'[8]

One major problem with user fees is that many people who pay property taxes in support of public services do not believe they should also have to pay user fees. They seem to forget that property taxes pay for only a portion of necessary public services.

Fewer political questions are raised over the practice of levying fines on wrongdoers; but the question of whether fines should be employed to deter law-breakers or to generate revenue for the municipality is occasionally raised.

Another small source of revenue, analogous to user fees, is described as "special assessments and charges for local improvements." In 1980 Alberta's cities derived two per cent and towns and villages four per cent of their revenue from this source. Building sidewalks, erecting street lighting, and paving alleyways and roadways are often paid for by individual property owners "on the basis of the total cost divided by the individual frontage of the properties." In some communities direct assessments in new subdivisions (i.e., the cost of servicing lots) is paid by the developer who passes the cost on to purchasers through higher prices. Although direct assessments and local improvement fees tend to hold down property taxes, at times they have been controversial. First, it is argued that older areas being upgraded contain many lower income people who cannot afford charges for local improvements; second, that since the upgrading of a deteriorating area benefits the whole community, the costs should be borne by all property owners through the property tax. Developers argue that passing on the costs of servicing in new subdivisions puts the housing out of reach of lower-middle-class and working-class people. The argument made for assessments and charges for local improvements is simply that the direct beneficiary of public services should pay.

Only Edmonton and Calgary receive substantial revenue from the business tax: it accounted for seven per cent of total revenue for each city in 1980. That year, most towns and villages in the province did not tax businesses and those that did received insignificant amounts. There are two reasons councils in smaller communities are reluctant to enact a business tax. First, a business tax prohibits the municipality from taxing machinery and equipment, and many municipalities derive substantial revenue from taxes on equipment, stored oil and coal, and lumber company machinery. Second, many councils feel that a business tax would drive business out of the community.

Some municipalities derive a small amount of revenue from the sale of services to adjoining communities. For example, in 1980 Edmonton received a total of $9,663,000 from such sales, with the greatest portion coming from the sale of water. Other communities derive revenue from contracting diverse services to other governments, such as snow removal and cleaning hospital laundry. As one would expect, since villages normally have only a skeletal service structure, they sell few services to other governmental units.

Grants from federal and provincial governments constituted approximately 45 per cent of municipal revenue in 1980. From the perspective of the municipalities, grants are ideal: monies received from senior levels of government are viewed as being free. Obviously, the more "free monies" municipalities obtain, the less dependent they are on property taxes, business taxes and user fees. Just as important, grants do not produce controversy in the community; if there is any controversy, it is with the granting government. There is an inherent tension between the provincial government and local municipalities: the municipalities want larger percentages of their revenue from grants, while the provincial government's policy is to reduce the dependence of municipalities on grants so that they can "stand on their own feet."

Basically, there are two types of government grants, conditional and unconditional. Understandably, municipalities prefer unconditional grants. Each year, the Municipal Assistance Grant Program administered by the Department of Municipal Affairs, provides an unconditional grant to every municipality in Alberta on the basis of relative need.[9] The purpose of the grant is to enable local governments to provide a range of municipal services without unduly burdening their citizenry with taxes and user fees. In 1981-82 the province gave municipalities $78,914,000 under this program.

Conditional grants are given to a municipality on a cost-shared basis. That is, the provincial government provides a certain percentage of funds for a specified purpose and the municipality is required to provide the remaining funding. A 1979 study of provincial-municipal financing in Alberta found the province shifting from unconditional to conditional grants. The report states:

> In 1965 only 43.1% of grants were specific but by 1977 over 70% were conditional. . . . In 1959 transfers were made only for transportation and social welfare. By 1965 grants for recreational and cultural purposes made a modest beginning. By 1968 there were six separate conditional program areas and seven by 1975. While transportation still remains the most important conditional grant program area, grants for protection (policing) and for recreation and culture have become relatively large.[10]

From the provincial government's perspective, this shift has several advantages: it enables the provincial government to establish province-wide municipal policy in such areas as recreation, highways, sanitation, etc.; it allows the province to implement province-wide municipal policy "on the cheap," since programs are cost shared; and it gives the province some control over municipal policy and fiscal priorities, which enables it to control what are seen as "irresponsible municipal councils."[11] On the other hand, the municipalities would like to see a return to primarily unconditional grants, since cost-shared grants tend to alter local spending priorities and erode local autonomy.[12] Since the municipality has to cost-share a new conditional grant program, it must either raise additional revenue or shift funds from an established program. Local decision makers find both alternatives undesirable since the community's budget priorities often result in controversy. In short, local decision makers argue that new cost-shared programs distort local revenue and expenditure policies. They reject the counter-argument that they are free to turn down any grant program, saying that they are always under pressure to obtain additional revenue. They further argue that conditional grants with stringent use guidelines merely make municipalities a conduit for the administration of provincially designed programs.

Municipal politicians logically conclude that this process lessens local autonomy and weakens local democracy.

Equally important is the fact that conditional grants tend to increase property taxes over time since a substantial number of cost-shared conditional grants are for capital facilities that the municipality must bear the burden of operating. When cost-shared conditional grants are made for operating expenses, the provincial policy normally ties the grant to a higher level of service. As a consequence, the municipality usually finds itself spending even more on a service than it spent before receiving the grant.

The federal and provincial governments and their agencies are generally exempt from taxation by urban and rural municipalities. However, it is the practice of both governments to make payments, i.e., grants, to municipalities in lieu of school and general purpose taxes. These grants are an important source of revenue for Alberta communities containing large numbers of federal and provincial government buildings and enterprises. Calgary, with the largest number of federal and provincial installations, has been the biggest beneficiary of this source: in 1980, eight per cent of the city's revenue came from them. Overall, in 1980, five per cent of cities' revenue, three per cent of municipal districts' revenue, and two per cent of the revenue of towns, villages and counties came from grants in lieu of taxes.

Although federal government properties are exempt from taxation by local municipalities, municipalities are given grants in lieu of taxes in recognition of municipal services. The federal government has generally been a good corporate citizen in Alberta communities and given grants equivalent to the amount of property taxes that would otherwise be assessed.[13] However, under the federal Municipal Grants Act the Minister is given the power to reduce the grant substantially almost at his or her discretion. The parallel provincial act, the Crown Property Municipal Grants Act makes it clear that grants are made at the province's discretion. Each year, a municipality must apply for the grant and section 2(3) of the Act states: "No municipality is entitled as of right to a grant under the Act." Moreover, the Act exempts a substantial number of properties, including parks, museums, monuments, hospitals, mental institutions, trade, forestry and agricultural schools, and colleges and universities.[14] In practice, the provincial government, like the federal government, has generally been a good citizen and paid for its share of municipal services. But the refusal to pay grants in lieu of taxes for non-profit accommodation for senior citizens or the physically or mentally disabled has been a sore point with municipalities. In both 1980 and 1981, the Alberta Urban

Municipalities Association adopted a motion requesting the province to reverse this policy. Then, in the spring of 1982, a study carried out by Edmonton's Real Estate and Housing Department on the impact of residential tax exemptions found that:

> In 1979, the Assessment Department estimated the total amount of municipal tax lost to be $980,000 for roughly 2700 apartment and bedsitting units in 36 projects. By 1981, this figure had risen to an estimated $1.8 million for approximately 4300 units in 74 subsidized housing projects. . . .

> Extrapolating this trend through to 1984, unless current provincial policy is amended, the City will be required to forego an estimated $5.2 million in that year alone for this purpose. This would be exclusive of an increasing annual amount paid by the City for direct operating subsidies associated with the Senior Citizen Lodge and Community Housing Programs. . . this latter subsidy by itself is expected to comprise 1% of the City's overall annual mill rate from 1982 through 1984.[15]

The Minister of Municipal Affairs' response to the AUMA and to Edmonton has been that the negligible amount of money at stake meant no hardship for any community.

Alberta's municipalities occasionally need to borrow to finance capital projects. Two urban economists succinctly sum up the argument for issuing debentures for this purpose.

> Quite apart from the theoretical merits of borrowing for capital projects, issuing bonds is often the only practical way to finance local capital expenditures, since it would be very difficult to use current revenues such as property taxes to make such large outlays in any given year. One capital project might account for a very large proportion of the budget in some municipalities for the year. By spreading the costs of a project over a period of time, there would be much less variation in tax rates on an annual basis. There appears, then, to be a strong case for financing capital projects at the local level through debt finance.[16]

The Alberta Municipal Finance Corporation was established in 1956 to purchase municipal debentures at a very favourable interest rate, thus enabling small villages as well as large cities to develop worthwhile capital projects. Local governments in Alberta floated debentures and sold $844 million in 1981 and $1.12 billion in 1982 to the corporation, which sheltered the interest rate at 11 per cent despite surging rates in the private sector. This high level of borrowing indicates a substantial increase in capital projects that will provide improved services in the future.

In spite of these successes, however, there are two signs that many local governments are having second thoughts about continuing to fund capital projects at the same level. First, with the dramatic downturn of Alberta's economy in 1981 and 1982 the government announced, in April of 1982, that the Interest Stabilization Programme that kept the cost of municipal debentures artificially low would be continued for only five years. Second, when it seemed that the provincial economy would remain buoyant with ever-increasing population, property values and property taxes, most municipalities had little concern about substantially mortgaging their futures. For example, between 1979 and 1980 Calgary's debenture debt increased from $399,311,000 to $659,045,000, and Edmonton's long-term debt increased from $832,382,000 to $943,676,000. And it was not only the major cities that incurred substantial debts. In 1980 there were seven villages with long-term debts of well over $1 million. Moreover, it is unlikely that the provincial government will make another $1 billion one-time grant to local governments for long-term debt reduction (payable at the rate of $500 for each individual living in a municipality) as it did in a 1979 election handout. With all of this in mind, in 1982 both Calgary and Edmonton began to give second thoughts to debenture financing for major projects.

Until Alberta's economy revives, only the most foolhardy municipal council will be willing to continue doubling its long-term debt year after year in order to finance capital projects. And even the most foolhardy council would be unlikely to pursue this policy, for the Local Authorities Board must give its approval before a municipality can borrow money for capital projects. On the other hand, a short-sighted council unwilling to borrow for capital projects that would make the community more attractive may be jeopardizing its future by driving a segment of its population into adjoining communities with more attractive services and amenities. When this happens the community's tax base and, consequently, its services begin to decline, leading to further erosion of population and economic vitality.

Housing and Land Development

Closely related to municipal fiscal policies and intricately linked to the planning and delivery of hard services are housing policies.

During the 1970s, with Alberta communities among the fastest growing of any in Canada, serviced land and housing became increasingly
scarce. Two factors were involved: the building industry was unable
to build housing fast enough to keep up with demand and, particularly in Edmonton and Calgary, a small number of companies held a
virtual monopoly on outlying development lands and manipulated
prices.[17] In Edmonton and Calgary housing prices escalated so quickly
that a large segment of working- and middle-class families were
priced out of the market. Alberta municipalities had faced housing
crises in the past and, with fiscal help from the provincial and federal
governments, had formulated policies to deal with them, but the
1970s crisis was particularly acute with unabated population growth
in almost all of Alberta's large towns and cities.

A few far-sighted municipalities have bought undeveloped land,
held it until there was a demand for it, then sold it on the open market, competing directly with private developers. Communities with
this policy of "public land banking" have broken the monopoly of the
private developers and held down the price of serviced land, and
have also turned a tidy profit. In Alberta, Red Deer pioneered land
banking; between the inception of the policy, in 1958, and 1972 Red
Deer bought 750 acres for $1.3 million, serviced it for $3.7 million,
then sold it for $9 million. By 1982 the city had a land inventory
worth $50 million that had cost $19 million. Land banking was so successful that, in 1978, the Red Deer branch of the Urban Development
Institute (the provincial association of private property developers)
complained that the city was selling lots at $5,000 to $6,000 below the
price private developers could profitably charge.[18] Medicine Hat has
also had a public land banking policy, both to keep land prices from
being unduly manipulated by the private sector and to provide for
orderly residential development. After the city bought 1,197 outlying
acres in 1981 the mayor said, "the city will use the land eventually. It
doesn't matter if you're talking 100 years, the city of Medicine Hat
will get there one day."[19]

In 1968 the provincial government established a program administered by the Alberta Housing Corporation (AHC) to assist municipal
land banking. Factors determining municipality eligibility are
whether 1) in the municipality "monopoly situation has developed to
the point where the private sector is charging prices far exceeding
cost and a reasonable profit"; 2) the municipality is unable to pursue a
land acquisition policy "because of financial or technical inadequacies"; 3) the private sector in the area either does not have the ability
to develop land or is unwilling to act; 4) the municipality's location is
such that its growth would further "the Province's balanced

industrial growth program"; and 5) there is a need for residential development to "relieve the demands being placed on large urban centers."[20] The AHC acquires land for residential development; the municipality can later buy this land, paying the original cost plus holding costs.

The AHC has the authority to acquire land without notifying the municipality. For example in 1979 the province began to buy 7,000 acres of land northeast of Edmonton, between Namao and Fort Saskatchewan. Edmonton was unaware of the AHC's activities until June, 1981, when the province notified the city. Meanwhile, unknown to Calgary, the province had acquired 10,000 acres between Calgary's northern city limits and the town of Airdrie.

In most cases, however, the AHC acts in concert with a municipality in the planning and acquisition stage. In 1969 the province, using the Alberta Housing and Urban Renewal Commission, bought 4,864 acres southeast of Edmonton. Shortly thereafter the city bought the land from the province and began to develop it. The first lots were sold to the public in the new Mill Woods subdivision in 1973. Although the city could not bring its lots onto the market fast enough to thwart large developers, the Mill Woods project was considered a qualified success. The only less than successful land banking project is the Timberlea project in Fort McMurray. During the heady days of planning for the Alsands Project, the AHC, in conjunction with the city's administration, began to develop 35,000 lots in the Timberlea subdivision with backup plans for an additional 5,000 lots. When Alsands collapsed, the AHC estimated that it would be 15 to 20 years before it recovered its initial investment.

Despite success in Alberta, land banking is controversial. When Edmonton was marketing Mill Woods lots at prices slightly below the market prices, there was sporadic debate on city council over whether the city should be competing with the private sector and attempting to beat down its prices. After the province bought 17,000 acres northeast of Edmonton some council members were strongly opposed to the city's acquiring the land and developing it. In 1981 Grand Prairie's council was almost evenly split over continuation of the city's land banking policy. One councillor summed up the opposition when he stated, "I have always felt that land acquisition and development is better left to private enterprise."[21] With a strong free enterprise ethic in the province, controversy over land banking is unlikely to diminish.

In addition to its land banking program, the province has several housing programs that provide fiscal assistance to municipalities to increase their flexibility in devising housing policies. One of the most important is the Community Housing Program, which allows municipalities to provide rental housing for low- and moderate-income families. The capital cost is borne by the AHC, which borrows 90 per cent of the funds from the Central Mortgage and Housing Corporation (CMHC) and 10 per cent from the provincial government. On completion, operating deficits are shared 50-40-10 respectively by CMHC, AHC and the municipality. In 1981-82 the province spent $59,400,000 on this program. Three smaller programs are the Municipal Housing Incentive Program, the Senior Citizen Lodge Program and the Lodge Assistance Program. The Municipal Housing Incentive Program provides municipalities with grants ranging between $500 and $2,000 for each new housing unit "based on the rate of new housing production in relation to production in previous years and the number of eligible units built."[22] In 1981-82 municipalities received $12 million under the program. The Senior Citizen Lodge Program was designed to provide for affordable senior citizen housing. A lodge is usually sponsored by a foundation consisting of a number of municipalities within an area, although a single municipality may sponsor one. The AHC provides 100 per cent of the costs of constructing and equipping the lodge for occupancy. The foundation then is responsible for the lodge's operation. A sister program, the Lodge Assistance Program, provides financial assistance to lodge foundations to help cover operating expenses.

Although cost is usually the most controversial question, other housing policy issues may divide a community. In 1972 Calgary and Edmonton adopted a policy of dispersing subsidized housing projects throughout the city to avoid creating an inner city ghetto.[23] Since developers were required to dedicate five per cent of the land in a new area for public housing, many projects were located in new subdivisions. The policy excited little controversy until 1980, when it was decided to locate a public housing unit in Edmonton's new middle-class suburb of Wolf Willow. The residents' objections were summed up by city councillor and Wolf Willow resident Oliva Butti who said, "I don't know how you can put people who can barely afford to eat next to people who can do their landscaping immediately."[24] Faced with well-organized, articulate opponents, the city and the AHC (which was to finance the project) decided not to locate public housing in Wolf Willow.

Transportation

A central characteristic of contemporary Alberta life is dependence on the automobile. Tens of millions of dollars are spent yearly by the provincial and municipal governments to build and maintain streets and highways. At the same time, municipal property tax bases are reduced as more and more "paved land" is taken off the tax rolls. Municipal councils and downtown businesspeople in larger cities curse the automobile for draining the middle class out of the central city to the suburbs. Concern is expressed over the 35-50 per cent of the core city devoted to servicing, moving and parking automobiles. Smaller municipalities view the province's outstanding roadway system as a mixed blessing. On one hand, it allows their residents the same access to cultural, health and educational facilities as the residents of larger communities; on the other hand, it gives people the mobility to spend their dollars in communities other than their own.

In the last decade, the provincial and municipal governments have been roundly criticized for massively funding automobile transportation and neglecting other modes of transportation. Ironically, in Edmonton and Calgary plans to develop freeway systems led to the deployment of massive amounts of money for public transportation systems that may never be fully used. In 1963, with its Metropolitan Transporation Study (METS), Edmonton embarked on a 25-year plan to build a comprehensive freeway system. In the same year, the Calgary Transportation Study (CALTS) proposed an equally comprehensive network of roadways. Escalating gasoline prices and concerns that the freeways would carve up neighbourhoods combined with the development of policies to revitalize the core city and curb low density suburban development to bring about billion-dollar LRT (Light Rail Transit) systems in each city in the 1980s.[25]

In Edmonton a mayor and council in the early 1970s, enamoured of a fixed rail transit system, sidetracked freeway planning in favour of an LRT system with virtually no study of transportation needs, usage, or costs.[26] Using an existing railway right of way, the city was able to construct a 4.5-mile northeast leg for $64 million.[27] However, a 3,000 foot extension under the city's main street cost an additional $120 million. With capital and operating costs escalating, LRT usage remaining relatively constant and, as neighbourhoods are beginning to realize how LRT may affect them adversely, future LRT legs are in a nebulous planning stage, although a southern leg has been approved in principle. Calgary embarked on an LRT system later, after city planners convinced Mayor Rod Sykes of its merits. A $167 million 12.5-mile southern line has been completed and a $180 million northwest line was approved by council and then halted by angry neighbourhood citizen groups. Mayor Ralph Klein, being committed to preserving downtown business and determined to rid the city of cars, then proceeded with a northeast LRT leg estimated to cost $239 million but being constructed at 30 per cent below estimates.

Both Edmonton and Calgary depend on the provincial government for the capital costs of their LRT systems. Up to now, there does not seem to have been a shift from the automobile to the LRT system, both systems are running far below their capacity, and the Department of Transportation has been asking the two cities some difficult questions. Is there any indication this trend to underuse will change? Will the cities be able to absorb what seem to be ever-increasing LRT operating deficits or will the province be forced to subsidize operating costs? Finally, is there any indication that Calgary and Edmonton's low population density areas will grow to the point that the LRT system will not incur such heavy per capita operating losses? The LRT proponents answer that, until a city has a comprehensive LRT system in place, there will be no substantial movement from automobile to public transit. It is further argued that the mere existence of an LRT line will increase population density along the route.

The public transportation versus private automobile controversy has taken an entirely different direction in Alberta's medium-sized cities. Although the numbers of people using public transportation are small, they are vocal. Inter-urban railways are proposed to lessen the dependence of residents on their automobiles. But critics point out that the capital costs of a province-wide rail system are exceedingly high and there are no definitive studies showing that people will desert their automobiles to travel by rail. The fact that VIA Rail has cut back passenger service in the province is an equally important consideration.

Smaller communities and rural areas, accepting the automobile as the primary mode of transportation for most of their residents, take a more pragmatic approach and work with the provincial Department of Transportation, regional planning commissions and municipal planners to plan and build roadways. Although these communities are not beset with LRT versus roadway and rail versus highway controversies, they are not without contention over transportation issues. Generally included under transportation policy are pedestrian control, on and off street parking, and street and bridge cleaning and maintenance. In some smaller communities policies on street lighting and parking have been particularly controversial and divisive. In other communities controversies have raged over which streets should be paved.

Although municipalities criticize the provincial government for underfunding transportation, there is a close working relationship on transportation issues between all Alberta municipalities and the province. Such co-operation is necessary because responsibilities are intermeshed: the maintenance of secondary highways and local roads and streets is the responsibility of the municipality, while the province is responsible for all primary highways except those within cities.

Provincial government transportation grants clearly favour the larger population centres: seven major grant programs and two minor ones are earmarked solely for cities.[28] A major source of funding for Edmonton and Calgary is the Public Transit Capital Assistance grant "to assist urban municipalities in providing public transit services in an efficient and cost effective manner." The program, which began in 1979 and will continue until 1985, is budgeted to provide the province's cities with $253.3 million, of which Edmonton and Calgary will receive $118 million each. The fact that there is no cost-sharing provision in the grant is a particularly important feature. Another smaller public transportation grant, the Grant-in-Lieu of Public Transit Operating Assistance, provides a grant either to reduce public transit operating deficits or to provide specialized transportation services for the disabled and senior citizens. In 1981 the province made grants totaling $13.7 million under this program.[29] Three similar programs for upgrading and building city roadways are the Arterial Roadway Capital Assistance program, the Major Continuous Corridors program and the Primary Highway Maintenance program.[30] The province's funding for the programs in 1981-82 was $38.4 million, $41 million and approximately $2 million, respectively.

The province gives much less recognition through grants to the transportation needs of towns and villages. Under a new program implemented in 1982 communities with populations under 10,000 receive a basic grant of $10,000 plus $60 per capita, while those having over 10,000 inhabitants receive a basic grant of $30,000 plus $60 per capita. In 1982-83 the government dispersed $14.2 million under this program. One transportation grant is restricted to counties and municipal districts for upgrading and improving roadway networks. Using a complicated formula, the Department of Transportation funds 100 per cent of a project's cost, up to the amount of its formula eligibility. In 1981-82 counties and municipal districts received $20.9 million under the program.

Despite the province's commitment to adequate municipal transportation and the municipalities' studies and plans devoted to transportation problems, neither governmental level has gone beyond conventional transportation thinking. For example, in Calgary there has been no serious attempt to integrate taxis into the public transportation system, although it would seem an ideal policy to pursue.[31] In neither Edmonton or Calgary, nor in smaller, low-density communities, has thought been given to outfitting a fleet of small, radio-equipped jitney buses to provide the convenience of door-to-door taxi service at low cost to the consumer and the municipality. In all communities, the integration of public and private transportation would substantially reduce costs and increase efficiency. Finally, thoughtful integration of particular kinds of industry, housing and retailing in a number of geographical sectors would eliminate many transportation problems.

Fire and Police Services

Many people consider fire and police protection the most important services provided by local government. Fire protection is the less controversial by far, since, while the encounters most people have with police are unpleasant, ranging from warnings about jaywalking to arrest, firefighters are seen as benefactors during trouble, saving lives by putting out fires and rescuing the cat stuck in the tree.[32]

Despite the importance people place on fire protection, under the Municipal Government Act a municipality is not required to have a fire department or even to adopt the National Fire Code of Canada: council is given the discretion to create a fire department and enact fire codes. However, all Alberta's large municipalities and most smaller ones do have fire departments. There are eight departments staffed by paid professionals, 25 staffed by at least one full-time paid professional plus volunteer firefighters, and 276 completely volunteer fire departments. In addition, a few municipalities have a contract with an adjoining fire department for fire protection. Edmonton and Calgary have modern fire departments that match any in Canada. Many smaller municipalities have placed a high priority on fire protection and have sophisticated, modern fire equipment.

With the pall of a fiscal crisis hanging over Edmonton and Calgary in 1982 and 1983, the costs of fire protection provoked controversy. In the early spring of 1983, in a political scenario reminiscent of the late 1920s and early 1930s, Edmonton laid off 87 firefighters as part of a fiscal package to limit property tax increases to no more than eight per cent. Some members of the public and the firefighters' union predicted that it was "only a matter of time before tragedy [would] strike." Calgary's cost-cutting measures were less dramatic; however, many people became alarmed over what they saw as a deterioration of the city's fire department.

A difficulty in evaluating the effectiveness of fire protection is that there have been few studies of the issue. However, a comprehensive study of American fire departments found four factors that increase efficiency:

(1) make the fire department more professional by such practices as providing incentives to fire fighters to get more education (e.g., pay for the time in school), (2) decrease maximum response time, (3) assign the number of personnel to apparatus on a variable rather than constant ratio (e.g., high ratio during times and in areas of high demand, otherwise a concomitantly lower ratio), and (4) reduce the number of mutual aid agreements [with other municipalities].[33]

But there seems to be a factor more fundamental than these four: namely, the lack of innovations in equipment or techniques among fire departments in North America. From the turn of the century until the Second World War, fires were fought using the same techniques. Then, with many aircraft fires during the war, the military devised new methods to put out fires quickly; these methods were soon adopted by municipal fire departments. Since the Second World War, there has been little innovation. It has been argued that, since fire departments are a public monopoly, there is no incentive to develop innovative machinery and techniques. The counter-argument is that there is little likelihood that innovations would improve fire fighting.[34]

An Alberta municipality with over 1,500 population is responsible "for providing and maintaining an adequate and efficient police force," unless it has contracted for policing with the RCMP.[35] Only 11 larger municipalities in the province have their own police forces, as a modern force is very expensive to maintain.[36] But whether a municipality contracts with the RCMP or maintains its own force, the province gives recognition to the costly nature of policing by providing several policing grants. The most comprehensive is the Law Enforcement Grant, which is available to all municipalities with at least 1,500 population. If the municipality contracts with the RCMP, the amount of the grant is $12 per capita; a municipality with its own police force receives $18 per capita. There are several other smaller and more specialized policing grants. The Summer Village Policing program provides a grant of $400 a month from May 15 to September 15 to summer villages to help pay for a special constable. A Liquor Control Act program gives smaller municipalities a small sum of money to defray the cost of sobering up intoxicated people in jail. Yet another small program provides funds to repair or build a police station.

Despite the importance of law enforcement, the citizenry has little say about policing policy or procedures. There are two major reasons for this lack of citizen control. First, the RCMP, although providing policing for most Alberta communities, is not responsible to either the municipality or the provincial Solicitor General; it is subject only to federal control.[37] Second, even a municipality maintaining its own police force has little control over policing policy; the responsibility lies with the municipal police commission required of every munici- pality with its own police force.[38] The police commission, which may vary in size from three to 12 members, is appointed by council for a term of office not to exceed three years. But since council cannot fill many of the commission's positions with council members, it has little control over the commission. Section 23(4) of the Police Act states:

> If 4 or less members are appointed . . . one of them may be a member of the council or a municipal employee, and if 5 or more members are appointed . . . 2 of them may be members of the council or municipal employees, but in either case no member of the council or municipal employee may be chairman of the commission.

The commission thus insulated from council is a powerful body, since it is responsible for: 1) policing policy in the municipality; 2) the ap- pointment of all members of the police force (the appointment of the chief of police has to be ratified by the council); 3) conducting hear- ings on the administration, operation, and requirements of the police force; and 4) at its discretion, making rules for the police. These rules include regulations relating to

> (a) the conduct, dress, deportment and duties of members of the police force, (b) the prevention of neglect or abuse in the discharge of duties, (c) the efficient discharge of duties by the members of the police force, and (d) punishment for contravention of the rules.

In the winter of 1982 a controversy erupted in Edmonton over the powers of the police commission. With the city facing a fiscal crisis, city council decided to terminate the employment of 94 police con- stables, and the Edmonton Police Association took the city to court. It was ruled that the city did not have the power to fire police officers but that its role was to provide funds which the commission could allocate as it saw fit. Although the court was silent on whether the commission had the power to fire police officers, the implication of the decision was that the commission had such power.

Edmonton's attempt to slow the escalating costs by cutting back on policing is a manifestation of a general trend taking place in all Alberta's larger municipalities in the 1980s. There are three reasons that municipalities consider cutting a service as important as policing rather than services generally regarded as less important. The first is that the results of the limited research that has been carried out indicate that the number of police officers on the streets seems to make little difference to the crime rate.[39] Thus, it is possible to reduce the number of police without jeopardizing public safety. Second, since policing is labour intensive and arbitration awards have recently increased salaries much faster than total budget, municipal administrations are forced to decrease police services just by holding the line on costs. For example, while other municipal employees were under salary constraints, in the fall of 1982 Edmonton police officers received a 32 per cent wage increase over two years and Lethbridge officers received a 28.5 per cent increase over the same period. Such settlements make the average pay of a first class constable $35,000 a year; top ranking officers make in excess of $60,000. The third reason for cutting back policing services is also fiscal. In 1981 the federal government reduced its share of RCMP policing costs. For the 62 Alberta municipalities with populations between 1,500 and 15,000 with RCMP policing contracts, the federal share was to begin to decrease from 44 per cent in 1981 to 40 per cent by 1985 and to 30 per cent by 1990. For municipalities over 15,000 the federal share was to decrease from 19 per cent to 10 per cent by 1990. The federal cost-cutting measure has forced all Alberta municipalities with RCMP contracts to reevaluate their policing policies.

As Alberta municipalities begin to place a lower priority on policing, two demographic factors will militate against any surge in crime. First, the migration of large numbers of young, single men (especially those in the 16 to 25, crime-prone age group) decreased dramatically as the bloom faded on oil-related enterprises. Second, the percentage of the population in the 16 to 25 age category was already decreasing during the 1970s and 1980s since the overall population is aging. As this trend continues, there will be a smaller and smaller percentage of the population in the age group that commits the most crimes. These two demographic factors alone indicate that crime will slowly decrease, regardless of changes in policing policy.

Garbage Collection and Disposal

Garbage collection and disposal, euphemistically called "solid waste management," has low priority in low density rural areas where farmers have traditionally used their own garbage pits. It becomes a problem when population density increases to the point where private garbage pits are not feasible. An indication of the magnitude of the problem is the 905,265 tons of garbage generated in Edmonton and the 1,052,000 tons generated in Calgary in 1982.[40]

Such controversy as occasionally erupts over the collection of garbage tends to be relatively minor. For example, in the fall of 1982 the residents of Calgary's affluent Mount Royal district became incensed when an economy measure forced them to carry their garbage to the street for collection rather than having it picked up from their back lanes. Equally minor controversies occasionally occur over the frequency of collection: whether it is to be once a week or twice a week. What can become extremely controversial is the location of a garbage dump. Such a controversy erupted in Edmonton in 1982 and 1983. With the city's Clover Bar dump expected to be filled by 1986, the city administration hired a consultant to recommend a new location.[41] Twelve sites were recommended, two within the city's boundaries, five in the County of Strathcona and five in other surrounding municipal districts. When acreage owners angrily protested against having to live near the city's garbage dump, the administration was forced to choose a site within Edmonton. With the rumour that the site was to be adjacent to southeast Edmonton's Mill Woods, a Mill Woods Anti-Dump Action Committee quickly organized and threatened political reprisal in the upcoming municipal election. Council backed down and struck the Mill Woods site from its list. Then, almost in desperation, the council decided to locate the new dump at a different location in Clover Bar, even though the location was not recommended by the consultant. After 10,000 residents of the adjoining community of Clareview signed a petition protesting the location of the new site, council backed down again. Currently, the city seems to be waiting for the organization of the Edmonton Regional Service Commission, whose initial mandate included garbage disposal, to solve the problem. A similar controversy, but with a different outcome, occurred in High River during the summer of 1982. The towns of High River and Okotoks and the Municipal District of Foothills, in conjunction with Alberta Environment, located a regional garbage dump in a sparsely populated area northwest of High River. Although the small number of affected rural residents were unable to change the dump's location, they were able to delay its operation several times. The location of dump sites is a perennial problem, for every community recognizes the need for an adequate dump site but no one is willing to live beside one.[42]

With the province becoming more and more urbanized and industrialized, the provincial government has become increasingly concerned about the disposal of residential and industrial waste. The Reclamation Program for Derelict Land and the Alberta Solid Waste Management Assistance Programs provide 100 per cent funding to assist municipalities with waste disposal. The program to reclaim derelict land funds any municipality reclaiming abandoned garbage dumps and sewage lagoons, while the waste management assistance program funds the purchase of sanitary landfill sites. In the latter program, funding preference is given to "two or more urban municipalities plus a rural municipality forming a regional authority."

Through these programs the provincial government implicitly recognizes garbage disposal, if not its collection, as a public activity. And in Alberta's larger municipalities garbage collection and disposal is almost always categorized as a public activity. But a closer examination reveals that it is a "mixed activity": residential garbage is collected by the municipality and commercial refuse is collected by private firms who often dispose of it in private dumps.

A recent study of collection costs in 126 Canadian cities found that the yearly cost was $42.29 per household when carried out exclusively by public collectors, $32.31 when carried out jointly by public and private collectors, and $28.02 when carried out exclusively by private collectors.[43] With such findings, the question is occasionally raised about whether all garbage collection should be turned over to the private sector, since it would be cheaper and private collectors seem to do a reasonable job for commercial establishments. However, just raising the issue incurs the wrath of politically powerful unionized public service workers who are justifiably concerned about job security. As a consequence, a comprehensive cost-benefit study of garbage collection for Alberta municipalities has not yet been done. However, if Alberta's cities continue facing fiscal crises, the possible role of the private sector in garbage collection will be examined much more closely.

Water and Sewage

In a small community with dispersed population, each family tends to its own water supply and sewage disposal with a well and a septic tank. As population becomes more concentrated, the close proximity of wells and septic tanks begins to constitute a serious health hazard.

Hence, the provincial government has established mandatory water safety standards for municipalities.

Water delivery and sewage disposal systems are exceedingly expensive; without provincial assistance the average municipality would be unable to cope unless it placed an unbearable burden on its ratepayers. Alberta Environment, through its Water Supply and Sewage Treatment Grant Program and the Regional Water and Sewage Grant Program, funds up to 90 per cent of the costs of water and sewage plants on the basis of per capita grants ranging between $250 and $2,100. The municipal share is normally raised through long-term debentures repaid by the users through service and user fees.[44] A somewhat simpler and less costly method is employed by communities near Edmonton that purchase their water from the city.

An important water policy issue is pricing. In the typical policy, the price for water is lowest per unit for the heaviest users and highest for the lightest users. As Bird and Slack point out, such a policy leads:

> to small users subsidizing large users. Sometimes lower-income consumers in this way subsidize higher-income consumers who have dishwashers, bigger lawns to sprinkle, two cars to wash and so on. More importantly, as a rule, all residential consumers tend to subsidize industrial users . . . . One of the most important results of pricing water below its marginal cost is to encourage overinvestment in water supply, with consequent unnecessary strain on municipal exchequers.[45]

A somewhat similar approach is employed by Calgary, which charges residential users a flat rate for water whether they use large or small amounts. In effect, the low-income homeowner with a postage-stamp lawn subsidizes Mount Royal homeowners in keeping their oversized lawns lush and green throughout the summer.

A much more controversial water policy issue involves the level and cost of sewage treatment. Since one community's cleansed waste waters are another community's water supply, there is continuing controversy over the adequacy of water treatment and the taste and smell of waters in the province's large rivers. The Bow River southeast of Calgary, the South Saskatchewan River east and west of Medicine Hat, the Oldman River east of Lethbridge, the Red Deer River east of Red Deer, and the North Saskatchewan River east of Edmonton (all of which are used for recreation and drinking water by smaller communities) have all been called heavily polluted. For example, in the early spring of 1983, a consultant hired by Calgary's administration concluded that the city was acting irresponsibly in dumping partially treated sewage into the Bow River thereby subjecting farm families and recreational users to the risk of cholera and typhoid fever. The city said it could not afford a higher level of sewage treatment.[46] Until the province enforces a much more stringent level of water purity and provides greater funding for treatment plants, animosity among many Alberta municipalities will continue.

In the past, one of the most divisive issues facing community councils was the fluoridation of water, a measure instituted to decrease tooth decay among children. For many communities during the late 1950s and early 1960s, fluoridation was the key political issue. Communities were deeply divided, with immediate neighbours becoming life-long enemies since both sides were unbending. Fortunately, councils had an escape hatch in the provincial Public Health Act, which made it mandatory that a plebiscite be held after a council passed a fluoridation by-law. Unless a majority voting on the plebiscite supported the by-law, it was nullified. Almost invariably, however, when a plebiscite lost, the proponents of fluoridation would call for another plebiscite which, under the Public Health Act, could not be held for two years. In Edmonton, plebiscites on fluoridation were held in 1957, 1959, 1961 and 1964; each time, fluoridation went down in defeat. Then, in a 1966 plebiscite, the issue passed and fluoridation equipment was installed the following year.

The reason this seemingly innocuous issue rocked community after community was that it contained not only health but ideological overtones. Anti-fluoridation forces in Alberta brought in speakers from the United States and based many of their arguments on anti-fluoridation literature coming out of that country. Many American anti-fluoridationists, closely tied to ultra-conservatives, argued that fluoridation was a communist plot to subvert the population of North America.[47] Both sides marshalled evidence to show that fluoridation was either a deadly poison, causing cancer and chromosome damage, or a completely safe chemical that, in minute amounts, did nothing more than prevent tooth decay. It is important to note that the reputable American Dental and American Medical associations came down on the side of fluoridation.

Despite the strong case made for fluoridation only 48 Alberta communities had fluoridated water systems by 1983; Calgary has not yet fluoridated its water supply. Councils avoid the fluoridation issue in the 1980s just as carefully as they did 20 years before. For example, in 1982 the town council of Mayerthorpe referred the issue to plebiscite (it had passed by community plebiscite in 1964). The mayor's explanation for council's action was that it "wasn't for or against fluoridation; it's for the people to decide." Until fluoridation becomes less ideologically charged, it is likely that other councils will emulate Mayerthorpe's stance and attempt to avoid the issue.

Public Health and Welfare

In Alberta's early years municipalities were solely responsible for public health. The Public Health Act established a Provincial Board of Health that was given wide-ranging responsibilities, from enforcing sanitation in slaughter and ice houses to preventing roller towels in public restrooms from being used by more than one person. The Provincial Board of Health delegated its responsibilities to local boards of health. Burdened by the costs of regulating public health practices, a number of Alberta municipalities received funds from the American Carnegie and Rockefeller foundations to improve local public health standards. Then, after the Second World War, in response to public demand for better public health services, the provincial government began to take over some health functions by initiating a cost-sharing program under which it funded 80 per cent of local health board costs with the municipality putting up 20 per cent. In January, 1973, the current funding formula was put into place: the 27 local health districts across the province received 100 per cent of their funding from the provincial government.

The boundaries of two local health districts coincide with the boundaries of Edmonton and Calgary; each of the other 25 encompasses a large geographic area coinciding with county, and improvement and municipal district boundaries. With the exception of the Edmonton and Calgary districts, each district is divided into wards, each ward being represented on the health district's board, its governing and administrative body. Under section 2(4) of the Health Unit Act, "When a municipality is included in an operating health unit . . . the board of the health unit shall be the local board of health . . . ." Municipalities are represented on the district board under the provision of section 6 of the Health Unit Act, which states:

1. if a ward of a health unit lies entirely within one municipality, the council of that municipality shall appoint a member of the council to be the member of the board representing the ward.

2. if a ward contains all or part of 2 or more municipalities, the council representing the greatest number of residents in the ward shall appoint a member of that council to be the member of the board representing the ward.

Despite this municipal representation, councils spend little time and effort on public health matters as the province closely prescribes the activities of district boards and provides all their funds.

Initially welfare, like health, was solely the responsibility of the municipalities. However, burdened by welfare responsibilities, the municipalities soon turned to the province for assistance. Cost-shared programs were implemented as early as 1919, when the province helped municipalities provide assistance to widows. But the desperate plight of municipalities during the "Dirty Thirties" clearly indicated that their fiscal resources were inadequate for supporting welfare programs. After the Second World War large numbers of people were demanding better welfare programs than the municipalities could afford and others argued that social services largely funded by municipal property taxes were not "a legitimate charge against real property."[48] Responding to the demand for more and better social services, the senior levels of government began to take over social welfare from the municipalities. Local governments did not resist this erosion of their power and autonomy; they were happy to be rid of the increasing financial burden. An indication of this attitude was the request, made in 1965 by the Union of Alberta Municipalities, that the provincial government assume all community welfare services.

In 1966 the Social Credit government took over child welfare services from the municipalities and initiated a unique, locally administered, preventive social service (PSS) program. The major goals of the government were:

1. *Preventive Welfare*: To prevent people from becoming dependent on government programs of financial assistance; as understood by the Welfare Minister and his colleagues, to 'prevent welfare'.

2. *Prevent Marriage Breakdown*: To prevent separation and divorce, which were perceived as leading to dependence on government and to child welfare problems.

3. *Reduce Child Welfare Intake*: soaring illegitimacy rates and a structural flaw in the child welfare program were flooding the province's child welfare system. PSS and associated reforms were intended to slow this influx.

4. *Promote General Social and Physical Well-being*: although its

meaning was not specified, a general statement of this kind was presented in most public justifications of the new PSS program.[49]

Funded 80 per cent by the province and 20 per cent by the participating municipality, the program allowed the municipality wide latitude in developing and administering its own preventive social service programs although, ultimately, it was necessary for the province to approve each program.[50] Equally important, the province was so committed to the program that no upper spending limits were placed on it. In order to gain support and the greatest benefits at the lowest cost, the program was to use private social agencies as a key component, with the municipality funding them for delivering specific services.

Both large and small municipalities responded by developing such diverse programs as drop-in centres and a job placement service for transients, home care programs for the elderly, day care centres for working class and handicapped children, family planning clinics, alcohol and drug counselling centres, and support programs for children of single parents. Edmonton and Calgary almost immediately incorporated many existing programs into the new PSS program. Initially, this practice meant savings since the cities were paying for the same services with 20-cent dollars. Very shortly, however, the two cities began new PSS areas. Under the legislation smaller communities had the option of establishing a regional PSS program with two or more of them providing joint funding. Although initially hesitant to get involved in PSS, in a short time many smaller and rural communities opted in.

With the Progressive Conservatives taking power in 1971 a ceiling was placed on provincial funding. The only other change at the time was a cosmetic one: the program's name was changed to Family and Community Support Services (FCSS). There have been only minor changes to the program since 1971.

One unintended consequence of the PSS/FCSS program has been that the communities, being free to devise their own programs, have produced substantial experimentation and innovation. Some innovative programs were very successful and others less so, but the communities have been useful laboratories for the province. In fact, the province has adopted several very successful programs initially developed by communities. A co-ordinated home care program and a particularly innovative method of delivering day care services initiated by Edmonton were adopted throughout Alberta. Similarly, a community developed school readiness program has also been adopted province-wide.

Undoubtedly, Family and Community Support Services is one of the provincial government's most successful cost-shared grant programs. It allows municipalities wide latitude in program development, has resulted in a number of innovations in the preventive social service field, and has given the province a large number of inexpensive pilot programs to examine, some of which have been adopted province-wide. All of these ends have been achieved without violating the principle of municipal autonomy, although occasionally a municipality will complain that the FCSS program undermines its local autonomy and makes it nothing more than an administrative conduit of provincial welfare policy.

A plethora of public welfare policy options has been made to increase the effectiveness of existing programs, to enable welfare recipients to become "meaningful and working citizens," and to make welfare programs more humane. However, since all welfare services, except the FCSS program, are now delivered by the federal or provincial governments, these policy options are outside the purview of municipalities. And it is extremely unlikely that welfare programs taken from the municipalities will ever be returned, for municipalities do not have access to sufficient revenue to support even a minimally acceptable welfare program.

Recreation and Culture

Traditionally, community recreation programs have focused on children and teenagers. Both the public and its elected representatives perceived recreational policy in terms of providing facilities to amuse youth and keep them out of trouble. The community's contribution to culture was a library catering primarily to a youthful clientele. More recently, community recreation and cultural programs have changed to take adult needs into consideration. Today, municipalities provide a wide variety of recreational facilities and programs from the more traditional parks and playgrounds to tennis courts, skating rinks, swimming pools with elaborate wave makers, golf courses, and adult hobby and skill courses.

The Department of Culture and the Department of Recreation and Parks have been active in promoting recreational and cultural facilities throughout the province. The most significant grant program for municipalities is the Major Cultural/Recreational Facility Development Program administered jointly by Culture and Parks and Recreation. Under this program, municipalities are provided a $100 per capita grant given on a 50 per cent cost-shared basis to help develop facilities with regional use, such as libraries, visual arts centres, theatres, museums, and art galleries. In 1981-82 the province allocated $23 million under this program.[51] Another provincial program assists municipalities in the day-to-day operation of recreational programs. Under the Operational Financial Assistance Program a municipality with a recreation board is eligible for a grant of $3.00 per capita for operational expenses. In 1981-82 municipalities received $6,600,000 through this program. A host of specialized grant programs administered through the Department of Culture have been particularly beneficial to smaller communities. One of the most successful is the Historical Publications Assistance Program that gives municipalities the incentive to delve into their past and promote civic pride by funding 50 per cent of the cost of producing a local history book up to a maxium of $5,000. In 1981, 75 municipalities took advantage of the program.[52]

Until recently provincial financial assistance for operating municipal libraries was inadequate. The two largest urban centres and many towns and villages castigated the province for its marginal support of libraries, with the result that the province substantially increased its library grants. In 1982-83 for every $2.00 per capita spent by a municipality for library services the province provided a grant of $3.00 to a maximum of $3.85 per capita.[53] Virtually every municipality with library services receives the maximum provincial grant.[54]

Even though the province has a number of recreational and cultural facilities and program grants, the demand for recreational and cultural programs has outpaced communities' abilities to provide them. Consequently, some councils have devised non-discriminatory user fees to help fill the fiscal void, while others have leased public facilities to the private sector. In yet other communities, service clubs have raised monies and voluntarily staffed facilities. Of all service areas, recreation and culture has been that in which local governments have been most successful in involving the citizenry in financing and operating.

Economic Development and Tourism

Virtually every council in Alberta is concerned with the community's economic vitality and, especially during the 1980s, its ability to weather a sustained downturn. Although a growing local economy and population places additional pressure on all municipal services, it also expands the community's business and property tax base. Every community has its "conservers" who prefer no growth in order to maintain the community's charm; however, they tend to be in the minority. For the business sector, economic and community growth is essential; a decline in population and business activity is a disaster. For example, the population of Brooks grew from 3,858 in 1971, to 6,820 in 1977, to 9,049 in 1981, and then declined to 8,060 in 1982. With the collapse of the region's oil and gas industry and a loss of 1,000 people, 60 businesses either went bankrupt or closed their doors in 1982.

It is not uncommon for both older, expanding businesses and newer businesses just gaining a foothold to over-extend themselves financially in anticipation of rapid community growth that will enable them to reap large profits and repay their loans. When population and economic growth begin to slow, stagnate, or decline, the business community greatly increases its efforts to influence council to implement growth-oriented policies. These policies invariably focus on developing tourism, promoting new industries, expanding existing ones, and inducing the provincial and federal governments to develop facilities in the community.

Edmonton and Calgary both have well staffed and professional business development departments that aggressively promote their respective cities across North America, Europe, and the Far East. Occasionally, a mayor will make a selling junket, as Calgary's mayor did in the summer of 1983, to extoll the virtues of investment opportunities in the city to Chinese entrepreneurs in Hong Kong. In smaller cities and towns, economic development promotion is handled either in the administration or directly by the council. In a few cases it is delegated to the local Chamber of Commerce. In addition, the Alberta Department of Tourism and Small Business has a small grant program for municipalities of less than 75,000 population that helps defray the cost of bringing prospective business representatives to the community or sending a community representative to visit businesses that might locate in the community.

The heart of almost any community's economic development policy is the establishment of a fully serviced industrial park. Generally, this is done through the provincial government's Industrial Land Program: the AHC assembles a parcel of land that the municipality can buy in portions, at the AHC's cost plus holding costs, over a 15-year period. The municipality then develops the park in stages by servicing one portion at a time. Under this program, every Alberta city has developed a sizeable industrial park, as have communities as small as Lac la Biche, which has a population of 2,069 and a 40-acre industrial park. An example of how a city uses its industrial park to promote economic development is provided in a 1980 interview with the director of Calgary's Department of Business (the predecessor of the

Calgary Economic Development Authority).

> There is no question, the City of Calgary is the major developer
> of industrial land . . . . Planning and Land Development are the
> ones [departments] we deal with mostly. For the simple reason
> that our clients are looking for a piece of property. They come to
> us and say, O.K., we're ready to settle in Calgary. Where do we
> go from here? We are the unofficial sales agent for the city. Our
> Land Department as well, merchandises land . . . . Most realtors
> realize that they are not going to get a commission from the city
> on city owned land, so they don't show it. And quite often the
> client will come in to see us, and find out that we do in fact have
> property in our industrial parks.[55]

For Calgary and Edmonton, convention dollars form another important component of economic development. Both cities have a convention centre. Despite continuing criticism from some community groups and charges that the structure would never cover its operating costs, the Edmonton council completed an $82 million convention centre in 1983.

A much more controversial economic policy is revitalizing the downtown core in older cities. In Edmonton, the decline of downtown retail shopping began in the late 1960s, particularly after the opening of Southgate Shopping Centre in a suburban area. The opening of the 2.2 million square foot West Edmonton Mall, with over 400 retail shops on the city's western perimeter, further accelerated the decline of downtown retail sales. Council responded by easing downtown parking restrictions, allocating a small amount of funds to upgrade the downtown with street planters, etc., encouraging high-density residential development, and discouraging non-retail businesses such as banks and financial institutions from locating on "shopping streets." In Red Deer the council attempted to halt decline in 1982 by reducing downtown business and heavy industrial taxes by 38 per cent and increasing the tax in outlying strip and shopping centres by 12 per cent. In 1981 Medicine Hat located the new provincial courthouse and city hall in the core. It is doubtful that such policies will reverse the trend towards the decentralization of retailing operating in all Alberta's larger cities.

General Government

All the governmental activities and policy areas examined so far have a direct impact on the citizenry; other governmental activities, labeled general government functions, have no such direct effect, but are, nevertheless, essential to governmental operation. The principal general function is the internal administration of city hall. While the public services discussed above are eligible for funding through provincial grants, Alberta municipalities bear almost the entire burden of financing general government expenditures — the only function assisted by the provincial government is property assessment. The cost of administration is affected by such factors as the number of administrative personnel, their salaries and fringe benefits, general administrative expenses (e.g., costs of supplies, equipment, postage, etc.), and costs incurred in holding public meetings and elections. These costs are often a source of stress between council and its civil servants, the more so as it is obvious that holding administrative expenses to a minimum frees funds for public services or may permit council to reduce taxes.

While proposals to increase the salaries of elected officials almost always cause controversy, and the cost of internal administration at city hall has occasionally become election fare in Calgary and Edmonton, there tends to be much less controversy over the salary of clerk-treasurers in the smallest of municipalities, the villages. Perhaps the reason is that both council members and the public are in direct contact with the clerk-treasurer and see that he or she is generally competent and hardworking.

Ironically, it is at the village level, where the public seems to be the most satisfied with administration, that the costs of administration represent the largest proportion of the total municipal budget. In 1980, expenditures on general government constituted 12 per cent of total expenditures for Alberta villages, nine per cent for towns, and five per cent for cities. The common-sense explanation of this inverse relationship involves the economy of scale. The specialized professionals characteristic of bureaucracies in large cities are more efficient, in economic terms, than are the "generalist" administrators found at the village level. In addition, fixed costs are proportionately larger in villages than in larger cities.

Symbolic and Ceremonial Functions

The governmental activities examined so far have dealt with fiscal policies, the delivery of services or the internal functioning of government. Certain other governmental activities and policies do not fall into any of these categories but are symbolic and ceremonial in nature, and are used to further a sense of community identity and to affirm patriotic, ethnic and community values. Municipalities across the province have their own flags, crests, mottos and official flowers. Edmonton even has its own official tartan.

At the community level "symbolic" policies may involve designating a particular day to honour one of the community's ethnic groups or a prominent citizen, or naming new neighbourhoods, streets and playgrounds. It is common for a council or one of its committees to spend many hours deciding upon appropriate names. Councils like to make symbolic policies since, besides being generally uncontroversial, they may lead to substantial support from an "honoured group or individual" in an upcoming election. But, occasionally, a seemingly innocuous symbolic policy will stir up political controversy. For example, in 1975, shortly after the death of Mayor Hawrelak, some members of the Edmonton community wanted to honour his memory by changing the name of Mayfair Park to Hawrelak Park. Although Hawrelak was revered by many Edmontonians, others felt that he had been irresponsible, and yet others argued that the name "Hawrelak" was too difficult to pronounce. Finally, after a year of controversy, on October 12, 1976, the council voted six to five to rename the park.

Ceremonial functions, also generally uncontroversial, are felt to be advantageous for the political future of council members. Medicine Hat celebrated its June 10, 1983, centennial by funding a day-long party of dancing, games and sports. When Leduc's legal status was changed from town to city in 1983, the council voted to fund a celebration picnic. During the summer of 1983, after Edmonton's administration had laid off a number of firefighters, bus drivers and police officers for fiscal reasons, the city honoured the short visit of Prince Charles and Princess Diana by spending approximately $50,000 on a barbeque, accommodations and a gift. With tens of thousands of people lining the streets to catch a glimpse of the royal couple, the very small number of people criticizing the expenditures were barely heard.

Provincial recognition of the importance of the symbolic function is made through Alberta Culture's Heritage Day grants. The Alberta Heritage Day Act of 1974 proclaimed the first Monday of August a day for celebrating cultural heritage (the celebration can also be held on the preceding Saturday or Sunday). Heritage Day activities are one of the most important symbolic functions performed in the community, largely because the Department of Culture funds up to 50 per cent of the cost of a municipal celebration. In 1982 and 1983 slightly over $100,000 was allocated under this program.

Summing Up the Functions of Local Government

At present, almost all Alberta's units of local government seem to be thriving. Their patron, the Department of Municipal Affairs, monitors their activities, provides help if it can and is continually devising programs and making recommendations to the cabinet and the legislature to make local governments better able to perform their functions. At the same time, many important functions either have been taken over from the municipalities or are being strictly controlled through a greater use of conditional grants.

One can only speculate whether local governments in Alberta have been harmed irrevocably by relinquishing one major function after another to the provincial government. On the one hand, it can be argued that turning over such "tax-draining" functions as health and welfare better enables local governments to meet public needs in other service areas. On the other hand, the contention is that giving up health and welfare and other important functions will ultimately result in the loss of public confidence in local institutions. The more functions local governments lose, the more will local institutions be perceived by the public as skeletal shells for playing "sandbox politics."

Rather than absorbing important functions or imposing unduly strict controls over local programs, the province has a feasible option that would provide adequate service delivery and greatly strengthen local institutions. One hundred per cent conditional grants with the wide latitude of the FCSS program could be given to local governments. Such a granting scheme would strengthen their administrative capabilities to manage programs and would ensure acceptable levels of program funding. To permit a modicum of control over municipal programs these grants could be allocated to general functional areas such as fire protection and prevention, recreation, and governmental administration. The inclusion of an equalization formula would slowly eradicate many of the disparities found between poor and wealthy municipalities. Any slight increase in program administration costs would be more than compensated for by the increase in local autonomy. This policy would link local decision making and knowledge of local conditions to the community's needs. At present, provincial policies tend to strengthen the powers of distant, senior policy makers and administrators while they weaken the service delivery function of local institutions and, ultimately, their major strength, democratic self-determination.

Notes

1. An example of the difference between intended and unintended policy outcomes would be a municipality opening a park in the evening in order to provide additional recreational facilities for teenagers. The policy's intended effect would be to provide worthwhile recreation for teenagers and keep them off the streets and out of amusement parlours; its unintended effect might be a slight increase in park crimes.

2. Wildavsky, *The Politics of the Budgetary Process*, 2.

3. In Canada in general and Alberta in particular, the proportion of municipal revenue derived from the property tax has been declining. A recent study of local public finance explains: "In 1960 . . . property taxes provided two-thirds of the total revenue of Canadian municipalities; by 1977, this proportion had fallen to one-third . . . . " A major factor in this reduction was "the willingness of provincial governments to increase transfers to municipalities—in effect to finance property tax reductions (or prevent increases). . . . " Although the absolute number of dollars paid in property taxes rose over this period, inflation and growth in real income was such that the relative importance of property taxes fell. Bird and Slack, *Urban Public Finance in Canada*, 60-61.

4. Another interpretation of the regressiveness of property taxes is found in Bird and Slack's study of local finance: ". . . it is probably safe to conclude that the conventional view almost certainly overstates the regressivity of the property tax, in part because it considers only the 'uses-of-income' side, while ignoring the effects on the sources of income; and in part because it takes too extreme a position on the relevant elasticities. While this ancient levy is certainly not the best of all possible taxes, it is, it now seems, not necessarily the hopeless fiscal villain it has sometimes been made out to be." *Ibid.*, 68.

5. There is another point of view on this issue. After the Edmonton city council passed a motion, in April of 1983, requesting the province to pass legislation absolving the city from having to collect school taxes, the city school board demonstrated that such legislation would be extremely costly to the citizenry. It was pointed out that it would cost an additional $200,000 for the school board to send out separate tax bills. In addition, it was argued the city's separate school board would be forced to hire an additional 100 staff members to collect their own taxes. *Edmonton Journal*, April 30, 1983.

6. In 1983 a political columnist in Edmonton wrote: "Probably, nobody knows exactly how much the city foregoes in property taxes each year, but in only one category—senior citizen and handicapped housing—the estimate is $3.7 million [for Edmonton] in 1983. Calgary, which has fewer projects than Edmonton, estimates that it will be losing $1.57 million in taxes on housing for the elderly and handicapped this year." *Edmonton Journal*, May 11, 1983.

7. In 1982 Medicine Hat's Economic Development Department conducted a survey of 15 cities and towns of approximately the same size in western Canada. The survey showed that Medicine Hat had the lowest property taxes of eight Alberta cities and towns. In 1981 the average tax bill for a three-bedroom, detached house in Medicine Hat was $638.83; the average utility bill, $828. *Edmonton Journal*, August 25, 1982. Medicine Hat's "mid-pricing" policy for its natural gas and electricity has been so successful that the city purchased an adjoining gas field for $46 million in 1982 in order to boost its reserves and to be gas self-sufficient well into the 21st century. *Medicine Hat News*, February 15, 1982.

8. Thompson, "The City as a Distorted Price System," 31.

9. With the exception of Edmonton and Calgary, the formula used to allocate unconditional grants to municipalities in the 1979-1982 period consisted of three components: 1) each municipality was given a base amount of funds that could not be less than the previous year's assistance; 2) a municipality's fiscal capacity was used in equalizing grants on a per capita basis; and 3) if a municipality's population increased five per cent or more in the previous year an additional sum was allocated to it on a per capita basis. Unconditional grants made to Edmonton and Calgary were based on the grants given in 1979 plus the level of inflation each year. In 1983 the province simply used a municipality's 1982 funding as a base and increased the amount by five per cent.

10. MacMillan and Plain, "The Reform of Municipal-Provincial Fiscal Relationships," I-19.

11. MacMillan and Plain argue persuasively that provincial bureaucrats benefit with the government's move towards greater use of conditional grants. ". . . provincial bureaucrats also favor conditional programs which, because they require considerably more bureaucratic involvement, afford a fertile area for bureaucratic empire building. . . . Between 1969 and 1977, transfers to Alberta municipalities grew . . . 26%. Provincial departmental employment over this same period [had] a growth of 27%. This suggests that as the provincial grant system became more complex, the provincial government bureaucracy grew relative to the provincial population thereby imposing a heavier burden on the Alberta taxpayer. Clearly other factors must be taken into account in considering these trends, however, one suspects that there is a grain of truth in the high correlation between the growth of the bureaucracy, the increase in the conditional grant system and the loss of municipal autonomy." *Ibid.*, III-16.

12. MacMillan and Plain cite a report by Edmonton, "whose conditional funding rose from 44% to 84% of transfers between 1966 and 1976"; the consequence there was "the loss of control over policy, the reduction of local autonomy, the distorted decisions, and the reduced flexibility of their operations." *Ibid.*, I-29.

13. In a discussion of the federal government's grant in lieu of taxes for the

city, Calgary's director of assessment said, "there is no difference between the tax assessment the city would charge for the land and buildings, if they were owned by private citizens or businesses, and the amounts granted to the city by the federal government. It is substantially identical to what one would collect from the same property if you or I owned it." *Calgary Herald*, September 30, 1982.

14. Properties of the Alberta Liquor Control Board and the Alberta Telephone Commission are also exempt under the Act, but section 18 of the Liquor Control Act and section 44 of the Alberta Government Telephones Act provides for grants to be paid in lieu of property and business taxes for these installations.

15. Report by the City of Edmonton's Real Estate and Housing Department, 2.

16. Bird and Slack, *Urban Public Finance in Canada*, 11.

17. In 1973 the development firms in Edmonton, with the number of acres they controlled, were: Nu-West 158, Bramalea 44, Western 3923, Dawson 58, MacLab 911, BACM Ltd. 1,500, Great Northern 2,807, Allarco 8,803 and Melton 1,815. In Calgary the firms and numbers were: Campeau 37, Nu-West 1,759, Bramalea 211, Western 2,063, Dawson 1,400, Paragon 30, Carma 4,500, Melton 920. Spurr, *Land and Urban Development*, 204-205. Spurr explains how the land monopoly occurred in Edmonton. "As most of Edmonton's private land banks were assembled in the 1960s at prices below $4,000 per acre, and held at relatively low interest rates, their production costs are greatly exceeded by current prices. This relationship between costs and prices translates, in the view of other actors in land (such as financial institutions, governments and sub-contractors) as relatively low risk, so the land-bank owners obtain a self-perpetuating competitive advantage over other developers. In other words, concentration in land markets leads to further concentration at the expense of competition and particularly, the entry of new, smaller developers. *Ibid.*, 155.

18. *Red Deer Advocate*, July 31, 1982.

19. *Medicine Hat News*, March 13, 1981.

20. *Provincial Housing Programs in Alberta*, 30.

21. *Grand Prairie Herald Tribune*, September 9, 1981.

22. The grant formula is as follows:

> (a) For production between 0% and 50% of the base level, [base level is defined as the average number of new dwellings started in the municipality over the previous three years] $500 per eligible unit.
>
> (b) For production in excess of 50% but less than 75% of the base level, $1,000 per subsequent unit.
>
> (c) For production from 75% but less than 100% of the base level, $1,500

per subsequent eligible unit.

(d) For production equal to or exceeding 100% of the base level, $2,000 per subsequent eligible unit.

Provincial Housing Programs in Alberta, 33.

23. Neighbouring St. Albert and the County of Strathcona solved the "public housing creation of ghetto problem" quite simply: they decided not to have any public housing.

24. *Alberta Report*, May 9, 1980.

25. Lightbody discusses the province's role in sparking opposition to roadways in Edmonton. He writes: ". . . it was a provincial statute that became the unintended catalyst for citizen opposition. The province now required that municipal applicants for conditional grants in support of transportation designs hold public hearings prior to approving a general transportation by-law. Hearings on the METS proposals served to spark a citizen revolt. In contrast to the three individuals opposed to the MacKinnon freeway in 1964, twenty-two groups or individuals demonstrated before the meeting in 1971. . . ." Lightbody, "Edmonton," 269.

26. The city administration and citizen groups committed to developing the LRT system have frequently justified it on the basis of a booklet entitled *The Immorality of the Motorcar*, produced in 1971 by a professor in the Faculty of Extension and his students. In fact, the booklet did nothing more than present a series of arguments proclaiming the efficiency of an LRT system in such areas as capacity and cost. The booklet did argue, with no factual or empirical basis, that once an LRT system was in place people would use it rather than their own automobiles. A report by the City Planning Department in 1979 found that the LRT "has not attracted a noticeable amount of new ridership [and] . . . rapid transit patronage increases are due to residential growth rather than from increased ridership from the established neighborhoods." City of Edmonton Planning Department, *North-East LRT Evaluation Study*, 3.

27. The first leg of the LRT was extended into the northeast area because Mayor Ivor Dent wanted to have a showplace system to transport people between the Commonwealth Stadium, where the 1978 Commonwealth Games were to be held, and the downtown area. Evidently, the fact that the northeast inner part of the city had been experiencing a decline in population since the late 1960s was not a factor in the decision.

28. The hamlet of Sherwood Park is also eligible for the Grant-in-Lieu of Public Transit Operating Assistance and the Public Transit Capital Assistance Program.

29. Cities with "approved" public transit systems receive $9.00 per capita yearly while cities without "approved" systems receive $2.00.

30. The Arterial Roadway Capital Assistance Program assists the

development of major arterials that directly support the primary highway system. The province funds two-thirds of the cost up to a specified annual maximum. The Major Continuous Corridor program is "to promote and ensure the planning and construction of one continuous roadway connection . . . to the Province's primary highway system." The province funds 90% of the program's cost. The Primary Highway Maintenance program is an unconditional grant given to a city to maintain the portion of the provincial highway system within its boundaries.

31. Edmonton is much more innovative in phasing taxis into the public transportation system. In its river valley, taxis are used late at night and on holidays to connect with regular buses.

32. Few if any fire departments send out expensive equipment and leave a firehall under-staffed in order to rescue a stray animal.

33. Coulter, MacGillivray and Vickery, "Municipal Fire Protection Performance in Urban Areas," 256.

34. The Rural/Metro Fire Department Inc. is a very innovative private fire department operating in Arizona. It contracts with Scottsdale and other communities in the area (it provides fire protection for one-seventh of the state's population) for fire protection, with the communities providing the fire halls. In order to cut costs the company has been very innovative in several areas. It developed "The Snail," a remote-controlled track vehicle to fight fires too hot for firefighters to approach. The company also developed its own modern and innovative fire truck at half the cost it would have had to pay on the market. With these innovations, and because the community need provide no fringe or retirement benefits to its firefighters, expenditures in Scottsdale are approximately 25 per cent of the national average for cities of its size; per capita fire losses, approximately 37 per cent.

35. If the Solicitor General believes that a municipality has a substandard police force and is providing inadequate policing, he may notify the municipal council and request it to remedy the situation. If the council refuses to act the Solicitor General has the power, under section 21(2) of the Police Act, to: "(a) appoint municipal constables . . . at salaries he considers proper, or (b) do any other thing necessary to create an adequate and efficient police force. . . . The costs are borne by the municipality. If it refuses to pay for the policing, costs are picked up by the province and, under section 21(3) of the Act, "may be recovered by the Government by deducting the amount from any grant payable by the Government to the urban municipality or by an action in debt." Needless to say, municipalities in Alberta have acted responsibly and it has not been necessary for the Solicitor General to resort to such drastic measures.

36. After the municipal police force in the Town of Hinton was rocked in 1980 with charges of harassment, favouritism and incompetence, the town administration reviewed the costs of maintaining its own police force and concluded that it could save $116,000 a year by contracting for police services

with the RCMP. Such savings were possible since the federal government provided a 43 per cent subsidy for the cost of law enforcement to towns with populations of less than 15,000. *Calgary Herald,* February 6, 1982.

37. The RCMP is not answerable to citizens' complaints. In a controversial case in which an RCMP officer strip-searched a man in front of two women companions, a complaint was laid with the province's Law Enforcement Appeal Board. The RCMP refused to appear before the board, claiming that it was allowed to handle its own internal affairs under federal legislation. The case was finally resolved in the summer of 1981, when the Supreme Court of Canada ruled that the RCMP is not subject to provincial police conduct boards.

38. Municipalities contracting with the RCMP for police services may also establish police commissions but, since the RCMP is only answerable to federal authorities, such a commission would be virtually powerless. In 1981 the council of the Town of Strathmore, which contracted for police services with the RCMP and also had a police commission, questioned the value of the commission since it was unable to exercise any control over the RCMP. One council supporter of the commission argued that the commission could investigate complaints against the RCMP and pass the information on to the force. *Calgary Herald,* September 3, 1981.

39. Robert Lineberry and Ira Sharkansky summarize the results of a study carried out in Kansas City, Missouri, in 1972-1973. "The police department in Kansas City divided one section of the city into three kinds of beats. In each case, beats were matched by socioeconomic profiles. *Reactive* beats were those where *no routine patrol* activities took place. Police came in response to calls, but were instructed not to engage in random patrol operations. In *proactive beats,* neighborhoods were saturated with patrol cars—three to four times as many as normal. And in *control beats,* patrol was carried on just as it had been in the past. After a year of the experiment, the experimentors concluded that:

> 1.There were very few significant differences in crime rates among the three neighborhoods.
>
> 2.Citizen surveys of victimization revealed few differences among the three neighborhoods.
>
> 3.Traffic death and accident rates did not vary much from one type of beat to the other."

Lineberry and Sharkansky, *Urban Politics and Public Policy,* 294-295.

40. In the United States it has been estimated that each resident of a municipality generates 2.39 pounds of waste each day. When the total of all components of municipal solid waste is divided by municipal population, the figure varies between 3.36 and 4.92 pounds of waste per day, depending on the municipality. Savas, "Solid Waste Collection in Metropolitan Areas,"

206. It is not unreasonable to conclude that similar figures would be found for Canadian cities.

41. Edmonton's Utilities and Protection Service Commissioner, Phil Walker, made a distinction between garbage dumps and landfill sites, declaring that the city has had dumps in the past but today the landfill sites are smoothed and packed with landfill material and ground garbage, making landfill sites much more aesthetically acceptable than the old dumps. *Edmonton Journal*, June 10, 1982. Unfortunately for Walker, the public does not seem to make the same distinction.

42. Several years ago the problem became so acute in Los Angeles that the city administration seriously examined the possibility of shipping the city's garbage daily by rail to a remote site in Arizona. The idea was dropped when Arizona emphatically stated that it would prohibit California garbage shipments into the state.

43. McDavid, "Residential Solid Waste Collection Services," 24. McDavid cautions: "Although costs per household vary with collection method, it is important to remember that the comparison does not control for the influence of other variables. In other words, when we examined the difference between public and private collection costs, we assumed . . . that everything else was held constant. That is, technologies and service levels were equalized for public and private producers. Clearly that assumption needs to be relaxed. Private companies, for example, use a larger percentage of larger hauling vehicles, which could itself influence costs per household. *Ibid*, 27. It should also be noted that one study of New York City found "that it costs the city more than twice as much as the private sector to collect a ton of garbage—$39.71 compared to $17.28!" Savas, "Municipal Monopolies Versus Competition in Delivering Urban Services," 477. However, since New York City's political and administrative characteristics are far different from those in any Canadian city, it would be naive to jump to the conclusion that a similar situation is to be found in Canada. New York's public service unions are very closely allied with the city's ruling Democratic Party. Consequently, the administration has looked the other way at featherbedding practices in the Department of Sanitation.

44. The cost of the water and sewer hookup from the street to the household is borne by each homeowner.

45. Bird and Slack, *Urban Public Finance in Canada*, 90.

46. *Alberta Report*, February 21, 1983, 10.

47. The basis of this assertion was: ". . . it [fluoridation] has a harmful effect on the human nervous system and weakens the memory. It has been asserted that the Russians use it on their slave laborers to rob them of their will to resist, and that the campaign for fluoridation is the work of Communists who want to soften the brains of the American people and make them pushovers for communism." *New York Times*, April 11, 1955. At a New York

State Legislative Committee hearing, a representative of a citizen's anti-fluoridation committee testifying on fluoridation said, "You can call this forced mass medication, but it might turn out to be mass liquidation." *New York Times*, March 5, 1953.

48. Those making this argument maintained that property taxes should pay only for services used either directly or indirectly by the property owner. Since the recipients of welfare rarely owned property, it was argued that property owners were paying for a service for which they received no benefit.

49. Bella, "The Goal Effectiveness of Alberta's Preventive Social Service Program," 144.

50. In addition to covering 20 per cent of program costs, the municipality was responsible for providing housing and furnishings for administrators and clerical staff.

51. A somewhat similar program, the Project Cooperative Program, was devised to encourage joint recreational facility development by two or more municipalities. The province expended $3,300,000 on the program in 1981-82.

52. Other specialized and less used programs are as follows:
1. The Local Restoration Assistance Program that gives municipalites an incentive to restore a local historical site by funding 50% of the cost of the project to a maximum of $5,000. Nineteen municipalities received funds in 1981 under the program.
2. A related program, the Inventory Assistance Program, funds 50 per cent of the cost for compiling materials on a local historical site to a maximum of $1,000. Three communities participated in this program in 1981-82.
3. The Cemetery Restoration Assistance Program gives municipalities 50 per cent of the cost of restoring a cemetery to a maxium of $2,000. Twenty municipalities participated in the program in 1981-82.
4. The Special Historical Project Assistance Program provides 50 per cent of the cost, to a maximum of $1,000, of putting on a local historical conference. Thirteen municipalities received funding under this program in 1981-82.

53. There are also grant programs for regional and community libraries. Under the regional library program, for every dollar spent by the participating municipalities the province provides a grant of two dollars to a maximum of $2.25 per capita. Under the community library program, the provincial grant is up to one and a half times the previous year's grant, to a maximum of $3.85 per capita.

54. Alberta's larger municipalities consider libraries to be very important and provide funding far greater than the minimum needed to receive the maximum provincial grant. For example, in 1981 when the maximum provincial grant was $3.37 per capita Edmonton spent $7,849,000 for libraries and received a provincial grant of $1,856,658. Calgary's expenditure was

$6,948,248 and its grant was $2,007,048. Lethbridge spent $886,013 for its libraries and received a government grant of $279,020.

55. *Business Life*, 8, 33.

9

PLANNING

AND

THE POLITICAL PROCESS

Planning: The Integrative Mechanism in Local Government

In the previous chapter the more important municipal service functions were examined in some detail. Intuitively we know that, if all the service functions are to mesh and departments are not to be working at cross-purposes, the elected and appointed personnel responsible for them must follow a comprehensive plan. Theory tells us that municipal planning is the key that determines whether governmental functions work together efficiently. Some scholars maintain that, in its broadest sense, municipal planning is the rational model of decision making practised by professional bureaucrats. Within the parameters laid out by elected decision makers, municipal planners identify community goals and resources and develop strategies to attain these goals. Equally important, planners are responsible for identifying members of the public who will be advantaged and those who will be disadvantaged by any particular planning strategy or goal. This function is a recognition that no single strategy or plan benefits everyone, that is, there is no such thing as a public interest, rather there are several diverse and conflicting group and class interests within a community.

Ideally, planning integrates all of the municipality's service functions; in practice, regional and municipal planning deal almost exclusively with land use.[1] Moreover, even within this narrow focus, key community resources are often overlooked, elected decision makers often are presented with a narrow range of community goals, and attempts to integrate land-use planning with a municipality's other functions are rare.[2]

Intellectual Development of Planning in Canada

The city planning movement in Canada has two intellectual roots, one of which died some 60 years ago. Shortly after the turn of the century, many Canadian students who had travelled extensively while training in Europe lamented the image of the Canadian city: they saw it as ugly and unplanned compared to European cities. Other Canadian architects were excited by the architectural wonders displayed at the 1893 Chicago World Fair. In fact, "in later years, when leaders in the Canadian planning movement talked of its beginnings, they often traced the North American planning movement back to the Chicago World Fair." [3] This notion of introducing beauty into the city, called the "City Beautiful Movement," emphasized broad thoroughfares, large parks, and graceful neo-classic public buildings and amphitheatres. But, beginning in the century's early years and peaking shortly after the First World War, the proponents of the "City Beautiful Movement" were attacked for not dealing with the most important problems in the city: housing for the poor and for the working class, and rampant suburbanization spurred by private greed and public boosterism.[4] During the latter quarter of the nineteenth century, new immigrants and the poor were housed in crowded and unsanitary slums and shantytowns that were periodically ravaged by disease. In their headlong rush for profits, the captains of industry, often among the city's civic elite, had little interest in creating liveable environments for their employees. [5] By the late 1920s the "City Beautiful Movement" had collapsed, although some of its tenets are still found, occasionally, in municipal and regional plans in Alberta.

The second and more important intellectual tradition, a concern with social ills, was intertwined with the imposition of a code of moral behaviour on the poor and uneducated. This concern was based on Jeremy Bentham's philosophy of utilitarianism, the basic tenet of which is that the greatest happiness should accrue to the greatest number. It was believed that the greatest happiness could be achieved through reason; for the planner, this philosophy meant that a single best solution to society's ills could be found through reason.

In 1914, an English planner with a utilitarian bias, Thomas Adams, was recruited to serve on the federal government's Commission of Conservation and, within a few short years, his social philosophy had had a major impact on Canadian planning. With his concern for housing reform, public health and professionalization of planning, he helped to mould the Town Planning Institute of Canada, established in 1918. Influenced by Adams, town planners with a social conscience emphasized that they were as concerned with economic and social problems as with the aesthetics of the city. Although Adams' ideas on the mechanics of planning, which were rooted in an English tradition, were rejected as inappropriate for Canada, his basic philosophy is still found in a segment of the Canadian planning profession today." He regarded the city as primarily an economic organism in which 'the first concern of a town plan should be to provide for the proper and efficient carrying out of business'. Mindful, however, of his reformist background, he added that 'complementary to the business side of a city is the provision of satisfactory and healthy living conditions for the people'."[6]

Yet another set of ideas on government and planning was introduced from the United States at about the same time that Adams and his disciples were providing a counterbalance to the "City Beautiful Movement." To eliminate the evils of the municipal party machine, American reformers advocated changing the structure of municipal government "to take politics out of government" and to "govern scientifically." Their program of change included, among other things, value-free comprehensive master planning. American planners adopted the philosophy that master planning was a rational technical exercise that could identify a single universal public interest. However, since politics connotes divisiveness and controversy over community goals, it is the antithesis of a single public interest. Thus, master planning and the planner were seen as being above the give and take of municipal politics. One manifestation of this anti-political stance was an attempt to insulate planning from politics by placing it in the hands of a semi-independent planning commission. In a Canada influenced by the dogma of the American reform movement, it was but a short step from a concern with alleviating social ills to a concern with the reform of the local political system considered partially responsible for those ills. Paul Rutherford writes of this new movement in Canada:

> At the institutional level, the bureaucratic method required the creation of an autonomous and trained administration dedicated to the twin ideals of economy and efficiency. To the reformers expert knowledge was a near panacea. This was the beginning of the age of the specialist and the professional. The reformers hoped to minimize the influence of the amateur in all departments of civic government, to take administration out of politics. . . . Responding to reform pleas, especially after 1900, municipal governments did create formidable civic bureaucracies to control police, public health, utilities, parks

and recreation, and social welfare. To a degree, this appeared to be a devolution of authority; in fact, it was a centralization of authority in the hands of professions, well-nigh independent of the electorate, with a vested interest in the success of the reform movement.[7]

In short, an American package of political and administrative reforms was modified and adapted to the Canadian political environment in order to cure social ills. This dose of American ideas advocated a "public interest" thought to be morally superior to the interests of "bickering transitory parochial politicians."

From the onset of the Depression until after the Second World War, city planning in Canada lanquished as the "nation turned to priorities other than cities."[8] And yet it was during this lull that still another set of planning ideas and goals, albeit radical ones, were advanced; they are found today among a small minority of radical planners. In 1935, the League for Social Reconstruction (LSR) published *Social Planning for Canada* in which they advocated a system of socialist planning. LSR discussed the city's ills caused by capitalism and proposed a number of solutions. Kent Gerecke, in an examination of their program, identifies their solutions:

1. public housing estates for low income families;

2. government housing corporations;

3. socialist housing plans based on the "neighbourhood unit";

4. comprehensive plans based on surveys; and

5. housing designs "to liberate the housewife from the monotonous servitude of domestic chores."

In addition they supported the elimination of "rake-offs" by promoters, the breaking of monopolies in building supplies and the compulsory purchase of inner-city lands below their "fictitious" value.[9] In addition to adopting a socialist approach to planning, today's radical planners espouse decentralized government and grass-roots democracy, especially where it benefits poorer neighbourhoods. More often than not, the radical planner is found at the neighbourhood level acting as its advocate.

Although important in its own right, a radical approach to planning is on the fringe rather than in the mainstream of Canadian planning. The planning profession today believes that planning should take place within the confines of the existing political and economic system. One virulent critic of the Canadian planning profession, Ron

Clark, argues that British-trained planners hired by planning departments and universities since the 1940s misdirected the profession. He
writes:

> Perhaps, most serious of the deficiencies in the British approach
> to planning was the relentless desire to accumulate, centralize
> and legislate more and more planning power and control.
> Accompanying this . . . the British ignored the role of the public
> in planning . . . what emerged . . . was a planning model in
> which planners were totally detached from the dynamics which
> characterized urban issues. The British belief that planning is a
> value-free, apolitical science to be practiced with rigorous
> precision, employing a grab bag of pseudo tools and having a
> "New Town" fixation was the unfortunate legacy that British
> planners bequeathed to Canada.[10]

Thus, today, both the American reform movement and the orienta-
tions of British planners contribute to the apolitical stance exhibited
by Canadian planners. In a 1976 cross-country survey of Canadian
planners, the respondents were almost evenly split over their conception of the public interest. Forty-two per cent believed there was a
single public interest "that overrides narrower parochial interests."[11]
Of this view Matthew Kiernan writes:

> . . . it [a unitary public interest] in fact bespeaks a distinct
> idiosyncratic sociopolitical outlook . . . the unitary public
> interest ideology implicitly adopts a fundamentally consensual
> rather than conflictive view of society. . . . Nor is this merely
> harmless rhetoric; it actually obscures from both the planners
> and the public the crucial fact that the benefits and disbenefits
> of planning interventions tend to fall disproportionately upon
> different socioeconomic classes and groups.[12]

The same study found that many Canadian planners were proponents
of value-free comprehensive planning guided by scientific principles. Sixty-six per cent of the respondents believed that the comprehensive plan ought to provide a general guide to community planning.[13] There is nothing wrong with comprehensive planning that is
part of a larger process of deciding upon the allocation of resources to
diverse groups in the community. In this process, several comprehensive plans are sketched out, each with a different allocation of
public goods to differing socio-economic, ethnic and geographic
groups in the community. However, the survey showed that only 16

per cent of Canadian planners felt that planners should be a part of a larger process governed by political considerations.[14]

The conception of the public interest and of comprehensive planning as apolitical is in itself of little consequence. A more important question is whether, in the foreseeable future, planners' attitudes about their role in policy making will change. The indications are that they are now changing rapidly. In their survey of Canadian planners, Page and Lang found, "as a whole, we see a young, well paid, predominantly male professional group. . . . The past 10 years has been a period of rapid growth and change for the planning profession, accompanied by shifts in background from the dominancy of engineering/architecture to that of geography/social sciences."[15] As greater numbers of planners obtain an undergraduate education in the social sciences, which tend to focus on the problems of societal inequities, rather than in engineering, with its focus on scientism, it is likely that planning will become increasingly liberalized and politicized.

History and Intellectual Development of Planning in Alberta

In 1914, heavily influenced by the "City Beautiful Movement," the Calgary City Planning Commission hired an English firm to prepare a plan for the city "which turned out to be a grandiose fantasy." At about the same time, Edmonton was considering a city beautification program that was to include an elaborate system of urban parks and tree-lined streets. But the real estate bust of 1913 left Alberta's cities with a more than ample supply of subdivided land. This development, coupled with a redirection of civic effort toward winning the "Great War," caused enthusiasm for planning to decline. Then, with a 1920s mini-boom in growth and building, interest in planning and civic beautification revived.

Alberta's second premier, Arthur Sifton, left an imprint of utilitarianism on the intellectual development of planning in the province that is still with us today. The premier's brother, Clifford Sifton, was the originator and chairman of the Commission of Conservation, established in 1910, that, according to P. J. Smith, "combined, in a single organization, the two mainstreams of progressive social philosophy, environmental conservation and urban improvement. It also epitomized the adaptation of utilitarian doctrine to the Canadian setting."[16] Arthur Sifton was the province's representative on the commission during his 1910-1917 tenure of office.

Alberta's first Planning Act seemed to be uncontroversial at the time—it passed through all three readings on the last day of the 1913 spring session. It received little press coverage and even less fanfare.

The new Alberta Act was based, with some slight changes, on New Brunswick's Town Planning Act of 1912, the first planning act in Canada. Since New Brunswick's planning legislation was closely modelled on the town planning section of the British Housing and Town Planning Act of 1909, Sifton indirectly brought English utilitarianism to planning in Alberta.

The year the new planning legislation was enacted, the province's cities were at the end of a major land boom. Working with developers, city administrators in Edmonton and Calgary committed millions of dollars to street, streetcar, water and sewer lines to service newly planned areas which, as it turned out, would not be settled for many years. By mid-1913 Edmonton had incurred a debt of $22,313,968 and Calgary one of $20,633,605. Since the province's major cities needed a long and continuing land boom to justify their excessive capital spending, it was unlikely that the new planning legislation would be used as a deterrent to speculation and growth.

While containing no definition of planning, the new Act focused on the "legal procedures by which town planning was to be implemented," and was very specific as to what area of the community was to be planned and regulated. Section 1(1) clearly stated that the Act applied only to underdeveloped land on the community's periphery.[17] Despite this prohibition on core city planning, the Act contained a small number of innovative provisions that have been incorporated into subsequent acts. One provided a mechanism "for individual property owners to combine their land holdings for planning purposes," which made it "possible to prepare a single unified design for quite large tracts of land, commonly of a thousand acres or more." It went a step further: "the town planning scheme was also able to incorporate non-economic features in the public good, such as parks and open space. . . . In short, it offered the aesthetic order of unified design rather than the mechanistic order imposed by zoning and grid subdivision."[18] The only substantial addition to the Act was a provision for a dedication of up to five per cent of land for open space and public lands *with no compensation* in a newly planned area. Compulsory dedication of lands was not to become part of planning legislation in other parts of Canada for 40 years.

In the Alberta Act, the Minister of Municipal Affairs was given an extraordinary amount of power over municipal planning. To begin with, the Minister's approval was necessary before any municipal planning scheme could be implemented. More importantly, the Act gave the Minister the power to require a municipality to prepare a planning scheme "in a case where a town planning scheme ought to be made." But, as Smith notes, "no Minister was ever put to the test."[19]

The onset of a recession in 1913 destroyed all interest developers or municipal administrators might have had in planning outlying developments. Bettison, Kenward and Taylor aptly describe the period when they write, "paradoxically, the 1913 Act was introduced at the very time when its authority was hardly needed. Rapid expansion of towns and cities had ceased and the next twenty years were to be largely consolidating, with slow but steady development in selected urban areas."[20] Although of little significance in regulating planning for a number of years, the importance of the 1913 Act is stated succinctly by Smith.

> The only significance of the Town Planning Act . . . is its place in the history of the idea of planning and, particularly, its contribution to the Alberta view of planning that is in place today. The central point is simple: the principle of utility [utilitarianism] continues to be served. . . . Unwittingly, Sifton's government set a doctrinaire hand on the evaluation of planning thought in Alberta, and the gospel of efficiency continues to be the only explicit ethic that supports the institution of planning.[21]

During the 1920s Edmonton and Calgary once again were beginning to expand and to infill some of the partially developed areas created by the 1913 land bust. But conditions in the 1920s were far different from those prevailing when the first Planning Act was implemented in 1913. The municipalities responded pragmatically "by replacing or revising those parts of the planning system that were no longer thought to be effective; by filling critical gaps in the original system; and by adopting innovative responses to new concerns (or to renewed expressions of old concerns)."[22] By the late 1920s it became clear that the 1913 Act was outmoded. With the impetus provided by the government in power (i.e., the United Farmers of Alberta), the City of Edmonton, the United Farm Women of Alberta and the Edmonton Local Council of Women, the 1913 Act was repealed in 1929. The UFA was committed to maximizing the quality of rural life and a "central planning agency designed to help the local communities to help themselves . . . was the obvious solution."[23] Edmonton felt that the 1913 Act was badly outdated and the United Farm Women of Alberta and the Edmonton Local Council of Women were concerned about the lack of legislation to prevent unsightly billboards along roads and highways. In 1928 "An Act to Facilitate Town Planning and the Preservation of the Natural Beauties of the Province" was passed, and then repealed and reintroduced in an amended form in the new

1929 Town Planning Act.

The 1929 legislation was an amalgam of sections of the 1928 Act, the British Columbia Act, and some of the latest ideas in American planning theory and practice. Smith sums it up, writing: "[it was] the longest and most complex piece of planning legislation . . . in Canada. It was also the most thorough illustration, to that time, of the process of cumulative adaptation and, in its new provisions, the most complete expression of American planning techniques in Canadian law."[24] It provided for the establishment of a Town and Rural Planning Board and a Provincial Director of Town Planning to establish provincial planning guidelines. It gave municipalities zoning powers by enabling them to prescribe permissible land uses in various areas of the community and to control densities, lot size requirements, and building heights and floor areas. The 1929 Act also gave cities, towns, villages, municipal districts and improvement districts in a region powers to establish a regional planning commission. As might be expected in a rural-dominated legislature, small municipalities were favoured over very large ones: no governmental unit was allowed more than three members on a commission; however, under section 18(4) of the Act, the costs of a regional planning commission were borne "by the councils in the proportion which the total value of the assessable property in their respective municipalities as shown on the assessment rolls bear to one another." Thus proportionality was woven into the composition of a regional planning commission, but only on its cost side! Despite the onset of the Depression in 1929 there was a great deal of interest in planning. Planning commissions were organized and professional staff hired in Edmonton and Calgary, and some 50 municipalities adopted planning by-laws. But as the Depression continued and money became increasingly scarce, interest in planning waned. No regional planning commissions were established and the province disbanded the newly created provincial planning branch to save money.

Fueled by a revival of agricultural prices shortly after the beginning of the Second World War, the province's economy began to pick up and again there was an interest in planning. In 1942 the few amendments passed during the 1930s were consolidated; the result was the 1942 Town Planning Act.

The 1947 Leduc oil discovery prevented a potential postwar slump in the province's economy and the cities of Edmonton and Calgary, again experiencing growing pains, did not want to repeat the mistakes of past expansions. In 1949, the Edmonton Local Council of Women petitioned city council to unravel the snafus in the city's planning process and to establish a department of town planning.

Two consultants were hired to examine the city's problems and their report, which was of crucial importance, was submitted to the provincial government as a justification for changing the Planning Act to facilitate planning in Edmonton. The government responded with yet another rewrite. The culmination was the Town and Rural Planning Act of 1950; its major contributions were provisions for the formation of district planning commissions, which were the direct forerunner of the province's regional planning commissions.[25] In a nutshell, the district planning commissions, voluntary associations of municipalities, were given primarily advisory powers in a region. A recent Department of Municipal Affairs' publication sums up the limited powers of the district planning commissions.

> A Commission was responsible upon the request of a municipality for the preparation of general plans and zoning by-laws for municipalities situated within the boundaries of the District, and for advising on planning matters of a general nature or involving two or more municipalities.[26]

Shortly after the passage of the Act, the Edmonton District Planning Commission was established, followed by the Calgary DPC in 1951, the Red Deer DPC in 1952, the Medicine Hat DPC in 1954, the Oldman River DPC in 1955, the Peace River DPC in 1958, and the Battle River DPC in 1960. By the end of the decade, although seven district planning commissions had been established, it became clear that with only advisory powers, they could not control land use effectively. This weakness was exemplified by the development of Edmonton's satellite community, Sherwood Park, in the County of Strathcona. Since a district planning commission could not make a decision unless a representative of the affected municipality was present at the hearing, the County of Strathcona simply did not send a representative to the meetings when the question of whether residential development should proceed in Sherwood Park was discussed. Development proceeded by default.

In 1957, the Planning Act was amended to require municipalities with populations in excess of 50,000 to prepare a district general plan. This provision established the precedent that, under certain conditions, planning was mandatory. A second important amendment delegated final subdivision approval to regional and municipal authorities.

In 1961, a review of planning legislation begun by the Minister of Municipal Affairs culminated in a rewriting of the Planning Act. Partially influenced by the McNally Commission's recommendations on the need for providing orderly development in Edmonton and Calgary, the Act changed the name of district planning commissions to regional planning commissions and required that all commissions prepare a regional plan; no deadline was mentioned. It also reduced the number of bodies dealing with planning appeals and subdivision approvals. In 1968, an amendment directed each regional planning commission to complete a preliminary regional plan by 1972.

By the end of 1971, only the Edmonton and Calgary Commissions had complied. Since lack of funds seemed to be a major problem everywhere, the Alberta Planning Fund was established in 1971.[27] All municipalities were required to contribute to the fund an amount determined by a formula that took into account the inherent differences between small and large, and rural and urban municipalities.

The Progressive Conservative government, elected in 1971, took an increasing interest in environmental concerns through an expansion of the Department of Environment. This government also realized that an effective planning mechanism was essential to control the accelerating urban trend in the province. Throughout the early 1970s the Department of Municipal Affairs conducted a complete re-examination of planning in Alberta. The Act was rewritten a number of times; finally, it was all incorporated into the 1977 Planning Act.

P.J. Smith has made a convincing argument that all planning in Alberta, both municipal and regional, has been based on utilitarian principles. These principles assumed that there was "one best way" to plan and that the "public good" is easily determined by the citizenry. A recent Department of Municipal Affairs discussion paper considered that the utilitarian approach had been successful until planning became more complex in the 1970s.

> A particular philosophy of planning was evident in the early Acts, a philosophy characterized by planning as a technical activity 'to be carried out by experts whose scientific knowledge equips them to judge that certain courses of action are 'best' because they maximize utility.'

> This approach proved successful until the Seventies, when the RPC planners were joined by provincial planners in the management of regional resources. The old utilitarian approach proved less useful in the face of the increasing complexity of planning. [28]

Smith would disagree with the assertion that there has been a move away from "the old utilitarian" approach in the 1977 Planning

Act. He argues that utilitarianism is as pervasive in the 1977 Act as in earlier ones. His principal argument is that the fundamental fault of this method is that "it does not incorporate a principle of justice." He explains what he means:

> Planning . . . is an allocative process in which scarce resources, notably land and public funds, have to be distributed among rival claimants. Conflict . . . is inherent in the situations. . . . To resolve conflict, there has to be an ethic, and that ethic has to incorporate a principle of justice independent of utility [utility loosely defined as the greatest good of the greatest number], since it will rarely be possible to prove, objectively, that the desires of one individual or interest group would contribute more to the general welfare than those of another.[29]

Smith further says that we live in a complex pluralistic society in which different groups (ethnic, occupational, income, etc.) are continually making claims on one another. Whether recognized or not, the effect of urban and regional planning is to take benefits (and sometimes liabilities) from one group and give them to another. But, since neither the provincial government nor many planners realize this fact, there has not been a conscious attempt to develop a set of principles for equitable distribution of benefits and liabilities.

Although Smith is very critical of the "scientism" of the utilitarian approach and is candid about the difficulty of determining the public good/public interest, he does not reject utilitarianism out of hand. Rather, he believes that, if a principle of justice were incorporated into the utilitarian approach, many of its shortcomings would be rectified. Finally, he argues that even the most recent Planning Act in Alberta is a manifestation of utilitarianism in planning without an explicit principle of justice.

The 1977 Planning Act and the Planning Process Today

In one sense the 1977 Planning Act can be seen as merely an evolution of the utilitarian approach to planning: section 2 states, "the purpose of the Act [is to] achieve the orderly, economical and beneficial development and use of land and patterns of human settlement . . . without infringing on the rights of individuals except to the extent that is necessary for *the greater public interest*." [Emphasis added]. An Edmonton legal authority maintained that the 1977 Act was largely no more than a refinement of the 1970 Act it replaced. However, since the new Act gave municipalities far more discretion in planning, she believed that it would "offer planners greater opportunities for creative planning."[30]

At the apex of the planning authorities is the Alberta Planning Board; just below it are the province's 10 regional planning commissions with authority over more than 90 per cent of the province's population. Although the Act directs a commission to act as a resource body on which its member municipalities can call for assistance in drawing up a municipal plan or a land-use by-law, its most important function is to prepare a regional plan to which all its members must adhere.[31] The regional plan is a potentially powerful instrument since it provides "for the present and future land use and development of the planning region" and "may regulate and control the use and development of land" in the region. In practice, the regional plan first establishes goals (the preservation of agricultural land, industrial development, etc.), then develops broad but firm guidelines determining how the region's municipalities are to manage their land. A common problem is that regional plans have been far too detailed and technical, and have been seen as being too regulatory. Some such plans, reviewed by the Alberta Planning Board, were turned back to the commissions to be rewritten as broad policy instruments.[32]

One administrative function of a regional planning commission is acting as the subdivision approving authority for most of the region's municipalities.[33] This duty requires that the commissioners examine a developer's subdivision scheme to ensure that it does not conflict with the regional plan's guidelines for the area. The commission then has three options: it can approve, approve conditionally or disapprove the application. As the name implies, conditional approval stipulates conditions that must be met before the developer can subdivide.[34]

Since each commission board is composed of representatives from its member municipalities, it would seem that regional goals and planning directives are the collective goals of all of the region's municipalities and that regional policy making is a grass-roots process. This is the case at one stage in the process, but a regional plan formulated by the commission board must be ratified by the Alberta Planning Board. The reason is explained in a forthright statement by the Board.

> The process of approving a regional plan provides an
> opportunity to reflect Provincial goals and objectives in a
> statutory document. The regional plan cannot be a definitive
> statement of Provincial policy and the Provincial government is
> not legally bound by it. Nevertheless, it provides a vehicle for
> interpreting Provincial goals and objectives at a regional level

in its areas of legitimate concern, and for coordination both
between municipal and Provincial levels of administration.[35]

Thus, one of the primary functions of the Planning Board is to bring a
locally devised regional plan into conformity with broad provincial
government policy. One of the difficulties the Board has is that these
policies are often unclear.

The Board's power seems almost all-encompassing since, if a plan
does not meet its approval, it is sent back to the regional planning
commission for revision.[36] The Planning Board has exercised this
power a number of times. Once a plan has been approved, all subsequent amendments need Board approval. In addition, the Board is the
appeal body for subdivision appeals; its decisions are subject only to
an appeal to the Appelate Division of the Alberta Supreme Court and
then only on questions of law, not on the planning substance of the
decision. [37]

Since the Alberta Planning Board can be viewed as the provincial
government's agent for ensuring that planning conforms to government policy, it is to be expected that the Board's members are appointed by the government and serve at its pleasure. Until recently,
the Board was composed entirely of senior civil servants, deputy ministers, assistant deputy ministers and departmental directors, all of
whom represented departments with a direct interest in land-use
planning. Then, with Marvin Moore's assumption of the Municipal
Affairs portfolio, a number of appointments were made on the basis
of political considerations. The rationale for actively politicizing the
Board with these new members, designated "citizens at-large," was
that regional planning commissions and municipal councillors "had,
for some years expressed dissatisfaction that Provincial servants
could, on subdivision appeals, overturn decisions that had been made
by municipally elected people."[38] Of the Board's 18 members, six are
considered political appointees.[39] Although the political appointees
constitute a minority, their influence is greater than their numbers
would indicate; they seem to play a greater role on the Board's committees than do civil-service appointees, and professional civil servants seem to be increasingly reluctant to participate actively in the
Board's activities. The long-term effect of politicizing the Board is to
give the province even greater control over regional and municipal
planning decisions. A Board composed entirely of civil servants has
as much commitment to professionalism in planning as to ensuring
regional and local conformity to provincial guidelines. Political appointees, much less hampered by ideals of professionalism, can be expected to focus almost entirely on furthering what they perceive as

provincial goals.

The regional planning commissions establish broad provincial and regional planning guidelines. It is the professional planners in the Planning Service Division of the Department of Municipal Affairs and those attached to the regional planning commissions who work closely with municipal councils in preparing general municipal plans and writing land-use by-laws. It is much less common for a municipality to employ private consultants to prepare its general plan. Larger municipalities are allowed to do their own planning and the cities of Calgary, Edmonton, Leduc, Lethbridge and St. Albert have established their own planning departments.

Every municipality in Alberta with a population of 1,000 or more and every county and municipal district with a population of 10,000 or more is required to have a general municipal plan describing the municipality's land uses and proposals for future development. A council has the discretion to "designate or describe the areas of the municipality that would . . . be suitable for an area structure plan or an area redevelopment plan or both."[40]

In order to make the general plan work it is necessary for a council to enact a very specific land-use by-law. The 1977 Planning Act combined a municipality's zoning powers and its somewhat more flexible development controls into land-use by-laws. A land-use by-law divides a municipality into a number of districts with designated permitted and conditional uses of land and buildings. The by-law can be very specific, limiting floor areas and building heights, specifying their character, appearance, lighting and myriad other details. The by-law can regulate the height of fences, placement of billboards, etc. The other parts of the machinery necessary for carrying out a municipality's general and area plans are the subdivision control system and the direct control exercised by the municipality over public works programs.

Avenues for public participation in the municipal and regional planning process are limited. The citizenry can participate only in an advisory capacity; there is no point at which members of the public are directly involved in the formulation of planning policy. Under section 62 of the Act, "a council shall, during the preparation of a general municipal plan, provide an opportunity to those persons affected by it of making suggestions and representation." Then, in section 139, more explicit instructions to council direct it to hold a public hearing before giving second council reading to a proposed general municipal plan by-law, area structure plan by-law, area redevelopment plan by-law, or a by-law that either amends or abolishes any of the above.[41] In section 49 of the Act, a regional planning commission is directed to hold one or more public meetings before a regional plan is adopted.

Since much planning deals with technical matters, members of the public are often hesitant to make presentations for fear of appearing ignorant. In addition, since professional planners often feel threatened by attacks on "their" plans, a public meeting to discuss a proposed plan often becomes adversarial. The prospect of such a confrontation inhibits many citizens. A recent development in the planning profession is the emergence of the "advocate planner" who uses his or her expertise on behalf of citizen groups attempting to prevent the enactment of what they see as an ill-conceived plan. At public meetings the advocate planner provides technical information and arguments to counter the proposals of municipal and regional planners.[42] Both Edmonton and Calgary moved into community-based advocate planning when they became participants in the federal government's Neighborhood Improvement Programme.[43]

Regional Planning Commission Conflict and Dissension

Alberta's 10 regional planning commissions range in size from the Mackenzie Commission, with 15 members, to the Oldman River Commission with 45 members. Although membership on a planning commission is not automatically bestowed on every governmental unit within a commission's boundaries, in practice, the Minister of Municipal Affairs has given representation to practically all affected municipalities.[44] Even the Blood and Peigan Indian Reserves each have one vote on the Oldman River Commission.

Political posturing and conflict are to be found on all planning commissions, but the greatest conflict is found on those containing a major urban centre. Conflicts between urban and rural municipalities revolve around both money and issues reflecting traditional urban and rural values. Land-use planning invariably specifies locations for industry, with its strong tax base. Although rural municipalities will compete among themselves over the location of an industry, the cleavage is normally an urban-rural one. Since, in most cases, the regional planning commission is the authority that approves subdivision, rural municipalities often charge that an urban-dominated commission approves outlying subdivisions with little concern for the effects on school growth, roadway usage and the depletion of agricultural land. On the other hand, urban municipalities maintain that the property taxes from suburbanites commuting from bedroom communities belong to the urban centre since the suburbanites use urban services without paying for them. Urban municipalities favour regional parks while rural municipalities maintain that parks deplete the stock of shrinking agricultural land and attract undesirable urbanites to rural areas, where they engage in crime and vandalism.

The Appendix to this chapter gives the composition of each planning commission: its municipal members (with population figures) and the number of votes allowed each jurisdiction. It will be noted that, although there is no proportional representation on the governing boards of regional planning commissions, the larger urban centres have been given multiple commission votes. Even with multiple votes, however, the larger centres are under represented on the commissions. For example, although Calgary's 16-member commission gives Calgary three votes, each of these three delegates represents 207,711 people; the Village of Beiseker has one delegate for its 637 residents. On the 24-member Red Deer Commission, Red Deer, population 48,562, has two delegates, each representing 24,281 people, while the Summer Village of Half Moon Bay, with a population of 31, has one delegate. The City of Edmonton has been particularly unhappy over this kind of disparity. Until the Commission was restructured in 1981, Edmonton had three members. With the formation of the new 27-member Edmonton Metropolitan Commission, the City of Edmonton was given nine votes;[45] the City of St. Albert, two votes; the County of Strathcona, two votes; and all other municipalities, one vote each.[46] Even with this larger representation, each Edmonton member still represents 61,257 people, while the delegate from the Town of Bon Accord represents 1,425 people. The crux of the problem is that the larger urban centres maintain that representation on regional planning commission boards should be based on population, while smaller units of government maintain that representation should be on the basis of individual units of government. This dilemma is summed up in a report titled "Municipal Attitudes Towards Regional Planning in Alberta," prepared in 1980 by the Alberta Association of Municipal Districts and Counties and the Alberta Urban Municipalities Association.

> Representation on the RPCs and the voting pattern of rural and urban members was a source of contention for both. There is a perceived urban domination in the eyes of the rural municipalities, and a small town and rural bias in the eyes of the larger urban municipalities.[47]

At the Alberta Planning Board's annual seminar, held in April, 1983, the provincial government's quandary over representation on regional planning commissions was apparent to all RPC delegates. When the Minister of Municipal Affairs, Julian Koziak, was asked what his position was on planning commission representation, he could only respond by saying that the present system recognizes local responsibility and that a balance had to be struck between the interests of urban and rural municipalities.[48] While the Department of Municipal Affairs has attempted to resolve the problem by giving larger municipalities slightly more representation, this compromise has satisfied neither the larger nor the smaller units.

Table 9.1
Evaluation of Regional Planning Commissions

Major Issues of Commissions	% of Total Urban Responses	% of Total Rural Responses
Advantages and Benefits	45	15
Disadvantages and Shortcomings	32	49

Section 51 of the Planning Act requires that two-thirds of the membership of a regional planning commission vote to approve a regional plan. This provision was designed to prevent an urban-rural split; it was thought that, where there was a slight majority of rural or urban members, the requirement for a two-thirds majority would force the majority to negotiate compromises with the minority for the sake of obtaining plan approval.[49]

Considering that smaller urban and rural municipalities are over represented on regional planning commissions, one would expect the commission's most outspoken critics to be the larger urban centres. With the exception of Edmonton, this is not the case.[50] The survey of "Municipal Attitudes Towards Regional Planning in Alberta" found rural municipalities to be much more critical of regional planning commissions. Table 9.1 presents a summary of responses from 59 urban and 17 rural municipalities.[51] Table 9.2 presents a breakdown of the regional planning commission issues that respondents from urban and rural municipalities commented on most frequently.[52] As can be seen from Table 9.2, rural and urban municipalities each felt that the commissions were biased in favour of the other. However, the most important finding is the major reason for rural criticism: as they have evolved from being purely advisory to exercising real power, regional planning commissions have forced municipalities to conform to planning schemes that undermine municipal autonomy. An example is found in the comments of a town member of the Battle River Regional Planning Commission. After citing five occasions on which the town council had been overruled by the Commission, the members concluded that, "the present Commission authority robs the local Council of making effective planning decisions." Several rural municipalities used the term *dictatorial* to describe their planning commissions.

Table 9.2
A Comparison of Urban and Rural Responses on
Regional Planning Commissions

Issue	% of Total Urban Responses	% of Total Rural Responses
Doing a good job	19	5
Availability of planning expertise	13	5
Encourages organized regional development	6	5
Slow to respond	8	3
Rural and small town membership bias	3	0
Urban membership bias	1	13
Too dictatorial — loss of local autonomy	9	13
Members lack information about other member issues	2	7
Should be more advisory	5	7
RPC should be primarily subdivision approving authority	3	0
Subdivision approving authority should be delegated to local governments	1	8
A need to clarify the role of RPCs	1	7
Need for a change in membership	1	5

Concern with local autonomy is also manifested by the number of respondents from rural municipalities who wanted subdivision approving authority delegated back to local governments from the planning commissions.[53] Another important finding is that urban municipalities are much more aware of the importance of involving professionals in planning than are rural municipalities.

This dissatisfaction with planning commission powers was made plain in a resolution passed at the annual convention of the Alberta Association of Municipal Districts and Counties in 1979. The resolution stated:

> WHEREAS as it was the purpose and intent of the original Regional Planning Commission to act as an Advisory Body; and WHEREAS, the same Regional Planning Commissions have over the years obtained more and more authority in the subdivision and development of Municipalities; and WHEREAS, local autonomy of rural Municipalities is being eroded,
> NOW THEREFORE BE IT RESOLVED that the Government of the Province of Alberta be requested to implement legislation which would stipulate that the regional planning commissions are created for the sole purpose and intent of The Planning Act . . . without infringing on the rights of individuals.

A Municipal Affairs representative responded to the Association's resolution by saying that, "a certain amount of local autonomy must be sacrificed in the interest of securing the policy objectives which are of common concern to the municipalities within a given region." These objectives are the preservation of agricultural land, curbing "wasteful" urban sprawl, and preventing and controlling development in "environmentally sensitive areas." Since 1979, however, the provincial government seems to have modified this policy to accommodate the concerns of municipalities that feel they are losing their autonomy. At the Alberta Planning Board's 1983 seminar, the Department of Municipal Affairs presented a discussion paper that stated:

> When the Board speaks of regional planning commissions in the years ahead, it is referring to the utilization of non-regulatory and non-control-oriented methods of achieving regional goals and objectives.
> Recognizing that the key decisions in a region are implemented by municipal governments, the development industry, private citizens as they go about the business of living, and the Provincial Government, the Board believes that the most effective long-term benefits for the community will be

achieved if those with the responsibility for making decisions are allowed to do so, with as little interference from outside as possible.

The Government has constrained the extent to which Regional Planning Commissions can intervene in local decision-making, to those occasions when the regional concern dictates it, and then only in specific and defined ways.[54]

The paper then suggested a "possible breakdown" on the time and work of a regional planning commission. The suggestion was:

Provision of land-use-related planning advice and assistance to municipalities, as requested [once a regional plan is in place]	60%
Subdivision approval and related matters	30%
Regional plan monitoring and review	10%

From this it seems that the Alberta Planning Board sees the future function of a planning commission as providing professional advice to municipalities rather than making administrative rules to confine municipalities to a regional plan.

The irony of this exchange between the rural municipalities and Municipal Affairs is that a great deal of controversy was generated by section 85 of the 1977 Act that provided municipalities with far more control over planning than they had had since the early 1950s. With the Minister's authorization, either a council or its municipal planning commission was given the power to act as its own subdivision approving authority. As the 1977 Act sets the stage for decentralization, rural municipalities would be better advised to convince the Minister that they have the expertise to be their own subdivision approving authorities than to focus on the "evils" of regional planning commissions.

Farmland preservation, urban sprawl and environmental problems are the three areas in which regional planning commissions are expected to follow broad provincial guidelines through review by the Alberta Planning Board. However, in fact, various government departments are increasingly making policies with adverse effects on planning commission goals, a situation that causes concern to urban and rural municipalities alike. From the Department of Transportation to the Department of Culture, province-wide policies are enacted with little or no consultation with regional planning commissions. Even in the specific stages provided to allow provincial departments to be brought into the initial formulation of a regional plan, the departments provide "inputs" rather than consulting and negotiating with planning commissions as equals. In the most recent *Revised Guidelines for Regional Plan Preparation and Review*, the regional planning commission is told that, in the first phase of developing a regional plan, all provincial departments are notified "that a plan process has been initiated and the departments have a responsibility, when asked, to provide support whenever possible to the regional planning commissions on those relevant interests."[55] The key phrase is "provide support"; i.e., the departments are not instructed to "co-ordinate, consult and compromise." In the second phase, the purpose of contact is "to allow the Province to comment on the consistency between Provincial and regional policies." Planning commissions are asked to provide the Board with technical and policy reports. Then:

> Any reports submitted through this process will be sent through
> the office of the Deputy Minister of each department to
> designated liaison officers. Once identified, the names of these
> departmental contacts will be sent to the commissions for future
> reference and so contact can be established directly.[56]

In this phase the onus is on the planning commissions to provide relevant materials for evaluation by various departments to determine whether planning commission goals are congruent with departmental programs. This process brings the commissions into contact with government departments, but only in the context of ensuring that their planning goals do not conflict with provincial goals; they are not consulting and negotiating over policies as equals. Finally, although there may be a modicum of consultation in the formulation of the regional plan, there are no provisions for ongoing consultation once the plan is in place.

Department regional offices do consult planning commissions, but these consultations focus primarily on how provincial policies are to be implemented at the regional level. Policy formulation is carried out at the Edmonton headquarters of most provincial departments, offices which have no formal consultative links with regional planning commissions. And, since upper-level decision makers have little information on the peculiarities of particular regions, their policies often work at cross-purposes with the commissions' long-range planning goals. If the provincial government's policy on regional planning and the maintenance of local autonomy is to succeed, it will be necessary to establish a formal mechanism to co-ordinate the policies of provincial departments with those of regional planning commissions.

Reducing Regional and Municipal Planning Conflict

The provincial government implicitly recognizes that virtually every planning decision advantages people in one geographical area and disadvantages those in others. Regional planning commissions are composed of municipalities with diverse interests that must be balanced against one another, especially as a two-thirds majority is needed for ratification of a regional plan. At the municipal level, public hearings must be held before a municipal plan can be approved. With opportunities for all interested parties to participate at various stages, the planning process has become increasingly political. But this politicization has occurred because the provincial government has been unwilling to fund municipal activities at a reasonable level rather than because it has "opened up" the planning process.

The root cause of the animosity between large cities and their outlying municipalities is money. With municipalities dependent upon inadequate provincial grants and locally derived property taxes for most of their revenue, and with regional planning commissions trying to make binding decisions on the location of industry, it is not surprising that the politics of planning often becomes bitter. If municipalities had an adequate revenue base there would be less competition for revenue-producing industries and, consequently, there would be a greater emphasis on developing regional plans that would mitigate social problems in the area. At the municipal level there would be a greater focus on producing municipal plans oriented to "livability" rather than to ensuring an industrial presence in every community. An adequate revenue base would allow redevelopment schemes to upgrade deteriorating housing without having to impose a redevelopment levy on developers and builders, who pass it on to consumers.

The argument that a lack of fiscal resources distorts planning decisions and causes an inordinate amount of hostility among and within governmental units is not new. It was made implicitly by Bettison, Kenward and Taylor in their *Urban Affairs in Alberta* in 1975.[57] More recently, a Department of Municipal Affairs' discussion paper has made the argument again.

> Under the present arrangements, the regional planning system becomes the battle ground for what are essentially fiscal matters perhaps more appropriately handled through tax sharing, grants aimed at low or no-growth areas, and so on . . . .

Recommendation The Study recommends that the [Provincial Planning] Board, as a part of its role vis-a-vis the planning system encourage the Government to find ways of reducing intermunicipal conflicts over tax resources, through tax sharing regionally, grants to communities and so on, so that good regional planning is not jeopardized by what is essentially a fiscal problem.[58]

Perhaps the best case for such fiscal policies as sharing provincial income tax revenue and oil and gas revenue with municipalities, making provisions that would allow a municipality to enact its own sales tax, and providing for substantially larger conditional and unconditional municipal grants can be made on the basis of the effect on regional and municipal planning. Until the provincial government devises a fiscal system that enables municipalities to meet their responsibilities, the planning process at all levels will be fraught with hostility and political in-fighting.

Notes

1. The Canadian Institute of Planners defines planning as "the planning of the scientific, aesthetic and orderly disposition of land, with a view to securing physical, economic and social efficiency, health and well-being in urban and rural communities." For a discussion of the reaction of Canadian Planners to this definition, see Sells, "Selected Material from the Report on the Questionnaire on the Future of the Planning Profession."

2. A good discussion of the tensions generated between planners and the elected decision makers is found in Catanese, *Planners and Local Politics.*

3. Van Nus, "The Fate of City Beautiful Thought," 163; for a general discussion on the evolution of city planning see Brunt, *The History of City Planning*, and Kaplan, *Reform, Planning, and City Politics.*

4. Van Nus cites an article in the 1911 *Canadian Municipal Journal*, one of the organs of the then planning profession: "Magnificent avenues, leading to grand buildings, are desirable. Lovely and artistic parks should be in every city. But the dwellings in which those live who cannot get away from their homes the whole year long, really decide whether any city is to be healthy, moral and progressive. The common people are in the great majority; their proper accommodation is the greatest problem." "The Fate of City Beautiful Thought," 171.

5. For graphic examples of these conditions see: Artibise, *Winnipeg: A Social History of Urban Growth.*

6. Simpson, "Thomas Adams in Canada, 1914-1930," 5.

7. Rutherford, "Tomorrow's Metropolis," 379. Also see Kaplan, *Reform, Planning, and City Politics*, 113-209.

8. Gerecke, "The History of Canadian City Planning," 13.

9. *Ibid.*, 22.

10. Clark, "Planners as Professionals," 51.

11. Page and Lang, "Canadian Planners in Profile," 8.

12. Kiernan, "Ideology and the Canadian Planning Profession," 18.

13. Page and Lang, "Canadian Planners in Profile," 8.

14. *Ibid.* Studies of American planners have found that many are not just apolitical but anti-political. In a 1963 survey of student planners at the Massachusetts Institute of Technology, it was found that "76 per cent saw politicians as selfish. Not one respondent believed politicians could be more than 'slightly' altruistic." Rabinovitz, *City Politics and Planning*, 135. A manifestation of the apolitical stance of American planners is found in the questionnaire results from a 1974 comprehensive survey of the American Institute of Planners' members. In answering a series of questions designed to determine the role planners should play in the political process, 48 per cent indicated a technical preference with the belief the planner should not be involved in the political process. Thirty-two per cent took a moderate position and only 20 per cent believed planners should take positions on political issues. Vasu, *Politics and Planning*, 34.

15. Page and Lang, "Canadian Planners in Profile," 3.

16. Smith, "The Principle of Utility," 202-203.

17. P. J. Smith explains how this omission of planning for the community's core area came about. He writes: "This may seem paradoxical, since the original emphasis in British urban reform was on the improvement of existing conditions, but it reflects the peculiar evolution of the British legislation. In fact, earlier versions of the housing act had already given substantial powers of intervention to local governments, including the right to carry out slum clearance and redevelopment schemes. The special contribution of the 1909 Act was to extend that right of intervention beyond the existing built-up areas. Whether out of ignorance, or because they were not thought to be relevant in Canada, the planning powers of the housing section of the 1909 Act were ignored in both New Brunswick and Alberta." *Ibid.*, 209.

18. *Ibid.*, 210-211.

19. *Ibid.*, 208.

20. Bettison, Kenward and Taylor, *Urban Affairs in Alberta*, 44.

21. Smith, "The Principle of Utility," 213.

22. Smith, "American Influences and Local Needs," 7.

23. *Ibid.*, 11.

24. *Ibid.*, 16.

25. It is worth noting that at this time the provincial government was making substantial changes in its local governments. In the same year, the County Act was enacted to streamline rural government and, in the following year, the City Act was passed to provide the province's cities with uniform charters.

26. *Planning in Alberta*, 2.

27. Prior to the establishment of the fund, the province contributed 60 per cent of the support for regional planning commissions and the member municipalities 40 per cent, based on a formula adopted by the local commission.

28. "A Summary of Preliminary Findings of the Regional Planning System Study," 12.

29. Smith, 215-216.

30. Phyllis Smith, "The New Planning Act in Alberta," 120-123.

31. Section 46(1) of the Act reads as follows. "Each regional planning commission shall, on or before December 31, 1982, adopt a plan for the planning region under its jurisdiction in accordance with this Act. . . ." For a variety of reasons, by the summer of 1983, only the Battle River RPC and the S.E. RPC had completed regional plans. The Yellowhead RPC and Mackenzie RPC did not have a preliminary plan in place by summer of 1983.

32. The Alberta Planning Board's Director of Administration's explanation of why regional plans have been unacceptable to the Board is as follows. "Generally speaking the proposed regional plans were too lengthy, too repetitious, too prescriptive and were seen by the Board as infringing upon the autonomy of their member municipalities and over-lapping into the exclusive jurisdictions of the Provincial and Federal governments in some respects and in some instances. Most of the proposed plans were management and control documents as opposed to providing guidance and direction to their municipalities and some contained policies which would control economic and social development which are seen by the Board as going beyond the mandate and jurisdiction of regional planning commissions." Suelzle, letter to Jack Masson, July 12, 1983.

33. A small number of the larger municipalities have been given the authority to act as their own subdivision approving authorities. For areas of the province not served by regional planning commissions, Municipal Affairs' Planning Service Division is the approving authority.

34. Under section 92(1) of the Planning Act a subdivision approving

authority can impose "(a) any conditions that may be necessary to ensure that this Act and the regulations and any regional plan, ministerial regional plan, statutory plan and land use by-law or land use regulations affecting the land proposed to be subdivided are complied with." The section then goes on to say that a developer can be required to construct a roadway and/or a pedestrian walkway system, install or pay for the installation of utilities, and provide off-street parking and loading facilities as a condition of subdivision approval.

35. *Revised Guidelines for Regional Plan Preparation and Review,* 3.

36. Section 52(2) of the Planning Act reads: "on receipt of a proposed regional plan adopted by a regional planning commission, the Board shall review it and may (a) return it to the regional planning commission with suggestions for changes, or (b) approve it and send the plan to the Minister with or without recommendations."

37. Section 109(2) of the Planning Act reads: "In determining an appeal the Board (b) may confirm, revoke or vary the approval or decision on any condition imposed by the sub-division approving authority or make or substitute an approval, decision or condition of its own."

38. Suelzle, letter to Jack Masson, July 12, 1983.

39. The board's political appointments are Brian Stecyk, former executive assistant to Marvin Moore, when he was Minister of Agriculture; Bill Boyd, former councillor of the County of Grande Prairie; Ron Clement, former mayor and councillor of the City of Medicine Hat; Lawrence Kluthe, former commissioner of the M.D. of Sturgeon; and Peter Polischuk, former mayor and councillor of Mundare. Denis Cole's appointment is also considered to be a political one, although he was a former planner and former City of Calgary commissioner.

40. According to a Municipal Affairs publication, an area structure plan "can be viewed as an intermediate step between a general plan and a plan of subdivision. While a general municipal plan encompasses an entire municipality, an area structure plan covers only a portion; yet this portion is large enough to ultimately include several plans of subdivision. . . . An area structure plan deals with blocks of land and their assignment to general land use classes, while subdivision plans are concerned with individual lot development." *Planning in Alberta,* 21. The publication describes the purpose of an area redevelopment plan as follows: "to assist municipalities in effectively planning the redevelopment of their old neighborhoods." *Ibid.,* 21-22. It should be noted that the area structure plan is the modern equivalent of the town planning scheme found in the 1913 Act.

41. Horace Seymour, appointed in 1928 as the province's first Director of Town and Rural Planning, "believed that all members of a community should be given an opportunity to express their views about the community needs and future before any by-law was adopted. His concern, however, was

more for the technical qualities of the planning policies, and their acceptability, than for the principles of participation and popular control." Smith, "American Influences and Local Needs," 22. Seymour's ideas were incorporated into the 1929 Act that required public hearings as one of the preconditions for the adoption of a comprehensive plan. But as Smith notes: "In general, the public hearing was thought to be most applicable to zoning by-laws or ordinances, and . . . it was designed to protect individual interests in real property." *Ibid.*, 23.

42. "The advocate planners . . . reject both the notion of a single 'best' solution, and the notion of a general welfare which such solution might serve. They take the view that any plan is the embodiment of particular group interests, and they therefore see it as important that any group which has interests at stake in the planning process should have those interests articulated in the form of a plan. Planning in this view becomes pluralistic, and partisan, in a word, overtly political." Peattie, "Reflections of an Advocate Planner," 81.

43. Of course, it is not in the government's interest to activate citizen groups or to provide them with resources so that they will impede and frustrate "the workings of government." Undoubtedly, it is for this reason that Alberta and other provinces have been very cool to suggestions that advocate planners be hired and funded by the province or municipality to provide assistance to community groups. The few American communities that have employed advocate planners have had an extremely strong commitment to grass-roots democracy.

44. Under section 22 of the Planning Act the Minister of Municipal Affairs designates which governmental units will be given representation and how many representatives each will have on the commission:

> the Minister shall:
>
> 1. a.designate the councils that are to appoint the members of the commission . . .
>
> b. specify the number of members of each council designated under clause (a) that are to be appointed by the council as members of the commission.
>
> 2. The Minister, may, with respect to an improvement district or special area situated in a planning region, appoint one or more residents of the improvement district or special area, as the case may be.

45. Especially significant is the fact that a two-thirds majority is required before a regional plan can be adopted or amended. Thus, the city only need gain the support of one small municipality to veto the commission's activities in this area.

46. After Edmonton had managed to obtain nine votes on the new planning commission, the city council suddenly realized that, under section 22 of the Planning Act, only council members were eligible to sit on the commission. This provision meant that nine Edmonton council members would have to attend every meeting of the commission. A worried council member, Olivia Butti, told the Alberta Planning Board, "With the workload of council, we certainly couldn't do that." The city has proposed that three councillors, each having three votes, attend the commission meetings. The response of Edmonton's neighbours was summed up by the Parkland County Reeve who said, "If they can't handle it [the representation], tough." *Edmonton Journal,* August 29, 1981.

47. "Municipal Attitudes Towards Regional Planning in Alberta," 22.

48. Alberta Planning Board Annual Spring Seminar, 1983.

49. In a convoluted argument, rural municipalities have contended: "with this requirement [the two-thirds rule] the regional plan could potentially be employed by those municipalities representing the majority interest (frequently the urban interest) of the region to control land use and development in municipalities which are in the minority position." Found in "A Summary of Preliminary Findings of the Regional Planning System Study," 34. The rural municipalities recommended that the Planning Act be changed to allow a simple majority to pass a regional plan. *Ibid.,* 62.

50. "Municipal Attitudes Towards Regional Planning in Alberta," 19.

51. Most urban centres in Alberta attempt to reconcile their differences with their smaller outlying rural neighbours through negotiation and compromise. In contrast, the City of Edmonton has adopted a strategy of confrontation and rigidity in dealing with neighbouring municipalities, although in the 1980s this seems to be changing. Even with nine members on the Commission the city can still be outvoted; this situation makes the city uncomfortable and generally critical of the commission.

52. "Municipal Attitudes Towards Regional Planning in Alberta," 20.

53. In 1980 and 1981, Thomas Burton examined the perceptions of regional planning commissions by developers, citizen groups, planning-related professions (surveyors/architects/engineers), regional planning commission planners and planners in the private sector. Altogether, 60 people were extensively interviewed. In his summary, Burton writes: "The most contentious issue . . . had to do with the Commissions' subdivision approval authority. The developers were about equally divided on whether or not this authority should be transferred from the Commissions to the municipalities, as were the citizens. The other three groups favoured its retention by the Commissions, although the planning-related professionals did suggest that the municipalities should be given greater autonomy (but *not* subdivision approval authority)." Burton, *The Roles and Relevance of Planning Commissions,* 87-88.

54. "Era of the Regional Plan."

55. *Revised Guidelines for Regional Plan Preparation and Review*, 3.

56. *Ibid.*, 4.

57. Bettison, Kenward and Taylor, *Urban Affairs in Alberta*, 502-509.

58. "A Summary of Preliminary Findings of the Regional Planning System Study," 53.

Appendix

Southeast Alberta RPC

Members (Pop.)	Votes
Medicine Hat (40,380)	3
Bassano (1,200)	1
Bow Island (1,427)	1
Brooks (8,060)	1
Irvine (360)	1
Redcliff (3,814)	1
Burdett (238)	1
Duchess (429)	1
Foremost (576)	1
Rosemary (328)	1
Tilley (367)	1
Co. of Forty Mile (3,451)	1
Co. of Newell (6,199)	1
I.D. No. 1 (5,029)	1
Alix (837)	1
Bentley (637)	1
Blackfalds (1,488)	1
Big Valley (360)	1
Bowden (1,021)	1
Caroline (431)	1
Cremona (402)	1
Delburne (555)	1
Donalda (266)	1
Elnora (243)	1
Gadsby (49)	1
Mirror (552)	1
Penhold (1,518)	1

Calgary RPC

Members (Pop.)	Votes
Calgary (623,133)	3
Airdrie (9,981)	1
Canmore (3,689)	1
Crossfield (1,217)	1
High River (4,941)	1
Okotoks (4,521)	1
Strathmore (3,199)	1
Three Hills (1,879)	1
Trochu (880)	1
Beiseker (637)	1
M.D. Foothills (8,725)	1
M.D. Kneehill (5,761)	1
M.D. Rocky View (17,362)	1
Co. Wheatland (5,513)	1
I.D. No. 18 (9,605)	1

Battle River RPC

Members (Pop.)	Votes
Camrose (12,809)	1
Wetaskiwin (9,896)	1
Bashaw (875)	1
Daysland (691)	1
Hardisty (680)	1
Killam (1,005)	1
Ponoka (5,221)	1
Rimbey (1,880)	1
Sedgewick (879)	1
Ferintosh (155)	1
Forestburg (968)	1
Lougheed (261)	1
Millet (1,087)	1
Warburg (541)	1
Ma-Me-O Beach (82)	1
Co. Camrose (7,564)	1
Co. Flagstaff (4,507)	1
Co. Leduc (13,258)	1
Co. Ponoka (7,536)	1
Co. Wetaskiwin (9,026)	1
I.D. No. 10 (9,201)	1

Mackenzie RPC

Members (Pop.)	Votes
Fairview (2,869)	1
Grimshaw (2,488)	1
Manning (1,262)	1
Peace River (6,043)	
High Level (2,354)	1
Rainbow Lake (739)	1
Berwyn (632)	1
Hines Creek (575)	1
Nampa (334)	1
M.D. Peace (1,520)	1
M.D. Fairview (1,889)	1
I.D. No. 17 (11,699)	1
I.D. No. 22 (4,250)	1
I.D. No. 23 (5,837)	1

Edmonton Metropolitan RPC

Members (Pop.)	Votes
Edmonton (551,314)	9
St. Albert (32,982)	2
Calmar (1,061)	1
Beaumont (2,927)	1
Bon Accord (1,425)	1
Devon (3,931)	1
Fort Saskatchewan (12,455)	1
Gibbons (2,592)	1
Leduc (12,471)	1
Morinville (4,943)	1
Redwater (2,174)	1
Spruce Grove (10,784)	1
Stony Plain (5,105)	1
Co. Strathcona (48,024)	2
Co. Leduc (13,258)	1
Co. Parkland (23,626)	1
M.D. Sturgeon (13,682)	1

Red Deer RPC

Members (Pop.)	Votes
Red Deer (48,562)	2
Carstairs (1,725)	1
Castor (1,123)	1
Coronation (1,268)	1
Didsbury (3,256)	1
Eckville (872)	1
Innisfail (5,444)	1
Lacombe (5,723)	1
Olds (4,888)	1
Rocky Mtn. House (4,735)	1
Stettler (5,136)	1
Sundre (1,750)	1
Sylvan Lake (3,779)	1
Birchcliff (43)	1
Gull Lake (80)	1

Palliser RPC

Members (Pop.)	Votes
Drumheller (6,508)	1
Hanna (2,828)	1
Oyen (1,002)	1
Cereal (252)	1
Consort (632)	1
Delia (211)	1
Morrin (245)	1
Munson (148)	1
Rumsey (89)	1
Veteran (107)	1
Youngstown (297)	1
Empress (200)	1
M.D. Acadia (604)	1
M.D. Starland (2,068)	1
I.D. No. 7 (1,258)	1
Special Area 2 (2,565)	1
Special Area 3 (1,701)	1
Special Area 4 (1,776)	1

Oldman River RPC

Members (Pop.)	Votes
Lethbridge (56,500)	2
Cardston (3,267)	1
Claresholm (3,493)	1
Coaldale (4,597)	1
Ft. MacLeod (3,139)	1
Granum (399)	1
Magrath (1,576)	1
Milk River (894)	1
Nanton (1,647)	1
Picture Butte (1,404)	1
Pincher Creek (3,757)	1
Raymond (2,837)	1
Stavely (548)	1
Taber (5,988)	1
Vauxhall (1,048)	1
Vulcan (1,474)	1
Crowsnest Pass (7,577)	2
Arrowwood (151)	1
Barnwell (359)	1
Barons (323)	1
Carmangay (277)	1
Champion (357)	1
Coalhurst (1,111)	1
Coutts (400)	1
Cowley (304)	1
Glenwood (259)	1
Grassy Hill (211)	1
Hillspring (200)	1
Lomond (204)	1

Milo (119)	1
Nobleford (555)	1
Stirling (688)	1
Warner (477)	1
Co. Lethbridge (8,779)	1
Co. Vulcan (3,715)	1
Co. Warner (3,460)	1
M.D. Cardston (4,292)	1
M.D. Pincher Creek (2,970)	1
M.D. Taber (5,637)	1
M.D. Willow Creek (4,534)	1
I.D. No. 6 (119)	1
Blood Indian Reserve	1
Peigan Indian Reserve	1

South Peace River RPC

Members (Pop.)	Votes
Grande Prairie (24,263)	3
Beaverlodge (1,937)	1
Falher (1,204)	1
High Prairie (2,506)	1
McLennan (1,176)	1
Sexsmith (1,184)	1
Spirit River (1,104)	1
Valleyview (2,061)	1
Wembley (1,209)	1
Donnelly (362)	1
Eaglesham (207)	1
Girouxville (325)	1
Hythe (681)	1
Rycroft (649)	1
Wanham (266)	1
Co. Grande Prairie (12,078)	1
M.D. Smoky River (2,858)	1
M.D. Spirit River (2,858)	1
I.D. No. 16 (5,350)	1
I.D. No. 17 (11,699)	1
I.D. No. 19 (1,757)	1
I.D. No. 20 (3,000)	1

Yellowhead RPC

Members (Pop.)	Votes
Half Moon Bay (31)	1
Norglenwold (84)	1
Rochan Sands (51)	1
Co. Lacombe (8,783)	1
Co. Mountain View (8,832)	1
Co. Paintearth (2,495)	1
Co. Red Deer (13,664)	1
Co. Stettler (5,092)	1
I.D. No. 10 (9,201)	1
Barrhead (3,736)	1
Drayton Valley (4,867)	1
Edson (6,291)	1
Hinton (8,819)	1
Mayerthorpe (1,475)	1
Swan Hills (2,497)	1
Whitecourt (5,408)	1
Fox Creek (1,978)	1
Grande Cache (4,624)	1
Onoway (669)	1
Co. Barrhead (5,517)	1
Co. Lac Ste. Anne (7,614)	1
Co. Parkland (23,626)	1
I.D. No. 14 (9,238)	1
I.D. No. 15 (2,670)	1

10

PARTIES

AND

PARTISANSHIP

Introduction

Previous chapters have discussed political bargaining, the balancing of group demands by council, and the political relationship between councillors and professional administrators. This chapter focuses on the electoral mechanisms and processes that bring the ordinary citizen into local politics. The early twentieth-century American reform movement had the greatest effect in shaping Alberta's political institutions, which in turn have structured political participation. Ironically, while the reform movement's orientation was conservative, it introduced ideas into Alberta that furthered grass-roots democracy by justifying the citizenry's right to have a direct say in policy making.

Partisan and non-partisan electoral systems, plebiscites, at-large, ward and proportional representation all work to the advantage or disadvantage of segments of the public. There has been a historic tension between the business community and organized labour in the province's larger municipalities, each lobbying for its own ends. Business has been more successful for the American reform proposals, eventually endorsed by most Albertans and adopted by municipal governments across the province, helped business to control municipal councils. Although for half a century labour was active in the municipal politics of many larger cities, in recent times it has made only sporadic, half-hearted attempts to capture political power. More recently, the new class of professionals active in local political parties and neighbourhood organizations have begun to question control of council by business interests and have proposed institutions that would give the advantage to themselves.

Non-partisanship and Political Reform

A pervasive characteristic of the electorate in Alberta's communities is a commitment to keeping politics out of local government. This commitment to non-partisanship has long and tenacious roots originating in the American municipal reform movement and reinforced by an anti-party philosophy found in the United Farmers of Alberta and Social Credit parties.

In the late nineteenth century the large eastern American cities were controlled by party machines whose power base was new immigrants. These party machines played an important role in assimilating non-English-speaking immigrants into a hostile urban environment by providing them with welfare not offered by federal or state governments. In return for providing a bag of groceries, a sack of coal, help in obtaining housing and, often, a job in an ever-expanding city bureaucracy, they demanded only total loyalty — and votes. The party machine was effective because it was a true grass-roots organization, organized, in fact, down to the block level. Councils were controlled by neighbourhood leaders of the working and lower-middle classes who tended to be saloonkeepers, owners of small hotels, semi-skilled white-collar workers and politically shrewd unskilled workmen. These council members were political brokers who used their friendships and contacts in the party's hierarchy to help their constituents.

To maintain power, politicians were vociferous spokesmen for their communities. A student of this period writes of their activities:

> They spoke for the local areas, the economic interests of their inhabitants, their residential concerns, their educational, recreational, and religious interests—i.e., for those aspects of community life which mattered most to those they represented. They rolled logs in the city council to provide streets, sewers, and other public works for their local areas. They defended the community's cultural practices, its distinctive languages or national customs, its liberal attitude toward liquor, and its saloons and dance halls which served as centers of community life.[1]

In short, municipal councils were composed of pragmatic grass-roots politicians from the working and lower-middle classes, each controlling a neighbourhood fiefdom. This decentralized political structure was unconcerned with efficiency and corruption since inefficiencies, "sweetheart" municipal contracts and the diversion of public funds to supporters kept it in power.

During this period (and parallel with the arrival of millions of immigrants) there were ominous rumblings from a labour movement intent on organizing immigrant industrial workers and making timid steps to exercise a modicum of local political power. In many American cities the party machine and organized labour existed in a symbiotic relationship, each using the other to further its own ends.

The corrupt political machine, skyrocketing deficits, city bureaucracies bloated with political appointments, councils composed of neighbourhood- or ward-oriented politicians seemingly unconcerned with the city's public interest, and attempts by labour to be a major power at the local level, all were anathema to the business community, the upper middle class and many elitist academics. An astute observer of the American political scene writes of these reformers:

> . . . profound in their implications for the content and
> consequences of reform, were two strongly held beliefs. The
> first was the view of most reformers that urban problems were
> apolitical, requiring little more than the application of honesty
> and good business practices. This perspective manifested itself
> in an emphasis on efficiency and economy as the prime goals of
> city government. Moreover, many reformers held a pervasive
> belief that certain citizens—professionals, experts, and the well
> educated—were more fit to govern than others. These two
> mutually reinforcing predispositions gave the municipal reform
> movement an elitist spirit and effect.[2]

They saw the political machine with its attendant evils as the problem; the solution was its replacement by a business-oriented approach. Specifically, the reformers advocated: 1) party politics to be replaced by non-partisan elections; 2) neighbourhood/ward representation on council to be replaced by councillors elected from the city at-large; 3) the political franchise restricted solely to the middle and upper-middle classes, i.e., to people who had a property stake in the community and paid property taxes; and 4) municipal government streamlined to operate like a private corporation.

The reform movement swept across the country. At the turn of the century "nonpartisan elections were almost unheard of, but by 1929 they could be found in 57 per cent of the cities with more than 30,000 population."[3]

Parallel with the rise of non-partisanship was a movement towards at-large electoral representation by the municipal council; working-class and lower-middle-class members of council were replaced by business people, professionals and members of the middle class. Although the reformers were less successful in restricting the political franchise, they were able to maintain the status quo at a time when many states were enlarging the franchise. The council-manager form of government, meant to bring efficiency and economy, was introduced in 1908 and was quickly adopted by large numbers of medium-sized American cities. A less successful reform government was the commission form,[4] which was developed in 1901 and, by 1917, had been adopted by almost 500 smaller municipalities. Shortly thereafter it waned as reformers became enthralled with the virtues of the manager form of government.

Canadian civic and economic elites were not immune to the persuasive proposals of American reformers that would "put things right" in the city. Although party machines never developed in Canadian cities, late in the nineteenth century, partisan community politics was as common in Canadian communities as in the United States, and caused occasional spates of municipal scandal.[5] But more importantly, the business community was becoming alarmed by the beginnings of labour's quest for political power and, to a lesser extent, by the large number of poor and propertyless Europeans settling in the country's major cities. With the restriction on the franchise and the abolition of mechanisms enabling the "underclass" to gain power (i.e., the political party and neighbourhood/ward electoral representation) it was felt that the community would be safe from the political activities of "less responsible" segments.

It was in the Canadian west that the reformers had their greatest influence, penetrating the region "through the medium of periodicals, newspaper reports, and books as well as more directly by virtue of the trips by leading western reformers."[6] An urban historian found the Calgary newspapers preoccupied with reports that had filtered up from the south of municipal corruption in American cities.[7]

Alberta's civic and business leaders were determined to rid their communities of political machines (which were nonexistent) and to bring a businesslike approach to government by restructuring it and tightening their control. Calgary's economic elite shaped the new city charter in 1893, raising property qualifications for council positions from $600 to $1,000.[8] Edmonton's city charter, in 1904, adopted at-large representation and a "cumulative voting clause which allowed holders of property to cast up to four votes on referred money by-laws; and a property qualification for municipal voters."[9] Both Lethbridge and Calgary abandoned neighbourhood/ward representation in 1913 and embraced at-large representation. The American commission form of government was adopted in Lethbridge, while council-commission government, promising professionalism and efficiency, was adopted in Edmonton in 1904 and was soon copied in Calgary and Red Deer. But it was in the almost complete eradication of parties from the municipal scene that the Alberta reformers had their greatest success. With the exception of Calgary, Lethbridge, Edmonton and one or two smaller communities, all of which will be examined shortly, municipal political parties were wiped from the provincial scene. The ex-mayor of Red Deer presented a paper before the 1909 Union of Alberta Municipalities Convention summing up the prevailing feeling among Alberta reformers.

> Our Municipal Councils know nothing of party politics and its baneful influence, dividing men on lines having no bearing upon the interests of the Municipality; neither bossism nor the vested rights of Public Service Corporations have yet thrown about us their demoralizing influences.[10]

A major reason the electorate was so receptive to the reformers' call for non-partisanship was a basic anti-party tradition pre-dating the establishment of the province itself. C. B. Macpherson's exhaustive analysis of Alberta politics documents this tradition.[11] From 1888 through 1905 the territorial government operated along strict non-party lines; party politics came to the province only after incessant pressure from the federal parties to create party organizations. Macpherson notes that, even when party politics was introduced at the time of provincehood, "As long as the provincial administration elected by party methods devoted itself officially to the provision of the desired physical helps to the rapidly growing economy it served well enough. But it was supported less for its party principles than for its business efficiency."[12] The ideology of the American Non-Partisan League, whose ideas captured the imagination of Albertans and swept across the province in 1916 and 1917, exemplified the idea that the outmoded party system should be replaced by a "business government." Macpherson carefully shows how the United Farmers of Alberta (UFA) included many of the Non-Partisan League's anti-party ideas. When the UFA gained power in 1921, it had a strong anti-party ideology.[13] The political theory of Social Credit was as anti-party as that of the UFA: its conception of the party system being that it was designed "to direct public attention to a profitless wrangle in regards to methods."[14] Even after being in office for a number of years, William Aberhart, the party leader, was as adamantly opposed to political parties as he had been earlier. In a 1942 speech he said that the party system was a "vicious and alarming negation of democracy in its true essence."[15]

A province-wide survey conducted in 1971 found that most respondents opposed party politics at the local level. The results, given in Table 10.1, show that less than a third of municipal residents in Alberta were favourably disposed to party politics. A surprising finding is the small variation between the responses of residents of large cities and those of inhabitants of small villages. One would expect to find much stronger support for parties in large cities with diverse and competing socio-economic and ethnic groups than in smaller, relatively homogeneous communities. [16]

Table 10.1
Attitude Towards Party Politics by Size of Community
(in per cent)

Favour Parties at the Local Level	Large City	Small City	Town	Village
Yes	32	28	26	28
No	68	72	74	72
N	391	182	135	145

A more recent study (1977) in Calgary's ward seven suggests that the electorate may be growing somewhat less hostile to municipal parties. While a survey of a sample of the ward found only 38 per cent of respondents agreeing "with the idea of locally-based political parties contesting local elections," another series of questions dealing with the advantages and disadvantages of local parties in Calgary revealed much stronger support. Table 10.2 showing the survey results indicates that, in every case, more respondents felt that the advantages of parties outweighed their disadvantages. Particularly surprising is the very small percentage of respondents (11.3 per cent) who felt that local parties would hinder "keeping corruption out of city government." Since one of the underlying assumptions of the reform movement was that corruption was associated with municipal parties, one would expect a substantial number of respondents to make the same association. However, despite this lessening of hostility, one would expect that the relatively high percentage of respondents who indicated their belief that parties "make no difference" would oppose their introduction into Calgary politics since there would be no reason to disturb the status quo.[17]

The Calgary study seems to indicate that the legacy of the reformers' non-partisan proposals and a strong provincial tradition of "antipartyism" is being replaced by an attitude of indifference to municipal political parties. With the exception of the largest cities and a scattering of smaller municipalities, elections are non-partisan and municipal councils are bereft of councillors with partisan identifications. A 1983 survey of Alberta municipal senior administrators, which asked whether party organizations contested elections in their community, found that only three cities, three towns and one village had any form of party politics.[18]

Table 10.2
Advantages of Local Political Parties
(in per cent)

	Would Help	Would Hinder	Make no Difference	No Opinion
Keeping the costs of city government low	25.7	13.4	39.7	21.2
Reducing bickering in city council	38.4	12.0	31.8	17.8
Keeping corruption out of city government	22.9	11.3	44.9	20.9
Providing long-term planning for the city	46.6	7.5	21.9	24.0
Providing better social services, e.g. welfare	33.6	6.5	36.3	23.6

Despite the overwhelming number of municipalities in the province with non-partisan elections and councils, partisan political factors still operate on councils: it is impossible to take partisan considerations out of local politics. As one of New York's politicians once said: "There is no such thing as nonpartisanship. If there were there would be no need for elections."[19] Quite simply, different philosophical outlooks on raising and allocating fiscal resources are found at the local level as well as the federal and provincial levels. Thus, local political decision making has a partisan component, even though it is covert rather than overt.

A number of studies in the United States examine the "partisan bias of non-partisan elections." Most conclude that Republicans are advantaged and Democrats are disadvantaged in non-partisan elections.[20] Willis Hawley sums up arguments and findings as follows.

They suggest that Republicans in general are more highly motivated politically and are more likely, in the absence of party provided cues, to make their correct linkages between their own self interest (as they perceive it) and their voting choice. Even if community organizational structures are not Republican dominated, Republicans are more likely to vote and more likely to vote for those who share their values (i.e., other Republicans) than are Democrats. In short, the Republican benefit thesis rests on the belief that Democratic candidates need parties more than Republican candidates do.[21]

The "partisan bias of non-partisan elections" in Alberta has been alluded to by at least two students of the Alberta municipal scene. James Anderson maintains that, in the province's early years, Liberals and Conservatives covertly running on civic slates were able to thwart the attempts of socialists and labour representatives to capture city halls. "On balance, the non-partisan camouflage appeared to have benefitted Liberal and Conservative business-oriented interests in prairie cities during the reform era."[22] James Lightbody, making a similar point for Edmonton's more recent period, writes: "Throughout the 1950s, the Citizens' Committee was extensively infiltrated by Liberals who employed their federal organization to advance municipal candidates, perhaps as a surrogate to realistic hopes elsewhere."[23] More recently, in October, 1983, a federal Liberal less than covert in identifying his party affiliation won the Edmonton mayoralty election by a landslide. Shortly after the election, the provincial Liberal party stated that 55 mayors and school board chairpeople elected across the province were, or had recently been, Liberal party supporters.[24]

The 1983 survey of senior municipal administrators attempted to determine whether the Progressive Conservative, Liberal, NDP and Social Credit parties were over represented or under represented on municipal, county and municipal district councils and school boards. Thus, the administrators were asked to give the federal and provincial party affiliation of elected representatives. Despite a general reluctance to reveal party identification, the limited responses indicated that, in the province's cities, the Liberal party was over represented and the NDP under represented on councils in comparison to votes received in federal and provincial elections. In towns, villages, counties, municipal districts and school divisions, extremely fragmentary data indicated almost all members to be provincial and federal Progressive Conservatives. With their extremely high percentage of "don't know" responses, these results must be considered highly tentative. Yet, in the province's cities, there seems to be a partisan bias on council. Furthermore, one can speculate that, with the NDP winning 18.5 per cent of the province's popular vote in the November, 1983, provincial election, it is substantially under represented on municipal councils throughout Alberta. However, until there is a further examination of the federal and provincial party affiliation of municipal councils, the extent and strength of the partisan bias of non-partisanship in Alberta municipalities can only be a subject of speculation.

Party Politics in Local Government

At the local level, parties can perform functions that are just as important in making government responsive and accountable as are those fulfilled at the provincial and federal levels. At election time they provide a comprehensive platform so that individual voters can make reasoned votes based on a prediction about the direction of municipal policy making. While a non-partisan, independent candidate might offer a comprehensive platform, it is practically impossible to predict the effect on the direction of municipal policy making that his or her election would have; the person would be only one among many on council, each with different ideas on policy direction.

A majority party can be held accountable for its actions; if it doesn't perform as promised, the electorate can pinpoint responsibility and sanction the party by not voting for its members in the next election. On the other hand, a non-partisan system lends itself to diffused responsibility since the electorate cannot pinpoint responsibility. At election time each incumbent can legitimately claim that support from other council members would have produced a much better set of policies.

Another important function of parties is to provide greater council representation by running candidates who appeal to diverse socioeconomic components. A well-balanced party ticket includes representatives from business, labour and various ethnic factions. In short, the party recruits many people who otherwise might be financially unable to run for office or be reluctant to do so. The spinoff effect is a heterogeneous council representing a variety of diverse interests and groups, which democratizes the political process.

Another spinoff effect is a higher level of political participation. There are several reasons for this development. First, parties use media more cost-efficiently, since their candidates' point of view is presented collectively at a much lower cost to each candidate. Thus, the electorate is exposed to more political messages, which raise their political awareness and stimulate their desire to vote. Second, parties have far greater resources, allowing them to carry out door-to-door campaigning, a thing impossible for independent candidates in a non-partisan system. Personalized campaigning is a major factor in stimulating the electorate to vote. Third, the political party presents a capsulized program to the electorate who have a low level of interest in local politics and little knowledge of political issues. Cues given by such party slogans as "for the businessman," "for fiscal responsibility," or "for the working man," simplify the issues for individuals and present them with an opportunity to participate without having to spend an inordinate amount of time becoming politically knowledgeable.

Finally, a perceptive observer of the municipal political process, James Lightbody, notes that under the non-partisan system found in municipalities across Canada "a major part of the provincial government's distrust of local politicians has been based on the suspicion that they are neither very representative nor can they be held effectively responsible by electors for services under their administration." He then suggests that, although party politics at the municipal level will not immediately change municipal-provincial power relationships, it would probably lead to important changes benefitting the municipality.

> What is likely to occur in the larger metropolitan areas
> following the routinization of the municipal party system is the
> gradual return of functions to local council control as parties,
> finding themselves subjected to a rigorous competition for
> office, expand their programs in the form of pressure on the
> province to maximize their responsibilities for all local
> services.[25]

As was shown in the previous section, the rationale for local non-partisan political systems is not nearly as persuasive as that for municipal party politics. The bossism and political corruption argument is not applicable to Canadian municipalities. The argument that non-partisan government takes the politics and divisiveness out of local government is fallacious. The primary difference between non-partisan and partisan systems is that, under the former, politics is covert and political decisions masquerade under labels of efficiency and the public interest; under the latter, politics is open to the scrutiny of the public. The argument that a political party puts its own interests before those of the community has been shown to be equally fallacious.

Although there are isolated examples of non-partisanship at the municipal level in other western industrialized democracies, it is only in Canada and the United States that there are concerted efforts to foster non-partisanship. In both countries, the strongest advocates of non-partisanship tend to be "rock-ribbed conservatives" and rural dwellers. Both groups fear that a move toward partisan government would erode their control over the political establishment.

Overall, the merits of party politics in promoting responsible and responsive democratic government far outweigh the arguments and rationale for non-partisan politics borrowed from nineteenth and early twentieth century American reformers attempting to remedy problems of their time. Partisanship opens government up to greater participation, which ultimately furthers democratic ideals.

Partisan Municipal Politics in Alberta

In the early days, in a small number of communities, a militant labour movement acted as a counter-balance to the success of the reform movement in convincing Alberta's citizenry of the "evils" of political parties at the local level. Labour made a concerted effort to gain a foothold on, if not to capture, councils in Edmonton and Calgary; these cities also saw isolated instances in which provincial parties successfully ran municipal candidates. However, in Edmonton and Calgary, and in Lethbridge, a more common phenomenon was the multitude of quasi-local parties that would appear and disappear almost at will. They were spawned by the business community both as a device to promote civic and business boosterism and as a response to labour's efforts.

For the first three decades of the century the labour movement in Alberta was deeply divided between radical unskilled and semi-skilled workers anxious to improve working conditions on the railroads and in the coal mines, and moderate skilled workers in the trades. Control of the labour movement seesawed between the two; however, both groups knew that success depended on electing labour members to municipal councils and the provincial legislature.

James Anderson, documenting the close relationship between William Irvine's Non-Partisan League and organized labour, writes:

> . . . Irvine and other League members were involved in setting up the Labour Representation League in Calgary in 1917 in co-operation with the Calgary Trades and Labour Council. By 1919 the Labour Representation League had evolved into the Independent Labour Party and later in the same year, it became

the Calgary branch of the Dominion Labour Party. These parties . . . succeeded in electing a few candidates to municipal [office] . . . . At the urging of the Labour Representation League of Calgary, an organization with the same name was set up in Edmonton by . . . the Trade and Labour Council of the capital city. It, too, was transformed into the Independent Labour Party and then the Dominion Labour Party by 1919. It also achieved a measure of success in Edmonton civic elections in the post-war years.[26]

During the 1920s a short-lived alliance between democratic social-ists and communists resulted in impressive gains for labour in Ed-monton and Calgary that alarmed the business communities. In 1923 labour had six representatives on the Calgary council and, in 1928, a majority of the seats on the Edmonton council.[27] In a discussion of the period, Warren Caragata writes:

> In both communities, candidates of the Canadian Labour Party contested and won seats on local school boards. . . . After the defeat of Joe Clarke (who was not a labour party member but depended on labour support) in Edmonton in 1920, business interests kept a firm grip on the mayoralty office. That situation lasted until the early Thirties when two typographers [in Edmonton and Calgary] . . . were elected to the posts.[28]

Except in Blairmore in the Crowsnest Pass, labour had little success in Alberta's smaller communities, most of which had a non-partisan, "businesslike" approach to civic administration. Some of the bitterest labour strife in Alberta's history occurred in the Crowsnest Pass when coal miners violently protested infrequent employment, dan-gerous and generally abysmal working conditions, and low pay. In 1932 striking workers in company housing had their water and elec-tricity cut off during a seven-month strike. In a municipal election immediately following the strike, Blairmore workers ran a labour slate and took control of the council with the purpose of striking back at the management and owners of the coal mine. "A dog licensing tax was imposed, but only on purebreds, on the grounds that only the bosses could afford purebred dogs."[29] The town's solicitor said that council:

> worked out a taxation system whereby . . . the whole burden of taxation fell on the company. Under law, we put up these miners' homes and shacks for auction but nobody would bid

when we told them not to and these miners lived there and
drew rent relief. They'd give it to council; we applied it to their
debts and in two or three years they got their houses back with
taxes paid off.[30]

With newpapers throughout the province referring to "Red Blairmore" and the spectre of similar results in Edmonton and Calgary,
business became increasingly alarmed. In Edmonton, Calgary and
Lethbridge, business had earlier organized professedly non-partisan
political parties with alphabet names, e.g., CGA (Civic Government
Association) and UCA (United Citizens Association), to counter
labour's activity, but the labour threat had not seemed nearly as serious as it seemed in 1932. Business redoubled its efforts to provide financial support to attractive candidates for council. This move only
intensified the activities of labour and its supporters. However, it was
some time before labour realized that it would increase its electoral
success by running candidates under non-partisan political party labels rather than on a formal party ticket.

The practice of running candidates under the banner of "alphabet
parties" continues today. In recent years a number of community citizens' groups, initially organized as broadly based lobbying groups,
have transformed themselves into alphabet parties. Far more transitory than the organizations created by business and labour, they seldom last more than a few months.

These quasi-party organizations only partially fulfill the requisite
function of a political party, i.e., winning elections in order to transform their supporters' demands into public policy. These local parties
have a loose, often nonexistent, organizational structure that is not
suited to transforming the demands of the electorate into public policy. It has been argued elsewhere that:

> Three prerequisites need to be fulfilled in order to ensure both
> responsible and democratic policy-making at the local level.
> First, the political organization needs to possess temporal
> continuity. Continually to change an organization's name,
> while searching for the right combination of name and platform
> to ensure electoral success, results only in thoroughly confusing
> the electorate. . . . Second, when local party candidates are
> elected to council they must function as a political bloc to
> implement their campaign platform into policy. This simply has
> not been the case in Alberta cities, even though certain local
> political organizations have been in power for years. Finally, in
> order to give the electorate a choice of potential policies it is

necessary to have at least two viable political parties competing for power. In Alberta, seldom does one find competitive politics at the local level. Consequently, the electoral options are limited to one policy perspective, or the alternative of voting for independent candidates who are either unable to implement policy or unwilling to offer clear-cut policy choices.[31]

The reason these alphabet party organizations do not function as responsible parties is that they have been used mainly as electoral vehicles by candidates who act as independents when elected. Faced with the fact that an overwhelming majority of Albertans are opposed to local party politics, members of electoral slates have been extremely reluctant to exercise party discipline and impose bloc voting on council. Their lack of discipline is exemplified by a comment made by a local party candidate in the 1968 Lethbridge electoral campaign, who stated that his party's candidates "would work as a team although occasionally there would be differences of opinion and they would be on the opposing sides."[32] Moreover, the party's loose organizational structure and lack of sanctions precludes the exercise of party discipline. Thus, the party organization would usually lanquish between elections, only to revive just before the next election. Then, the party would often either splinter, with dissidents spawning yet another electoral organization, or adopt another name, often that of a defunct local party. Yet another factor weakening local parties is that they seldom run enough candidates to capture a majority of council seats, let alone a full slate. In Edmonton, Calgary and Lethbridge there are many instances of a party running a single candidate.

Edmonton Party Politics

In Edmonton quasi-parties, commonly referred to by their initials, arose in response to a militant labour movement that seemed to be achieving momentum. In 1907 the Edmonton Labour Council endorsed candidates pledged to fight for equal municipal expenditures in all areas of the city.[33] The establishment responded when the mayor, addressing an Alberta municipal convention, warned "the trade union's political party may place a man on council irrespective of his fitness."[34] In 1914 the president of the Edmonton carpenters union became the city's first labour councillor. Joe Clarke, an avowed reformer, tied his political fortunes to an emerging labour movement committed to changing the social order. With labour's support, Clarke was elected mayor, in 1919, along with three council candidates under the banner of the Dominion Labour Party. On the heels of the Winnipeg General Strike in May of 1919, organized labour called for a general strike in Edmonton. Mayor Clarke was sympathetic and, a few months later he was re-elected mayor with labour's support.[35] Later, in James Lightbody's words, "the resultant mobilization of conservative interests produced the Citizens' Progressive League [CPL] and Clarke's defeat."[36] Undeterred by this defeat, labour ran municipal candidates throughout the 1920s and several times gained control of city hall. The reaction to labour's involvement is summarized by Lightbody.

> This forced a resurgence of the good burghers, initially in the form of the Civic Government Association (CGA), which campaigned on slogans of 'sound business government' and representation 'of all classes of our citizens.' The north and east were predominantly labour; the south, central and west, CGA. The CGA retained a slim majority on council until 1929 and held the mayoralty until labour's smashing victory in 1931. The declining fortunes of the CGA initially reflected internecine divisions but, as the Depression worsened, the electorate clearly sought an alternative.[37]

Throughout the 1930s and 1940s the pendulum swung back and forth between labour-endorsed candidates, labour-sponsored alphabet parties, and the alphabet party organizations originating in the business community and the middle class. Deep-seated political cleavages within both labour and the moderates led to their splintering into a number of short-lived political organizations.

Labour was especially prone to this phenomenon. For example, in 1934 the Communist Party, the Independent Labour Party (ILP) and the Canadian Labour Party (CLP) all ran candidates for council. In 1935 the Communist Party abandoned the municipal field and the ILP disappeared. Then, in 1936, all labour candidates ran under the banner of the short-lived Edmonton United Peoples League (EUPL), which folded after the election. Its sucessor in 1937 was an umbrella organization, the Progressive Civic Association (PCA), which ran candidates supported by labour, liberals and the Cooperative Commonwealth Federation (CCF). With the exception of 1939 when it remained dormant, the PCA ran candidates yearly until 1944, when it folded, its supporters throwing their votes behind a full slate of CCF candidates. In both 1942 and 1943 the CCF ran candidates that split the labour-liberal vote; one CCF candidate, Harry Ainley, was elected to council in 1943 for one term. After its minimal success in three years of effort, the CCF abandoned municipal politics in order to put its energies into provincial and federal elections. The vacuum was filled by the newly created, labour-backed Civic Democratic Alliance (CDA), which also folded after running candidates in 1945, 1946 and 1947, and capturing one seat each year.

In terms of electoral success, the moderates fared somewhat better, although they created and dismantled organizations at will in order to work out a winning combination of issues and candidates. The business-oriented CGA ran full slates until 1936 when, chameleon-like, the Citizens Committee (CC) replaced it, claiming support from "businessmen, working men and other responsible citizens."[38] It was Social Credit's entry into municipal politics that led to the realignment. In his discussion of this period of Edmonton politics, George Betts writes:

> Following the sweeping provincial victory in 1935 of S.C., it would have been surprising if S.C. had not toyed with the idea of entering the municipal field directly. In October 1935, shortly before the civil election campaign opened, the Social Credit Advisory Board met to decide whether it should follow up its signal success at the provincial level by entering the municipal field. It was decided to run three aldermanic candidates. In spite of the fact that many S.C. members thought an S.C. candidate for mayor would stand an excellent chance of election, it was decided not to run one. All three S.C. nominees were elected handsomely.[39]

In 1936 the party ran three candidates for council and two for the Public School Board; all went down to ignominious defeat, despite strong support from the provincial party. Broken at the municipal level, Social Credit withdrew from the Edmonton scene, most of its numbers backing the newly created fusion PCA party, the rest supporting CC candidates. From 1936 through the 1940s the CC fielded almost a full slate of candidates in every election and managed to elect more candidates to council than any other group. In addition, throughout the period, they contested the city's public school elections and consistently placed a majority on the board.

With the demise of the CDA, labour was quiescent from 1948 until the Edmonton Labour Council ran two candidates in 1951; both lost, placing 11th and 13th in a field of 14 candidates. The leadership of the CC was attempting to co-opt labour, and labour was attempting to infiltrate the CC; thus, it is not surprising that, in 1952, one of the Edmonton Labour Council candidates defeated in 1951 was elected as a CC candidate. By 1954 three of the five CC candidates identified themselves with labour.[40] The business community split; some of its members supported the CC slate and others founded the Committee for Sound Civic Administration (CSCA) that supported only non-labour CC candidates. While labour's conservative wing was infiltrating the CC, its liberal wing formed the Civic Reform Committee (CRC) and ran the secretary of the Alberta Labour Progressive Party and a previously defeated federal Labour Progressive for council. When their candidates finished 17th and 18th in a field of 18, the CRC quietly dissolved.

The CC began to unravel a bit more in 1955 when a CC councillor deserted the party to form the Civic Voters Committee (CVC). He lost and disbanded his one-man party. In 1957, realizing that it had been co-opted by the CC, labour allied itself with certain liberals to form yet another party, the Edmonton Voters Association (EVA), which ran a full slate of candidates, all of whom lost.[41] The CC further splintered when a long-time CC councillor forsook the party to run against the CC's Mayor Hawrelak, and large numbers of small property owners who had been CC supporters formed the Edmonton Property Owners Association (EPOA) and ran a full slate of candidates.[42] With all of their candidates losing, the organization dissolved. EVA again fielded a full set of candidates in 1959; they all lost, leading to such disillusionment among party members that EVA could field only three candidates in 1960. The candidates lost again, and EVA folded.

CC's death knell came in 1959 when the organization completely splintered over the Porter Royal Commission's revelation that CC's Mayor Hawrelak was involved in a land fraud. A fusion organization, the Civic Reform Association (CRA), was founded by dissident CC members along with a faction of the NDP, with Elmer Roper heading its ticket. The CRA split both the EVA and the CC vote and captured four of the six contested council seats and the mayor's chair.[43]

Like a phoenix rising from the ashes, in 1960 the Civic Government Association (CGA) made another appearance, its first since 1936. The CRA had bifurcated: some of its members supported candidates running under the CGA label; the rest, the CRA slate. The CGA won three council seats, the CRA two.[44] In 1961 the CRA splintered when some of its members founded the League of Edmonton Electors (LEE); predictably, both LEE and CRA candidates lost and the organizations disbanded.[45] In 1962 the Civic Rights Protective Association (CRPA) was founded by members of the defunct EVA and ran four candidates, all of whom were defeated. With the CGA capturing all of council's seats, the CRPA was quietly dismantled. In 1963 two more alphabet parties were formed and Hawrelak returned to the electoral scene running for mayor as an independent and besting the CGA mayoralty candidate. The defunct CRPA supporters founded the

United Voters Organization (UVO), which won two council seats. Former alderman and mayoralty candidate Ed Leger returned to the scene, founded the Citizens Council (CC) and successfully ran for office as its only candidate.[46]

By virtue of a 1962 plebiscite the electoral system in Edmonton was changed for the 1963 and subsequent elections: instead of six candidates elected each year for a two-year term, all 12 members were to be elected every two years. With more positions to contest, there was a flurry of local party activity. The CGA changed its name to the Better Civic Government Committee (BCGC) and ran a full slate of candidates who captured five council seats.[47] The UVO also ran a full slate of candidates, including Leger who switched from CC to UVO. The resurrected CRA did surprisingly well, capturing two council seats.[48] Almost immediately after the election, the UVO announced that it was disbanding, and the two members elected under its banner became independents. In 1966 the BCGC captured seven council seats in a bitter campaign in which it was repeatedly charged with being undemocratic and "the mouthpiece for the czars of downtown business."[49] Stung by these allegations, the BCGC disbanded shortly after the election and its members proclaimed themselves independents. The CRA managed to elect one member, and three candidates running under a Labour banner lost badly.

In 1968 the CVO, BCGC and CRA (the more recent alphabet parties) disappeared. However, several incumbents elected under the BCGC label in 1966, along with other members of the business community, established the United Civic Action Party (UCAP), which ran eight candidates for council and a mayoralty candidate. Although it failed to win the mayoralty contest, the new party captured five council seats. By this time the revolving door antics of the alphabet parties during the 1960s had thoroughly confused not only the public but also some candidates. For example, the *Edmonton Journal* reported:

> Alderman Morris Weinlos . . . qualified for the Most
> Embarrassing Moment of the Civic Election award—he forgot
> which slate he is running on . . . Dr. Weinlos was in the process
> of telling voters of his pride to be associated with . . . stumbled,
> then came out with: 'Better Civic Action Committee.' Dr.
> Weinlos in the past, ran on the Better Civic Government
> Committee slate. The group has disbanded and he is now a
> member of Les Bodie's United Civic Action Party.[50]

With new legislation enacted in 1968, the Municipal Government Act changed the term of tenure of a municipal office from two to three years. Therefore, it was 1971 before another municipal election was held in Edmonton.[51] The unique characteristic of the issueless 1971 election was the total absence of municipal parties.[52] A new organization, the Concerned Citizens, endorsed candidates, as did the Edmonton and District Labour Council, but no candidate ran under a party label. Then, in 1974, parties once again emerged. The ever-increasing "new class," composed of professionals and middle-class bureaucrats concerned with the lack of citizen participation, the lack of city amenities and the low priority given to environmental issues, were represented by the newly created Urban Reform Group Edmonton (URGE). Two of its strong slate of candidates were elected. In addition, a popular student leader from the University of Alberta (and an avowed socialist) resurrected EVA, ran as its sole candidate and captured a seat.[53]

In 1977 a group of conservative incumbents and new office-seekers, searching for a name, adopted a variation on the CGA label that had not been used for 15 years and called themselves the Edmonton Civic Government Association (ECGA). After capturing a majority of council seats, the organization was allowed to disappear quietly. Although the EVA incumbent elected in 1974 decided not to run again, five candidates ran unsuccessfully on the party label. URGE again ran a strong campaign and increased its council members to three.

Flushed with their mounting success, URGE ran 11 candidates in 1980, electing four. EVA was finally successful, placing one member on council. A far right Fort Saskatchewan businessman created the People for Independent Aldermen (PIA) which, although endorsing candidates, spent most of its money railing against the "left wing socialist" tendencies of URGE and EVA. In 1983 the business community spawned the Responsible Citizens Committee (RCC), which ran an almost full slate of candidates and elected two of them. The PIA came back into existence, repeating its 1980 warnings about the socialist leanings of EVA and URGE. The fortunes of URGE began to slide when it elected only two members; as the campaign progressed, many candidates were reluctant to mention their URGE affiliation. EVA continued its on-off existence with the election of one candidate.

Calgary Party Politics

Calgary's early civic councils were completely dominated by the business community; during this period of unbridled capitalism, with a council concerned with only real estate and business expansion, the plight of the working class was ignored by council after council. In a discussion of Calgary's early political history, Max Foran writes:

. . . 40 men, 38 of them merchants occupied the 72 available positions on council. In addition these same 40 individuals comprised 50 per cent of all unsuccessful candidates and on no occasion did artisans or labourers run for office. In 1889, 10 individuals who occupied Council positions were among the 20 biggest ratepayers in the town.[54]

Until 1915 labour was frozen out of the municipal political process by a franchise requirement restricting the vote to owners of property with assessed value of at least $200, or personal property of at least $400. Until 1918 a candidate for council required real property with a value of at least $1,000, or personal property of at least $2,000.[55] Only after the franchise was extended to all residents of the city did labour become politically active; even then its involvement was tepid. The Calgary Trade and Labour Congress encouraged its members to run for council but was hesitant to establish a labour party for fear of alienating the business community. Calgary's mayor from 1915 to 1918 had been a member of the Typographical Union but espoused non-partisanship while in office. A member of the Machinist Union was elected to council in 1916 and served for two years; a member of the same union, elected in 1917, served for three years. Then, in 1918, a Calgary Trade and Labour Congress executive was elected to council and served continuously for 17 years.

After an abortive city general strike in 1918 and in the face of increasing labour militancy, the business community created the Civic Government Association (CGA) in 1920 to ensure that city hall would not fall into labour's hands. "Election campaigns, especially between 1920 and 1923, were advertised in the press as struggles between business and labour, and as such were replete with class rhetoric."[56] Despite the business community's fear that the "socialists" were making gains at city hall, the number of labour councillors remained constant, at three or four, election after election; the CGA consistently controlled council.[57] Foran offers a number of reasons for labour's lack of success: "1) the relative weakness of the union movement in Calgary, both in terms of its actual members and its success in securing the working man's vote; 2) the low level of voting turnout; and 3) the system of proportional representation which it is argued did not advantage labour."[58]

Throughout the 1920s and into the 1930s, labour continued to restrict its activity to endorsing candidates. Candidates would receive the endorsement of the Calgary Trade and Labour Congress and the Dominion Labour Party, but neither group was willing to confront the CGA directly with a formal slate. Not until the depths of the

Depression in 1933 did labour wrest control of council from the CGA. Labour councillors controlled the council for only a very short period; Social Credit's entry led to labour's loss of control.

Social Credit was much more successful in Calgary municipal politics than it was in Edmonton or Lethbridge. In 1935 they had seven candidates for council and several for the public school board. With three council and two school trustee candidates winning, the party immediately began to prepare for the 1936 election. Again it contested both areas and placed two more members on council and two more on the school board. In 1937 the party fell into disfavour; all its candidates, including incumbents, lost. Undiscouraged, the party continued to run candidates with some success until 1940. In 1938 and 1939 there were two Social Creditors on council and two on the school board. Then, in 1940, the Social Credit Advisory Board decided to stop running party candidates in Calgary.

Neither the CGA nor the labour movement was deterred by the entry of the ruling provincial party into city politics. Labour captured three council seats and one school trustee position in 1935. At the height of Social Credit's popularity in 1936, when there were five Social Creditors on council, labour still occupied two positions. The low ebb for labour was 1937 when all its candidates lost and it held only one council seat. From 1938 through 1940 there were two labour council members; there were two school trustees in 1938, one in 1939 and two in 1940. Buffeted first by the success of labour and then by that of Social Credit, most of CGA's candidates went down to ignominious defeat in 1935 and 1936. Then, from 1937 through 1940 it placed two or three of its members on council in each election.

In 1941 and 1942 no elections were held since the federal and provincial governments followed the example of Great Britain in declaring a "political truce"; elections were suspended to avoid political controversies during the war. The CCF in Alberta, bitterly opposed to this suspension of the democratic process, succeeded in having municipal elections in Calgary and other municipalities in 1943. Perhaps encouraged by this triumph, the CCF ran three candidates for the Calgary council in 1943 and elected one; labour ran several candidates, also electing one. In 1944 the city's labour movement threw its support behind CCF candidates rather than running its own. The CCF captured two council seats and two school trustee positions. Shortly thereafter, the party withdrew from the municipal scene and neither labour nor the CCF ran candidates in the 1945 election.

Almost immediately after the Second World War, the labour movement in Calgary splintered, with the left wing running civic candidates under the Labour Progressive Party label (the Canadian

Communist Party) and the moderate wing running candidates under the United Civic Labour Group (UCLG) label.[59] With labour splintered, the CGA, almost monotonously, won one election after another. Not until the mid-1950s was the CGA's tenacious hold on the Calgary council broken. In 1953 labour unified and ran a single slate, capturing two seats; CGA's candidates won three seats. The 1954 and 1955 elections were a re-run, with the CGA pitted against a united labour slate. The demise of the CGA came in the autumn of 1956 when its supporters became alarmed over council's intense party politics. For the first time in a number of years, both CGA and labour members were beginning to act like true political parties and vote as blocs. The remedy was to restructure the CGA and change its name to the United Citizens Association (UCA), which would encompass both labour and business positions and candidates. The UCA did have several trade unionists on its slate in the 1957 election and was successful in its strategy, electing five members. However, labour's left was not to be mollified and a labour slate elected two council members.

Until that time, the Calgary Labour Council would sometimes endorse labour candidates and, at other times, would not. There were times when Labour Group candidates had been nominated by council. Just days before the 1957 election, the Labour Council announced that it would no longer endorse labour candidates. This declaration sounded the death knell for the Labour Group and it soon vanished from the civic scene. Shortly thereafter, the Labour Council, in yet another policy shift, announced that for the 1959 election it would run a Calgary Labour Council (CLC) slate; it was only marginally successful, capturing one council seat.

At about the same time, another event occurred, which alarmed labour and has had a lasting effect on its civic political strategy. In 1958 anti-labour members of council convinced the council to scrap proportional representation, ostensibly because it confused the voters and made it difficult for the administration to count the votes. Their main reason was to cut labour's representation on council. After much political manoeuvring and an eventual plebiscite, proportional representation was abolished and (with changes in the province's City Act) replaced by a two-member, six-ward system of representation, which began in the 1961 election. The anti-labour strategy paid off: in the 1961 election, in which all 12 council seats were up for grabs, the CLC captured only one and, ever since, labour's representation has been considerably diminished.

An unforeseen consequence of the ward system was the sporadic emergence of community-based political organizations contesting council elections. A group of dissatisfied businesspeople in north

Calgary founded the North Hill Businessmens Association (NHBA) and fielded two candidates in 1962, 1963 and 1964; one or both was elected in each year.[60] Another community group, which considered running candidates but then decided simply to endorse them and provide some financial assistance, was the Bridgeland-Riverside-Renfrew Ratepayers Association.

Despite the appearance of these community political organizations, the UCA obtained a majority of council seats throughout the 1960s; however, once elected, their members seemed to splinter on voting as often as they voted together. The executive of the UCA made no apology for the behaviour of its candidates; in 1967 it announced that the UCA existed only "to place good men in local government," not to give them policy direction: "Our sole function is to get responsible people and to get them to run for election. We assist in a financial way."[61] After labour was bested with the abolition of proportional representation, the UCA no longer found it necessary to include labour members on its slate. During the 1960s the typical slate consisted of businesspeople, oil executives, realtors, and a sprinkling of housewives and teachers.

Labour decided that, in order to exercise power on council, it had to expand its support base. The CLC, replaced in 1965 by the Civic Labour Association (CLA), appealed to home owners, tenants and small businesspeople as much as to labour. Despite labour's attempt to broaden its appeal, the CLA seated only one person on council in 1965 and 1966. The organization folded and yet another was founded to make a wide appeal to the electorate. The Civic Action League (CAL), dubbed a "non-partisan civic political body," announced it was going "to bring democracy back into civic elections."[62] After running five candidates unsuccessfully in the 1967 election the organization was disbanded. The 1960s ended with labour so dispirited that it ran no candidates after 1967 and left the field clear for a string of UCA electoral successes.

With the term of office for council members being three years, 33 candidates ran for 12 council seats in 1971. Labour's demise left the field clear for the UCA, which elected four members. The rest of the seats were captured by independents. In 1974 UCA candidates won three council seats and promptly disbanded. In 1977 the Calgary Urban Party (CUP) was born and attempted to capture the vote of the city's new professionals with a platform of social and planning policy reforms. Its six candidates all went down to ignominious defeat.[63] In the spring of 1980 the CUP executive decided that the city was not ready for party politics and, to all intents and purposes, disbanded. With no parties involved, the election contest revolved around disparate campaign promises made by 34 council and eight mayoralty candidates. The 1983 electoral campaign was equally bereft of party involvement and a record 73 independent candidates ran for council.

Lethbridge Party Politics

Local party politics developed somewhat differently in Lethbridge than in Edmonton and Calgary. A party representing the city's business interests maintained continuity over almost half a century, changing its name only once. At the same time one alphabet party after another burst forth on the electoral scene only to disappear after a short period of time.

Lethbridge's population tripled, growing from 2,313 to 8,060, between 1906 and 1911, and newly chartered unions had equally impressive growth. Although organized labour did not run candidates for municipal offices, the Lethbridge Labour Council endorsed candidates during this early period. With the 1913 recession, the city's buoyant economy and growth began to decline. In an attempt to avert a fiscal crisis and to halt the growth of labour's influence, the nonpartisan American commission form of government was adopted in 1913.[64] Weakened by a loss of membership and internal divisions, labour still endorsed municipal candidates sporadically for the next 14 years. Then, in 1927, faced with another fiscal crisis and desiring to put a complete halt to labour's political activities, the electorate, in a plebiscite, voted to adopt the city manager form of government.[65] The *Lethbridge Herald* enthusiastically supported this new form of government and, in an editorial printed during the plebiscite campaign, stated:

> It does away with civic politics and in this respect must tend to efficiency. It's only natural that men elected to office . . . for a term of three years have to depend on the vote of the people. . . . They have to consider that the element for tenure in office rests in the final analysis on the vote of the people. It is only natural for men to seek to hold their jobs and there must be a human element of what is known as playing politics for this purpose. With an appointed manager this would be eliminated.[66]

Ironically, it was in the 1928 election, after the adoption of the city manager form of government, that Lethbridge's first local political parties came into being. The Dominion Labour Party (DLP), loosely affiliated with the federal party of the same name, ran a full slate and elected two to council. The Citizen's Slate, committed to "business administration for conserving [city] capital assets," also elected two members. Independents took the rest of the seats. With three council seats to be filled in 1929, the DLP ran three candidates, all of whom lost. The Citizen's Slate had disbanded shortly after the 1928 election but threw its support behind another new party. Independents running in 1928 created the Lethbridge Civic Government Association (LCGA) and, with the endorsement of the business community and the *Lethbridge Herald*, captured all three seats. In 1930 the defunct Citizen's Slate was resurrected and merged with the LCGA, which captured three seats, the fourth going to the DLP. In 1931 the DLP was shut out, with the LCGA capturing all three seats. Then in 1932 the DLP and the LCGA entered into a curious agreement designed to ensure that neither would have to campaign. With four council seats vacant the two civic parties agreed that the LCGA would run three candidates and the DLP one, thus negating the necessity of an election, as the candidates would win by acclamation. However, the plan failed since, at the last minute, an independent filed, forcing an election. Still, the two parties captured all council seats. In 1933 the two parties again ran a full complement for three seats, all taken by the LCGA.

The 1934 election saw a backlash against the LCGA, which had consistently controlled council since its formation in 1929. With taxes in arrears, an inadequate welfare program and municipal service cuts, the electorate turned on the LCGA, which won only a single council seat, while the DLP won three. Although after the election the LCGA controlled council with four seats to the DLP's three, labour was certain that it would be in control after the 1935 election. It was the entry of a full slate of candidates running under the Social Credit banner that upset labour's plans. Despite a platform similar to LCGA, Social Credit candidates picked up substantial labour support. A candidate running under the Communist Party label added to labour's woes, although he received only 185 votes. With labour splintered, the LCGA won all three council seats. Failing to win a single seat and chastised by the *Lethbridge Herald* for bringing provincial party politics to the local level, Social Credit formally abandoned the Lethbridge scene shortly after the election. With four council vacancies in 1936, both the DLP and the LCGA ran a full slate of candidates. The Communist and Social Credit candidates defeated in 1935 allied and ran under a newly created Civic Progressive Association (CPA), advocating a city industrial policy to reduce unemployment. This odd alliance of right and left alienated large numbers of Social Creditors who threw their support behind the LCGA, which won all four seats. In 1937 there was again a bizarre alliance of Communists, Social Creditors and a breakaway wing of the DLP all running under the banner of the Lethbridge Citizen's Educational League — Non-Partisan (LCEL-NP). With the labour vote splintered between the DLP and the LCEL-NP, and with substantial numbers of Social Creditors throwing their support to the LCGA, the last party won all three seats, with the result that every seat on council was held by an LCGA member.

With LCGA's opposition dispirited by successive defeats, the 1938 and 1939 elections were lackluster. A former LCEL-NP member running under an Independent Progressive Candidate (IPC) label was soundly defeated. The LCGA won all four seats in a 1938 election and all seats in 1939 by acclamation. In 1940 the DLP and LCGA entered into an agreement similar to the 1932 one; each would put forward only two candidates for the four vacant seats, to let the electorate devote its energies to the war effort rather than to an electoral campaign. In 1941 the DLP changed its name to the Labour Party (LP) and ran a full set of candidates, all of whom were ignominiously defeated by the LCGA. In 1942 the LP and the LCGA again agreed that each would put forward only two candidates for the four council vacancies in order to forestall an election. In 1943 three LCGA candidates were elected by acclamation. In 1944 organized labour disbanded the LP and supported independent labour candidates who won one council seat to the LCGA's three. In 1945 all independent labour candidates lost to the LCGA slate.

As Lethbridge emerged from the war years its political complexion began to change. The LCGA dropped "Lethbridge" from its name and became the CGA. More importantly, in the 1946 election, labour healed its internal dissent and supported the Civic Labour Organization (CLO), which captured two of four vacant seats (a popular independent candidate captured one seat and the CGA the other). Labour's momentum was stopped in 1947 when the CGA won all three vacancies. In 1948 the independent who had won in 1946 created the Independent Civic Welfare Association (ICWA) and was reelected under its banner. The CLO captured two seats, the CGA one. For 1949 the election was issueless and lackluster, with the CGA besting the CLO and taking all three council seats. For the 1950 election, candidates blossomed like spring flowers with the CGA and the CLO running full slates, a full slate running under the banner of the Independent Civic Welfare Association (ICWA) (which folded after the election) and nine candidates running as independent labour. Each group elected a single candidate.

In 1951 eight candidates ran for three council seats. First, the CGA and CLO fielded a full slate of candidates and then, shortly before the election, the Lethbridge Citizen's Association (LCA) was founded by a coalition of women's groups to elect a woman to council. It fielded only a single candidate, however, and, as a woman had never sat on council, women across the city strongly supported her and she was elected. The CGA captured the other two positions. Interest waned for the 1952 election and only five candidates, running under the CGA and CLO banners, contested four seats; each group won two. In 1953 the LCA changed its name to the Lethbridge Women's Citizens Association (LWCA) and ran the LCA incumbent who won her race. The CGA captured the other two seats. For the 1954 election the CGA and CLO each ran three candidates and the LWCA one; one independent ran as well. For the first time in a number of years, an independent was elected, along with one CLO and two CGA members.

In 1955 the local political parties again played their name-changing game. The LWCA underwent a metamorphosis and became the Inter-Club Council for Women in Public Affairs, which would endorse candidates but would not run them under its own banner. It made a single endorsement, the woman incumbent who had successfully run in 1951 and 1953 and was running in 1955 as an independent. The *Lethbridge Herald* reported that it was the strong support she received from the city's women that guaranteed her re-election. In addition, the CGA and an independent each won a seat. The CLO went through its own metamorphosis, became the Lethbridge Citizen's Organization (LCO) and attempted to broaden its support by making an appeal to the business and professional community. The strategy backfired, alienating the left wing of labour and being ineffective in attracting members outside the labour community; the new party elected no one to council. In 1956 the LCO ran two candidates on a straight labour platform and elected one after labour's left wing returned to the fold. The CGA captured two seats, and one independent was elected.

The Lethbridge electorate must have been perplexed in 1957 as 13 candidates filed for four council positions. The Council for Women in Public Affairs endorsed four independent women but was unwilling to endorse the woman councillor, who subsequently lost. The LCO had angered the Lethbridge Labour Council, which promptly founded the Civic Labour Committee (CLC) with two candidates running under its banner. With labour split, neither party placed a member on council. The Lethbridge Taxpayers' Association (LTA) entered the fray and ran three candidates, one a conservative labour member. The LTA elected one, the CGA two. Also elected was a woman who had received the endorsement of the Council for Women in Public Affairs. Shortly after the election, the CLC disbanded and labour's divisive factions were again reunited.

In 1958 eight candidates ran for four council seats and the CGA, LCO and LTA each elected one. An independent candidate was also elected. The 1959 and 1960 campaigns were dull as a result of labour's absence from the political scene. Failing to place a candidate on council in either election, the LTA retired from electoral involvement. Almost predictably, the CGA held a majority on council after each election.

The 1961 political campaign was another lethargic one, with the CGA running candidates for three seats and winning two; again labour sat out. With the mayor directly elected for the first time since 1913, three local parties and a host of independents contested the 1962 election. The CGA endorsed the incumbent mayor and two council candidates ran under its label. For the first time in a number of years, the Lethbridge Labour Council (LLC) ran a candidate (who lost) under its own banner. Yet another short-lived party came into existence when a number of people concerned with "the evils of planning" founded the Civic Improvement Association (CIA) and ran a full set of candidates. The CIA captured the mayor's chair but the CGA won two of the three council seats. In 1963 the CIA died as suddenly as it had been born when its advertising bills for the 1962 election remained unpaid. Labour, licking its wounds from its 1962 defeat, decided not to run candidates. The CGA filled the vacuum with party candidates but managed to elect only one. The 1964 election found only the CGA running candidates; all won handily. The 1965, 1966 and 1967 elections were almost repeat performances, with only CGA candidates running. The party captured two of three council positions in 1965 and 1967 and one of three in 1966; an independent mayor was elected by acclamation.

For the 1968 election council was increased from seven to nine members, with five council seats and the mayor's position up for election. Charges of fiscal squandering and a heated controversy over the University of Lethbridge's new location spawned the Independent Civic Association (ICA) with a full slate from disenchanted Social Creditors and organized labour. The CGA, taking the high ground, received the endorsement of the *Lethbridge Herald* and took every council seat while the ICA dissolved after the election. The next year, a lackluster election saw four CGA candidates take four seats with little opposition.

In 1971, with the mayor's chair and eight council seats open, there were 17 candidates: 15 for council and two for mayor. Opposed only by independents, the CGA, with a full slate, captured the mayoralty position and four council seats. The 1974 election was almost a re-run: the CGA mayor won by acclamation and four CGA candidates took council seats, the only opposition again being independents. In 1977 the *Lethbridge Herald*, reversing its long-time policy of giving tacit support to CGA candidates, editorialized that the CGA had become too partisan and advocated a return to non-partisan campaigns.[67] The party quietly disbanded and its council incumbents ran as independents. Satisfied that partisanship had been stripped from the local scene, the *Herald* endorsed all the ex-CGA members. The Lethbridge Labour Council endorsed six candidates (two of whom were elected) for their "excellent work" in the community, whether they were pro-labour or not. The 1980 election was again lackluster with the mayor elected by acclamation and 15 independents vying for eight council seats. Although the 1983 election produced vigorous campaigns by three mayoralty candidates and a host of would-be councillors, no political parties were involved as all candidates campaigned as independents.

The Politics of At-Large and Ward Representation

There are two basic forms of political representation: ward and at-large. Under a ward system a member represents a geographical area; in at-large systems, a councillor's constituency is the whole city. Under an at-large system each voter is given the opportunity to vote for any council candidate; under a ward system each voter is restricted to the candidates in the voter's ward. Some ward systems require candidates to reside in the ward they run in. The ward system and the at-large system differ significantly in their implications for both election campaigns and politics on council.

The advocates of at-large elections contend that a council will share a community-wide view that diminishes council conflict and promotes unanimity in policy making. They argue that ward representation means that representatives take a parochial view of the public interest in order to get re-elected. This attitude will manifest itself in "council logrolling," where one representative supports another ward in return for something for his or her own ward. Even more telling is the intensification of racial, ethnic and class feelings, creating even deeper cleavages in the community and council and corroding the council bargaining process. All of these factors make efficient policy making very difficult. The advocates of ward representation respond that a councillor elected from a ward represents a smaller number of people and therefore knows the people and their problems much better than someone elected at-large. They also point out that the smaller ward allows the person with limited financial resources to carry out a successful electoral campaign; success in a large city at-large election requires an expensive media campaign. Finally they argue that, since most communities are geographically segmented by race, ethnic origin and class, only wards enable the diverse groups to be adequately represented.

One difficulty in evaluating these arguments is that they rest on different premises. The proponents of at-large elections start from the premise that the important value is efficiency in government; the proponents of wards believe in democracy and participation. Each system is used by various community interests and politicians to justify a form of representation that will give them an electoral advantage. This can be seen in a brief examination of representation, first in the United States and Canada, and then in Edmonton and Calgary.

In the nineteenth century in both Canada and the United States, wards provided representation for the immense pockets of new, working-class, ethnic immigrants in larger cities. In the United States, wards were used as building blocks to develop political machines. A machine's lieutenant in the ward would be the person constituents would see to obtain a city job or have a teenager bailed out of jail. In return, those so assisted were expected to vote *en masse* for the machine's ward candidate. Thus ward representation was closely linked with the party politics of the times and at-large representation was linked with non-partisan politics. To eradicate the political machine and ensure that the "right kind" of people were elected to council, reformers proposed that ward representation be replaced by at-large elections.

As the reform movement swept into Canada, at-large versus ward representation became an issue in a number of cities. However, there was little debate in Edmonton, for its 1904 city charter incorporated the major principles of reform advocated by the American National Municipal League, thus institutionalizing at-large representation from the beginning. James Anderson, comparing the effects of the at-large system in Edmonton and the ward system in Winnipeg, writes:

> . . . in the absence of a ward system in Edmonton, labour and Eastern European immigrant groups concentrated in the eastern section of the city were largely unsuccessful in obtaining representation on city council despite organized attempts to do so. In Winnipeg, however, labour groups and Jewish and Slavic immigrant communities elected several spokesmen to Council early in the century.[68]

Organized labour was especially quick to recognize that the at-large electoral system diffused their potential power. Sporadically, for over half a century, labour unsuccessfully advocated the adoption of a ward system and, almost predictably, the *Edmonton Journal* opposed it, arguing that it would lead to divisions on council. Unstated was the fear that it would break the middle-class business community's hold on council and possibly lead to a full-blown party system in the city. Not until the late 1960s, with the city's greatly increased size, was serious consideration given to adopting a ward system. And, then, only through the shrewd manoeuvring of council by one of its liberal members was the issue referred to the electorate. In the October, 1968, ballot on the issue, 61.5 per cent favoured the ward system. The council's response was to devise four strip wards running north to south (completely ignoring community, economic and ethnic cleavages), with three councillors representing each.[69] With 65 per cent of the city's population north of the Saskatchewan River and seven of 12 councillors living south of the river, strip wards were the only way incumbent councillors could seek re-election in their home ward. Adding insult to injury, Mayor Ivor Dent proclaimed that the north-south wards would "mean the best distribution of socio-economic areas" for representational purposes.[70]

Even more important than the way in which incumbent councillors ensured themselves safe seats by adopting a strip ward system is how the system worked to the disadvantage of the city's poor and working-class areas. Whether it is a federal, provincial or municipal election, a variety of factors cause a substantial difference in the rate of voter turnout by social class. Middle-class areas almost always have a much higher turnout rate than poor and working-class ones. Therefore, in a strip ward with an equal number of middle-class, and poor and working-class people, the middle class will elect its candidate to council.[71] Although there has not been an analysis of the differential turnout rates by class in Edmonton, it is unlikely the electorate behaves differently than in other cities.

Even with four wards completely heterogeneous in socio-economic composition and with no requirement that councillors live in the ward they represented, some council members were dissatisfied. Another plebiscite, held in 1974 in conjunction with the 1974 civic election, asked voters, "Do you favour abolishing the Ward System and revision to a system of nomination and election of aldermen for the entire City of Edmonton?" Slightly more than 53 per cent rejected abolition of the ward system. The second mandate made it clear to council that the electorate wanted a ward system with wards representing "something." For more than four years the council debated and held hearings on restructuring ward boundaries, but to no avail. Then, in February, 1979, a Mayor's Task Force on City Government, composed of a cross-section of middle-class citizens, was created to review council's discussions and make recommendations on the ward system. The task force concluded that there should be eight two-member wards, approximately equal in population and representative of neighbourhoods. The council ignored the recommendations but did increase the number of wards to six, each with two members representing approximately 81,900 people. In 1983, ward representation was still an issue, with its proponents arguing that wards were far too large to represent neighbourhoods or to bring the representative and his or her constituents together.

Calgary had four wards, each with three members, from 1893 until 1913 when the electorate was asked whether or not the ward system should be abolished.[72] Influenced by the arguments of the American reform movement, the electorate voted 1,319 to 1,280 for abolishing the wards. With the city's move to proportional representation in 1917 (to be discussed in Chapter 11), labour was assured of representation on council.

There was little concern over the at-large system until 1958 when a pro-business council decided to abolish proportional representation. Labour responded by proposing that wards be re-introduced if proportional representation were dropped; the compromise was accepted. Since provincial legislation had no provision for ward representation, the government was asked for permissive legislation to allow a ward system to be established. The necessary ruling was finally passed in the spring of 1960. However, the Act required a municipality to have the approval of two-thirds of the voting electorate before it could establish a ward system. In the October, 1960, municipal election, with almost every area of the city strongly favouring wards, the outcome was 20,263 to 9,262, or 68.6 per cent, which met the provincial requirement. [73] With little controversy the council created six two-member wards in time for use in the 1961 election.

The by-law establishing the ward system required that "the number of electors residing in each ward . . . be substanially equal." This provision eventually required that some ward boundaries be restructured, for Calgary's dramatic population increase in the 1960s made some wards "unbalanced." However, the changes caused little controversy.

Ward representation was a dominant political issue until the late 1960s and early 1970s when it became entwined with demands for greater citizen participation in Calgary's government. Politically attuned to the demands for citizen participation, Mayor Rod Sykes established a Standing Policy Committee on Legislation and a Citizen's Open Government Study to determine how more citizen views and demands could be incorporated in the policy-making process. Both bodies made similar recommendations, including expanding to 18 single-member wards. As in Edmonton, council deliberations were fraught with discord. Stan Drabek, examining the council meeting that settled the controversy, writes:

> This meeting showed the difficulty for any group of people to arrive coherently and logically at what could be considered, in terms of numbers, a truly representative ward system. . . . Figures were bandied about with abandon—sixteen, twelve, eight. . . . Council, ever mindful of past demands for more citizen participation indicated a dissatisfaction with the existent twelve member council but on the other hand it felt that a sixteen member council would be too large a representative body. There is reason to believe that council felt that a single member and smaller size wards would satisfy citizen appetites for more representation. Ultimately, council on a close vote . . . decided on fourteen wards so that the new system would see one member elected per ward for a . . . total of fourteen. . . . [74]

Unlike Edmonton, Calgary had little controversy over drawing ward boundaries. The task was left to the City Clerk's Office, which has attempted to balance the number of wards north and south of the Bow River in order to defuse a north-south rivalry. Currently, there are six wards south of the river, six north of the river, and two straddling it. In addition, there has been an attempt to devise wards that represent communities of interest, although in some cases these are hard to define.

The major difference between the ward systems in Edmonton and Calgary is the number of constituents and the number of square miles each councillor represents. In Calgary, with 14 single-member wards, each councillor represents an average of 44,300 people (1983 census figures) and an average ward size of 15 square miles. Although this hardly allows a close working relationship between elected representatives and their constituents, it is far better than Edmonton's system where, with six two-member wards, each councillor represents an average of 93,300 people (1983 census figures) in an average ward size of 43 square miles. [75]

Some members of Edmonton's council, recognizing that the ward system is not adequately representative, have called for changes. After the geographical size of the city doubled in 1981, it was proposed that the number of wards be expanded to eight with two members from each. The proposal was bandied around council for over a year and then quietly dropped. This did not seem to bother Edmonton's quiescent public, for the lack of adequate ward representation was a non-issue in the 1983 municipal election.

One of the difficulties Edmonton and Calgary face in devising ward systems is that section 27 of the Municipal Government Act limits a city to no more than 20 councillors, which in effect limits single-member wards to 20.[76] Other provisions of the Act, in section 28, state that the number of electors in each ward be "substantially equal" and each ward must have the same number of representatives. A recent change in the Act allows a city council to have some of its councillors elected city-wide and others from wards.

Electoral representation of county and municipal districts must be geographically based on electoral divisions. Like city wards, these divisions are restricted in number. Under section 2 of the County Act the number of county councillors cannot exceed 11, all of whom are elected from electoral divisions. Surprisingly, there are no limitations on the number of a municipal district's electoral divisions or councillors. The reason is that section 13(4) of The Municipal Government Act states merely that when a municipal district is formed the Lieutenant-Governor shall divide the district into an unspecified number of electoral divisions. Then, section 27(1) of the Act states, "the council of a municipal district shall consist of the same number of councillors as there are electoral divisions." Despite the potential for such development, an electoral system with a large number of electoral divisions each represented by a councillor has not been inaugurated in any of the province's municipal districts.

Notes

1. Hays, "The Politics of Reform in Municipal Government," 161.

2. Hawley, *Nonpartisan Elections*, 9.

3. *Ibid.*, 14.

4. The commission form of government, not to be confused with the council-commission form, has a small number of popularly elected commissioners who collectively constitute the city council and exercise its legislative powers. Individually, each commissioner is the administrative head of one or more related departments.

5. James Anderson cites a number of such scandals. Greedy aldermen in Montreal, Toronto, Winnipeg and Calgary were found guilty of using their positions to further private gains. Anderson, "The Municipal Government Reform Movement," 92-93.

6. *Ibid.*, 85.

7. Foran, "The Calgary Town Council, 1884-1895," 42.

8. *Ibid.*, 44.

9. Anderson, "The Municipal Government Reform Movement," 85.

10. Gaetz, "Municipal Legislation," 26.

11. Macpherson, *Democracy in Alberta, 20-27.*

12. *Ibid.*, 24-25.

13. *Ibid.*, 28-61.

14. Major Clifford Douglas, *Social Credit*, cited in Macpherson, *Democracy in Alberta*, 127.

15. Aberhart, "The Democratic Monetary Reform Organization of Canada," cited in Macpherson, *Democracy in Alberta*, 204.

16. Masson, "The Ebb and Flow of Municipal Party Politics," 360.

17. Gibbins, *et al.*, "Attitudinal and Socio-Demographic Determinants of Civic Partisanship," 11.

18. The survey, carried out by the author in the early spring of 1983, consisted of a mail-out questionnaire with follow-up letters, postcards and telephone calls for those not responding. The response rate was 83 per cent for cities, 73 per cent for towns and 64 per cent for villages. The municipalities identified as having some form of party organization were Edmonton, Calgary, Lloydminster, High River, Hinton, Vulcan and, surprisingly, the small village of Ferintosh.

19. Safire, *The New Language of Politics*, 289, cited in Hawley, *Nonpartisan Elections*, 143.

20. Lee, *The Politics of Nonpartisanship*, 55-59; Adrian and Williams, "The Insulation of Local Politics," 1063; Rogers and Arman, "Nonpartisanship and Election to City Office," 941-945; Salisbury and Black, "Class and Party in Partisan and Nonpartisan Elections," 584-592; and Hawley, *Nonpartisan Elections*, 31-39.

21. Hawley, *Nonpartisan Elections*, 23.

22. Anderson, *"The Municipal Government Reform Movement,"* 95.

23. Lightbody, "Edmonton," 266.

24. *Toronto Globe and Mail*, January 13, 1984.

25. Lightbody, "The Rise of Party Politics," 200.

26. Anderson, "The Municipal Government Reform Movement,"94.

27. Caragata, *Alberta Labour*, 95.

28. *Ibid.*, 95.

29. *Ibid.*, 116.

30. *Ibid.*, 118.

31. Masson, "The Ebb and Flow of Municipal Party Politics," 357-358.

32. *Lethbridge Herald*, October 3, 1968.

33. *Minutes of the Edmonton Trades and Labour Council*, November 4, 1907, cited in Anderson, "The Municipal Government Reform Movement," 99.

34. Short, "Municipal Government by Commission," 95.

35. Lightbody, "Edmonton," 260. During the 1919 general strike in Edmonton the mayor was sympathetic to the demands of the strikers. The conservative and business-oriented *Edmonton Bulletin* said of his involvement: "Better to deal with the Soviet direct . . . than the Soviet reinforced by the authority of the mayor's office." Caragata, *Alberta Labour*, 76.

36. Lightbody, "Edmonton," 260.

37. *Ibid*

38. Ogilvie, CC council candidate 1936, cited in Betts, "The Edmonton Aldermanic Election of 1962," 31.

39. *Ibid.*, 40

40. *Edmonton Journal*, September 21, 1954.

41. Ivor Dent, who successfully ran for mayor in 1968 strictly as an independent decrying party politics in general and the Civic Party affiliation of his opponent in particular, was an EVA candidate in 1957. At that time, he was a strong proponent of parties at the local level. *Edmonton Journal*, October 2, 1957.

42. The original EPOA had its birth and demise in 1936. The defunct organization's name was adopted in 1957 by the CC dissidents.

43. Both the CRA and the CC endorsed Elmer Roper for mayor.

44. Yet another organization was founded in 1960 to contest the public school board elections. The Better Education Association (BEA) bested both the CRA and CC candidates and won all the positions on the school board.

45. For the first time in Edmonton's history an alphabet party contested the city's separate school board elections when, in 1961, the Separate School Voters Association (SSVA) ran a full slate of candidates.

46. In 1963 another new party formed to contest the public school board elections, the Quality Education Committee (QEC), ran four candidates and managed to get one elected to the board.

47. A UVO candidate caustically remarked of this name change: "Last year we had the CGA. This year it's the Better Civic Government Committee; maybe someday we'll have the Even Better Civic Government Committee." *Edmonton Journal*, October 9, 1964.

48. In 1964 the BEA, QEC, BCGC and independents were seeking seats on the public school board.

49. *Edmonton Journal*, October 11, 1966. Another candidate said, "I'm not sure what it [BCGC] stands for . . . Bandits and Crooks, Gangsters and Criminals?" *Ibid*.

50. *Edmonton Journal*, October 3, 1968.

51. A by-election was held in 1970 to replace a councillor who had died in 1969. Normally the vacancy would have remained open until the 1971 election. However, council wished to place an important plebiscite before the electorate and so it was decided to combine the plebiscite with a by-election. All candidates ran in the by-election as independents.

52. BEA did run candidates for the school board; however, most of them lost.

53. Lightbody offers an alternative explanation for the success of EVA's candidate. He writes: "His election was 'accidental' insofar as none of the three incumbents stood for re-election in the ward and in a non-partisan contest, where name recognition is important, many voters undoubtedly thought they were voting for his father, a very prominent Anglican clergyman. Mr. Leadbeater [the student leader] received 8.93 per cent of the total vote cast. His EVA successor in 1977 received but 2.7 per cent." Lightbody, "Edmonton," 287, n74.

54. Foran, "The Calgary Town Council, 1884-1895," 46.

55. Foran, "The Civic Corporation and Urban Growth," 175.

56. *Ibid*., 261.

57. Foran notes that "Labour's share of the popular vote hovered around twenty five per cent" throughout the 1920s. *Ibid*., 262.

58. *Ibid*., 264-265. The argument that proportional representation did not advantage labour is a controversial one, especially as proportional representation normally gives a minority an advantage in obtaining representation. The only way it could be determined whether Calgary's proportional representation advantaged labour would be to examine voting data of the period. Foran has not done that.

59. The UCLG became the Civic Labour Association (CLA) in 1951.

60. In the 1962 election one of the NHBA candidates received an endorsement from the CLC, although the person was not included on the CLC slate.

61. *Calgary Herald*, September 27, 1961. In 1964 a UCA spokesman, in a candid statement, said that the organization collected between $5,000 and $8,000 annually from private donors, using the money to provide partial financial support for UCA candidates. *Calgary Herald*, September 15, 1964.

62. *Calgary Herald*, September 18, 1967.

63. Perhaps one of the reasons for the defeat of party candidates is found in a ward seven Hillhurst-Sunnyside community survey. It was found that 67 per cent of respondents "preferred that their ward alderman stand alone and not be bound to any city-wide electoral organization." Drabek and Woods, "Calgary: The Boom Ends," 14.

64. The key feature of this form of government is a small number of representatives elected on a non-partisan ballot. In the case of Lethbridge, the number of representatives was seven. Each elected representative, known as a commissioner, is responsible for one or more municipal departments. This system is adopted to fuse the policy-making and administrative arms of city government. The commissioners elect one of their own members to be mayor. Normally the mayor is also the city's finance commissioner.

65. The commissioners became councillors, with the manager being held responsible to the council. The mayor was still elected internally by council's members. It was not until 1961 that the citizenry, in a plebiscite, decided that the mayor should be directly elected.

66. *Lethbridge Herald*, October 3, 1927.

67. *Lethbridge Herald*, October 19, 1977.

68. Anderson, "The Municipal Government Movement," 89. James Lightbody describes how, in 1920, Winnipeg's business community aided by an anti-labour, rural-based Manitoba legislature, managed to undermine the representation on council afforded to labour by the ward system. The number of wards was reduced from seven, with two members each, to three, with six members each. The effect was to diminish labour's council representation. See Lightbody, "Electoral Reform in Local Government," 312-319.

69. While the average area of a ward in other Canadian cities varied between 2.4 and 4.4 square miles, in Edmonton the average area of the ward was 30.25 square miles.

70. *Edmonton Journal*, March 18, 1969.

71. Jerry Hough presents a hypothetical example contrasting electoral outcomes using a strip ward system and one following homogeneous class boundaries. "Imagine an area populated in its northern half by 50,000 affluent persons and in its southern half by 50,000 poor persons, an area in which the northern half casts three times as many votes as the southern. If two electoral districts are created and the boundary is drawn along a north-

south line, then each district will have 25,000 persons of each income level. It might well be predicted that the representative or representatives in each district would be much more sensitive to the demands of the northern area with its larger number of effective votes. If the boundary is drawn east-west along class lines, however, then the poor will obtain representation equal to that of the affluent, despite their lower turnout rate." Hough, "Voters' Turnout and the Responsiveness of Local Government," 295-296.

72. Much of the information on Calgary's ward system was taken from Stan Drabek's unpublished paper, "The Calgary Ward System."

73. In an earlier plebiscite held on May 6, 1959, 64 per cent of the electorate had favoured wards. However, since provincial legislation was not yet in place, the plebiscite was not binding, although it was used by the city to show the need for changes in legislation.

74. Drabek, "The Calgary Ward System," 11.

75. The doubling of the city's size with its successful 1980 annexation bid somewhat distorts the size of the area represented by each ward, for few people were annexed into the city. The city's population is concentrated within its pre-annexation land area. However, even if the pre-annexation size figure is used, a councillor still represents almost 21 square miles.

76. Only cities have the option of adopting a ward form of representation; towns and villages are restricted to at-large representation.

11

MUNICIPAL ELECTIONS
AND
PLEBISCITES

Introduction

Despite the number of political interest groups, neighbourhood associations and local political parties in Alberta municipalities, large numbers of people are unaffiliated; only through the electoral process are they able to express preferences in public policy. Elections, however, often fall short of linking the electorate and the policy makers. As has been noted, non-partisanship, so prevalent in Alberta communities, has worked to depress participation and representation from among lower-income groups, and the transient local political parties have been either impotent or negligent in formulating clear public policies. Wards are far too large to represent minorities adequately; at-large elections are even less adequate. Just as provincial and municipal election rules have alternately discouraged or encouraged partisan elections and prohibited or allowed ward representation, other electoral rules give an advantage to one segment of the electorate over others and weaken or strengthen the electoral link between the elected official and the citizenry.

Electoral Systems

The municipal voting system in Alberta, like its counterparts at the provincial and federal levels, seems to be straightforward, a model of simplicity and lack of bias: the candidate with the most votes wins. The "plurality formula",[1] ratifies the election of the candidate who receives more votes than any other single candidate, but the successful candidate need not necessarily have a higher total than all other candidates combined. In reality, the plurality system does not necessarily produce a truly representative council, the first function of a democratic voting system.

In a non-partisan election, the effect of the plurality system is to elect candidates who often receive far less than a majority of the vote. An example of this phenomenon is seen in Table 11.1 which presents Calgary's 1980 mayoralty election results. Klein, the winner, received almost 45 per cent of the popular vote. This total, while close to a majority, still falls short; hence, only a minority of the electorate voted for the man who won.[2]

Table 11.1
Calgary Mayoralty Election Results, 1980

Candidate	Votes	Percentage
Klein	68,118	44.8
Algers	52,054	34.2
Petrasuk	27,614	18.1
Tennant	2,136	1.4
Curry	971	.6
Mason	380	.3
Jasienczyk	345	.2
Ashton	340	.2
TOTAL	151,958	100.0

In a municipality with a party system, such as Lethbridge, Calgary or Edmonton during the 1930s, the effect of the plurality system is to give an advantage to the strongest party out of proportion to the size of its electoral margins. For example, in the 1935 Lethbridge election, a sizeable minority of the electorate voted for the Social Credit candidates, who lost. Under the plurality system the business-dominated Civic Government Association elected all of its members to council. The quarter of the population expressing a preference for Social Credit candidates had no Social Credit representation whatsoever on council. An astute student of the electoral systems sums up the effect of a plurality system for political parties when he writes: "Like the Sheriff of Nottingham, electoral systems are apt to steal from the poor and give to the rich: strong parties usually obtain more than their proportionate share of legislative seats while weak parties receive less than their proportionate share of the seats."[3]

For a time, Edmonton and Calgary employed a complex system of proportional representation (PR) meant to rectify the inequities of the plurality system. The basic principle of PR is that candidates of both majority and minority community groups receive the percentage of seats on council equivalent to the percentage of votes they received in the election. In short, it guarantees minority representation.

In Edmonton and Calgary the proponents of PR were militant labour groups that felt unfairly disadvantaged under the plurality system. In both cities the citizenry, by plebiscite, brought the system into use. Calgary first employed PR in the December, 1916, election; Edmonton followed six years later for the election of December 1922. Both cities adopted a complicated variant of PR, i.e., the "single transferable vote" system, for selecting municipal and school board members. Although extremely complex, the single transferable vote system captured the imagination of the Calgary electorate and was used for more than 40 years before being discarded in 1961. From its inception, it confused the Edmonton electorate and was used only until 1927, when the city reverted to the plurality system.

The single transferable vote system, in conjunction with proportional representation, is always used in multi-member constituencies, such as a municipality that elects all of its council members in a city-wide election. The ballot lists all candidates and each voter ranks them in order of preference, marking a "1" for first choice, a "2" for second choice, and so forth, until every candidate is ranked. After all votes are counted, a quota is computed to set the number of votes a candidate needs to win a seat. The formula is total number of votes cast in the election divided by the number of seats to be filled plus one. After this figure is computed, one is added to complete the formula.[4] Then the first preference votes are counted; any candidate who reaches the quota is elected. Any surplus votes the winning candidates receives over the quota are redistributed proportionally to candidates who were the second preferences on the winning candidate's ballot.[5] In addition, the candidate with the fewest votes is declared defeated (dropped from the list) and the ballots on which the loser is listed as first preference are distributed to the other candidates on the basis of the second preferences on these ballots.[6] If this redistribution makes another candidate a winner, this winner's surplus votes are distributed as were those of the first candidate. Again the candidate with the lowest number of votes is declared defeated and the second preferences are re-distributed. If any second preferences are designated for candidates already elected or defeated, the third preferences are distributed. This process continues until winning candidates are selected for all the seats. It is worth noting that many voters will not express any more than a first preference. Therefore, it is impossible to distribute their votes after the first round of counting.[7]

Three problems plagued the cities' single transferable vote systems. First, many voters were confused about the ranking instructions on the ballot. In the 1923 Edmonton election a number of voters befuddled by the instructions dropped blank ballots in the box. Others marked either an "X" or a "1" by the names of all the candidates of their choice rather than ranking them. As a consequence, over 1,200 of the 13,000 ballots cast were spoiled.[8] The Edmonton electorate did not seem to understand the PR system any better the last year it was used than it had the first. In the 1927 election there were 3,842 spoiled ballots.[9] The second problem was that few people understood the system's mechanics; even newspaper descriptions as to how votes were transferred from one candidate to another were muddled. Especially confusing was the fact that, in several instances, a candidate received only a few first preferences but was elected after votes were transferred. For example, in the 1927 Edmonton election, 11 candidates were running for five council seats, and a quota of 2,116 votes was required for election. Following are the first preferences:

Bellamy (CGA)	2,193
Sloane (CGA)	1,951
East (Labour)	1,922
Bowen (CGA)	1,514
Keillor (CGA)	1,227
Findlay (Labour)	914
Dineen (Labour)	798
Pelton (Independent)	784
Rehwinkel (CGA)	550
Herlihy (Labour)	485
Thompson (Labour)	375

Bellamy won on the first count, but on the fifth count, Sloane was elected when he received 190 votes upon Rehwinkel's elimination. On the sixth count East reached the quota when he received a substantial portion of the eliminated Herlihy's votes. On the next count 110 votes were transferred from Findlay to Bowen, giving him his quota, and Dineen also received enough votes from Findlay to reach his quota.[10] Thus, the candidate who placed seventh in first preference votes was elected to council. The third problem was the length of time it took to count the ballots and transfer votes. The 1917 Calgary election was held on Monday, but the results were not known until early Tuesday morning. In both Edmonton and Calgary, candidates and the electorate became frustrated at having to wait so long for election results.

In Calgary there were sporadic newspaper comments on the complexity of the system and the time it took to count ballots, but never the spirited debate found in Edmonton. After using the PR system for four successive years, the public was still so confused that an "expert" was brought in from the United States in 1927 to explain the system; he was unsuccessful. By that time the public was completely disenchanted with PR and a campaign was mounted to abolish it. Labour defended the system, which maximized its council strength, but the electorate, in a plebiscite held in December, 1927, voted to revert to a plurality system. PR's demise in Calgary was orchestrated by the business community in the 1950s in order to clear the council of labour representation. As in Edmonton, labour opposed its abolition, but to no avail.

Electoral Rules

An electoral rule that explicitly benefits incumbents and wealthier candidates is section 29 of the Local Authorities Election Act, which allows municipalities to require all candidates to make a substantial deposit when registering their nomination papers. In 1983 the new Act allowed municipalities with populations of 100,000 or more to require a deposit as high as $500; those with a population of under 100,000 could require up to $100. The candidate's deposit is returned "if he obtains a number of votes at least equal to one-half of the total number of votes cast for the candidate elected with the least number of votes".[11] The justification for a substantial deposit is that it discourages the frivolous candidates, such as John Buttery who ran for mayor in the 1980 Edmonton election. Buttery boasted that he was "criminally insane" and sought to prove it by blowing "raspberries" during his free television commercials; he continually interrupted the other candidates at election forums and wore a black pantsuit with a bell attached as his electoral garb.[12] Although a $500 deposit may discourage the frivolous, it also deters serious working-class candidates and those on the ideological fringe who can ill afford to lose the money. At a time when property qualifications for holding office and voting have become almost an anachronism and widespread citizen activity has been legitimized by requirements that encourage citizen input into policy making, it is peculiar to see barriers erected to prevent "undesirables" from running for public office.

Another electoral rule that advantages some and disadvantages others is the Local Authorities Election Act's provision on voter eligibility. Under section 47(1) of the Act a person is eligible to vote in a municipal or school election provided that he or she is at least 18 years of age, a Canadian citizen, an Alberta resident for six months prior to election day and a resident of the jurisdiction on election day.[13] This is a substantial change from the municipal voting requirements in 1970. At that time section 34(1) of the Municipal Election Act stated:

> A person is qualified to vote . . . at an election in a municipality if he is of the age of 19 years and
>
> a. his name appears upon the last revised assessment roll in respect of land or business liable to taxation, or
>
> b. he is a Canadian citizen or British subject and has continuously resided in the municipality for 12 months immediately preceding polling day.

Since 1970 the age of eligibility has been reduced, British subjects who are not Canadian citizens are no longer given special preference and the property qualification has been dropped. In the past, money by-laws needed the assent of the proprietary electors, i.e., property owners.[14] Today, with two exceptions, the distinction between those who own property and those who do not has been eliminated. Section 324 of the Municipal Government Act reads, "no by-law for creating a debt not payable within the current year has any effect until it has received . . . the assent of the proprietary electors." The same section states that a petition for a vote on a money by-law needs the consent of a certain percentage of proprietary electors. However, under provisions of the Act's section 325 a municipality can waive this provision, and most have done so.[15]

With most barriers to local participation eliminated, one would expect the turnout rate for municipal elections to equal that for provincial and federal elections. However, this is not the case in Alberta, as can be seen from Table 11.2 which shows turnout rates for municipal elections in Edmonton, Red Deer and Fort MacLeod, and for Alberta provincial and federal elections. Turnout is highest in federal, next highest in provincial, and lowest in municipal elections.

A number of explanations have been offered to account for lower turnout rates in municipal elections. It has been suggested that a comparative lack of political opposition at the local level decreases electoral interest. The difficulty with this argument is that opposition in recent provincial and federal elections in Alberta has been minimal. It has been suggested that inclement October weather tends to keep the electorate away from municipal polls; however, bad weather has not discouraged the electorate in provincial and federal elections. It has been suggested that the electorate is more interested in federal and provincial issues than in municipal ones and, as a discussion in an earlier chapter showed, this is in fact the case in both Edmonton and Calgary. This relative lack of interest may account for some of the difference but, as has been shown, the major catalyst of political interest at any level is a well-developed party system. The party system is strong at the provincial and federal levels but exists in a fragmentary

Table 11.2
Federal, Provincial, and Municipal Electoral Turnout Rates, 1964-1983 (selected years for cities in per cent)
* indicates median

Year	Federal (Alberta component)	Alberta provincial	Edmonton	Red Deer	Fort Macleod
1964			47	26	n.a.
1965	74				
1966			59	27	40
1967		63*			
1968	73				
1971	67-73*	72	37	35*	43
1972	76				
1974	67		48	40	61
1975		60			
1977			38	36	59*
1979	68	59			
1980	61		21	39	acclamation
1983		66	42*	28	82

and transitory form in only three Alberta municipalities; in most of the rest, non-partisan political systems continue to depress electoral turnout.

An absence of electoral rules can distribute political advantages and disadvantages just as effectively as can an elaborate set of rules. For example, no campaign spending limits or mandatory declarations of funding sources are placed on municipal candidates; in contrast, provincial and federal candidates must declare the source of all campaign funds and provincial candidates cannot receive more than $1,000 from each donor.

Village and small-town politicians who carry out door-to-door campaigns would be little affected by such limits. Even in a city the size of Lethbridge the cost of successfully contesting a council seat has been only $1,500 to $2,000.[16] However, in Edmonton and Calgary, where serious candidates conduct high-profile media campaigns with extensive use of radio and television and the placement of thousands of lawn signs, campaign costs have become exorbitant. Disclosing the sources of campaign funding could be embarrassing and limiting donations would advantage door-to-door grass-roots politicians. In the 1980 Calgary mayoralty campaign, Ross Algers spent over $150,000 in an unsuccessful bid for re-election. In the same election, a University of Calgary professor, dropping out of the mayoralty race after raising only $25,000, announced: "we thought we could win on $100,000 and we could run a credible campaign on $40,000, which wouldn't even allow for television advertising."[17] In the 1983 Edmonton mayoralty election it has been estimated that Laurence Decore spent between $135,000 and $175,000 to unseat the incumbent. In a 1980 Edmonton council ward race, a gold broker estimated his campaign costs to be $20,000; he lost. In a discussion of the 1983 Calgary municipal campaign a political analyst for *City Magazine* wrote: "Six months before the October vote, there were reliable reports from several individuals . . . that packages of $10,000 each are being offered in key Calgary wards to ensure pro-business candidates are being elected."[18] Perhaps this was not such an excessive amount for large city campaign contributions: it was rumoured in the 1974 Edmonton election that a council candidate received more than twice that amount from the business community.

Ed Oman, a former Calgary councillor and unsuccessful mayoral candidate who later became the MLA for Calgary North Hill, has introduced several private member bills to limit municipal campaign spending. In 1981 an Oman bill would have limited individual campaign contributions to $2,000 in mayoralty races with a spending cut-off of $125 per 1,000 population; individual contributions to council candidates would be limited to $1,000 with a spending cut-off of $50 per 1,000 population. The Calgary council refused to endorse the bill in principle and other MLAs in caucus refused to support it because they felt it was too restrictive.[19] In the spring of 1982 and that of 1983, Oman modified his position and introduced private bills that would give municipalities the right to establish their own campaign spending ceilings. Once again he was unable to generate support. The idea of limiting municipal campaign spending has received only lukewarm support from municipal officials and seems to leave the public uninterested.

Perhaps the reason campaign spending has been of so little interest is that there are few municipalities in which it is seen as a problem. Most campaigns are low key, low cost, door-to-door events, with positions often filled by acclamation.[20] In the 1983 election, even in the province's 12 cities, where competition and interest were relatively intense, there were four cases where one council seat was filled by acclamation. Entire councils in the municipal districts of Kneehill and Spirit River were elected by acclamation. Although no county councils were entirely filled by acclamation, the County of Vulcan filled eight of 11 seats without a campaign. Of a total of 114 towns, 10 elected all councillors and the mayor by acclamation; 38 elected their mayor by acclamation; and two elected the council by acclamation. At the village level, 48 of 122 councils were filled by acclamation.

Elections and Council Turnover

In municipalities where electoral positions are consistently filled by acclamation (usually small towns and villages), the citizenry tends to have a common outlook, and holding political office is considered to be a civic duty to be rotated every three years. An example is the small town of Irvine that has had at least a 57 per cent turnover in councillors in the last four elections. This rate of change is not an indication of divisiveness since, in 1983, the whole council and the mayor were elected by acclamation.

Other small communities are bitterly divided, with the electorate feeling that councillors make a substantial difference in policy direction. The village of Bawlf, with a 1983 population of 323 and a five-member council, had eight candidates in the 1983 election. In each of Bawlf's last four elections there has been at least a 67 per cent turnover in municipal councillors, with a 100 per cent turnover in 1977. The even smaller village of Strome had six candidates for the three council seats in the 1983 election; in 1977 and 1983 there was a 100 per cent turnover in council; in 1980, 67 per cent.

One would expect larger towns with heterogeneous populations to be highly politicized. Table 11.3 presents relevant figures. Electoral activity was particularly intense, with a number of candidates running in Cardston, Cochrane and Westlock in the 1983 election; it was only slightly less intense in Beaverlodge, Carstairs and Drayton Valley. If figures were available for 1974, 1977 and 1980, they would probably show large numbers of candidates in each election. On the other hand, Bruderheim, Irvine and Mayerthorpe are examples of councils with high turnover not because the community is politicized but because community members take turns performing three-year stints. The number of candidates is just enough to fill council.

Table 11.4 shows the turnover of council seats for cities. One would expect cities, which tend to have larger councils and even more heterogeneity than towns, to have many candidates and a high turnover in every election. There are substantial numbers of candi-

Table 11.3
Alberta Towns Having more than 50 per cent
Council Member Turnover, 1974-1983
(includes mayor)

Town	Number of Council Members	Number of Council Candidates, 1983	% Change			
			1974	1977	1980	1983
Beaverlodge	7	13	57	100	71	86
Bruderheim	7	8	100	66	86	57
Cardston	7	15	86	71	57	57
Carstairs	7	12	86	57	100	57
Cochrane	7	15	86	86	86	86
Drayton Valley	7	12	71	86	86	57
Irvine	7	7	71	86	57	86
Lacombe	7	10	57	57	57	57
Mayerthorpe	7	8	57	57	86	57
Turner Valley	7	9	80	100	71	71
Westlock	7	17	71	86	71	71

dates in most cities, but turnover tends to be relatively low for two reasons. First, city campaigns tend to be impersonal; hence, name familiarity gives an advantage to incumbents who, after all, have been in the news for three years. Second, in larger cities the mayor's position is regarded as full time and, although council positions are considered part time, some incumbents make the position a full-time career. With higher stakes involved, the incumbent is willing to devote more time and money to retaining a council position. Turnover usually takes place because an incumbent decides not to run rather than because of an electoral defeat.

Plebiscites

Plebiscites bring the citizenry directly into the policy-making process.[21] The first chapter pointed out that, from the standpoint of the individual citizen, the ideal way to make governmental decisions is to hold a community meeting where each citizen casts a single vote. But, except in the smallest communities, such direct democracy is unwieldy and impractical. The plebiscite, usually employed to decide the most crucial public-policy issues, is a form of direct democracy and, therefore, has the same theoretical underpinnings. David Butler

Table 11.4
Turnover of Council Members in Alberta Cities, 1977-1983
(includes mayor)

City*	Number of Council Members	Number of Council Candidates 1983	% Change 1977	1980	1983
Calgary	15	70	47	40	55
Camrose	9	17	67	44	44
Drumheller	7	18	57	29	57
Edmonton	13	60	46	31	46
Grande Prairie	9	19	33	89	56
Lethbridge	9	25	33	22	22
Medicine Hat	9	22	44	44	44
Red Deer	9	20	78	56	33
St. Albert	7	17	57	43	14
Wetaskiwin	7	8	43	29	29

*Fort McMurray underwent a change of status and therefore is not
  included.
Lloydminster's election data is not available.

and Austin Ranney, in an exhaustive study of referendums, state two basic propositions of popular government. They are: "(1) all political decisions should be as legitimate as possible, and (2) the highest degree of legitimacy is achieved by decisions made by the direct, unmediated vote of the people."[22] Discussing why the referendum leads to legitimacy in government, they write:

> People may or may not trust legislators . . . but they certainly
> trust themselves most of all. Hence a decision in which all have
> participated (or at least had a full opportunity to participate) is
> more legitimate in their eyes than one in which they have not
> participated. Moreover, decisions in which popular
> participation is direct and unmediated by others, as in
> referendums, produce more accurate expressions of their will

than do decisions in which they participate only by electing
others who make the decisions for them.[23]

Alberta's use of the plebiscite is a legacy of the American
Progressive's attempts, in the first quarter of the century, to root
political parties and special interests out of the political process by a
mechanism enabling the people to make public policy.[24] Butler and
Ranney's discussion of Progressive beliefs notes that they felt "even
popularly elected legislatures and municipal councils are bad because
they are so easily purchased by special interests and dominated by
party bosses."[25]

The Progressive's fervent rhetoric extolling the virtues of direct
democracy was well received, appearing just when special interest
groups and party machines almost completely controlled the policy-
making process in many American states and municipalities. The
Progressives used three different types of plebiscite to re-democratize
government: the initiative, the referendum, and the recall. The *initiative* enables anyone to draft a proposed law and, when a number of
people (usually three to five per cent of registered voters) sign a petition, the proposed legislation is placed on a ballot for the electorate's
approval or rejection. [26] If approved, it becomes law. The *referendum*
allows a legislature that has passed a measure to refer it to the electorate for approval before it becomes law. In such extraordinary cases as
a state constitutional amendment, the legislation must be submitted
to the electorate; in other cases, referral is discretionary. The *recall*, a
device allowing the electorate to remove a public official from office,
is similar to the initiative in that it is initiated by a petition signed by
three to five per cent of registered voters. The petition to remove trig-
gers a special election a short time after the petition requirement has
been satisfied, at which time the electorate determines whether the
official is to be removed.

Like a whirlwind sweeping across the United States, initiative and
referendum legislation was adopted by 17 primarily western American states between 1898 and 1912. In 1913 Alberta's Liberal government, with the tacit support of its Conservative opposition, enacted
an Act to Provide for the Initiation or Approval of Legislation by the
Electors, which introduced a restrictive use of the initiative and referendum; the Act remained in effect until 1958, when it was repealed.
The same year, the new charter of the City of Lethbridge provided a
mechanism for the recall of the city's mayor or commissioner. If 15
per cent of those who voted in the previous election signed a petition
calling for the removal of the mayor or commissioner, a recall election was to be called immediately.

The newly formed United Farmers of Alberta (UFA), coming to power in 1919 with a membership composed of, among others, adherents to the American Non-Partisan League and advocates of the American Progressive movement, brought with them other ideas furthering direct democracy in the province. The UFA soon developed its unique ideology, one tenet of which was the rejection of the political party as a means of governing. Although parties were not to be replaced by direct democracy, this stance provided a fertile environment for direct legislation that by-passed the party system. In 1921 the UFA's provincial platform endorsed "the principle of the initiative, referendum and recall."[27] However, a motion to legalize the recall, presented at the UFA's 1924 convention, was defeated. The recall did not revive as a political issue until 1935 when it was embodied into the theory of the new Social Credit Party, which also had a strong anti-party bias. C. B. Macpherson, discussing Social Credit's theory of representation and responsibility, writes:

> The only proclaimed line of responsibility was that by which elected members of the legislature were to be made recallable by their constituents. The social credit provision for recall
> . . . [was] by petition signed by a stated percentage of all the voters in the constituency. This was quite in keeping with, though not required by, the social credit notion of a conglomerate electorate in each constituency. It was also quite in keeping with the fact that it was not by the constituency association that the elected member had originally been chosen as the social credit candidate.[28]

In March of 1936, An Act Providing for the Recall of Members of the Legislative Assembly was passed. Shortly thereafter, a bizarre attempt was made to recall three members of the Calgary council. Five councillors elected in December, 1935, had run as official Social Credit candidates. Before they were allowed to run under the Social Credit banner, the Calgary Social Credit Association required them to sign a document stating that they would vote as a cohesive Social Credit bloc and espouse Social Credit principles in the administration of the city.[29] Shortly after they were elected, Premier Aberhart gave them sometimes written and sometimes verbal instructions on how to vote. They were to vote against any increase in municipal unemployment relief, against a request to the provincial government for a reduction in municipal debenture interest and against a council proposal to tax provincial businesses. In November, 1936, three of the five bolted, saying they would no longer take instructions from

Aberhart or the Calgary Social Credit Association; henceforth, they would represent not only Social Creditors but "all classes of citizens in council matters".[30] Within days the three were told that the constituency association would trigger a recall election unless they recanted. Unrepenting, they were expelled from the party and again threatened with recall, although the provincial Act had no provisions for the recall of municipal officials.

Unsuccessful in ousting recalcitrant Social Creditors in Calgary, the party shifted its focus to Taber, where the mayor was also a sitting Social Credit MLA. The constituency association, charging him with not adhering to Social Credit principles at the municipal level, wanted to recall him as mayor, but the legislation provided for recall only from the provincial assembly. However, in a close reading of the 1936 Recall Act, the association found the number of signatures it needed on a provincial recall petition was sixty-six and two-thirds per cent "of the total number of voters who were upon the voters' list" in the constituency. Since it was almost impossible to collect that number of signatures, the association presented a resolution to the legislature to substantially reduce the number of signatures the Act required. The mayor of Taber also eluded attempts by "true" Social Creditors to discredit him through a recall election.

The attempts to use the recall to punish dissident Social Creditors quickly ceased in the summer of 1937, when a coalition of Liberals and Conservatives in Premier Aberhart's district of Okotoks-High River made an attempt to recall him. In October, 1937, the Act was quietly repealed and the repeal was made retroactive to April 3, 1936, to ensure that the attempt to recall the Premier was doomed to failure.

As the initiative and referendum became accepted as legitimate at the provincial level, direct democracy provisions were incorporated into legislation pertaining to policy making by local units of government. Today, plebiscite provisions are found in the Municipal Government Act, the Municipal Election Act, the School Act, the School Election Act and the Lord's Day Act.

Since education funds constitute a sizeable percentage of municipal expenditures (in the sense that school authorities requisition the municipalities for their funds) there are provisions in the School Act that allow the citizenry to intervene directly in the policy-making process. Under section 111, the board of trustees is given extensive power to finance major capital projects, such as erecting new buildings, adding to existing buildings and furnishing and equipping them, through the sale of long-term debentures. When the board decides upon such an action, it is required to give public notice of its intent. This is to allow any objector to submit a petition within 15 days calling for a vote on the issue.[31] If 10 per cent of the electors vote and a majority opposes an action, the board is bound by the decision for 12 months. The same procedure applies if a board decides to build or purchase at considerable cost a school building for non-educational use. Section 58 of the Act allows the electors of a separate school district to dissolve itself, either by having the board submit the question to the electorate or by 25 per cent of the electors filing a petition calling for an election on the issue. If a majority opt for dissolution the Minister of Education is bound by the vote to dissolve the board. Finally, the Minister is given broad powers under section 2 of the School Election Act to call for a plebiscite in a school district on "any matter or question specified by him."

Equally broad powers of direct intervention by the citizenry are found in section 324 of the Municipal Government Act. If a council passes a by-law creating long-term debt (not payable within the current year) it must have a copy of the by-law published in the municipality's newspaper at least once a week for two consecutive weeks.[32] If within 15 days of the by-law's last publication a petition[33] is filed with the municipal secretary for a plebiscite, the council must submit it to the proprietary electors for approval.

A much broader use of the plebiscite is found in section 125 of the Municipal Government Act which gives the electorate the right to submit by petition to council "a by-law dealing with any matter within its legislative jurisdiction."[34] The council is required to give the proposed by-law a first reading. Then the proposed by-law must be published within four weeks of the petition and a plebiscite is to be scheduled thereafter. If a majority of the electorate vote in favour of the by-law, council is required to give it third and final reading within four weeks.

Although the direct democracy provisions of the Act are crystal clear, in the late 1970s the Edmonton council twice refused to comply; each case went to court and the city lost. After the council voted itself a 60 per cent salary increase in December, 1977, a popular media personality, Fil Fraser, led a plebiscite petition campaign against the increase. Although more than enough names were secured to force the plebiscite, the council ignored the petition, maintaining that its actions were administrative rather than legislative and, thus, not subject to plebiscite. The *Edmonton Journal* forced the issue to court, where the city lost.[35] The council again ignored a plebiscite petition in 1979 when a group of citizens, incensed over the skyrocketing costs of a convention centre under construction, collected more than enough signatures to fulfill the legal qualifications.[36] Taken to court, the city was forced to hold a plebiscite.[37]

A major criticism of the plebiscite is that it short-circuits the established system of representative democracy. The argument goes that the more the citizenry turns to plebiscites the more reticent elected representatives will become in making controversial decisions. The result is a loss of respect for the legislative body so that competent and respected members of the community are less inclined to seek public office. But legislators have been much relieved by mandatory referral provisions in both the Alberta Lord's Day Act and the Public Health Act. The issues of Sunday openings and water fluoridation, which can completely polarize Alberta communities, have become "no-win" situations for legislators.

Under the 1907 federal Lord's Day Act virtually all activities, except the worship of the Lord, are prohibited between midnight Saturday and midnight Sunday. There is, however, a provincial "opt out" provision, which Alberta adopted by enacting the Alberta Lord's Day Act. In essence, the provincial Act allows municipalities to "opt out" of the federal act and permit Sunday attendance at movies, games, sports, lectures, cultural exhibitions, etc. A council can pass or amend a by-law providing for these activities but, after its second reading, it must be published in the community's newspaper for two consecutive weeks. If within 15 days the council receives a petition requesting a plebiscite (which is binding) it must comply. If a council is unwilling to pass or amend an Alberta Lord's Day Act there are provisions in the Act for the electorate to pass, amend and repeal it. Interestingly, the petition requirements are lower than the comparable ones under section 125 of the Municipal Government Act. Under the Lord's Day Act a petition has to be signed by at least 10 per cent of the municipality's electorate or 2,000 residents, whichever is less. After the petition is presented, council must give the proposed by-law a first and second reading and publish it in the community's newspaper for two consecutive weeks. If a second petition requesting that the electorate be given the right to vote on the by-law is not received within 15 days of the newspaper's last publication of the by-law, the council must give it a third reading and pass it. If a second petition is received within the requisite time, the electorate determines whether it shall become law. It is important to note that a Sunday by-law can be repealed only by plebiscite.

The Public Health Act gives a municipal council the power to give first and second reading to a by-law to fluoridate the community's water supply, but it must be referred to the electorate for approval before it receives third and final reading. If the electorate defeats fluoridation, the council is prohibited from initiating another fluoridation by-law for two years. In like manner, the council can terminate a fluoridation program only with the electorate's approval.

More recently, in Edmonton and Calgary, the referendum has been used to block fiscal policies rather than to initiate innovative policies. In the late 1970s a segment of the electorate made up of blue-collar workers and retired people on fixed incomes were becoming increasingly concerned by a decade of high inflation. They had been unable to muster support federally or provincially to curb government spending or increased taxation. Although property taxes in both cities were among the lowest in North America, this segment turned to the plebiscite. This tax revolt initiated plebiscite petitions in 1977 and 1978 to roll back substantial council wage increases in the two cities. The same frustrated members of the electorate collected enough signatures to force plebiscites on a massive $234 million downtown redevelopment project in Calgary and a $32 million convention centre in Edmonton. In each city the business community and civic boosters countered by spending well over $100,000 in highly professional campaigns. Nevertheless, by a razor-slim margin of 1,800 votes, Calgary's electorate voted down the redevelopment project. In Edmonton 63 per cent of the electorate, primarily from the city's middle-class polls, supported the convention centre. Elated boosters on city council embarked on a program to build a new $240 million city hall. Yet another grass-roots plebiscite campaign was launched and the electorate voted the city hall plan down. In both cities those who circulated petitions calling for plebiscites had little money, but mobilized broadly based grass-roots organizations to campaign door-to-door during both the petition and election campaigns.[38]

During these campaigns a study was carried out to determine why people signed the plebiscite petitions.[39] An examination of Table 11.5 shows that, in both cities, only a minority of the citizenry who signed the petitions were "tax-cutters." More importantly, 44 per cent of respondents in Edmonton and 54 per cent in Calgary were not opposed to the projects but thought the issue was so important that the electorate, rather than their elected representatives, should make the decision. In both cities, although blue-collar workers and the retired initiated the plebiscite petitions and worked in the electoral campaigns, the socio-economic characteristics of those who signed plebiscite petitions were little different from those of the general population.[40]

The results of the 1979 survey clearly indicate that support for using the plebiscite to make public policy is by no means restricted to tax-cutters. However, rather than encouraging the citizenry to use the plebiscite to provide citizens with a new perspective on policy making, within two years after the Calgary and Edmonton plebiscite elections the provincial government made it much more difficult to initiate plebiscites. At the 1979 annual meeting of the Alberta Urban Municipalities Association (AUMA), which came on the heels of the two cities' plebiscites, a recommendation was made to the Minister of Municipal Affairs to make it much more difficult to trigger a plebiscite election.[41] The government responded, in 1981, by substantially increasing the number of signatures needed to initiate a plebiscite and by stipulating that a petition for a plebiscite to amend or repeal a by-law had to be received by council within 60 days of the by-law's passage. Taken together, these two provisions may leave the structure of direct democracy intact, but they strip it of much of its substance.

Table 11.5
Reasons for Signing Plebiscite Petitions in Calgary and Edmonton (in per cent)

Reason for Signing	Edmonton	Calgary
Not opposed to project; wanted to show dissatisfaction with city government	11	11
Not opposed to project; think it should be put to a vote (some respondents also wished to show dissatisfaction with city hall)	44	55
Opposed to project for fiscal reasons	35	26
Don't Know	11	8
TOTALS	101%	100%

When the advantages and disadvantages of using plebiscites to make public policy and to further grass-roots democracy are weighed, the scale favours the plebiscite. The plebiscite's opponents are able to make a number of convincing arguments for its abolition. They point to the additional municipal expense involved in holding a special plebiscite election. They point to the plebiscite's frequent low voting turnout, arguing that it indicates that a vocal and politically active minority, rather than all of the community's members, makes public policy. They point to plebiscite elections with complex issues that are difficult to comprehend and argue that plebiscite outcomes often reflect the policies of an ill-informed electorate. Finally, they argue that the plebiscite short-circuits representative, democratic policy making. But, when these criticisms are weighed against the advantages of a mechanism that allows the citizenry to have a direct input into the policy-making process and to make grass-roots democracy work in the larger municipality as well as the smaller one, then clearly the use of the plebiscite should be expanded rather than restricted or abolished.

Notes

1. Another common name for this system of representation is "first past the post."

2. An even more striking example can be seen in the 1980 electoral results from Edmonton's ward four. It should be noted that Edmonton has two-member wards, which means that each voter marks two names on the ballot and the two candidates who receive the most votes are elected. It can easily be seen that the two winners represented only a minority of those voting in the ward. (Asterisk indicates the winning councillors.)

	Votes	Percentage		Votes	Percentage
Aiello	467	2.4	*Norris	3550	18.4
Bird	260	1.3	Nutter	3393	17.6
Broad	817	4.2	Patsula	2172	11.2
Eastcott	1490	7.7	Wasnea	1190	6.1
Meier	2486	12.9	*Wright	3461	17.9

3. Rae, *The Political Consequences of Electoral Laws*, 86.

4. For example, in a three-member constituency in which 600 votes are cast, the quota formula is [votes ÷ (members + 1)] + 1, i.e., [600 ÷ (3 + 1)] + 1, or 151.

5. An example would be candidate E in a five-man race in a three-member constituency, who received 200 votes, when the number needed to win, the quota, is set at 151. Candidates who were listed second on ballots cast for candidate E would receive part of a vote for each such ballot; i.e., (votes cast for E - quota) ÷ votes cast for E, or (200-151) ÷ 200 = 49/200 of a vote (for rounding purposes, one quarter of a vote). If candidate B and candidate C were each chosen second on 100 of candidate E's ballots, then 25 votes would be transferred to each one.

6. An example would be a five-man race in a three-member constituency, in which Candidate D, with the fewest first preference votes (the one to be dropped from the list), has 35 first preference votes. On these 35 first preference ballots candidate A is listed second preference on 20 of the ballots and candidate B on 15 of them. Twenty votes would be transfered to candidate A and 15 to candidate B.

7. For a detailed discussion of proportional representation and the single

transferable vote system see Mackenzie, *Free Elections*, 61-84.

8. *Edmonton Bulletin*, December 12, 1923.

9. *Edmonton Bulletin*, December 14, 1927.

10. *Edmonton Bulletin*, December 13, 1927.

11. There are two other provisions in the Act that allow the return of candidates' deposits. Under section 30(3) "If a candidate dies before the closing of the voting stations on election day, the sum deposited by him shall be returned to his estate." Section 30(2)(c) states that the deposit will be returned to a candidate who, "withdraws his name as a candidate in accordance with Section 32." Section 32 states, "if more than the required number of candidates . . . are nominated, any person . . . may, at any time within 24 hours after the close of the nomination period, withdraw his name as a candidate for the office for which he was nominated by filing with the returning officer a withdrawal in writing."

12. *Alberta Report*, October 17, 1980.

13. An important exception applies in summer villages. Section 11(1)(b) of The Local Authorities Election Act states:

> A person is entitled to vote at an election if he is:
>
> i. a proprietary elector of the summer village who is at least 18 years old,
>
> ii. at least 18 years old and the spouse of a proprietary elector of the summer village, or
>
> iii. at least 18 years old and not entitled to vote under sub-clause (i) or (ii) but is a Canadian citizen and has resided in Alberta for the 6 consecutive months immediately preceding election day and resides in the summer village on election day, but only an elector who is a resident of the summer village is entitled to vote at an election for school representatives.

14. In section 1 of the Municipal Government Act a "proprietary elector" is defined as:

> i. an elector whose name appears on the assessment roll in respect of land liable to assessment and taxation for general municipal purposes, and
>
> ii. an elector who is liable for the payment of a mobile unit license.

15. The section reads as follows: "(1) Notwithstanding anything in this or any other Act, a council may, by by-law, authorize all electors of the municipality to petition and vote on a specific by-law or on all by-laws requiring the assent of the proprietary electors. (2) When a council passes a

by-law pursuant to subsection (1), all references to proprietary electors in this or the Municipal Election Act shall, in relation to petitioning and voting on by-laws, be deemed to refer to and to include all electors."

16. *Lethbridge Herald*, April 25, 1983.

17. *Alberta Report*, September 19, 1980.

18. Shapcott, "Calgary: Pre-election Money Madness," , 7-8.

19. *Calgary Herald*, March 18, 1982.

20. Election by acclamation is discussed in section 34 of the Local Authorities Election Act. "(1) When at the close of nominations the number of persons nominated for any office is the same as the number required to be elected, the returning officer shall declare the persons nominated to be elected to the offices for which they were nominated."

21. For the purpose of this discussion the terms "plebiscite" and "referendum" are used interchangeably; however, some scholars have made a distinction between the two, noting that "plebiscite" is a much older term dating back to the fourth century B.C., while "referendum" did not appear until the seventeenth century. The Nazis used national "plebiscites" to justify their policies while the twentieth-century American reformers preferred to use the term "referendum."

22. Butler and Ranney, *Referendums*, 24.

23. *Ibid.*, 25.

24. However, it is important to note that the use of the plebiscite in Canada pre-dates the American Progressive movement, for example, the Canada Temperance Act of 1878 provided for the prohibition of retail liquor sales by local option. "This meant that the Act as passed in the regular way by Parliament was to go into force in a county or city if and when there was a favourable vote in that county or city under voting procedures provided for by the Act. In these circumstances, the electors of a county or city were confined to accepting or rejecting as a whole the statutory package of rules already fully determined by Parliament."Boyer, *Lawmaking by the People*, 26.

25. Butler and Ranney, *Referendums*, 29.

26. In the United States, voters must register before voting.

27. UFA, *Annual Report*, 1920, quoted in Macpherson, *Democracy in Alberta*, 71.

28. Macpherson, *Democracy in Alberta*, 162.

29. *Calgary Daily Herald*, December 2, 1936.

30. *Calgary Daily Herald*, November 30, 1936.

31. Section 113(1) of the Act states that the petition must be signed by at least:

   a. 2% of the electors in a district or division having 10,000 electors or more,

b. 5% of the electors in a district or division having less than 10,000 but 5,000 electors or more,

c. 10% of the electors in a district or division having less than 5,000 but 500 electors or more, or

d. 15% of the electorate in a district or division having less that 500 electors.

32. Councils have an escape clause in section 328 of the Municipal Government Act, which states that if the capital debt to be incurred is to be repaid in three years and "yearly payments of principal and interest . . . do not exceed . . . 5 mills" it does not require the approval of the proprietary electors.

33. Under section 324(3) of the Act the petition must be signed by: "(a) 5% of the population of a municipality . . . having a population of 1000 or more persons, or (b) 10% of the population of a municipality . . . having a population of less than 1000 persons."

34. Under section 125(2)(a) and (b) of the Act the minimum number of electors who sign the petition must be: "5% of the population of a municipality . . . having a population of 1000 or more . . . 10% of the population of a municipality . . . having a population of less that 1000."

35. *O'Callaghan v. Edmonton.*

36. In 1979 the Act read that only 3 per cent of the electors had to sign a petition to call for a plebiscite. The opponents of the direct democracy provision in the Act managed to convince the government to increase the minimum number of signatures needed to 5 per cent in 1981.

37. *Ewasiuk v. Edmonton.*

38. In contrast, the well-financed "Go Calgary" organization, established to extoll the virtues of downtown redevelopment, had almost no grass-roots support. "Thousands of buttons and posters were produced, but Go Calgary insiders report many were never distributed because there was not a network set up for that purpose." *Alberta Report*, December 7, 1979

39. Masson, "Some Preliminary Findings on the Plebiscite Petitions."

40. *Ibid.*, 12.

41. The attitude of municipal representatives is summed up by Edmonton councillor Bettie Hewes who said that citizens had a right to petition against capital spending projects but questioned "the wisdom of the provincial government act that allows them to do so." *Alberta Report*, June 5, 1981. Interestingly, this was said after the costs of the convention centre in

Edmonton had ballooned from $32 million to $90 million. It was the soaring of costs from $22 million to $32 million that had sparked the plebiscite campaign in the first place.

12

THE FUTURE

The Futurists

Social scientists attempting to predict the future of local government
are not much different from medieval soothsayers who attempted to
predict the future of the kingdom; both rely on social trends liberally
mixed with an active imagination. Sometimes the predictions are extremely accurate; at other times, totally inaccurate. Despite the pitfalls, such predictions are worthwhile as they provide a focus for
long-range policy proposals.

Today the "futurists," as they like to be called, develop "scenarios"
for policy makers. Suppose a municipality is interested in developing
long-range policy to promote stable economic growth. The futurist
might provide one scenario based on encouraging a heavy industry to
locate in the community, another based on developing tourism, and
yet another based on developing the community as a market centre.
In each case the futurist would predict increases in population, per
capita income and costs of governmental services, and attempt to anticipate social and technological changes. The policy makers are then
able to choose a scenario and formulate policies for moving the community in that direction. A major difficulty with scenarios is anticipating pertinent social and technological factors.

Some futurists base their predictions *solely* on past trends. In 1976
the Ministry of State for Urban Affairs commissioned John Kettle to
predict urban forms and social patterns to the year 2000. Following is
a portion of his scenario.

> About 1984 it first came to national notice that there were rival
> gangs of squatters in empty houses—and even in a large

348

apartment building abandoned by its landlord. . . . What started with looting and some vandalism soon turned to gangsterism. Those involved were long term unemployed, people pushed out of their resource industry jobs, people who could not survive in small villages that had depopulated below a viable level. The fierce gang war that wrecked downtown Chicoutimi occurred in the spring of 1985. . . . So far the troubles have been confined to depopulating cities and a few smaller places that were losing people quite rapidly. But many small towns have had to raise taxes for much larger security forces and special squatter squads, which in turn has caused some residents to move out and so make the problem worse. . . . In the countryside, of course, it's everyone for oneself; you may get your corporation to put in floodlights, hot wire sirens, and outside scanners. . . . Since 1981 the number of households has jumped by more than half while the population has grown by less than 20 per cent. The family can no longer be thought of as the typical unit, though of course there are still more family than non-family households in the 12,600,000 total. . . . There are reliable estimates that a third of the cohabiting couples under thirty are unmarried . . . at the bottom of the pyramid [social class structure] there was an uncomfortable gap where there should have been new workers coming in. Those who did come were pampered, overpaid, too conscious of their scarcity value, not keen to do the dirty work.[1]

John Kettle made a straight-line projection of social and economic trends: crime rate, birth rate, inter-urban migration, rural-urban migration and employment. Are Kettle's predictions accurate? Certainly his predictions for the early 1980s are completely erroneous. He made the mistake of extrapolating short-term social disorganization statistics of the late 1960s and early 1970s to long-range predictions.[2] Since this futurist made one critical error in judgment his other predictions must be examined carefully and charily. If Kettle had made his projections in 1890, taking them forward to the year 1940, he undoubtedly would have predicted that a sizeable percentage of the population in urban areas would travel by streetcar while in smaller towns the horse population would soon approach the size of the human population. Finally, the very small communities across Canada would be thriving.

An example of the way in which technology can change life-styles and population trends is advances in birth control, particularly the pill. In the past, large families were the norm; today, the large family is regarded as a curiosity. If a trend theorist of the 1940s had projected family size forward to the year 2000 the population estimates would have been much too high.[3] Such theorists do not anticipate technological breakthroughs that shake the social and economic structure of society and move it in entirely new directions.

Other futurists, almost completely disregarding social and economic trends, attempt to anticipate social upheavals caused by technological change. This is a "chancy" approach at best. Forty years ago, who could have foreseen a television in almost every home, with its impact on family structure, retailing, the selection of political candidates and the nature of political campaigns? Yet today one can see glimmers of a technology that has the potential of creating major urban change. For example, it is possible to build a self-contained living unit that produces its own power and completely recycles its own waste products. If the cost of such a unit were to become competitive it would have major ramifications on the spatial development of metropolitan areas. With living units no longer tied to electricity, water and trunk sewer lines, housing would become even more decentralized than it is today. "Tele-shopping," which radically updates the mail-order catalogue by allowing consumers to use television to shop, is now in its infancy. If it becomes widespread the end may be near for many traditional retail stores. Still, only a small number of futurists dealing with technological change are taken seriously by policy makers, perhaps because much of their work tends to be little more than glorified science fiction.

Although both kinds of prediction, that which anticipates technological breakthroughs and that which analyses trends, are fraught with pitfalls, more and more communities are relying on a combination of the two as a tool to formulate long-range policy goals. Policy makers attempt to anticipate birth rates and migration trends in planning new educational facilities. If accurate estimates are made of population growth, municipalities can build trunk sewer lines to service future populations rather than continually reacting to population pressures by replacing serviceable lines that are much too small every few years. With accurate population projections and innovative planning it is possible to stage growth in the community and to induce growth in certain areas and inhibit it in others. In addition, transportation needs can be determined and tremendous savings made by buying and reserving transportation corridor lands. Since planning and futurists' projections are inextricably linked, both must work together to anticipate changes in trends as well as technological advances. Thus, future estimates can be changed and community plans revised.

The 1980s: Reversal of a Trend

Alberta's sea of oil moved the province from an economy dominated by agriculture in 1940 to one dominated by oil, from discovery and re-fining to distillation. From 1947, when oil was discovered at Leduc, until 1971 the population of the province doubled, with the greatest growth occurring in the large cities. Migrants flocked in from the east for the economic opportunities offered by the buoyant economy. In 1980 Premier Lougheed said, "We have a province where almost half of our labour force is employed directly or indirectly, by the petro-leum industry."[4] With business and construction booming and public sector employment increasing every year, there was a shift in the composition of the labour force as a large professional and manage-rial class developed. When the Organization of Petroleum Exporting Countries (OPEC) flexed its muscles in 1973, raising its oil prices 70 per cent, and then kept raising prices every several months there-after, the oil-based Alberta economy was supercharged. Labour re-cruiters fanned out across eastern Canada seeking workers who found in Alberta skyrocketing housing prices and rental vacancies that, at one time dropped to less than one-tenth of one per cent in Ed-monton and Calgary.

Commencing in 1980, a series of events made the Alberta economy begin to falter and migration begin to slow. Even the most percipient futurist would have had difficulty predicting any single event, let alone the confluence of events, that changed the direction of the pro-vincial economy. A federal National Energy Policy capping Alberta oil prices, American interest rates forcing up Canadian rates and pinching off business spending, and a stabilization of oil prices all sent Alberta's undiversified oil economy into a nosedive. In 1981 and 1982 drilling companies either went bankrupt or moved their rigs to the United States. As unemployment mounted, business and residen-tial foreclosures escalated. Then, in the late spring of 1982, the $13 billion Alsands Project was cancelled and the $43 billion Alaskan gas pipeline project was put on hold. Fort McMurray was devasted, hav-ing planned for an additional 4,400 workers. The Alberta Housing Corporation, in conjunction with the city's administration halted the partially completed development of a giant housing tract that was to serve 45,000 new residents. By the spring of 1982, Calgary downtown land prices had dropped as much as 50 per cent in six months.

In the latter half of 1983 an end could be seen to the drift of the provincial economy. In early July the energy minister announced that $1.2 billion would be spent over five years to expand the Syn-crude plant at Fort McMurray. Two thousand jobs would be created at the peak of construction and 400 permanent workers would be employed in the new addition. Petro-Canada and BP Exploration announced a plan to develop an oil extraction project near Bonnyville that would employ 450 construction workers and a permanent work force of 200. Shell Canada announced that it was considering an oil extraction plant in Peace River if the technology could be worked out and the world oil market stabilized. Although the Alberta economy is expected to improve somewhat by the last quarter of 1984 or the first quarter of 1985, it will be many years before municipalities will have the almost unlimited funds they had in the 1970s. Thus, although the halcyon growth of the 1960s and 1970s cannot be ignored, it needs to be heavily discounted when predictions are made.

Population Trends

In 1975 it was projected that Calgary would have a 273 per cent population increase between 1971 and 2001: 642,500 by 1986, and 955,900 by 2001. It was estimated that Edmonton would also continue its high rate of growth, reaching a population of 898,800 by 2001.[5] Shortly after this projection was made, a super-heated economy led to a provincial population growth of approximately 4 per cent a year from 1977 through the first quarter of 1982. Population soared in Calgary, with 5.6 per cent increases in both 1980 and 1981; Edmonton's figures for the same years were 3.1 and 2.9 per cent. Then, when the economy lurched and wallowed in 1982 and 1983, the provincial increase dropped to 2.4 per cent in 1982. Edmonton's population growth slowed to 1.6 per cent (8,771 people) in the 1982-83 period and Calgary showed a decrease of 0.4 per cent (2,441 people) in the same period, the first time in the city's history that there had been a decrease. Moreover, during the summer of 1983, there were indications that the slight decline in Calgary's population was only the precursor of a general provincial decline. While there was a 17 per cent decline in the volume of household goods moved in Canada in the first six months of 1983 by the country's five largest van lines, the decline of goods moved into Alberta from outside the province was 43 per cent. The Edmonton offices of two of the largest van lines "estimated they were seeing 10 moves out of Alberta for each one in"; another van line spokesperson and the owner of a U-Haul agency estimated six to seven families were leaving the province for each one moving in.[6]

Although many of Alberta's smallest communities that serve as market centres for agricultural areas had little or no growth during the province's period of explosive growth, others that either service oil activity or are bedroom communities for the two major cities have experienced phenomenal growth. The Town of Airdrie, just north of Calgary, with a population of 1,414 in 1976 increased by almost 500 per cent to 8,414 by 1981 and, despite Calgary's slowdown, leaped to 9,981 in 1982. Another Calgary bedroom community, Cochrane, increased 138 per cent to 3,544 between 1976 and 1981. Edmonton's outlying communities also grew substantially although less spectacularly. Stony Plain jumped 69 per cent and Morinville 121 per cent in the same period. Oil and gas activity boosted Brooks by 47 per cent from 6,387 in 1976 to 9,421 in 1981; growth sagged to 8,060 in 1982 when oil activity dried up. The same thing happened in Grande Prairie, where the population increased 37 per cent between 1976 and 1981 and then abruptly stopped growing. Red Deer, with its exceptionally strong economy, is another city where population increase has begun to weaken. For some time the city benefited from Premier Lougheed's policy of economic decentralization and, more recently by the construction of three world-scale petrochemical plants at an estimated cost of $1.5 billion. Construction for the three projects commenced in late 1980 and, at its peak, employed 3,000 workers who pumped an estimated additional $3 million a week into the city's economy. Between 1980 and 1981 the population increased 10 per cent, then 7 per cent between 1981 and 1982, and 3.5 per cent between 1982 and 1983. With the construction phase of the large plants winding down in 1983 and the general weakening of the provincial economy in the second half of 1983, population began to level off and it is unlikely the city will ever repeat its rapid growth.

Some people have moved from smaller Alberta communities into Edmonton and Calgary; however, in the last two decades it has been migrants from other large Canadian urban centres who have been responsible for the substantial growth of the province's two metropolises.[7] Immigrants from other countries have had little effect on Alberta's population; they tend to settle in Montreal, Toronto and Vancouver. In the most recent period these three cities accounted for 70 per cent of foreign immigrants settling in Canada's 21 largest cities.

Natural population increases in recent times have been more important than foreign immigration in accounting for Canada's increasing population. For example, in the 1951-61 period, foreign immigration was 1,081,000 while the country's natural population increase was 3,148,000. In the 1961-71 period the natural increase was 2,592,000 while immigration accounted for 738,000. The rate of natural increase is exceedingly important for smaller Alberta communities outside the shadow of Edmonton and Calgary since it accounts for more than 80 per cent of their growth. Very few foreign immigrants settle in smaller communities and few people moving into the province settle in very small communities. Today, the fertility rate is so low in Canada that with zero migration the population would be unable to replace itself.[8] If this trend continues it will have an adverse effect on the small communities.

Unlike birth rates, Canadian mortality rates have consistently declined since records started to be kept. During the twentieth century, public health programs have reduced infant mortality and have practically eliminated fatal communicable diseases. Only recently has the downward trend in the mortality rate begun to level out as accidents and chronic disorders have become the principal causes of death.

With a decrease in both fertility and mortality rates, the Canadian population is beginning to age. While the median age is approaching 27 years, it is expected to increase to 35 years by the mid-1990s. Hence, it is reasonable to predict that communities will be spending less on youth and more on the middle-aged and the elderly. Spending on education will become less sacrosanct. With an older population it is likely that recreational spending will begin to shift from hockey to more sedate sports, such as lawn bowling, and to craft classes. If the present pattern of crime continues, as the median age of the population shifts upward, there will be a decrease in most crime categories. This factor should result in a substantial redeployment of municipal funds now spent on policing.

It would seem that the most important factors in structuring future municipal policy choices are the slowing in population growth and economic activity in the 1980s. Slower growing and declining populations are of even greater concern to city halls than they are to community business boosters. Municipalities depend on many per capita conditional grants, which become an integral part of the municipal budgeting process. When Calgary showed a net decrease in population instead of a predicted 20,000 increase, the budgetary process was thrown into a tailspin. For example, the transportation operating grants, based on a $9.50 per capita formula, dropped to $5.9 million instead of growing to an anticipated $6.18 million. The city opted to take its 1982 and 1983 provincial Major Cultural Recreational (MCR) grant in 1981 and, on the basis of a substantial projected increase in population, budgeted for an additional $2.3 million in grant money it expected to receive in 1983. With a shortfall in population and its per capita MCR grant, community association recreation funding was cut. Of more importance for the future is that, by 1983, Calgary had incurred a long-term debt in excess of $1 billion, with debt servicing charges in excess of $100 million annually. When the long-term debt began to mount, there was little concern, for the city expected to continue its explosive population and economic growth and the associated increase in city revenue. Now, with stagnant population and economic growth, coupled with a heavy debt and annual servicing charges, it is safer to predict that the city's revenue policy and policy in all service areas will be much different in the 1980s than it had been in the two previous decades.

Calgary is not an isolated example, nor is the problem restricted to larger cities. In the spring of 1983 Edmonton's general manager in the city's financial department said that, in planning for the 1983 budget, the city estimated that it would collect $167 million in tax revenue. However, because of a "stagnant assessment base" the city had come to expect to collect only $164 million.[9] At approximately the same time, the Red Deer city treasurer announced that $2,316,000 in 1982 commercial, industrial and residential property taxes had been unpaid at the end of the year. This figure was 11 per cent of the total 1982 property taxes and double the unpaid taxes in 1981.[10]

The Town of Stony Plain and the Village of Plamondon were in dire financial straits in 1983, difficulties caused by earlier municipal policies that assumed uninterrupted population and economic growth. In 1980 Stony Plain embarked on an ambitious plan to develop two industrial parks. With the downturn in the economy the project faltered and, in the fall of 1983, the town found itself with a $12.4 million debt including a $800,000 1983 deficit. To reduce the fiscal hemorrhaging, the council made substantial cuts in services and enacted fiscal conservation measures. Municipal salaries were frozen, the mayor and councillors' salaries were reduced by 20 per cent, and 12 of the town's 37 full-time employees were laid off. Substantial spending cuts were made on outdoor rinks and parks; business licenses were increased; and sewer and water rates increased 10 per cent. Despite this austerity program, the mayor announced that property taxes would have to be increased 47.7 per cent for 1984.[11] The Village of Plamondon (1982 population, 271) was encouraged in 1980 to upgrade its water and sewer system by a developer who proposed a 40-lot subdivision to house Fort McMurray workers. At the insistence of Alberta Environment a $1.2 million water and sewage system was built to handle 1,000 people. The village's share of the cost was to be $250,000, to be shared by the developer. However, the village council failed to obtain an agreement from the developer before starting the project and, with the cancellation of the Fort McMurray project, the developer vanished. The developer's failure to share the cost, combined with a substantial cost overrun, left the village with a $405,738 long-term debt and annual debenture payments of $60,220 for 22 years. In 1982 property taxes were increased 60 per cent with no end to further increases in sight. Although roads in the municipality are unpaved and recreational facilities nonexistent, in 1983 the property tax on a basic five-year old bungalow was $2,000, 75 per cent higher than the tax on an equivalent property in Edmonton. Rather than raise taxes in 1983 the mayor and council resigned and the village's administration was taken over by the Department of Municipal Affairs. The inspector who took over the village's financial affairs commented on its fiscal plight: "unless more money gets injected, I don't think they'll ever get out—except for higher taxes and I feel taxes are too high now. There's just no light at the end of the tunnel."[12]

The president of the Alberta Urban Municipalities Association has said there is no simple explanation for the recent financial plight of so many Alberta municipalities. He notes that some were lured into a "false sense of security" by the one-time, $500 per capita grant to municipalities in 1979, while others expected the high funding levels of the 1970s to continue through the 1980s. Instead, the government abolished street assistance and housing incentive grants and made cuts in other grant programs. With the province's economic downturn it became clear that many municipalities had been inefficiently managed during the buoyant 1970s and had paid overly high prices for everything, managed their investments poorly, ignored the low productivity of their municipal employees, and settled wage disputes quickly and expensively. Other municipalities hired poorly trained people while others provided little or no incentive for municipal employees to upgrade their qualifications, all of which led to poor morale and low productivity.[13]

The Fiscal Crisis and Remedies for the Future

Common sense dictates that a municipality's financial capability determines whether policies can be successfully carried out. An earlier discussion of the property tax indicated that it is one of the culprits in constraining a municipality's capabilities. Most Alberta municipalities have some of the lowest property taxes in North America; however, the province has recently eliminated interest shielding on debenture borrowing and this factor, combined with the fact that increases in provincial grants have lagged behind the overall rate of inflation, has placed greater fiscal pressure on municipalities.[14] In 1983, with the provincial government limiting increases in unconditional grants to five per cent, municipalities had to make substantial property tax increases even though they also made substantial cuts in services. For example, in 1983 tax increases in Medicine Hat were 9.5 per cent, in Calgary 9.4 per cent, in Fort MacLeod 8.5 per cent, and in Grande Prairie 7.7 per cent, with large increases promised in coming years.

There are two alternative fiscal futures for Alberta municipalities: either they will become merely administrative conduits for policies made by the provincial government or they will become viable units controlled by their residents. If the provincial government has a commitment to strong municipal government and grass-roots democracy, it must devise innovative means for municipalities to become much more fiscally self-sufficient. In the past, the provincial government has had a far greater commitment to fiscally sound and viable municipalities than it has today. Until the very end of the Social Credit regime, one-third of the revenue from the previous year's provincial oil and gas royalties was given to municipalities in unconditional grants. This policy was terminated in the spring of 1971 and, when the Progressive Conservatives came to power in the summer, no thought was given to re-establishing this revenue-sharing formula.

Convention after convention of the Alberta Urban Municipalities Association (AUMA) passes resolutions requesting the provincial government to increase unconditional grants. In 1981 a different tack was taken when an AUMA advisory committee to the Minister of Municipal Affairs recommended increasing the gasoline tax eight per cent at the pump and distributing the revenue to municipalities as an unconditional grant on a per capita basis. With the Minister's tacit support, a gasoline tax motion was brought to the convention floor, where it failed by a vote of two to one. The larger municipalities tended to support the resolution, the smaller ones opposed it. Delegates then proposed that municipalities be given eight per cent of the provincial government's oil and gas revenue for five years. The Minister rejected the proposal, explaining: "There just isn't a whole bunch of money lying around. The fund [Heritage Savings Trust Fund] is asset-rich and cash poor."[15] However, somewhat later the Minister suggested that if the AUMA should reverse its position and support an increase in the gasoline tax, the government might consider such a policy.[16] Since 1981 little has been heard about using a portion of the gasoline tax to fund municipalities.

In the early spring of 1983, Strathcona County's chief commissioner thought he had found a painless way for local governments in Alberta to raise funds for capital projects while maintaining a modicum of independence from the provincial government. Taking his cues from municipal bond financing in the United States, he proposed that the federal government allow municipalities to sell municipal bonds on which the interest would be tax free to private investors. Since the bonds would be tax free, municipalities would be able to sell them (borrow money) at substantially lower rates of interest than the market rate. With the endorsement of the provincial Minister of Municipal Affairs the proposal was sent to federal Finance Minister Marc Lalonde who responded non-committally, saying: "any comments or response . . . would only involve further speculation by the press as to what is or is not in the forthcoming budget."[17]

There are two reasons federal legislation allowing municipal tax free bonds is unlikely. First, the federal government would be deprived of revenue. Second, even if the federal government were sympathetic to the plight of Canadian municipalities and willing to make a financial commitment to them, it is improbable that it would favour tax free bonds, for, based on the American experience, they are seen by the public as a tax loophole for taxpayers in the upper income brackets. A person normally has to be in at least a 50 per cent tax bracket before it is advantageous to buy tax free bonds. Furthermore, if all of a wealthy person's capital is invested in tax free bonds the person's interest income, no matter how large, is exempt from taxation. At a time when federal and provincial taxes continue to creep upward, a tax scheme enabling the wealthy to escape taxation completely would be politically unwise and would probably lead to greater tax cheating and use of the underground economy by the working and middle classes, who already feel that the tax system is weighted to the advantage of businesspeople and the wealthy.

Another proposal municipalities have at times advocated is sharing provincial income tax revenue. There is a precedent for such a policy. Donald Higgins points out that "the Premier of Manitoba announced in his 1975 budget speech that the province's municipalities would be allocated a share of the province's income tax in 1976: 2 per cent of personal income tax, and 1 per cent of corporate income tax."[18] However, in Alberta, the provincial government has jealously guarded its income tax preserve and there has never been a hint from cabinet that the government would consider such a proposal. Not only is the province unwilling to share its income tax revenue with municipalities, as was indicated in an earlier chapter, it has increasingly moved away from giving unconditional grants to giving conditional ones: less than 10 per cent of municipal grant monies are unconditional.

With the federal government hesitant to help municipalities and the province unwilling to share its oil and gas or income tax revenue and increasingly limiting the use of unconditional grants, local government autonomy and grass-roots democracy face an uncertain future. Perhaps the provincial strategy is to help local governments through economic diversification by encouraging industries to locate in the province. With industries locating in municipalities throughout the province, the property tax base would be strengthened and fiscal crises averted. Unfortunately, the strategy has had mixed success, and the fiscal fortunes of a great number of municipalities are still tied to an oil and gas industry that is only beginning to recover in fits and starts.

Rebuilding the City Core

Alberta's cities are relatively young compared to those in eastern Canada; however, they are beginning to age, and sections of their downtowns are starting to look dowdy and run-down. At the same time, outlying shopping centres with department stores, specialty shops, restaurants, entertainment centres and movie houses have proliferated. Attracted by indoor shopping, free parking and proximity to their neighbourhoods, suburbanites have deserted the core city for the shopping centres. For the past 25 years city after city has attempted to upgrade its core and reverse this trend. In both Edmonton and Calgary, downtown business boosters wistfully hoped the LRT system, whose lines all funnel into the city core, would be the catalyst leading to downtown revitalization. In uneasy alliance, downtown merchant associations, core city land owners unhappy with declining investment, and sundry citizen groups nostalgic for the hustle and bustle of an active downtown area have lobbied city hall for incentives to upgrade the downtown core. It has been suggested that if middle-class housing were built adjacent to the core, decentralization could be reversed. Suggestions have been made to close off downtown streets to vehicles and to encourage free parking. Politicians have responded with a gamut of programs from hanging potted plants on utility poles to holding street dances to lure shoppers back downtown.

The city's core is not going to die, though undoubtedly it will look much different. Rather than serving as the city's retail centre, the core will provide specialized goods and services for a middle-class clientele of office workers. Despite the best efforts of the business boosters the city's core will never again play the dominant retail, entertainment, hotel and office role it played in the past. These activities will increasingly move to outlying shopping centres.

A glimpse of the future can be seen in an examination of the recently constructed 2.2 million square foot West Edmonton Mall complex located several miles from the city's core. With over 400 stores,

52 restaurants, a National Hockey League regulation size skating rink, a 50,000 square foot amusement centre, and free parking, the new mall has boomed. Once the third phase is completed in late 1985, the mall is expected to do 20 to 25 per cent of retailing in Edmonton.[19] Large outlying malls in other areas of the city will expand and, along with West Edmonton Mall, will continue to siphon off retail activity from the city core.

Retail activity in Calgary will follow a similar pattern. It can be safely predicted that the 950,000 square foot Chinook Centre will be enlarged, as will some smaller outlying malls. As in Edmonton, retail activity in Calgary's core will slowly decline as more activities move to the periphery.

Participation and Politics in the Future

Political upheavals in the last 20 years have had a major impact on local politics and portend substantial changes for the future. The emergence of grass-roots citizen groups, a lessening in the importance of owning property, increasing political activity of women, and a recognition of the importance of natives and the minority ethnic communities have been major alterations and, in all these areas, one can safely predict even more changes in the future. In only one area is change unlikely. The political franchise was recently extended to 18 year olds who argued that, if they were old enough to marry and serve in the military, they were old enough to make intelligent political decisions in their own communities. But more important than the arguments was the political reality: during the late 1960s and early 1970s, politicians attempted to court the unusually large numbers of young people in the population by extending them the franchise. During this short-lived generation the slogan was "never trust anyone over 30," and there were discussions on extending the franchise to 16 year olds. Today the bulge is aging and the median age of the Canadian population is increasing. There is little likelihood that the age to exercise the franchise will be reduced or that there will be an emphasis on youth-oriented municipal policies; youth just will not have the numbers to exercise the political clout they had in the past.

With the citizenry increasingly interested in having input into policy making there is little doubt that, in the near future, all property restrictions on voting will be abolished. No longer is there the belief that only property holders can be expected to make thoughtful and objective voting decisions because those without property have no stake in the community and vote on the basis of self-interest. Today, the general attitude of the public is that franchise restrictions based on property make second-class citizens out of the propertyless; equally important is the fact that non-owners of property are beginning to outnumber owners in the province's larger cities. If this trend continues, there will be even greater pressure to abolish all property qualifications for eligibility to vote.

Only after women had won the right to exercise the political franchise were they considered responsible citizens. At present, women use only a portion of their franchise. They are active in election campaigns and exercise their vote but, in almost all communities, they hold only a small minority of elective offices. Today, greater numbers of women are entering occupations such as law, business and education that have traditionally been the stepping stones to municipal office. Now, with women demanding all the advantages men have long enjoyed, one can safely predict that future women will share political offices equally with men, particularly at the municipal level.

At the community level, natives tend to be a hidden population that participates only minimally, if at all, in local politics. Native people are just beginning to demand what they consider a fair share of public goods and services. As natives gain a better understanding of the political process at the local level there will undoubtedly be a dramatic increase in their political activity. In the near future there will be a far greater number of natives contesting local office. One can only speculate on the nature of native political leaders' demands; whether they will demand separate but equal development or complete integration into the community's social and economic structure remains to be seen.

Alberta's heritage and social fabric is rich with the contribution of its minority ethnic populations: Ukrainians, French, Germans, Italians, Scandinavians, West and East Indians, Orientals and many others. Unfortunately, until recently many families who took pride in their ethnic traditions were shunned and condemned by "other" Canadians who maintained that ethnic customs should be abandoned. In Alberta there were instances of children being punished for speaking languages other than English at school. Today, with the support of provincial government policies, ethnic groups are renewing their customs and traditions. Although some communities have always experienced minority ethnic politics, if the current ethnic pride and cohesiveness continues, it is likely that minority ethnic candidates, voting and politics will be much more prevalent in the future.

In the last 20 years citizen groups in larger municipalities have begun to play major roles in the formulation of municipal policy. In the future there will be a sustained growth in their size and numbers if politicians and bureaucrats become even more remote and unresponsive. Environmental groups in large and small municipalities are becoming increasingly intolerant of polluted streams, open sewage lagoons, garbage dumps and industrial pollution. With a recognition of the importance of "the quality of life," demands will be made that high priority be placed on parkland and open space and lower priority be given to "land-eating freeways" and industrial parks for polluting heavy industry.

There are two quite different scenarios on the role of neighbourhood groups in the local political process. In one, highly politicized neighbourhood groups will demand decentralization of the city's administrative structure to make it sensitive to neighbourhood needs. These groups will probably demand more control over transportation planning, traffic control, zoning and educational policy. An alternative scenario is that neighbourhood groups are now at their zenith and their membership and importance will decrease. The argument runs that there is a decreasing attachment to neighbourhoods as people live in one, work in another, shop in another, and visit their friends in yet another. Related trends are the continuing decline in home ownership and an increasingly mobile middle class. If these trends continue, a family will have little more identification with the neighbourhood it lives in than with the others it frequents. In this scenario there will be citizen groups, but they will not be identified with geographical area.

Whether broadly based citizen groups will have a geographic identification or not, the educational establishment will likely become a major target. Unless this establishment makes major changes in policy, it can be safely predicted that dissatisfaction with the educational system will erupt in a demand for parental control of educational policy.

Policy Making in the Future

From the discussion throughout the previous chapters it becomes clear that a variety of government and non-government individuals and groups play key roles in making policy at one time or another. The most visible are the mayors and council members, for they are the ones who formally enunciate policy proposals and legitimize them by making them into law. Senior bureaucrats present policy alternatives to elected officials and both senior and junior bureaucrats often subtly change the intended direction of policy by the way they carry it out. Consultants are involved both in presenting policy alternatives and in legitimizing policy preferences of councils.

Business, labour and community citizen groups play an active role in policies that effect them. Merchant groups have been key actors in planning and development in many Alberta communities. Public sector unions have forced some municipalities to redeploy their economic resources. In communities with a strong commitment to grassroots democracy, ratepayer associations and broadly based citizen groups have presented policy proposals to their elected representatives. Even in communities without this commitment, concerned citizen groups have come into being to play a major role in the formulation of particular policies. In short, political interest groups, whether they represent narrow economic interests or broadly based citizen concerns, attempt to gain an advantage by resorting to public-sector decision making.

At the same time, all these individuals and groups are circumscribed in their actions by the policies and actions of the provincial and federal governments and by the general economic climate. Provincial and federal policies that effect community economic activity and general population movements are bound to have an important effect on the ability of a community to raise revenue and provide services.

To complicate further the policy process, economic and political decisions made in Brazil, Dubai, Hong Kong and other world centres have had unintended effects on Alberta municipalities far greater than the combined policies of the Alberta and federal government. A dramatic change in oil prices, a declaration of a moratorium on external debt payment by a debt-ridden country, or the dumping of a country's stockpile of gold will have an almost immediate effect on policy making in every Alberta community. Very recently the whole Alberta economy faltered as a result of international oil pricing agreements made in the Middle East. With the costs of municipal borrowing tied to monetary policies set in the United States and to the vagaries of gold pricing in Europe, the Middle East and Asia, it is clear that an individual municipality's policy is often directed by economic policy set in foreign lands.

The future is unlikely to see substantial changes in the way municipal policy is formulated. Policy making will be shared by a multiplicity of elected officials, bureaucrats and groups representing various interests.[20] Municipal policy making will continue to be constrained by a provincial, national and international economic and political framework. Shifting circumstances will continue to shape the options and thinking of municipal decision makers.

Regional Government

In Chapter 3 it was noted that Calgary, Edmonton and many of the province's medium-sized and smaller cities have expanded their boundaries through annexation and amalgamation. There is little doubt that the regional government concept will continue to be attractive to political leaders and civic boosters interested in expansion.

If the present trend of metropolitan government continues, Edmonton and Calgary will be much larger by the year 2000, at the expense of outlying communities; they will become city neighbourhoods with no political and little social and economic identity.

It is not inconceivable that the provincial government will divide populated areas into regional service districts delivering most traditional municipal government services. The effect would be to weaken greatly small municipalities, for they would have little reason to justify their existence. Their service functions stripped, they would become little more than political and administrative shells. Most assuredly, decision making would be much more centralized than it is today.

Since many people believe that centralized decision makers tend to be less responsive than decentralized decision makers, concessions will have to be made to community groups interested in local self-determination. One could foresee territorial representation on the regional government's legislative body; in short, a form of ward representation. The proponents of regional government argue that representation by wards takes into consideration concerns for grass-roots democracy and local self-determination. It is equally easy to foresee the creation of citizen advisory groups at the community level, ostensibly to suggest policy proposals to the elected representatives and to act as a sounding board for them. It is unlikely that these groups would ever be anything but advisory.

This scenario does not account for the growing interest many segments of the population are showing in grass-roots democracy. If the public begins to question the purported advantages of centralized decision making inherent in regional and metropolitan government, and demands a greater role in determining its own destiny, a much different scenario emerges. In this scenario, large and small communities across the province would solve their own problems and decide their own futures. Municipal decision making would be much less complacent than it is today, for it would be highly politicized with a multiplicity of community and other groups placing demands on local councils. If there is a strong sense of local community, zoning, local transportation and educational planning would probably devolve to neighbourhood groups. Recognizing the public's desire for decentralization, the provincial government would provide unconditional grants on the basis of need and fiscal capability. Municipalities would be given many responsibilities that, today, are carried out by the provincial government.

With a strong network of local governments, coupled with increased citizen activism, one would expect to find municipalities pursuing a variety of financial and planning policies. One would expect to find the citizenry of some communities opting for high levels of services while in others the citizenry would opt for minimal services and taxes. With financial support from the provincial government in the form of guaranteed unconditional grants, some municipalities would develop as strictly residential communities with no industry and a minimum of retail businesses, while others would develop primarily as industrial communities. The key words in the province's local government policy would be "diversity" and "experimentation."

The more likely scenario is neither domination by a few regional governments nor a completely decentralized system with a total public commitment to grass-roots democracy. Assuming that the present trends of support for regional government and local self-determination continue unabated, one can predict the continuance of metropolitan government in Edmonton and Calgary and of a number of restive groups and citizens unhappy with representation and policy making in these much larger units of government. Outside the metropolitan areas there will be continuing community conflict between those desiring local autonomy and control and those wanting all service functions transferred to either regional governments or the provincial government. The conflict will be sharpened by the province's unwillingness to provide municipalities with unconditional grants large enough to maintain their financial independence and stability.

Notes

1. Kettle, *Hindsight on the Future*, 19-26.

2. In the late 1960s and early 1970s an inordinate number of people in the population were between the ages of 16 and 24. Since this is also the group in the population that commits the most crimes, there was a substantial amount of crime at that time. Since this bulge in the population has aged, to be replaced by a much smaller percentage of young people, the crime rate has stabilized and has even begun to decline slightly.

3. A 1975 poll of preferred family size found that most Canadian couples felt the ideal family was two or fewer children. This finding is markedly

different from the results of a 1945 poll that found the majority of Canadians felt the ideal family was four or more children. *Toronto Star*, August 23, 1975.

4. *Maclean's*, September 15, 1980.

5. Gertler and Crowley, *Changing Canadian Cities*, 91.

6. *Edmonton Journal*, August 27, 1983.

7. Rural-urban migration trends in Alberta are similar to those in other Canadian provinces. "Net migration statistics force one to conclude that internal migration was responsible for remarkably little of the change that took place during the 1960s in the distribution of population between the rural and urban sectors of Canadian society. As an example, the 3.6 million internal migrants recorded during 1966-71 resulted in a net transfer of only 26,000 people from rural to urban areas in Canada. The balance between migration streams is best illustrated by observing flows between . . . the urban and the rural non-farm sectors. Of 800,000 people involved, 399,000 people took up residence along a township road or on a country estate, while an equivalent number 396,500 sought to establish a new home in an urban community." Gertler and Crowley, *Changing Canadian Cities*, 71.

8. The *total fertility rate* is defined as the number of children the average woman will have during her child-bearing years.

9. *Edmonton Journal*, March 22, 1983.

10. *Red Deer Advocate*, February 4, 1983.

11. *Edmonton Journal*, November 16, 1983.

12. *Edmonton Journal*, December 6, 1983.

13. *Edmonton Journal*, November 17, 1983.

14. Under the interest shielding plan the province would rebate the interest above a specified amount on municipal debentures. When the plan was terminated in 1983, the rebate to municipalities was on interest in excess of 11 per cent. At one point in 1982, the shielding amount was as much as 11 per cent.

15. *Grande Prairie Daily Herald Tribune*, October 2, 1981.

16. The AUMA is astute enough to realize that raising municipal revenue through a gasoline tax is a provincial government political boobytrap. When the government abolished its provincial tax on gasoline in March of 1978, it received widespread public support. Evidently Premier Lougheed felt this public support was worth the loss of $95 million in annual revenue. The province would disclaim any responsibility for a gasoline tax earmarked for municipalities and would direct an irate public's attention to the municipalities as the appropriate vent for its wrath.

17. *Edmonton Journal*, March 18, 1983.

18. Higgins, *Urban Canada*, 70.

19. *Edmonton Journal*, September 14, 1983.

20. In an inciteful analysis of Calgary's policy process Drabek and Woods discuss Mayor Klein's conception of his role in policy making. "He takes the position that the civic corporation is just one among a number of competing interests with which he must deal as the sole representative of Calgary's entire citizenry."Drabek and Woods, "Calgary: The Boom Ends," 32.

Bibliography

Articles

Adrian, Charles, and Oliver Williams. "The Insulation of Local Politics Under the Nonpartisan Ballot." *American Political Science Review* 53 (December 1959): 1052-1063.

Alexander, Alan. "The Institutional and Role Perceptions of Local Alderman. In *Emerging Party Politics in Urban Canada*, edited by J. Masson and J. Anderson, 124-140. Toronto: McClelland and Stewart, 1972.

Anderson, James. "The Municipal Government Reform Movement in Western Canada, 1880-1920." In *The Usable Urban Past*, edited by Alan Artibise and Gilbert Stetler, 73-111. Toronto: MacMillan, 1979.

Aucoin, Peter. "Theory and Research in the Study of Policy Making." In *The Structure of Policy-Making in Canada*, edited by G. Bruce Doern and Peter Aucoin, 10-38. Toronto: Macmillan, 1971.

Bella, Leslie. "The Goal Effectiveness of Alberta's Preventive Social Service Program. " *Canadian Public Policy* 8 (Spring 1982): 143-155.

Bourassa, G. "Les élites politiques de Montréal." In *Emerging Party Politics in Urban Canada*, edited by J. Masson and J. Anderson, 87-109. Toronto: McClelland and Stewart, 1972.

Burke, Edmund. "Address to the Electors of Bristol, November 3, 1774." In the author's *Works*, Vol. 2, 95-96. Boston: Little Brown, 1871.

Child, Alan H. "The Ryerson Tradition in Western Canada, 1981-1906." In *Egerton Ryerson and His Times*, edited by Neil McDonald and Alf Chaiton, 279-301. Toronto: Macmillan, 1978.

Clark, Ron. "Planners as Professionals." In *The City Book*, edited by James Lorimer and Evelyn Ross, 46-53. Toronto: James Lorimer, 1976.

Clarkson, Stephen. "Barriers to Entry of Parties in Toronto's Civic Politics: Towards a Theory of Party Penetration." *Canadian Journal of Political Science* 4 (June 1971): 206-223.

Coulter, Philip B., Lois MacGillivray, and William Vickery. "Municipal Fire Protection Performance in Urban Areas: Environmental and Organizational Influences on Effectiveness and Productivity Measures." In *The Delivery of Urban Services*, edited by Elinor Ostrom, 231-260. Beverly Hills: Sage, 1976.

Dahl, Robert. "The Concept of Power." *Behavioral Science* 2 (July 1957): 201-215.

Derthick, Martha. "Intercity Differences in Administration of the Public Assistance Program: The Case of Massachusetts." In *City Politics and Public Policy*, edited by James Q. Wilson, 243-266. New York: Wiley, 1968.

Dickerson, M.O., S. Drabek, and J.T. Woods. "A Performance Approach to Urban Political Analysis: The Calgary Case." In *Problems of Change in Urban Government*, edited by M.O. Dickerson, S. Drabek and J.T. Woods, 61-81. Waterloo: Wilfred Laurier University Press, 1980.

Easton, David. "An Approach to the Analysis of Political systems." *World Politics* 9 (1957): 383-400.

Easton, Robert, and Paul Tennant. "Vancouver Civic Party Leadership, Backgrounds, Attitudes and Non-Civic Party Affiliations." *B.C. Studies* (Summer 1969): 19-29.

Gardiner, John A. "Police Enforcement of Traffic Laws: A Comparative Analysis." In *City Politics and Public Policy*, edited by James Q. Wilson, 151-172. New York: Wiley, 1968.

Gerecke, Kent. "The History of Canadian City Planning." *City Magazine* 2 (Summer 1976): 12-23.

Gilsdorf, Robert. "Cognitive and Motivational Sources of Voter Susceptibility to Influence." *Canadian Journal of Political Science* 6 (December 1973): 624-638.

Greenberg, Bradley, and Brenda Dervin. "Mass Communication Among the Urban Poor." *Public Opinion Quarterly* 34 (Summer 1970): 224-235.

Hays, Samuel P. "The Politics of Reform in Municipal Government in the Progressive Era." *Pacific Northwest Quarterly* 55 (October 1964): 157-169.

Hirsch, Werner. "The Supply of Urban Government Services." In *Issues in Urban Economics*, edited by Harvey S. Perloff and Lowden Wingo Jr, 477-524. Baltimore: Johns Hopkins Press, 1968.

Hough, Jerry F. "Voters' Turnout and the Responsiveness of Local Government: The Case of Toronto." In *Politics Canada*, 3d ed., edited by Paul W. Fox, 284-299. Toronto: McGraw-Hill, 1970.

Kagi, Herbert. "The Role of Private Consultants in Urban Governing." *Urban Affairs Quarterly* 5 (September 1969): 45-58.

Kiernan, Matthew. "Ideology and the Precarious Future of the Canadian Planning Profession." *Plan Canada* 22 (March 1982): 14-24.

Knill, W.D. "Community Decision-Making in the Educational Area." *The Canadian Administrator* 6 (February 1967): 17-20.

Lightbody, James. "Edmonton: Gateway to the North." In *City Politics in Canada*, edited by Warren Magnusson and Andrew Sancton, 225-290. Toronto: University of Toronto Press, 1983.

_____. "Electoral Reform in Local Government: The Case of Winnipeg." *Canadian Journal of Political Science* 11 (June 1978): 312-319.

_____. "The First Hurrah: Edmonton Elects a Mayor, 1983." *Urban History Review* 13 (June 1984): 35-41.

_____. "The Rise of Party Politics in Canadian Local Elections." In *Emerging Party Politics in Urban Canada*, edited by Jack Masson and James D. Anderson, 192-202. Toronto: McClelland and Stewart, 1972.

Lindblom, Charles. "The Science of Muddling Through." *Public Administration Review* 19 (Spring 1959): 79-88.

Lipsky, Michael. "Street Level Bureaucrats and the Analysis of Urban Reform." *Urban Affairs Quarterly* 6 (June 1971): 391-409.

_____. "Toward a Theory of Street-Level Bureaucracy." In *Theoretical Perspectives on Urban Politics*, edited by Willis D. Hawley et al, 196-213. Englewood Cliffs N.J.: Prentice-Hall, 1976.

Long, J. Anthony, and Brian Slemko. "The Recruitment of Local Decison-Makers in Five Canadian Cities." *Canadian Journal of Politicial Science* 7 (September 1974): 550-559.

Long, Norton E. "The Local Community as an Ecology of Games." In *Urban Government*, rev. ed., edited by Edward C. Banfield, 472-483. New York: The Free Press, 1969. First published in *American Journal of Sociology* 64 (November 1958): 251-261.

Masson, Jack K. "Decision-making patterns and floating coalitions in an urban city council." *Canadian Journal of Political Science* 8 (March 1975): 128-137.

_____. "The Ebb and Flow of Municipal Party Politics in Alberta." In *Society and Politics in Alberta*, edited by Carlos Calderola, 356-368. Toronto: Methuen, 1979.

_____. "Edmonton: The Unsettled Issues of Expansion, Governmental Reform and Provincial Economic Diversification." In *Politics and Government of Urban Canada*, 4th ed., edited by Lionel D. Feldman, 431-447. Toronto: Methuen, 1981.

_____. "Labor Politics in Alberta." In *Society and Politics in Alberta*, edited by Carlo Caldarola, 271-283. Toronto: Methuen, 1979.

Maxey, Chester C. "The Political Integration of Metropolitan Communities." *National Municipal Review* 11 (August 1922): 229-253.

Peattie, Lisa. "Reflections of an Advocate Planner." *Journal of the American Institute of Planners* 34 (March 1968): 80-87.

Plunkett, T.J., and J. Lightbody. "Tribunals, Politics, and the Public Interest: The Edmonton Annexation Case." *Canadian Public Policy* 8 (Spring 1982): 207-221.

Rogers, Chester B., and Harold D. Arman. "Nonpartisanship and Election to City Office." *Social Science Quarterly* 51 (March 1971): 941-945.

Rutherford, Paul. "Tomorrow's Metropolis: The Urban Reform Movement in Canada, 1880-1920." In *The Canadian City*, edited by Gilbert Stetler and Alan Artibise, 368-392. Toronto: McClelland and Stewart, 1977.

Salisbury, Robert H., and Gordon Black. "Class and Party in Partisan and Nonpartisan Elections: the Case of Des Moines." *American Political Science Review* 57 (September 1963): 584-592.

Sancton, Andrew. "Conclusion: Canadian City Politics in Comparative Perspective." In *City Politics in Canada*, edited by Warren Magnusson and Andrew Sancton, 291-317. Toronto: University of Toronto Press, 1983.

Savas, E.S. "Municipal Monopolies Versus Competition in Delivering Urban Services. In *Improving the Quality of Urban Management*, edited by Willis D. Hawley and David Rogers, 473-500. Beverly Hills, Calif.: Sage, 1974.

_____. "Solid Waste Collection in Metropolitan Areas." In *The Delivery of Urban Services*, edited by Elinor Ostrom, 201-229. Beverly Hills: Sage, 1976.

Sells, James. "Selected Material from the Report on the Questionnaire on the Focus of the Planning Profession." *Plan Canada* Special Issue (June 1982): 26-30.

Shapcott, Michael. "Calgary: Pre-election Money Madness." *City Magazine* 6 (October 1982): 7-8.

Short, William. "Municipal Government by Commission." *The Canadian Municipal Journal* 3 (1907): 143-146. Cited in James Anderson, "The Municipal Government Reform Movement in Western Canada 1880-1920," in *The Usable Urban Past*, edited by Alan Artibise and Gilbert Stetler. Toronto: MacMillan, 1979.

Simpson, Michael. "Thomas Adams in Canada 1914-1930." *Urban History Review* 11 (October 1982): 1-15.

Smith, P.J. "American Influences and Local Needs: Adaptions to the Alberta Planning System in 1928-1929." Forthcoming in a collection of papers edited by Alan Artibise and Gilbert Stetler. [1985].

_____. "The Principle of Utility and the Origin of Planning Legislation in Alberta, 1912-1975." In *The Usable Urban Past*, edited by Alan Artibise and Gilbert Stetler, 196-225. Toronto: MacMillan, 1979.

Smith, Phyllis. "The New Planning Act in Alberta." *Plan Canada* 20 (June 1980): 120-123.

Thompson, Wilbur. "The City as a Distorted Price System." *Psychology Today* 2 (August 1968): 28-33.

Van Nus, Walter. "The Fate of City Beautiful Thought in Canada, 1893-1930." In *The Canadian City*, edited by Alan Artibise and Gilbert Stetler, 162-185. Toronto: McClelland and Stewart, 1977.

Vickers, Jill McCalla. "Where are the Women in Canadian Politics?" *Atlantis* 3 (Spring 1978): 40-51.

Wright, Deil S. "The City Manager as a Development Administrator." In *Comparative Urban Research*, edited by Robert T. Daland, 203-248. Beverly Hills: Sage, 1969.

_____, and Robert Paul Boynton. "The Media, the Masses, and Urban Management." *Journalism Quarterly* 47 (Spring 1970): 12-19.

Books

Adrian, Charles R., and Charles Press. *Governing Urban America*, 4th ed. New York: McGraw-Hill, 1972.

Artibise, Alan F. *Winnipeg: A Social History of Urban Growth*. Montreal: McGill-Queen's University Press, 1975.

Aubin, Henry. *City for Sale*. Toronto: James Lorimer, 1977.

Banfield, Edward C., and James Q. Wilson. *City Politics*. Cambridge, Mass.: Harvard University Press, 1965.

Benello, C. George, and Dimitrios Roussopoulos, eds. *The Case for Participatory Democracy*. New York: Viking Press, 1971.

Bettison, David G., John K. Kenward, and Larrie Taylor. *Urban Affairs in Alberta*. Edmonton: University of Alberta Press, 1975.

Bird, Richard M., and N. Enid Slack. *Urban Public Finance in Canada*. Toronto: Butterworths, 1983.

Black, Edwin. *Politics and the News*. Toronto: Butterworths, 1982.

Boyer, J. Patrick. *Lawmaking by the People*. Toronto: Butterworths, 1982.

Braybrooke, David, and Charles Lindblom. *A Strategy of Decision*. New York: The Free Press, 1963.

Brunt, Michael Hugo. *The History of City Planning*. Montreal: Harvest House, 1972.

Burton, Thomas. *The Roles and Relevance of Alberta's Regional Planning Commissions*. Edmonton: University of Alberta Department of Recreation Administration, 1981.

Butler, David, and Austin Ranney, eds. *Referendums: A Comparative Study of Practice and Theory*. Washington: American Enterprise Institute, 1978.

Caragata, Warren. *Alberta Labour*. Toronto: James Lorimer, 1979.

Caraley, Demetrios. *City Government and Urban Problems*. Englewood Cliffs, N.J.: Prentice-Hall, 1977.

Catanese, Anthony James. *Planners and Local Politics*. Beverly Hills, Calif.: Sage, 1974.

Caulfield, Jon. *The Tiny Perfect Mayor*. Toronto: James Lorimer, 1974.

Clement, Wallace. *The Canadian Corporate Elite*. Toronto: McClelland and Stewart, 1975.

Corry, J.A., and J.E. Hodgetts. *Democratic Government and Politics*. Toronto: University of Toronto Press, 1959.

Crawford, Kenneth Grant. *Canadian Municipal Government*. Toronto: University of Toronto Press, 1954.

_____. *Report of the Institute of Local Government*. Kingston: Queen's University, 1959.

Downs, Anthony. *Inside Bureaucracy*. Boston: Little Brown, 1967.

Dye, Thomas R. *Understanding Public Policy*. Englewood Cliffs, N.J.: Prentice-Hall, 1972.

_____, and Harmon Ziegler. *The Irony of Democracy*. Belmont, Calif: Wadsworth, 1970.

Easton, David. *A Framework for Political Analysis*. Englewood Cliffs, N.J.: Prentice-Hall, 1965.

Einsiedel, E. *Survey of Alberta Chief Municipal Administrators and Municipal Development Officers*. Edmonton: Local Government Studies, University of Alberta, 1983.

_____. *Survey of Planning Needs and Training Preferences of Alberta Elected Officials*. Edmonton: Local Government Studies, University of Alberta, 1983.

Engelmann, Frederick C., and Mildred A. Schwartz. *Canadian Political Parties: Origin, Character, Impact*. Scarborough: Prentice-Hall, 1975.

Etzioni, Amitai. *The Active Society*. New York: The Free Press, 1968.

Feldman, Lionel D., and Katherine A. Graham. *Bargaining for Cities*. Toronto: Institute for Research on Public Policy, 1979.

Fraser, Graham. *Fighting Back: Urban Renewal in Trefann Court*. Toronto: Hakkart, 1972.

Gertler, Len, and Ron Crowley. *Changing Canadian Cities: The Next 25 Years*. Toronto: McClelland and Stewart, 1977.

Hanson, Eric. *Local Government in Alberta*. Toronto: McClelland and Stewart Ltd., 1956.

Hawley, Willis D. *Nonpartisan Elections and the Case for Party Politics*. New York: John Wiley, 1973.

Higgins, Donald. *Urban Canada: Government and Politics*. Toronto: MacMillan, 1977.

Hunnuis, Garry, ed. *Participatory Democracy for Canada*. Montreal: Black Rose Books, 1971.

Hunter, Floyd. *Community Power Structure*. Chapel Hill: University of North Carolina Press, 1953.

Jones, Victor. *Metropolitan Government*. Chicago: University of Chicago Press, 1942.

Kaplan, Harold. *Reform, Planning and City Politics: Montreal, Winnipeg, Toronto*. Toronto, University of Toronto Press, 1982.

Kotler, Milton. *Neighborhood Government: The Local Foundations of Political Life*. New York: Bobbs-Merrill Co., 1969.

Lasswell, Harold, and Abraham Kaplan. *Power and Society*. New Haven, Conn.: Yale University Press, 1950.

Lee, Eugene C. *The Politics of Nonpartisanship*. Berkeley: University of California Press, 1960.

Lilienthal, David. *TVA: Democracy on the March*. New York: Harper & Brothers, 1944.

Lineberry, Robert L., and Ira Sharkansky. *Urban Politics and Public Policy*. 3d ed. New York: Harper, 1978.

Lorimer, James. *The Real World of City Politics*. Toronto: James, Lewis and Samuel, 1970.

_____, and Carolyn MacGregor, eds. *After the Developers*. Toronto: James Lorimer, 1981.

_____, and Evelyn Ross, eds. *The City Book*. Toronto: James Lorimer, 1976.

_____, and Evelyn Ross, eds. *The Second City Book*. Toronto: James Lorimer, 1977.

Lowi, Theodore J. *The End of Liberalism*. New York: W.W. Norton, 1969.

Lynd, Robert S., and Helen M. Lynd. *Middletown in Transition*. New York: Harcourt and Brace, 1937.

MacEwan, Grant. *Poking into Politics*. Edmonton: The Institute of Applied Art, 1966.

MacKenzie, W.J.M. *Free Elections*. London: George Allen and Unwin, 1958.

MacPherson, C.B. *Democracy in Alberta: Social Credit and the Party System*, 2d ed. Toronto: University of Toronto Press, 1962.

Martin, Roscoe. *Grass Roots*. Alabama: University of Alabama Press, 1957.

Panitch, Leo, ed. *The Canadian State: Political Economy and Political Power*. Toronto: University of Toronto Press, 1977.

Pateman, Carole. *Participation and Democratic Theory*. Cambridge, Eng.: Cambridge University Press, 1970.

Plunkett, T.J. *Urban Canada and its Government*. Toronto: MacMillan, 1968.

Prewitt, Kenneth. *The Recruitment of Political Leaders: A Study of Citizen Politicians*. Indianapolis: Bobbs-Merrill, 1970.

Rabinovitz, Francine F. *City Politics and City Planning*. New York: Atherton Press, 1969.

Rae, Douglas. *The Political Consequences of Electoral Laws*. New Haven, Conn.: Yale University Press, 1967.

Roussopoulos, Dimitrios, ed. *The City and Radical Social Change*. Montreal: Black Rose Books, 1982.

Safire, William. *The New Language of Politics*. New York: Random House, 1968.

Sayre, Wallace S., and Herbert Kaufman. *Governing New York City*. New York: W.W. Norton, 1965.

Selznick, Philip. *TVA and the Grass Roots*. New York: Harper and Row, 1966.

Sewell, John. *Up Against City Hall*. Toronto: James Lewis and Samuel, 1972.

Spurr, Peter. *Land and Urban Development*. Toronto: James Lorimer, 1976.

Studenski, Paul. *The Government of Metropolitan Areas in the United States*. New York: National Municipal League, 1930.

Truman, David. *The Governmental Process.* New York: Knopf, 1951.

Vasu, Michael Lee. *Politics and Planning.* Chapel Hill: University of North Carolina Press, 1979.

Weidenhamer, T.D. *A History of the Alberta School Trustees Association.* Edmonton: The Alberta School Trustees Association, 1971.

Wildavsky, Aaron. *The Politics of the Budgetary Process.* Boston: Little Brown, 1964.

Williams, Oliver, and Charles Adrian. *Four Cities.* Philadelphia: University of Philadelphia Press, 1963.

Wilson, S.J. *Women, the Family and the Economy.* Toronto: McGraw-Hill, 1982.

Wright, Gerald. *The Immorality of the Motorcar.* Edmonton: Community Resources Development, Division Department of Extension, University of Alberta, 1971.

Government Publications

Alberta Legislative Assembly. Alberta Hansard, various dates. Edmonton: Queen's Printer.

Alberta Municipal Affairs Urban Advisory Group and Special Projects Branch. *Municipal and Local Administrative Bodies in Alberta 1941-1981.* Edmonton: Alberta Department of Municipal Affairs, 1982.

The Banff-Jasper Autonomy Report. Edmonton: Alberta Department of Municipal Affairs, 1972.

Canada. *1981 Census Dictionary.* Ottawa: Supply and Services Canada, 1982.

_____. *Report of the Royal Commission on Government Organization* (The Glassco Commission) Vol. 2, *Supporting Services for Government.* Ottawa: Queen's Printer, 1962.

_____. *Sixth Report of the Standing Committee on Northern Affairs and Natural Resources, 1966.* Ottawa: Queen's Printer, 1966.

City of Edmonton. "About the Edmonton Boundaries." *Mainstream,* April 18, 1979.

City of Edmonton Planning Department. *North-East LRT Evaluation Study.* Edmonton: City of Edmonton, 1979.

City of Edmonton Real Estate and Housing Department. "Report," May 4, 1982.

Commemorative Brochure of the Alberta Urban Municipalities Association, 1980.

County of Strathcona. "A Proposed Boundary for Sherwood Park." Submission to the Minister of Municipal Affairs and the Edmonton Regional Planning Commission, October 11, 1983.

Edmonton: The Annexation Issue. Edmonton: City of Edmonton, 1981.

Edmonton Regional Utilities Study. Edmonton: Alberta Environment, 1978.

"Era of the Regional Plan: A Discussion Paper for the Annual Spring Seminar." Presented by the Alberta Planning Board at the Annual Spring Seminar, Jasper, April 26-29, 1983.

Ewasiuk v. Edmonton (1979), 23 A.R. (C.A.)

Hanson, Eric. *The Potential Unification of the Edmonton Metropolitan Area*. Edmonton: City of Edmonton, 1968.

Hickey, Paul. *Decision-making Process in Ontario's Local Governments*. Toronto: Ministry of Treasury, Economics and Intergovernmental Affairs, undated.

Kettle, John. *Hindsight on the Future*. Ottawa: Ministry of State for Urban Affairs, 1976.

Kratzmann, Arthur, Timothy C. Byrne, and Walter H. Worth. *A System in Conflict: A Report to the Minister of Labour by the Fact Finding Commission*. Edmonton: Alberta Department of Labour, 1980.

MacIntosh, G.H. "Opening speech to the fifth session of the second legislature of the Northwest Territories." In *Northwest Gazette*, Vol II (August, 1984).

Markusen, J.R., and D.T. Scheffman. *Speculation and Monopoly in Urban Development: Analytical Foundations with Evidence for Toronto*. Toronto: Ontario Economic Council, 1977.

"Municipal Attitudes Towards Regional Planning in Alberta." Joint report by the Alberta Association of Municipal Districts and Counties and the Alberta Urban Municipalities Association, October 7, 1980.

Municipal Counsellor 20 (1st quarter, 1976).

O'Callaghan v. Edmonton (1978), 6 Alta. L.R. (2d) 307,12 A.R. 563, 7 M.P.L.R. 140 (Dist. Ct.).

Planning in Alberta. Edmonton: Alberta Department of Municipal Affairs, 1980.

The Park Town of Banff: An Option for Local Government. Edmonton: Alberta Department of Municipal Affairs, 1980.

Parks Canada. *Resident Involvement in Park Townsite Administration, Western Region*. Ottawa: Queen's Printer, 1970.

Plunkett, T.J., et al. *A Form of Municipal Government and Administration for Banff Townsite*. Ottawa: Queen's Printer, 1964.

Province of Alberta. *Report of the Royal Commission on the Metropolitan Development of Calgary and Edmonton*. Edmonton: Queen's Printer, 1956.

Provincial Housing Programs in Alberta. Edmonton: Alberta Department of Housing, 1983.

Revised Guidelines for Regional Plan Preparation and Review. Edmonton: Alberta Planning Board, 1982.

Revised Statutes of Alberta, 1980, Edmonton: Queen's Printer, 1980.

Statutes of Alberta, 1956.

Submission to the Local Authorities Board of Alberta on Behalf of the City of Edmonton. Edmonton: City of Edmonton, 1980.

"Summary of Preliminary Findings of the Regional Planning System Study." Discussion paper prepared by the Inter-Agency Planning Branch of the Alberta Department of Municipal Affairs, September 15, 1981.

Task Force on Urbanization and the Future. Edmonton: Queen's Printer, 1972.

Miscellaneous

Betts, George. "The Edmonton Aldermanic Election of 1962." Master's thesis, University of Alberta, 1962.

Blake, Donald. "Role Perceptions and Local Decision-Makers." Master's thesis, University of Alberta, 1967.

Dean, Colin. Letter from Colin Dean, President of the Local Government Administrators' Association of Alberta, to Jack Masson, February, 10, 1984.

Drabek, S. "The Calgary Ward System." Unpublished paper, prepared for the City of Vancouver Electoral Reform Commission. University of Calgary, undated.

_____, and John Woods. "Calgary: the Boom Ends." Paper presented at the annual meeting of the Canadian Political Science Association, University of Guelph, June 10-12, 1984.

Foran, Maxwell. "The Calgary Town Council, 1884-1895: A Study of Local Government in a Frontier Environment." Master's thesis, University of Calgary, 1970.

_____. "The Civic Corporation and Urban Growth: Calgary, 1884-1930." Ph.D. dissertation, University of Calgary, 1981.

Gaetz, H.H. "Paper Presented to the Union of Alberta Municipalities Convention." 1909. Presented as "Municipal Legislation," in *Emerging Party Politics in Urban Canada*, edited by Jack Masson and James Anderson. Toronto: McClelland and Stewart, 1972.

Gibbons, R., S. Drabek, M.O. Dickerson, and J.T. Woods. "Attitudinal and Socio-Democratic Determinants of Receptivity to Civic Partisanship." Paper presented at the annual meeting of the Canadian Political Science Association, London, Ontario, June, 1978.

"Information Sheet." Urban Development Institute, Alberta Division, 1983.

Le Sage, Edward, and Charles Humphrey. "Alberta Administrator's Survey." Edmonton: 1977. Mimeographed.

Lougheed, Peter, "Alberta's Industrial Strategy." Speech presented before the Calgary Chamber of Commerce, September 6, 1974.

_____. Speech to the "Think West" Conference, September 28, 1977.

MacMillan, M.L., and R.H.M. Plain. *The Reform of Municipal-Provincial Fiscal Relationships in the Province of Alberta*. Report prepared for the Alberta Urban Municipalities Association, 1979.

Manz, Velma. Letter from Velma Manz, Executive Secretary of the Royal Alexandra Hospital, to C.J. McGonigle, City Clerk of Edmonton, May 4, 1982.

Masson, Jack. "Some Preliminary Findings on the Reasons People Signed the Convention Centre and Downtown Redevelopment Plebiscite Petitions." Paper presented at the Conference on Referenda and Plebiscites, University of Calgary, March 20-21, 1980.

McDavid, James. "Residential Solid Waste Collection Services in Canadian Municipalities." School of Public Administration, University of Victoria, 1983. Monograph.

Page, John, and Reg Lang. "Canadian Planners in Profile." Paper presented at the annual meeting of the Canadian Institute of Planners, Toronto, June 27, 1977.

Pilkington, Roger. Letter from Roger Pilkington, President of Bearspaw, Glendale Ratepayer Association, to Jim Rochlin, August 19, 1983.

Price, Richard. Letter from Richard Price, President of Leduc Residents Association, to Jim Rochlin, undated, 1983.

"Statement of Strategic Plan." Canadian Home Builders' Association, Alberta Council, 1983.

Suelzle, A.J. Letter from A.J. Suelzle, Alberta Planning Board Director of Administration, to Jack Masson, July 12, 1983.

Newspapers and Magazines

Alberta Report.

Business Life.

Calgary Daily Herald.

Calgary Herald.

City Magazine.

Edmonton Bulletin.

Edmonton Journal.

Edmonton Report.

Grand Prairie Herald Tribune.

Lethbridge Herald.

Maclean's.

Mainstream.

Medicine Hat News.

New York Times.

Poundmaker.

Red Deer Advocate.

Regina Leader Post.

St. Albert and Sturgeon Gazette.

Toronto Globe and Mail.

Toronto Star.

Index of Places

Index of Persons and Subjects